A DIFFERENT VISION

Since the civil rights movement of the 1960s, public discourse on race relations has tended to focus on political and social inequality rather than the economic impact of racism. *A Different Vision: African American Economic Thought* redresses this imbalance.

A Different Vision brings together for the first time, the ideas, philosophies and interpretations of North America's leading African American economists. Presented in two volumes, each of the thirty-five chapters focuses on various aspects of the social and economic experiences of African Americans, past and present. The volumes thus present a unique perspective on the most important contemporary economic issues. **Volume 1** includes:

- an in-depth discussion of the economics of race and gender;
- assessments of the contribution and influence of major figures in African American economics, including Booker T. Washington, Abram Harris, and Phyllis Wallace;
- an examination of racism within the economics profession; and
- an accessible approach which is free of technical jargon.

Volume 2, *Race and Public Policy*, focuses on issues of poverty, racial inequality and public policy, providing detailed analysis of the theory and method which underlie them.

The authors' findings clearly illustrate that African American economists do indeed have "a different vision." These volumes demonstrate that the impact of racial inequality is immense and race is an important variable in every sphere of American life. By investigating its various dimensions, the authors arrive at a common conclusion – race matters.

Thomas D. Boston is Professor of Economics at Georgia Institute of Technology. He is editor of *The Review of Black Political Economy*. He previously served as a Senior Economist to the Joint Economic Committee of Congress and was President of the National Economic Association. He has lectured and published widely on issues of race and economics.

A DIFFERENT VISION

African American Economic Thought,
Volume 1

Edited by Thomas D. Boston

London and New York

First published 1997
by Routledge
11 New Fetter Lane, London EC4P 4EE

Simultaneously published in the USA and Canada
by Routledge
29 West 35th Street, New York, NY 10001

© 1997 Thomas D. Boston

Typeset in Garamond by
Pure Tech India Limited, Pondicherry
Printed and bound in Great Britain by Clays Ltd, St. Ives PLC

British Library Cataloguing in Publication Data
A catalogue record for this book is available from the British Library

Library of Congress Cataloging in Publication Data
A catalogue record for this book has been requested

ISBN 0–415–09590–5 (hbk)
ISBN 0–415–12715–7 (pbk)

To Catherine Laverne Ross
My Best Friend, Closest Colleague, and Wife

CONTENTS

CONTENTS

ILLUSTRATIONS

FIGURES

TABLES

ILLUSTRATIONS

CONTRIBUTORS

Thomas D. Boston
Professor of Economics
School of Economics
Georgia Institute of Technology
Atlanta, Georgia

Andrew F. Brimmer
Economic & Financial Consultant
Wilmer D. Barrett Professor of Economics
University of Massachusetts at Amherst
Amherst, Massachusetts

Robert S. Browne
President
Twenty-First Century Foundation
Washington, DC

Lynn C. Burbridge
Assistant Professor
Department of Public Administration,
Rutgers (The State University of New Jersey)
Newark, New Jersey

John Sibley Butler
The Dallas TACA Centennial Professor of Liberal Arts (Sociology)
The Arthur James Douglas Centennial Professor of Entrepreneurship
and Small Business (Management)
The University of Texas at Austin
Austin, Texas

Cecilia A. Conrad
Associate Professor of Economics
Department of Economics
Pomona College
Claremont, California

Jerome McCristal Culp, Jr.
Professor of Law
Duke University School of Law
Durham, North Carolina

William Darity, Jr.
Cary C. Boshamer Professor of Economics
University of North Carolina at Chapel Hill
Chapel Hill, North Carolina

Julian Ellison
Economic Consultant
Mid. Atlantic Research Corporation
Gaithersburg, Maryland

Leonard Harris
Professor, Department of Philosophy
Purdue University
West Lafayette, Indiana

Herbert M. Hunter
Chair and Associate Professor of Sociology
Department of Sociology
Indiana University of Pennsylvania
Indiana, Pennsylvania

Julianne Malveaux
Economist / Writer / TV Host
Washington, DC

Manning Marable
Professor of History and Director
Institute for Research in African-American Studies
Columbia University
New York, New York

CONTRIBUTORS

George Sherer
PhD Candidate in Economics
Department of Economics
Columbia University
New York, New York

James B. Stewart
Vice Provost for Educational Equity and
Professor of Labor Studies and Industrial Relations
The Pennsylvania State University
State College, Pennsylvania

Vernon J. Williams, Jr.
Associate Professor of History and American Studies
Purdue University
West Lafayette, Indiana

PREFACE

These two volumes are designed to fill a major void in our knowledge of the African American economic experience. The chapters contained herein represent the thinking of some of America's most distinguished scholars on the topic. We have entitled the book, *A Different Vision*. As you read the various essays, you will see that the idea of a "different vision" is more than just a title. Indeed, these authors have a different set of scholarly priorities and interpretations that are grounded in the dissimilar life experiences and life chances of African Americans.

Each author was given the freedom to write on any aspect of the African American economic experience, but was asked to write in a style that is accessible to a wide audience. The contributions cover several well defined areas. These include economic philosophy and history, the political economy of race and gender, the history of African American economic thought, public policy and racial inequality, and economic method. They are organized into two volumes. Volume 1 is subtitled "African American Economic Thought" and Volume 2 is subtitled "Race and Public Policy".

This enormous undertaking has stretched over quite a long period of time. During this period, each author has graciously given of his or her time not only in developing the essays, but also in responding to editor's queries and even serving as reviewers of companion essays. This unusual level of commitment reflects the dedication of each author to the successful completion of this project.

To add a finishing touch to *A Different Vision*, we asked Atlanta artist Michael Ellison to illustrate the jacket covers of each volume. His two panel subtractive woodblock color prints, entitled "Everyday Life", capture the essence of contemporary urban black life. The background symbols and visual imagery he employs are haunting reminders of the past and present racial barriers.

We thank all contributors for their generosity. We thank the following individuals for serving as reviewers: Robert S. Browne, Robert Cherry, William Darity, Jr., Julian Ellison, Augustin K. Fosu, Herbert M. Hunter, Wilhelmina A. Leigh, Margaret C. Simms, and Stephanie Y. Wilson. Each made invaluable comments on various chapters of the two volumes. Graduate assistant Paula Stevens also provided extremely helpful editorial assistance.

This is the second time that I have had the opportunity of undertaking a project with Routledge and on each occasion, the experience has been very pleasurable. The editors have provided tremendous support and great optimism throughout. In particular, we thank Alan Jarvis, Alison Kirk and Ann King.

We hope the essays contained herein are useful to all individuals interested in learning more about the African American economic experience. Of course, a project such as this, no matter how ambitious, cannot cover all relevant areas. In this regard, we chose to sacrifice empirical and theoretical contributions for others focusing on philosophy, history, and public policy. In this way, the subject can be digested by a broader audience of readers.

Finally, we sincerely hope this project is worthy of the efforts of so many fine contributors. We thank you all.

Thomas D. Boston

1

EDITOR'S NOTES

Thomas D. Boston

We are pleased and honored to present this two volume book containing the philosophies, opinions and perspectives of some of this country's leading African American economists, sociologists, historians, philosophers, political scientists, and legal scholars. Each has contributed enthusiastically to this first ever compendium on African American economic thought.

The idea behind this book emerged three years ago following a panel discussion that was sponsored jointly by the National Economic Association and the American Economics Association. That discussion, entitled History of African American Economic Thought, generated a surprising amount of interest from the audience. Yet the subject is seldom discussed in scholarly journals in economics. This oversight means that only a small number of economists and non-economists are aware of the contributions and views of many of the country's most noted African American economists. We sincerely hope that this book helps to close this gap.

The thirty-five chapters presented in these two volumes provide a unique look at some of the most important economic issues of the day, as seen primarily through the eyes of African Americans. While economics is the central theme, these chapters are not written solely by economists, nor are they written exclusively by African Americans. In fact, two of the chapters are written by non-African American scholars and ten are written by scholars of other disciplines. These other disciplines include history, philosophy, political science, sociology, African American studies, and law.

A Different Vision is interdisciplinary, yet the authors share a common perspective. Each examines economics not for its own sake, but to address the broader socio-economic disadvantages confronting African Americans. Their writings are not confined to the abstract boundaries of general equilibrium analysis where theory takes precedence over practical dynamics. Instead, the chapters in this book have a methodological resemblance to political economy and economic sociology.

Authors were invited to make a contribution because of their past research on the African American economic experience. The topics they chose are classified under the following headings: Race, gender and

1

economics; The economic philosophers and their vision; Poverty, inequality and public policy; Historical perspectives on race, economics and social transformation; and, Theory and method. It is interesting that they chose not to analyze how racial earnings disparities can co-exist with markets that are in equilibrium; a topic that has received the most prominent attention in neoclassical economics.

The contributions are focused instead on the practical aspects of racial inequality. While the particular issues and insights vary from scholar to scholar, their perspective is surprisingly similar. W. E. B. Du Bois calls it, "the color line." This book documents how the country's leading African American economists, past and present, have been and are preoccupied with analyzing the "color line."

W. E. B. Du Bois (1868–1963) was the first African American trained at the PhD level in economics. Few people are aware of this, or of the fact that Du Bois studied economics at the University of Berlin under the direction of Gustav von Schmoller. Schmoller was a key figure in the Historical School of Economics. He supervised Du Bois's doctoral studies during the two years spent in residency at Berlin while on leave from Harvard University.

David Lewis's 1993 biography of Du Bois notes that Schmoller expressed enough satisfaction with Du Bois's work that the latter notified the Slater Fund, his sponsor, that "a fair possibility" existed of him being allowed to stand for his PhD examination in economics after having completed only three semesters in residence. Lewis notes that, "A doctorate in economics from Berlin ('the most difficult of German degrees') would represent the capstone of western academic preparation. Not just for himself, then, but 'for the sake of my race,' he must try to obtain this degree, he wrote Gilman" (Lewis 1993: 143).[1]

Du Bois's enthusiasm was soon tempered by the mischief of a chemistry professor who threatened to advance an early graduation petition for ten of his students if Du Bois were allowed to finish in three semesters rather than the required four. So despite Schmoller's, Adolf Wagner's and the Dean's strong support, this professor prevented Du Bois from receiving the doctorate degree in economics. His fate was ultimately sealed when the Trustees of the Slater Fund decided they would not renew his fellowship for a fourth semester of study in Berlin. Lewis notes that the Fund's displeasure with Du Bois's course of study suggests that it was "much too rarefied to suit the men who had the heavy responsibility of guiding Negro higher education into appropriate channels" (Lewis 1993: 146). Of course all of these men were white. They advised Du Bois to present himself instead for the PhD degree at Harvard. A transcription of the comments he recorded in his notebook concerning the affair reads, "Thou shalt forgo, shalt do without" (1993: 146). More than a half century later, Du Bois recalls in his *Autobiography*

Schmoller wanted to present me for my doctorate, despite the "triennium" required in a German university and my work at Harvard was not recognized. The faculty was willing in my case but was restrained by the professor of English who threatened to push the similar claims of several Britishers. I therefore regretfully had to forgo the chance of a German doctorate and wait for the degree from Harvard.

(Du Bois 1968: 175[2])

Du Bois's dissertation in history became the first volume of the Harvard Historical series. Three years later, he published *The Philadelphia Negro* (1899). Throughout the remainder of his long and active career, Du Bois made major contributions to the study of history, sociology and to literature. Despite this, he was never offered an appointment at a predominantly white university. In his *Autobiography*, he writes sarcastically that the University of Pennsylvania, where he was in residence while writing *Philadelphia Negro*, offered him a one-year position in the "unusual status of assistant Instructor" (1968: 194).

Economists are very familiar with *An American Dilemma*, written by Gunnar Myrdal, or the *Economics of Discrimination*, by Gary Becker. But few have ever heard of *The Philadelphia Negro*. This work is so penetrating in its insights and thorough in its method of examination, that Myrdal refers to it as the model study of black life in America.

Economists are somewhat more familiar with the work of Abram Harris, Jr. Darity writes that Harris was the first African American economist to attain academic prominence in the United States. After receiving a PhD degree in Economics from Columbia in 1922, he taught at Howard University until 1945 and afterwards at the University of Chicago. His most famous book, *The Black Worker* (1931), written jointly with Sterling Spero, is a definitive study of race and class within the context of the labor movement. Harris used his mastery of economic tools to elucidate society's racial ills.

Phyllis Wallace was a 1948 doctoral graduate of Yale University. Wallace attained prominence for her studies of race, gender and labor markets and will be remembered most for her abiding commitment to racial and gender equality. Julianne Malveaux notes that through a series of books and through her work as Chief of Technical Studies at the Equal Employment Opportunity Commission, Wallace shattered racial stereotypes and elucidated the workings of race and gender inequality in labor markets. She also pressed for the alleviation of poverty. From her position as President of the Industrial Relations Research Association, she urged her colleagues to consider the costs of maintaining racial and gender barriers. Malveaux writes that Wallace was usually the first and only African American woman in a particular role. Yet, "Wallace never relished that role or basked in it. 'You do your work and that's it' she said." A gifted and talented scholar, it is ironic, but not unusual for the times, that Wallace pursued the study of economics outside of her home state of Maryland because segregation laws prevented her from attending the all-white University of Maryland.

Other noted African Americans of earlier generations who were trained in the discipline of economics include Sadie T. M. Alexander, George Edmund Haynes, Oliver C. Cox and Robert Weaver. A variety of factors, usually associated with racial discrimination, led them out away from academic careers in economics and into public service or other academic disciplines. Yet in these new endeavors, the "color line" remained their primary focus.

The preamble to each volume of this work is written by Andrew F. Brimmer. Brimmer is one of the country's most distinguished economists. Born in Louisiana in 1926, Brimmer received a doctoral degree in Economics from Harvard University. After serving on the faculties of Michigan State University and the University of Pennsylvania, he entered public service; first with the Department of Commerce, and afterwards as the first African American Member of the Board of Governors of the Federal Reserve System where he served for eight years. In 1989, Brimmer served as Vice President of the American Economic Association and as President of the Association for the Study of Afro-American Life and History. One aspect of Brimmer's research reflects his keen understanding of financial markets. A second aspect reveals his abiding commitment to using his academic skills to elucidate issues pertaining to the "color line."

WHAT'S IN STORE FOR THE READER?

This book is not only about the lives and contributions of noted African American economists, it also discusses issues of law, philosophy, history, sociology, and public policy. You will find some of the most topical issues of the day discussed; topics such as affirmative action and the law, race and gender inequality, poverty and income disparity, the slave trade and African history, black business development, and economic growth in contemporary Africa. Three chapters are devoted to Booker T. Washington's philosophy and each takes a different view of its relevance today.

Most importantly, *A Different Vision* is not burdened with the technical jargon that characterizes most economics books. Instead, we have tried to make it readable to a general audience and yet appealing to scholars and policy makers.

As one reads these chapters, the different vision of African American economists will become apparent. To these authors, race is an important variable in the life chances of African Americans. Each arrives at a conclusion popularized by Cornell West – "Race Matters." This conclusion is evident in the contributions of economists, philosophers, lawyers, historians, political scientists, and sociologists. Whether the topic under discussion is the slave trade or urban housing, these authors demonstrate that the impact of racial injustice is immense. We hope this book will eventually find its way into the library of every reader who is interested in questions of the "color line."

For the preambles Andrew Brimmer was asked to write a few pages that would summarize his past research on the economic status of African Americans and his views on contemporary racial dynamics. He responded with a seventy-six page manuscript entitled "Blacks in the American Economy." This preamble now serves as an excellent introduction to the contemporary economic status of African Americans. It discusses trends in output, employment and income between 1960 and 1994 and how they have affected African Americans. Brimmer also provides a detailed discussion of African American wealth accumulation, consumer expenditure patterns and the economic costs of discrimination. Finally, he provides a penetrating look at the dynamics of African American entrepreneurship. The preamble to Volume 2 is entitled "The Economic Cost of Discrimination Against Black Americans." In it, he argues that the disparate treatment of African Americans cost the US economy $214 billion in 1993.

Volume 1 contains a preamble and two parts. Part I is entitled "Race, gender and economics" while Part II is entitled "The economic philosophers and their vision."

The chapters in Part I of Volume 1 are woven together by a common thread. Specifically, they reveal how the life chances of noted African American economists and would-be economists are affected by race and gender inequality. Robert S. Browne, the first author in this section, is the co-founder of the Black Economic Research Center, the National Economics Association, and *The Review of Black Political Economy*. Through a wide variety of professional activities, Browne has mentored an immense number of African American economists. He writes that he was propelled towards the study of economics by an "extraordinarily powerful urge to ease the plight of poor people and especially of blacks...." But this urge created an ambivalence during the earlier stages of his professional career. The ambivalence centered on his desire to address the problems of the African American community on one hand and his inclination to become immersed in more traditional theoretical research areas such as public finance, monetary policy and international economics. "I was not insensitive to the joy to be derived from sheer theoretical analysis and from the elegance of mathematical 'proofs' of obscure theorems," he observes, "but such scholarship, in isolation, had always struck me as an extravagance when there are so many genuine human problems crying out for our attention." So, Browne has devoted his life to public service. Thanks to him, the National Economics Association and *The Review of Black Political Economy* are now more than twenty-five years old. Robert S. Browne's life vividly reflects the career path chosen by many African American economists and scholars. Readers wishing to understand the personal conflicts and challenges that race imposes will find this chapter particularly enlightening.

Jerome McCristal Culp, Jr. describes how the courts and policy makers respond to race and gender inequality. They assume that color blind remedies are morally superior to race conscious policies. But he notes that racism is so well ingrained in everyday life, the very idea that the "law is or can be color blind" is a myth. Color blind remedies fail to correct racial injustice. Instead, they simply maintain the status quo.

Lynn C. Burbridge has a similar theme. But her particular focus is the neglect and inadequate coverage of African American women in scholarly research in economics. She notes that of the 7,041 titles indexed in the *Journal of Economics Literature* in 1993, only three had titles that referred specifically to African American women. This neglect stems from the shortage of African American scholars in the profession, a dominant paradigm that does not adequately address issues relevant to minorities, and the fragmentation of the profession into narrow sub-fields.

Julianne Malveaux discusses the lives of two prominent African American women economists: Phyllis Wallace (1921–93), who achieved significant stature in the economics profession during her lifetime; and Sadie T. M. Alexander (1898–1989), who was forced to pursue a career outside of the profession. Alexander was the first African American woman to receive the PhD degree in the United States. She graduated in economics from the University of Pennsylvania. But racial discrimination prevented her from pursuing an academic career except at a historically black college or university. As a result, Alexander earned a law degree and subsequently distinguished herself as a public servant and civic leader.

Philosopher Leonard Harris asks a very basic question. "What is it that economists are explaining when they explain the difference between Black and White incomes...?" Racial differences in earnings, he argues, assume that the social construct upon which the differences are predicated actually exists. While economists assume that race is the appropriate construct, Harris draws a sharp distinction between race and ethnicity and discusses the limitations of each. "If Blacks and whites are understood as a race, then explanatory causes, variables, and solutions relevant to race fail to capture ethnic features; if Blacks and whites are understood as ethnics, then explanatory causes, variables, and solutions relevant to ethnics fail to capture racial features. It is not that raciated ethnic groups are hard to explain; it is that they cannot be adequately explained if the explanation is strictly contingent on the use of a strict dichotomy between race and ethnicity," observes Harris.

Booker T. Washington (1856–1915) was not formally trained in economics. But his economic philosophies have had the greatest and most lasting impact on African Americans. Even today, his thoughts on economic advancement engender enormous theoretical and policy debate. Born a slave, he emerged to become the most influential African American of the early twentieth century. Manning Marable notes that his achievements as an educator are unparalleled. But his conciliatory political strategy has been credited with facilitating the establishment of the rigid system of Jim Crow segregation. Washington championed the formation of African American enterprise like none before him and few since. But Manning concludes that these strategies and policies were wrong. Still his ideas are permanently ingrained in many of today's African American leaders and organizations. For this reason, three chapters are devoted to Washington.

Vernon J. Williams, Jr. disagrees with Washington's philosophies and strategies. He argues that Washington "exonerated white Southerners of any responsibility for the so-called Negro problem, and placed it squarely on the shoulders of blacks." In Williams's words, Washington was "a consummate mythmaker." Although John Sibley Butler concedes that Washington's political strategy was wrong, he takes sharp exception to Marable and Williams. Butler argues that Washington's economic program for the future of the race was "simply right."

William Darity, Jr. notes that Abram Harris, Jr. was the first African American economist to obtain prominence within the academic profession. An individual with a broad-ranging intellectual curiosity, Harris made contributions in economic anthropology, black studies, institutional economics, and the history of economic thought. Darity further describes Harris's contributions to both radical and neoconservative economic thought. A 1930 graduate of Columbia University, Harris subsequently taught at Howard University and the University of Chicago. Julian Ellison notes that the better part of the last third of Harris's life was spent teaching philosophy. In addition, he argues that his philosophical thought is grounded in Hegelian and Marxian dialectical logic.

The remaining chapters of Volume 1 are also devoted to a discussion of the lives and contributions of four other prominent African Americans. Each was formally trained in economics, but not all remained in the discipline. George Edmund Haynes became the first African American doctoral graduate of Columbia University's economics program in 1910. Haynes was a charter member of the NAACP and a founder of the National Urban League. He also served as Director of Negro Economics for the US Department of Labor. James B. Stewart draws a close parallel between Haynes's ideas of social change and those of contemporary conservative economists such as Thomas Sowell and Walter Williams.

Herbert M. Hunter analyzes the political economic thought of Oliver Cromwell Cox (1908–74). Cox was trained at the University of Chicago in economics and sociology in the 1930s. While Cox is most noted for his seminal sociological treatise *Caste, Class and Race* published in 1948,

Hunter analyzes three of his relatively neglected books on the ascendancy and decline of leading capitalist countries. Hunter concludes that Cox's work predates the contemporary world systems theory popularized by Immanuel Wallerstein, and many of the arguments of the dependency–modernization debate in economic development literature.

Finally, Cecilia A. Conrad and George Sherer discuss the life of Robert C. Weaver (1907–   ). Weaver received a doctoral degree in economics from Harvard University in 1934. For the next ten years, he served the Roosevelt Administration as an advisor on Negro Affairs and on Housing. In 1966, he became the first African American to hold a Cabinet level post when he was appointed Secretary of Housing and Urban Development by President Johnson. He is a former President of Bernard Baruch College and is currently Professor Emeritus at Hunter College.

Volume 2 is divided into three parts: Part I has ten chapters addressing issues of "Poverty, inequality and public policy"; Part II is entitled "Historical perspectives on race and economics;" and finally, Part III is entitled "Theory and method." I will not belabor this introduction with a summary of the nineteen chapters contained in the second volume: the chapter titles clearly reveal their substance.

We thank all authors for their contribution. Several more authors committed themselves to submitting chapters for this work but are not represented in these volumes; unfortunately, other obligations interfered with their plans. Invitations were extended to African American economists regardless of their ideological views. However, several prominent conservative economists chose not to participate. We particularly thank Alan Jarvis, Economics Editor at Routledge, for initially proposing the book project and then waiting patiently throughout its long development. Finally, we thank our many colleagues who reviewed and commented on various chapters in these volumes. They include: Julian Ellison, William Darity, Jr., Wilhelmina Leigh, Herbert Hunter, Robert S. Browne, Robert Cherry, Augustin Fosu, Stephanie Wilson, and Margaret Simms. Finally, a special thanks is due to Paula Stevens for her detailed editorial comments.

NOTES

1 David L. Lewis (1993) *W. E. B. Du Bois: Biography of a Race* (New York: Henry Holt and Company).
2 W. E. B. Du Bois (1968) *The Autobiography of W. E. B. Du Bois* (New York: International Publishers).

2

PREAMBLE
Blacks in the American economy:
Summary of selected research
Andrew F. Brimmer

* * *

ANDREW FELTON BRIMMER

Dr Andrew Felton Brimmer is President of a Washington, DC-based economic and financial consulting firm, and he serves simultaneously as Wilmer D. Barrett Professor of Economics at the University of Massachusetts-Amherst. He is also Chairman of the Presidentially-appointed Financial Control Board which oversees the fiscal affairs of the District of Columbia.

Brimmer was born in 1926 in Newellton, Louisiana, a small town located in the northeast section of the State a few miles from the Mississippi River. His family had been long-time cotton farmers who were forced off the land as the boll weevil devastated the crops.

After graduating from the local, racially segregated high school, Brimmer joined an older sister and her family in Bremerton, Washington, in 1944. During the day, he worked as an electrician's helper in the Bremerton Navy Yard where war-damaged ships were repaired. At night, he continued his education at the equivalent of a community college. He was drafted into the US Army in May 1945, and served through November 1946. Ten months of that service was in Hawaii.

In January 1947, Brimmer enrolled in the University of Washington, Seattle. He completed his undergraduate work in three years. He first studied journalism; but, half way through, he switched his major to economics earning a BA in March 1950. He continued in the field and was awarded an MA in the summer of 1951. Brimmer won a Fulbright grant for the academic year 1951–52, which enabled him to study at the Universities of Delhi and Bombay in India. Between September 1952 and June 1955 he was enrolled in the doctoral program at Harvard University. He received his PhD in economics in March 1957, with a dissertation entitled "Monetary Policy, Interest Rates, and the Investment Behavior of Life Insurance Companies."

From June 1955 through August 1958, Brimmer was an Economist at the Federal Reserve Bank of New York. During three and a half months of that period, he served on a three-man mission to Sudan to help that country establish its central bank. He taught economics at Michigan State University from 1958 to 1961. He taught money and banking and macroeconomics at the Wharton School, University of Pennsylvania, during 1961–63. On leave of absence from the University, he served as Deputy Assistant Secretary and Assistant Secretary for Economic Affairs in the US Department of Commerce, from May 1963 until early March 1966. From March 9 of that year Brimmer began a fourteen-year term as a member of the Board of Governors of the Federal Reserve System – having been appointed by President Lyndon Johnson. He served for eight and a half years. He resigned in August 1974 to return to Harvard University, where he was appointed Thomas Henry Carroll Visiting Professor in the Harvard Business School. He held that position during the period 1974–76. In 1976 he established his consulting firm.

Brimmer is a director of a number of major corporations – including Bank of America and the Du Pont Company. He has published extensively and is the author of several books and many articles in economic and financial journals – with the main concentrations in banking and monetary policy, international finance, and the economic status of black Americans. Brimmer states that the economic research of which he is most proud is the Testimony he prepared when he was in the US Department of Commerce which demonstrated the burden of racial segregation on interstate commerce. The US Supreme Court cited it extensively in its unanimous opinion upholding the Public Accommodations Section of the Civil Rights Act of 1964.

Brimmer has been honored a number of times by the economics profession. He was the Richard T. Ely Lecturer of the American Economic Association in 1981, and he was Distinguished Lecturer on Economics in Government of the Association (joint with the Society of Government Economists) in 1988. He was Vice President of the AEA in 1989. He served as Westerfield Lecturer of the National Economics Association in 1990. He was President of the Eastern Economics Association in 1991–92, and he was elected a Fellow in 1993. He was President Elect (1996) of the North American Economics and Finance Association.

* * *

MACROECONOMIC DEVELOPMENT AND THE BLACK COMMUNITY

On several occasions, I have attempted to trace the impact of developments in the economy at large on the black community. These effects are illustrated by the behavior of employment and income over long periods of growth, as well as during recessions and recoveries.

Economic trends: 1960–72

The overall economic history of blacks in the United States during the 1960s mirrored that of the nation as a whole. However, blacks as a group did slightly better during those years – and considerably worse in the early 1970s – than the country at large.[1]

The principal changes in employment and income among blacks can be traced in Table 2.1. From 1961 through 1969, the black labor force rose in

Table 2.1 Trends in employment and income in the black community

Category	1960	1965	1969	1972
Employment (thousands)	65,778	71,088	77,902	81,702
Negro and other races[1]	6,927	7,643	8,384	8,628
White	58,850	63,445	69,518	73,074
Percentage of total				
Negro and other races	10.5	10.8	10.8	10.7
Unemployment (thousands)	3,852	3,366	2,831	4,840
Negro and other races	787	676	570	956
White	3,063	2,691	2,261	3,884
Percentage of total				
Negro and other races	20.4	20.1	20.1	19.8
Unemployment rate (per cent)				
Total	5.5	4.5	3.5	5.6
Negro and other races	10.2	8.1	6.4	10.0
White	4.9	4.1	3.1	5.0
Ratio: black:white	2.1	2.0	2.1	2.0
Median family income (current dollars)				
Total	5,620	6,957	9,433	11,116
Negro and other races	3,233	3,994	6,191	7,106
Black	n.a.	3,886	5,999	6,864
White	5,835	7,251	9,794	11,549
Income gap				
White/Negro and other Races	2,602	3,257	3,603	4,443
White/Black	n.a.	3,365	3,795	4,685
Ratio: Negro and other races:				
white	0.55	0.55	0.63	0.63
Black:white	n.a.	0.54	0.61	0.59

Source: Labor force, employment and unemployment: US Department of Labor, Bureau of Labor Statistics. Income: US Department of Commerce, Bureau of the Census
Note: 1   About 90 per cent of the persons in this category are black

line with the total civilian labor force; however, the participation rate (i.e., total labor force as a percentage of the non-institutionalized population) of blacks declined noticeably.

Blacks got a moderately larger share of the increase in employment during the 1960s than they had at the beginning of the decade. Within the black group, adult females got a relatively larger share of the expanded jobs than was true of black men. This general pattern paralleled that evident among whites, except that black men did slightly better than their white counterparts. On the other hand, black youths made virtually no progress toward improving their relative employment position during the decade. This was in sharp contrast to the situation among white youths, who expanded their share of the total.

Between 1960 and 1969, the total number of workers without jobs dropped by 1,021,000. Unemployment rose appreciably during the 1960–1 recession, but the subsequent growth of the economy during the decade was large enough to absorb an eleven million increase in the labor force and to take more than one million workers off the unemployment rolls. Over the same years, the black labor force rose by 1.2 million, but unemployment among blacks still declined by 217,000. This reduction was about in line with the decrease in joblessness in the economy generally. On the other hand, the distribution of unemployment within the black community changed significantly. Among adult black males and females, the level of unemployment decreased over the decade, as did unemployment among all components of the white group. But among black youths, the level of unemployment was 55,000 higher in 1969 than it was in 1960. The inability of the economy to meet the job needs of black youth was one of the main shortfalls in national economic policy during that decade.

The 1969–70 recession had a disproportionately adverse impact on blacks, and the subsequent recovery brought them a relatively small proportion of benefits. In fact, after two and one-half years of substantial economic expansion, blacks as a group ended up with a smaller proportion of the nation's jobs than they had at the time of the recession. The relative decline in their job shares was especially noticeable in lower-skilled occupations.

Income trends among blacks

The extent to which blacks benefited from the long period of economic expansion during the 1960s can also be traced in income trends. In 1959, blacks' money income amounted to $19.7 billion, representing 6.2 per cent of the total for the nation as a whole. By 1969, the amount for blacks had just about doubled (to $38.7 billion) – compared with a gain of 89 per cent for whites – and their share had edged up to 6.4 per cent. Although blacks did not participate in the recent recovery as fully as did whites, by 1972 their total income had climbed to $51.8 billion – or 6.7 per cent of the total of $773 billion.

Over the decade of the 1960s, the median family income of blacks just about doubled. The figure for these families in 1969 was $5,999, compared with $9,794 for whites. In 1959, median income was $3,047 for blacks and $5,893 for whites. The ratio of black to white median income rose from 0.52 in 1959 to 0.61 in 1969. In absolute terms, however, black families in 1969 received an average of $3,795 less than their white counterparts, whereas they had received $2,846 less in 1959. By 1972, the median income of black families had climbed to $6,864 compared to $11,549 for white families, but the black/white income ratio declined to 0.60 in 1971 and to 0.59 in 1972 – the level at which it had been in 1967. So the 1969–70 recession – like the recession in 1960–1 – resulted in a widening of the white/black income gap, which in absolute terms amounted to $4,685 in 1972. The explanation of these shortfalls in black income is widely known: a legacy of racial discrimination and deprivation limited blacks' ability to acquire marketable skills and barred them from better-paying jobs.

Economic trends in the mid-1980s

By the mid-1980s black Americans had resumed the moderate progress they were making before two severe recessions earlier in the decade set them back. The relative improvement in blacks' economic position was evident in expanding employment and rising income – especially among those blacks with skills that enabled them to get and hold jobs in a labor market where competition was becoming ever more vigorous.

In contrast, blacks who were truly disadvantaged – increasingly, because of a lack of preparation rather than racial discrimination – were falling further behind. In fact, the gulf between blacks at the bottom of the income scale and those who are better off even widened.[2]

Blacks in the labor market

Despite strong claims to the contrary, blacks did share substantially in the expansion of the American economy after 1982. Blacks asserted themselves more in the labor market; they got a somewhat larger proportion of the nation's jobs; and black unemployment decreased somewhat.

Changes in the black labor force

The relative improvement represented a marked turnaround from the experience blacks had during the two recessions that plagued the economy in 1980 and 1981–2. Before then, at the peak of economic activity in 1979, blacks had held 10.1 per cent of all jobs and had accounted for 20.8 per cent of total unemployment. But over the next three years of stagnation and recession, the black labor force rose by 7.5 per cent, compared with 3.7 per cent for whites and 4.4 per cent overall. The number of employed blacks fell by 291,000 – one-third of the net loss of jobs in the nation at large. Between December 1979 and December 1982, the rate of unemployment among blacks rose from 12.2 per cent to 20.9 per cent. The parallel increase in the white unemployment rate was from 5.2 per cent to 9.6 per cent, and for the total civilian labor force the unemployment rate increased from 6.0 per cent to 10.7 per cent. Thus, blacks bore a disproportionately large share of the overall loss of jobs caused by the recessions of 1980 and 1981–2.

Following the end of the recession in December 1982, the American economy rebounded vigorously. Over the next two years, the growth stimulated a strong increase (3.2 per cent) in the total civilian labor force. The increase among blacks was even greater (6.4 per cent), raising the black civilian labor force to 12.3 million. At that level, blacks constituted 10.8 per cent of the total civilian labor force at the end of 1983, compared with 10.4 per cent two years earlier.

The increase in the black civilian labor force reflected the degree to which the labor force participation rate among blacks had increased over the preceding two years. The black participation rate had been – and remained – below that for whites and other groups, but the gap between blacks and whites did narrow slightly over the two-year period.

For blacks as a group, the participation rate rose from 61.7 per cent at the end of 1982 to 63.1 per cent in December 1984 – a gain of 1.4 percentage points. The corresponding figures for whites were 64.4 per cent and 64.8 per cent – a gain of only 0.4 percentage points. Among blacks, the increased participation of black women in the labor force was particularly noticeable – an increase of 2.2 percentage points (to 56.6 per cent). The gain for black men was much more moderate (0.3 percentage points, to 71.2 per cent). In contrast, the participation rate for white women rose by 0.8 percentage points (to 53.5 per cent), and the rate for white men remained unchanged (at 77.2 per cent).

The faster expansion in the black labor force reflected the higher growth rate of the black population as well as a greater determination among blacks to search for jobs. The latter was especially true among black women. At the end of 1984, the number of black women in the civilian labor force (5,703,000) nearly equalled the number of black men (5,762,000). This was a male–female ratio of 1.01. In sharp contrast, reflecting the much lower participation rate of white women, the male–female ratio for whites was 1.34.

Gains in black employment

At the end of 1984, blacks held 10.5 million jobs – 9.8 per cent of total employment. At the trough of the recession, in December 1982, 9.2 million blacks were at work, accounting for 9.2 per cent of total employment. So, over the following two years of economic expansion black employment climbed by 1.3 million. That represented 18.1 per cent of the net increase of 7.2 million in civilian employment during the same period. Thus, whereas at the bottom of the recession blacks held just under one in every ten jobs, during the next two years they received just under one in six of the new jobs created by the strong pace of economic growth.

The jobs held by black adults were almost equally divided between men and women at the end of 1984: 4,998,000 for men and 4,977,000 for women. This was a male–female employment ratio of 1.004; the corresponding ratio for whites was 1.34.

But despite the relative improvement in black employment over the following two years, the blacks' job deficit remained substantial. For example, at the end of 1984, blacks represented 10.8 per cent of the civilian labor force but held only 10,462,000 jobs – equal to 9.8 per cent of the total. If parity had prevailed, blacks would have had an additional 1,015,000 jobs. In other words, the level of black employment would have increased by 9.7 per cent.

Reduction in black unemployment

The strong expansion of the economy during 1982–4 not only created job opportunities for new entrants into the labor force, but it also cut deeply into the backlog of unemployment, including black unemployment.

At the end of 1984, 8.1 million persons were unemployed, a decrease of 3.7 million from the level recorded in December 1982. Among black workers, unemployment at the end of 1984 amounted to 1.8 million, compared with 2.4 million two years earlier. This reduction of 568,000 in black joblessness represented 15.4 per cent of the decline in total unemployment. Nevertheless, blacks still bore a disproportionate share of the burden of unemployment. Although constituting 10.8 per cent of the civilian labor force, they represented 23.5 per cent of all persons unemployed at the end of 1984.

The overall civilian unemployment rate declined from 10.7 per cent at the end of 1982 to 7.2 per cent at the end of 1984. Over the same period, the unemployment rate for whites decreased from 9.6 per cent to 6.2 per cent; for blacks the reduction was from 20.9 per cent to 15.0 per cent. These figures suggest that, although economic expansion considerably reduced joblessness for both blacks and whites, the relative improvement for blacks was not quite as dramatic as it was for whites. Accordingly, the black–white unemployment ratio was 2.42 at the end of 1984, compared with 2.18 two years earlier.

Economic development in the 1990s

The 1990–1 recession had a noticeably negative impact on black Americans. The adverse effects showed up in a disproportionate decrease in jobs and a sharp rise in unemployment. Blacks' money income also stagnated.

In the economy at large, gross domestic product corrected for inflation (real GDP) reached a peak of $4,906.5 billion (seasonally adjusted annual rate) in the second quarter of 1990. At the trough in the first quarter of 1991, GDP was recorded at $4,837.8 billion. Thus, from peak to trough real GDP declined by 1.4 per cent.

The decline in output led to a parallel reduction in the civilian labor force and employment and to a rise in unemployment. At the peak in May 1990, the total civilian labor force stood at 124.9 million; total employment amounted to 118.3 million, and unemployment was recorded at 6.7 million. The unemployment rate was 5.3 per cent.

At the peak, the black civilian labor force equaled 13.6 million; black employment was 12.1 million, and black unemployment was 1.4 million. The black unemployment rate was 10.6 per cent. Blacks accounted for 10.9 per cent of the total civilian labor force; 10.3 per cent of total employment, and 21.6 per cent of total unemployment. The black unemployment rate, at 10.6 per cent, was twice the rate for the total labor force (5.3 per cent).

At the labor market low point, in June 1992, the total civilian labor force stood at 127.3 million; employment at 117.5 million, and unemployment had risen to 9.8 million. The unemployment rate was 7.7 per cent. From peak to trough, unemployment climbed by 3.1 million (or 46.9 per cent).

Among blacks, at the recession's labor market trough, the civilian labor force amounted to 14.0 million; employment stood at 12.0 million, and unemployment was 2.0 million. The black unemployment rate was 14.5 per cent. In the case of blacks, the level of unemployment rose by 586,000. Therefore, blacks accounted for 19.0 per cent of the rise in unemployment. Consequently, blacks absorbed a disproportionate share of the adverse effects of the 1990–1 recession.

On the other hand, blacks' participation in the employment recovery following the recession was not exceptional. Between the recession's labor market trough in June 1992, and December 1994, the civilian labor force expanded by 4.4 million to 131.7 million (or 3.5 per cent); the number of jobs rose by 7.1 million to 124.6 million (or 6.0 per cent), and unemployment decreased by 2.6 million – to 7.2 million. The unemployment rate fell from 7.7 per cent to 5.4 per cent. Among blacks, the corresponding changes were: civilian labor force rose by 540,000 to 14.5 million (or 3.9 per cent); employment rose by 1.1 million to 13.1 million (or 9.6 per cent), and unemployment decreased by 608,000 to 1.4 million. The black unemployment rate fell from 14.5 per cent in June 1992 to 9.8 per cent in December 1994.

Consequently, during the recovery through December 1994, blacks accounted for 12.2 per cent of the rise in the civilian labor force; for 15.5 per cent of the increase in jobs, and for 23.1 per cent of the reduction in unemployment. So, on balance, blacks' overall labor market situation, after $2\frac{1}{2}$ years of economic recovery, was essentially unchanged from what it was when the 1990–1 recession began.

INCOME, WEALTH, AND INVESTMENT BEHAVIOR

I have undertaken more than a dozen studies of income and wealth in the black community.[3] Several conclusions reached in these inquiries stand out clearly: blacks suffer from a significant income deficit, and the gap has closed very little over time. Moreover, within the black community the distribution of income has become increasingly unequal. Finally, the distribution of wealth is biased even more against blacks.

Over time, as blacks' incomes have risen they have increased their saving rate to the point where it is only slightly below that of whites (e.g., 9.60 per cent for blacks vs. 10.91 per cent for whites in 1984). The greater margin of saving has enabled blacks to enlarge their accumulation of assets. However, blacks' share of wealth is much smaller than their share of income.

The profile of asset accumulation by blacks generally parallels that in the economy at large. Yet, a few striking differences in asset preferences – distinguished by the degree of risk involved – are evident when blacks' portfolios are compared with those held by whites.

Members of the black middle class have made the most progress in improving both their income and wealth. Among them, the pattern of asset ownership is more similar to that of their white counterparts than is the case of the black community as a whole.

Blacks have little knowledge of the stock market, and they have developed only a weak demand for equity securities. However, over time, as their incomes rise further and as they acquire more familiarity with common stock, more blacks will include these issues in their investment portfolios.

These general conclusions were documented in a comprehensive study completed in 1987.[4]

Income, wealth, and asset choices

The black community lags much further behind in the accumulation of wealth than one might have expected from a familiarity with the money income figures available annually. The magnitude of the deficit in black wealth could be measured for the first time in 1987, on the basis of information published by the US Bureau of the Census.

Using these basic data, I prepared detailed estimates of the amount and composition of wealth held by households in the United States in 1984. The households were divided by race. The estimates are in Table 2.2. In compiling the data, the Census Bureau did not include the assets which individuals have accumulated in the form of pension funds and life insurance policy reserves. Individuals' accumulated contributions to Social Security (which will generate future retirement income) were also excluded. The Census Bureau data show 'net worth', the measure which represents the market value of the specified assets owned by households minus the households' total liability.

Level of accumulated wealth

In 1984, the wealth of the black community (measured by net worth) amounted to $208.2 billion. Thus, blacks owned 3.0 per cent of the accumulated wealth in the United States – which totaled $6,912.2 billion. By

Table 2.2 Money income and net worth, by types of assets owned and by race, 1984 ($ million)

Types of asset	All households Amount	White households Amount	White households Per cent of total	Black households Amount	Black households Per cent of total	Other races Amount	Other races Per cent of total
Regular checking accounts	43,131	40,598	94.1	1,823	4.2	710	1.7
Interest-earning assets at fin. insts.	985,512	958,084	97.2	13,057	1.3	14,371	1.5
IRA/Keogh retirement accounts	149,794	145,865	97.4	1,669	1.1	2,260	1.5
US savings bonds	32,443	31,829	98.1	387	1.2	227	0.7
Other interest-earning assets	213,653	209,797	98.2	1,735[1]	0.8	2,121[1]	1.0
Stocks and mutual fund shares	466,357	459,028	98.4	1,443	0.3	5,886	1.3
Equity in business or profession	706,501	680,293	96.3	12,919	1.8	13,289	1.9
Motor vehicles	410,754	380,537	92.6	21,300	5.2	8,917	2.2
Homeownership	2,822,332	2,633,619	93.3	124,592	4.4	64,121	2.3
Vacation homes and other real estate	298,853	288,258	96.5	4,529	1.5	6,066	2.0
Rental property	613,389	561,854	91.6	23,953	3.9	27,582	4.5
Other assets	169,484	168,156	99.2	782[1]	0.5	546[1]	0.3
Total: Net worth	6,912,202	6,557,918	94.9	208,189	3.0	146,095	2.1
Memorandum: Money income	2,391,693	2,160,203	90.3	171,649	7.2	59,841	2.5

Source: Analysis and calculations by Brimmer & Company, Inc. Basic data from US Department of Commerce, Bureau of the Census, "Household Wealth and Asset Ownership: 1984," Current Population Reports, Series P–70, no. 7
Note: 1 Estimated by Brimmer & Company, Inc

comparison, in 1984, blacks received 7.2 per cent of total money income in the country. Therefore, their share of wealth was less than half their share of income.

The Census Bureau estimated that there were 9,509,000 black households in the nation in 1984, representing 11.0 per cent of the 86,790,000 total households. In that year, black money income amounted to $171.6 billion – 7.2 per cent of the total. If blacks had received their proportionate share of income (11.0 per cent), they would have gotten $263.1 billion – or $91.4 billion more than they actually received. Thus, blacks had an income deficit of 34.8 per cent. Their deficit in wealth was proportionately much larger. If blacks had owned 11.0 per cent of the total wealth in 1984, their net worth could have amounted to $760.3 billion – or $552.2 billion more than they actually held. Thus, their wealth deficit amounted to 72.6 per cent.

Types of assets

The assets in Table 2.2 are arranged by the degree of liquidity. The first four categories grouped together represent mainly bank accounts and liquid savings. In combination, they accounted for 17.7 per cent of the net worth of all households in the country in 1984. The corresponding fractions were 17.9 per cent for white households and 8.2 per cent for black households. The second group consists of financial investments. The interest earning assets in this group include mainly money market funds, US government securities, municipal obligations, and corporate bonds. Stocks and mutual fund shares represent household ownership of corporate enterprises. Blacks' investment in these categories was quite meager. They held only 0.8 per cent of the bonds and money market funds and only 0.3 per cent of

Table 2.3 Distribution of net worth, by race and asset type, 1984 (percentage)

Type of asset	Total	White	Black
Total net worth	100.0	100.0	100.0
Interest-earning assets at financial institutions	14.4	14.7	6.8
Other interest-earning assets	3.1	3.2	0.7
Checking accounts	0.6	0.6	0.9
Stocks and mutual fund shares	6.8	7.1	0.8
Own home	41.3	40.5	64.7
Rental property	9.0	8.6	12.4
Other real estate	4.4	4.4	2.4
Motor vehicles	6.0	5.9	11.1
Business or profession	10.3	10.5	6.7
US Saving bonds	0.5	0.5	0.2
IRA or Keogh accounts	2.2	2.2	0.9

Source: Prepared by Brimmer & Company, Inc. Data from US Department of Commerce, Bureau of the Census, "Household Wealth and Asset Ownership: 1984," Current Population Reports, Series P–70, no. 7, p. 5

stocks and mutual fund shares. Such assets also accounted for a small fraction (0.8 per cent) of blacks' total wealth (Table 2.3).

In a similar vein, the equity accumulated by blacks in the form of business or professional assets was quite modest. Their share amounted to 1.8 per cent of the total held by all households. This category represented 6.7 per cent of the total wealth of black households – a proportion only three-fifths of the 10.3 per cent recorded for all households in the country.

The ownership of physical assets is reflected in the value of motor vehicles, homes, vacation homes, rental property, and other real estate. In 1984, blacks owned 5.2 per cent of the motor vehicles held by households. This category represented their largest share of all of the different types of assets shown in Table 2.2. Motor vehicles also accounted for 11.1 per cent of blacks' total wealth. The corresponding fractions were 6.0 per cent for all households and 5.9 per cent for white households.

As one would expect, the equity accumulated in their homes represented the most important form of wealth held by blacks. This equity was valued at $124.6 billion in 1984 and equaled 4.4 per cent of the value of all homes in the nation. For blacks, homeownership accounted for 65 per cent of their total wealth compared with 40 per cent for whites and for all households in the country. Blacks owned only 1.5 per cent of the vacation homes and other real estate. The value of these properties represented 2.2 per cent of blacks' wealth versus 4.4 per cent of the wealth of all households combined. Rental property is relatively more important as a form of investment for blacks than it is for whites or for all households in the country. Blacks owned 3.9 per cent of the rental property, and the latter accounted for 12.4 per cent of their total wealth. The corresponding fractions were 9.0 per cent for all households and 8.6 per cent for whites.

Income and wealth

The data published by the Census Bureau also show the distribution of wealth by level of income. For example, in 1984, the median annual income of all households was $20,124 (which means that half of the households had incomes above this figure and half had incomes below this amount). The median income for whites was $21,120, and that for blacks was $13,056. Thus, the white–black income ratio was 1.62. Also in 1984, the median net worth of all households was $32,666. The corresponding figures for white and black households were $39,135 and $3,397, respectively. Therefore, the white–black wealth ratio was 11.52. This meant that the average white household was more than ten times as "rich" as the average black household.

Not surprisingly, the relative position of blacks with respect to wealth accumulation varied with income. Among households with annual incomes under $10,800, the median net worth of white households was $8,443 (Table 2.4). The corresponding figure for black households in the same

Table 2.4 Median net worth, by race and annual household income, 1984 (dollars)

Category	All households	White households	Black households	Black as percentage All households	Black as percentage White households
Median income	20,124	21,120	13,056	64.9	61.8
Median net worth	32,667	39,135	3,397	10.4	8.7
Annual income					
under 10,800	5,080	8,443	88	1.7	1.0
10,800–23,999	24,647	30,714	4,218	17.1	13.7
24,000–47,999	46,744	50,529	15,977	34.2	31.6
48,000 and over	123,474	128,237	58,758	47.6	45.8
Type of household					
Married couples	50,116	54,184	13,061	26.1	24.1
Female householders	13,885	22,500	671	4.8	3.0
Male householders	9,883	11,826	3,022	30.6	25.6

Source: Calculations by Brimmer & Company, Inc. Data from US Bureau of the Census, op. cit., p. 5

income class was $88. The black–white wealth ratio was 0.01. In the income range of $10,800 to $23,999, the median wealth of white households was $30,714 compared with $4,218 for black households. The resulting black–white wealth ratio was 0.14. White households with median incomes between $24,000 and $47,999 had a median net worth of $50,529. The parallel figure for blacks was $15,977 – yielding a black–white wealth ratio of 0.32. At the upper end of the income scale (in excess of $48,000), the median net worth of white families amounted to $128,237, and that for black families amounted to $58,758. This represented a black–white wealth ratio of 0.46.

The distribution of wealth was even more striking when the asset holdings of different types of households were compared. For instance, in 1984, white married couple households had a median net worth of $54,184. Among black married couple households, the median net worth was $13,061. The black–white wealth ratio was 0.24. In sharp contrast, white female householders had a median net worth of $22,500, and the corresponding figure for black female householders was $671. In this case, the black–white wealth ratio was 0.30. Among male householders, the median net worth for whites was $11,826, and it was $3,022 for blacks. These figures yielded a black–white wealth ratio of 0.26.

The distribution of wealth within the black community is far more uneven than it is among whites in the nation at large. For example, among all households combined, the net worth of those at the top of the income scale was 24 times as large as the net worth of those in the lowest income category. Among white households, the multiple was 15 times, but among blacks it was 67 times. A similar pattern – though less extreme – prevailed when types of households are compared. Thus, the wealth held by married couples in the

21

nation at large was nearly four times that held by female householders. Among whites, married householders had about 2.5 times the wealth held by female householders. In sharp contrast, the wealth held by black married couples was 19.5 times as large as that held by black female householders.

In summary, the ownership of wealth by blacks reflects the same pattern of deficits evident when one looks at money income. However, the shortfall in wealth is much larger. To a considerable extent the latter can be traced to a long history of deprivation in this country. This means that blacks have had much less opportunity than whites to earn, to save, and to invest. Because of this historical legacy, black families have had few opportunities to accumulate wealth and to pass it on to their descendants.

RACIAL DISCRIMINATION AND CONSUMER BEHAVIOR

In the summer of 1963, when I was Deputy Assistant Secretary in the US Department of Commerce, I was asked to undertake a study to assess the burden of racial discrimination on interstate commerce. The results were presented as testimony before the Commerce Committee of the US Senate when it was considering the Public Accommodations section of the measure which became the Civil Rights Act of 1964. Later the United States Supreme Court cited that testimony in upholding the constitutionality of the Act.

The research showed that, in the past, the pattern of expenditures among blacks had diverged sharply from that of the general population. This divergence had resulted from a number of circumstances, but low incomes and the restrictions of racial discrimination had been principally responsible. Because of low incomes, the typical black family had to spend a somewhat larger proportion of its paycheck for basic necessities – such as food, clothing, and housing – than white families. Because of limited access to public accommodations, blacks tended to entertain more at home than white families in the same income group. Moreover, blacks seem to be particularly brand conscious; and (when they could afford them) they appeared to lean toward higher priced items in any specific line. Finally, expenditures for personal care (including the costs of cosmetics and patronage at beauty and barber shops) normally ran much higher for blacks than for whites in the same income category.

In some cases it was possible to obtain a reasonably good quantitative estimate of the effects of racial discrimination on black consumption expenditures. The effects were particularly noticeable in the pattern of spending for the services of the amusement, restaurant, hotel, and motel industries. Here the availability or nonavailability of desegregated facilities seems to outweigh any special kinds of taste or conspicuous consumption in shaping the behavior of black consumers. The differential effects of the segregated market are clearly discernible in Table 2.5, showing average

Table 2.5 Average family expenditures for admissions, food eaten away from home, and automobile operations, for three income classes, large northern and southern cities, by race, 1950 (dollars)

Income class and region	Admissions			Food eaten away from home			Automobile operations		
	Black	White	Blacks percentage of whites	Black	White	Blacks percentage of whites	Black	White	Blacks percentage of whites
2,000 to 3,000:									
Large Northern cities	31	29	107	148	184	80	52	86	60
Large Southern cities	23	36	64	113	194	58	52	95	55
Northern expenditures as percentage of Southern	135	81	–	131	95	–	100	91	–
3,000 to 4,000:									
Large Northern cities	45	37	122	138	170	81	67	158	42
Large Southern cities	37	39	95	117	180	65	86	170	51
Northern expenditures as percentage of Southern	122	95	–	118	94	–	78	93	–
4,000 to 5,000:									
Large Northern cities	57	48	119	182	234	78	148	220	67
Large Southern cities	39	45	87	166	257	65	136	225	60
Northern expenditures as percentage of Southern	146	107	–	110	91	–	109	98	–

Source: "Study of Consumer Expenditure Income and Saving," tabulated by Bureau of Labor Statistics, US Department of Labor, for Wharton School of Finance and Commerce, University of Pennsylvania, Philadelphia, PA, 1956–7 black and white family expenditures for "admissions," which is a good proxy for patronage of theaters and recreational facilities; "food eaten away from home", which covers restaurants, diners, and other eating places; and "automobile operations," that is, the cost of driving and maintaining a car – a key to travel, including the use of hotels and motels. From these data it is clear that blacks in large Northern cities spent considerably more than Southern blacks of the same income bracket for each of the services listed in the table. On the other hand, Northern city white families spent less than Southern city families. Within the same income class, blacks in the North spent more than whites in the North for "admissions." But Southern blacks spent less than either Southern whites or Northern blacks. In both the North and South, blacks spent less on "food eaten away from home" than white people in the same income categories. However, the differential was much greater in the South. The table also indicates that both Northern and Southern blacks spent much less than whites of the same income class on "automobile operations" – 40 to 60 per cent less.

These summary statistics certainly suggest that blacks were less likely than whites to be patrons of cultural events, customers of restaurants, or tourists along the open road. Since blacks spent close to the same amount, on the average, for the purchase of automobiles as did whites of the same income level (and proportionately more for food) it seems evident that their limited access to adequate facilities historically had distorted their overall pattern of consumption.

THE ECONOMIC COST OF DISCRIMINATION

The disparate treatment of blacks cost the American economy about $241 billion in 1993. This figure is equal to roughly 3.8 per cent of that year's gross domestic product (GDP). While part of the loss can be attributed to the lag in blacks' educational achievement, the bulk of the shortfall appears to be related to continued discrimination, which limits their access to higher-paying jobs. Furthermore, over the last quarter-century, the relative cost of discrimination seems to have risen. And, given the slow rate at which blacks are being absorbed into managerial, professional, and technical positions, the income deficit they face – and the corresponding economic cost to the nation – will probably narrow very little in the years ahead.[5]

Economic impact of racial discrimination

The earliest assessment of the economic cost of discrimination against nonwhites in the United States was prepared by the President's Council of Economic Advisers (CEA) in 1962. The CEA estimated the cost at approximately $17.8 billion, or 3.2 per cent of gross national product

(GNP) – which totaled $554.9 billion in that year. (Note that GNP, the value of total production of goods and services measured at market prices, was the official measure of economic activity in use in 1962.)

In 1965, when I was Assistant Secretary of Commerce, at my request the US Bureau of the Census made estimates of the cost of discrimination against nonwhites for the years 1949 through 1963. The Census Bureau's estimating procedure was more comprehensive than that employed earlier by the CEA. The Census Bureau's estimates sought to account for the economic losses originating from two sources: inefficiencies in the use of the labor force arising from failure to use fully the existing education, skills, and experience of the population, and failure to develop fully potential education, skills, and experience. The losses were described in terms of the gains that might accrue to GNP if discrimination were eliminated – or had been eliminated in the past. However, the Census Bureau recognized that, because the legacy of past discrimination affects the contemporary occupational, geographic, and capital structures, as well as the education, training, and skills of the nonwhite labor force, the gains would accrue only over time as the labor force is upgraded and the economy adjusts.

Based on the Census Bureau's analysis described above, I estimated that discrimination against nonwhites cost about $20.1 billion in lost GNP in 1963, equal to 3.5 per cent of that year's total GNP of $583.9 billion. Roughly $11.1 billion (1.9 per cent of GNP) reflected the failure to use fully nonwhites' existing skills, and $9.0 billion (1.6 per cent of GNP) arose from the failure to improve and fully use their educational achievement.

Applying the Census Bureau's technique as used in 1965, in 1994, I updated the estimates for the economic cost of discrimination against blacks. The results for four years (1967, 1973, 1979, and 1993) are summarized in Table 2.6.

Table 2.6 Economic cost of discrimination against blacks, 1967–93 (estimated loss of Gross Domestic Product) ($ billion)

Year	Gross Domestic Product	Gain from full use of present education		Gain from full use of improved education		Total gain from full use of present and improved education	
		Amount	Percentage	Amount	Percentage	Amount	Percentage
1967	814.30	12.10	1.49	11.10	1.36	23.20	2.85
1973	1,349.80	22.90	1.70	19.40	1.43	42.30	3.13
1979	2,488.60	45.80	1.84	38.20	1.53	84.00	3.38
1993	6,374.00	137.00	2.15	103.90	1.63	240.90	3.79

Source: Prepared by Brimmer & Company, Inc. Data for GDP from the US Department of Commerce, Bureau of Economic Analysis. Percentage increases in compensation and other income estimated by Brimmer & Company, Inc., based on data from the US Department of Commerce, Bureau of the Census

Trends in the economic cost of discrimination

The figures show that, over the last twenty-five years or so, the American economy has been losing between 1.5 per cent and 2.2 per cent of GDP because racial discrimination against blacks limits the full use of their existing educational attainment. In 1967, this loss amounted to 1.5 per cent of GDP or $12.1 billion. Another 1.4 per cent ($11.1 billion of GDP) was lost because of the failure to improve and fully utilize blacks' educational level. In combination, lost GDP amounted to $23.2 billion, equal to 2.9 per cent of the 1967 total of $814.3 billion. By 1993, the shortfall in GDP due to the failure to use blacks' existing education amounted to $137.5 billion (2.2 per cent of GDP). Failure to improve their education cost $103.9 billion (1.6 per cent). The aggregate loss was estimated at $204.9 billion – 3.8 per cent of GDP.

The statistics in Table 2.6 enable one to apportion the loss in GDP between contemporary discrimination against blacks (failure to use fully their existing education) and the legacy of past discrimination (failure to improve their education). The figures suggest that, while no dramatic shifts have occurred over the last two and a half decades, the proportion of the loss that can be attributed to current discrimination has risen slightly. The latter component varied from 52.2 per cent in 1967, to 54.31 per cent in 1973, to 54.44 per cent in 1979, and to 56.87 per cent in 1993.

ECONOMICS OF BLACK ENTERPRISE

Most of my research on black-owned businesses has sought to explain why black firms have played such a marginal role in the American economy. The question has been examined in both theoretical and empirical terms. The conclusions reached can be stated succinctly: blacks in business have been both beneficiaries and victims of racial discrimination, but the latter had the greater impact. The evidence also suggests that, while blacks have made modest progress in recent years, the overall situation is not likely to improve very much in the years ahead.

During the last decade, black-owned firms saw a rapid expansion of their share of the American economy. This was a reversal of the declining trend that had been evident since the end of official racial segregation in the mid-1960s. Black businesses initially failed to keep pace with the national economy and their growth fell considerably short of that experienced by the black community as a whole.

The turn-around in the expansion of black-owned businesses began in the early 1980s. It was due primarily to the entry of newly established firms in fields far removed from the black consumer market to which racial segregation and its legacy had restricted the typical black-owned enterprise. Historically, the latter was confined mainly to the provision of personal services and retail trade in segregated neighborhoods. In addition, a number of existing black firms have diversified into the general consumer market and the provision of business services – especially to large corporations and to government agencies.

Long-term trends in black businesses

The pattern of black business expansion can be traced in Table 2.7. The figures show the level of receipts of black-owned businesses in selected years during the period 1969 through 1993. These are compared with the level of business sales in the nation at large, as well as with a number of measures of overall economic activity. The check points are the years 1969, 1972, 1977, 1982, and 1987. Those are the years in which the US Bureau of the Census conducted *Surveys of Minority-Owned Businesses*. Receipts of black-owned firms in 1993 were estimated by Brimmer & Company.

Several features of these data stand out. Between 1969 and 1982, the status of black-owned businesses deteriorated noticeably – no matter what measure is used to compare their position. For example, in 1969, black-owned firms had receipts of $4.5 billion, equal to 0.362 per cent of total business sales. By 1982, their receipts had risen to $12.4 billion,[6] but the amount represented 0.301 per cent of total business sales. Compared with overall economic activity, black firms' receipts decreased from 0.466 per cent of Gross Domestic Product (GDP) in 1969 to 0.395 per cent in 1982.

Black firms also fell short of the improvement which the black community as a whole was making in its relative economic position. For instance, the money income of blacks climbed from $39.6 billion to $146.1 billion between 1969 and 1982. This raised blacks' share from 6.517 per cent to 7.088 per cent of the total. Moreover, since the largest fraction of black businesses' receipts comes from the black community, their sales can be compared with black income. In 1969, such receipts equaled 11.291 per cent of blacks' money income. By 1982, the figure had decreased to 8.515 per cent.

The data also show that the decline in black businesses' relative position had been reversed by 1987. It is estimated that their receipts amounted to $25.6 billion in the latter year. At that level, they accounted for 0.474 per cent of total business sales. Their receipts represented 0.563 per cent of GDP, and 11.368 per cent of black money income.

The accelerated expansion of black-owned businesses since the mid-1980s can also be traced. Black firms' receipts were estimated at $34.3 billion in 1993. At that level, such receipts were equal to 0.510 per cent of total business sales. They also represented 0.569 per cent of GDP and 11.496 per cent of black money income.

Another indication of the more rapid growth of black-owned businesses is provided by the figures showing the sales of firms on *Black Enterprise*

27

Table 2.7 Economic growth and the expansion of black-owned businesses, 1969–93 ($ millions)

Category	1969	1972	1977	1982°	1982^R	1987°	1987^R	1993°	1993^R
US economy									
Gross Domestic Product	959,500	1,207,000	1,974,100	3,149,600		4,539,900		6,020,200	
Personal income	773,700	980,500	1,601,300	2,690,900		3,802,000		5,375,100	
Money income	607,982	777,552	1,238,910	2,061,691		2,988,548		3,922,100	
Sales: manufactures and trade	1,237,612	1,560,400	2,755,500	4,130,200		5,394,000		6,717,600	
Black community									
Money income	39,624	53,330	88,775	146,130		224,893		298,100	
Percentage of personal income	5.121	5.439	5.544	5.432		5.915		5.546	
Percentage of total money income	6.517	6.859	7.088	7.525		7.601			
Sales: black enterprise									
BE-200s	–	473	897						
Black-owned businesses				2,170,000		6,156,334		10,280,801	
Receipts	4,474	5,534	8,645	12,443,600^O	9,619,055^R	25,566,000[1]	19,762,900^R	34,269,337[1]	25,702,003[2]
Percentage of GDP	0.466	0.458	0.438	0.395	0.305	0.563	0.432	0.569	0.427
Percentage of personal income	0.578	0.564	0.540	0.462	0.357	0.672	0.516	0.638	0.478
Percentage of total money income	0.736	0.712	0.698	0.604	0.467	0.855	0.657	0.874	0.655
Percentage of black money income	11.291	10.377	9.738	8.515	6.583	11.368	8.728	11.496	8.622
BE-200s sales, percentage of black business	–	8.547	10.376	17.439	22.559	24.080	31.364	30.000	40.000
Percentage of total business sales	0.362	0.355	0.314	0.301	0.233	0.474	0.364	0.510	0.383

Source: Data on US economy from US Department of Commerce, Bureau of the Census. Data on black-owned businesses from US Bureau of the Census, *Survey of Minority-owned Businesses: Black, 1969, 1972, 1977,* and *1987.* Data on BE-200s from *Black Enterprise* Magazine

Notes: O For 1982, data for black-owned businesses as published by the US Bureau of the Census

R For 1987, the US Bureau of the Census revised data for black-owned businesses to exclude regular corporations. Data for 1982 were revised to conform to the new methodology

1 Estimated by Brimmer & Company using the original 1982 methodology

2 Estimated by Brimmer & Company using the 1987 methodology

magazine's list of 200 top black-owned businesses. In 1987, the BE-200 had sales of $6.2 billion, equal to 0.137 per cent of GDP and 0.115 per cent of total business sales. By 1993, the BE-200 sales had increased to $10.3 billion, and the corresponding percentages were 0.171 and 0.153, respectively. On the other hand, the sales of the BE-200 rose from 24.1 per cent of total black business receipts in 1987 to 30.0 per cent in 1993. The BE-200 firms are the largest of the companies owned by blacks, and they are also the most innovative. They – and smaller firms like them – have been the main drivers behind the rapid expansion of black-owned businesses in recent years.

Origins and evolution of black businesses

Black businesses in the United States are mainly the by-product of racial segregation. The latter acted like a protective tariff. This was especially true with respect to most services. It served simultaneously to keep blacks out of many markets used by white consumers, and it provided a protected market for black-owned businesses.[7]

The origin and behavior of black-owned firms are reflective of blacks' adaptation to the malfunctioning of the market place caused by racial segregation and discrimination. The latter created two markets. One was open to the white public essentially without limitations, and whites were able to purchase both goods and services with complete freedom of choice. For blacks, however, access to this general market was extremely restricted. They enjoyed considerable freedom of choice in the purchase of goods (except housing), but a wide range of services (particularly personal services) offered in the general market was not available to them. Therefore, a second market emerged. This was basically a black consumer market, and local retailing and the provision of personal services lay at its core.

The structure and functioning of these segmented markets are illustrated in Figure 2.1. It will be noted that blacks earned income in the same way as did other households; they offered their labor and capital in the market for productive factors (Stage I). They were paid in the form of wages, rents, interest, and profit (Stage II). However, after this point, the two flows diverged. The business sector (Stage III) divided into two segments: one (B_C) generated output for the general market for consumer goods and services (Stage IV, M_C), and the other (B_N) produced mainly for black consumers (M_N).

The way in which the components of the structure were linked together can be traced from black households (H_N in Stage I) through the black consumer market (M_N in Stage IV) to black-owned businesses (B_N in Stage III). This parallel structure was the predominantly segregated black consumer market. It was basically a market for services and local retail trade. It

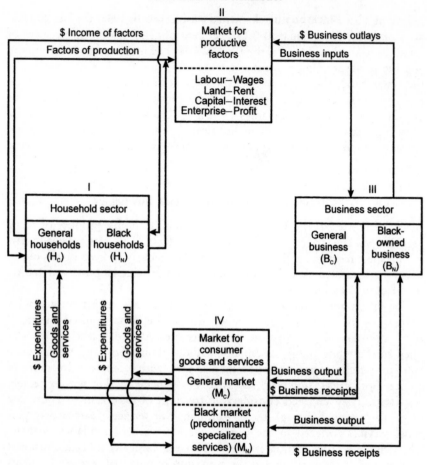

Figure 2.1 Blacks in the American economy
Source: The American Negro Reference Book, edited by John P. Davis, Englewood Cliffs, NJ: Prentice Hall, Inc., 1966, p. 253

was the place of practice for black professionals (lawyers, physicians, dentists, undertakers). It was the counter for blacks in business (owners of retail outlets, real estate dealers and brokers, life insurance companies, cosmetic manufacturers). Above all, it was the source of personal services purchased by blacks (barber and beauty shops).

Thus, this segregated market, serving as a protective tariff, was the foundation for black businesses. However, blacks did not have exclusive hold on black consumers. Firms catering to the general market (especially sellers of automobiles and other durable goods) always tried to attract black buyers. This competition also served to restrict the opportunities open to black firms.

Black businesses at the end of segregation

The model of black business evolution described above had been thoroughly validated by the time official racial segregation ended in the mid-1960s. The situation prevailing at that time is illustrated by the data in Table 2.8. The figures show self-employed businessmen, by race and industry, in 1950 and 1960, as reported in the US Census of Population. Since the vast majority of black firms were proprietorships, the data on self-employment provide a fairly complete profile of black-owned businesses.

In 1960, there were 46,400 black businessmen, and they represented 2.4 per cent of the total in the nation at large. Almost three-fifths (56.7 per cent) of the black businessmen were engaged in retail trade – which was primarily serving black consumers. Within that category, food stores accounted for 18.8 per cent and eating and drinking places for 24.4 per cent of the total. Personal services represented 9.4 per cent. Areas serving the general market accounted for smaller fractions of self-employed blacks: construction (8.6 per cent), manufacturing (3.0 per cent), and transportation (2.7 per cent).

An alternative comparison shows the same degree of concentration by blacks on the segregated consumer market. For example, while blacks represented 2.4 per cent of all self-employed businessmen, they made up 5.6 per cent of all those operating eating and drinking places. Other above-average comparisons were: food stores (4.1 per cent), personal services (3.4 per cent), transportation (3.2 per cent), and automotive repair (2.8 per cent). In the case of business services, blacks accounted for 2.4 per cent – equal to their share of the total self-employed. In all other lines, blacks fell short of the average representation.

Black capitalism

In the early 1970s, it became fashionable to stress a strategy of "black capitalism" as a means of stimulating economic development for blacks. This strategy had an intuitive appeal to varying shades of political opinion. To the black militant it was appealing because it promised community ownership of property and an end to "exploitation" by outside merchants. The strategy was appealing to white conservatives because it stressed the virtues of private enterprise capitalism as the path to economic advancement instead of reliance on public expenditures, especially for public welfare. Since this strategy received explicit approval and encouragement in the federal government and led to the creation of various governmental bodies, it merited a critical examination of the contribution which it might be expected to make to minority economic development in the United States.[8]

The selection of a strategy centered on black ownership of business enterprises raised several fundamental economic questions which this paper attempted to answer:

Table 2.8 Self-employed businessmen, by race and industry, 1950 and 1960

| Industry | 1950 | | | 1960 | | | Annual average percentage rate of growth 1950–60 | | Median income (dollars) | | | |
| | | | | | | | | | 1949 | | 1959 | |
	Total[1]	Black	Black as percentage of total	Total	Black	Black as percentage of total	Total	Black	White males	Non-white males	White males	Non-white males
Construction	191,820	3,390	1.7	222,601	3,978	1.8	1.7	1.6	3,873	1,922	6,756	3,239
Manufacturing	231,210	1,050	0.4	168,395	1,376	0.8	-3.1	2.7	4,700	2,250*	7,998	3,503
Transportation	50,940	2,430	4.7	38,223	1,241	3.2	-2.9	-6.5	3,535	2,250*	6,638	2,792
Communications, utilities and sanitary services	4,260	270	6.3	4,812	82	1.7	1.2	-11.2	3,316	2,500	7,138	3,500*
Wholesale trade	174,240	2,640	1.5	133,607	2,610	1.9	-2.6	-0.1	4,336	1,838	7,813	2,693
Retail trade	1,349,190	38,730	2.8	994,425	26,303	2.6	-3.0	-3.8	3,277	1,838	5,332	3,511
Food and dairy products	376,350	14,520	3.9	214,758	8,740	4.1	-5.5	-4.9	2,875	1,819	4,464	3,487
Eating and drinking places	270,720	15,030	5.5	203,830	11,344	5.6	-2.9	-2.9	3,114	1,870	4,990	3,170
Genl. merchandise and limited price variety	63,690	750	1.2	46,406	640	1.3	-3.1	-1.6	3,211	2,000	5,416	2,500*
Apparel and accessories	82,140	600	0.7	56,722	321	0.6	-3.6	-5.9	4,725	1,250*	7,292	4,500*
Furniture and home furniture	66,210	360	0.5	49,946	182	0.4	-2.9	-6.1	3,931	2,250*	6,923	5,500*
Motor vehicles and accessories	58,590	180	0.3	55,476	163	0.3	-0.5	-0.9	6,367	2,000	7,460	3,500*
Gasoline service stations	143,010	1,290	0.9	152,294	2,153	1.4	0.6	5.3	2,906	2,250*	4,657	4,030
Hardware, building materials	79,020	120	0.2	67,002	80	0.1	-1.6	-3.9	4,427	1,750*	6,552	2,500*
Other retail trade	209,460	5,880	2.8	147,991	2,680	1.8	-3.3	-7.5	3,330	1,717	5,794	3,737
Banking and finance	20,910	90	0.4	22,076	41	0.2	0.6	-7.5	8,277	nr	14,527	12,500*
Insurance and real estate	44,910	600	1.3	49,232	794	1.6	1.0	2.8	5,727	2,250*	10,393	5,500*
Business services	33,390	570	1.7	37,020	890	2.4	1.1	4.6	4,250	2,250*	7,626	4,500*
Automotive repair and garages	59,610	870	1.5	38,528	1,083	2.8	-4.2	2.2	3,183	2,000	5,237	3,564
Miscellaneous repair services	29,070	450	1.5	19,317	414	2.1	-4.1	-0.8	2,713	1,750*	4,851	3,500*
Personal services	135,720	5,970	4.4	127,356	4,349	3.4	-0.7	-3.1	3,114	2,174	5,060	3,296
Other industries	97,080	2,760	2.8	95,311	3,239	3.4	-0.2	1.6	3,433	1,250*	5,777	2,508
Total	2,422,350	59,820	2.5	1,954,903	46,400	2.4	-2.1	-2.4	3,502	1,860	5,932	3,368

Sources: U.S. Census of Population, 1950, Special Reports, "Occupational Characteristics," 1956, IB Table 13. U.S. Census of Population, 1960, "Occupational Characteristics," 1963, Table 3

Notes: 1 White and black only   * Estimated at mid-point of income class interval   nr not reported

- What is the nature of the economic environment in which black businesses operate?
- What are the types of businesses that are likely to evolve from this environment?
- What are the main economic forces at work in the national economy that are influencing the number and scale of operation of the types of firms in which black businessmen are concentrating?
- Can black-owned businesses offer reasonable employment opportunities to a sizable proportion of the black population?
- In terms of individual opportunities, which career path is the more promising – a career as a self-employed businessman or a career as an employed manager or official in a larger corporation? Expressed differently, which economic choice is superior – one involving investment in a business firm or one involving investment in human capital?

The general conclusion from this analysis was that the strategy of black capitalism offers a very limited potential for economic advancement for the majority of the black population. The ghetto economy as we understood it does not appear to provide profitable opportunities for large-scale business investment, and any economic advances made by residents of this marginal sector of the economy in all likelihood will not materially alter the investment prospects. This situation is in large part due to a tendency for affluent blacks to shop in the more diverse national economy.

The strategy of black capitalism fails, however, for an even more fundamental reason; it is founded on the premise of self-employment. Our research has indicated clearly that self-employment is a rather rapidly declining factor in our modern economy because the rewards to employment in salaried positions are substantially greater. Self-employment may be the path to affluence for the fortunate few who are very successful, but for the great majority of the black population it offers a low and rather risky expected pay-off.

At this juncture, we pointed out that our disenchantment with the strategy of black economic development through black capitalism was not based simply on its limited economic potential. We were also concerned that reliance on such a strategy may substitute for efforts in vital areas which are of the utmost importance to the black population. In the long run, the pursuit of black capitalism may retard blacks' economic advancement by discouraging many from the full participation in the national economy with its much broader range of challenges and opportunities. A strategy of black capitalism may also prove deleterious to the black community because, in the words of two observers, "the programs would place those least capable of accepting risk in the position of accepting large risks." New ghetto enterprises would certainly be more prone to failure than already established firms, and their failures would leave a lasting burden on the individuals starting these firms and on those employees who had been induced to work in such enterprises rather than in businesses not dependent on the ghetto economy.

Growth and diversification of black businesses

Over the last two decades, black-owned businesses have exhibited uneven progress in shifting away from the pattern of activity established during the era of racial segregation. In general, the greatest strides have been made by those which have diversified into the general market while lessening their dependence on black consumers.

These conclusions are based on the statistics on black business ownership in 1972, 1977, 1982, 1987, and 1993. The number and receipts of black-owned businesses in 1972, 1977, and 1982 are shown in Table 2.9. The same figures for 1982 and 1987 are shown in Table 2.10.

Several striking changes occurred during the decade 1972–82. Between those years, the total sales of black firms rose by 124.9 per cent. By comparison, nearly all of those firms concentrating on traditional black consumer markets fell short of this average growth rate. For example, the

Table 2.9 Number and receipts of black-owned firms, 1972, 1977, and 1982 ($ thousands)

	1972		1977		1982	
Market segment and industry	Number	Receipts	Number	Receipts	Number	Receipts
Black consumer market						
Manufacturing	764	98,863	825	180,136	1,093	369,321
Printing and publishing	690	*59,666	788	122,193	1,055	190,391
Chemicals and allied products	74	39,197	64	57,943	38	178,930
Retail trade	26,233	1,007,668	23,687	1,358,107	20,816	1,557,967
Food stores	11,887	570,572	10,679	785,776	9,187	882,737
Eating and drinking places	14,346	437,088	13,008	572,331	11,629	675,230
Finance, insurance and real estate	7,669	393,987	9,805	641,372	14,829	748,136
Insurance carriers	70	199,371	58	249,201	51	254,469
Insurance agents, etc.	1,906	34,548	2,639	44,183	5,548	70,001
Banking	99	40,416	152	140,497	354	156,418
Real estate	5,071	85,140	6,606	141,267	8,637	198,992
Other, fire	523	34,512	350	66,224	239	68,256
Selected services	50,702	611,992	79,380	1,346,693	74,486	2,215,245
Hotel and other lodging places	2,196	49,995	1,733	61,349	1,285	78,555
Personal services	34,693	320,125	35,035	399,274	40,394	560,809
Health services	2,367	61,464	14,560	432,534	17,195	594,619
Amusement and recreation services	4,460	58,772	5,535	109,664	7,836	121,059
Legal services	–	–	2,442	77,393	3,445	127,141
Motion pictures	151	2,873	241	14,372	342	9,321
Educational services	1,942	27,441	1,837	20,835	2,947	26,431
Social services	–	–	810	33,828	287	34,460
Misc. services	827	91,323	12,840	136,094	755	662,850
Sub-total	85,368	2,112,508	113,724	2,889,936	111,224	4,142,532

Table 2.9 (cont.)

Market segment and industry	1972		1977		1982	
	Number	Receipts	Number	Receipts	Number	Receipts
General open market						
Construction	19,120	627,026	21,101	757,691	23,061	994,816
Manufacturing	4,737	437,540	5,675	705,273	4,897	989,802
Food and kindred products	109	59,716	89	95,025	76	154,657
Lumber and wood products	1,497	45,038	1,935	83,992	1,533	63,662
Electric and electronic equipment	78	35,032	81	56,412	82	68,970
Fabricated metal products	129	30,168	149	26,562	102	38,902
Transportation equipment	24	2,643	30	9,753	26	44,972
Other manufacturing	2,900	264,943	3,391	433,529	3,078	618,639
Transportation and public utilities	18,819	308,924	19,640	424,777	20,194	617,887
Trucking and warehousing	9,938	245,215	11,552	353,216	13,029	530,049
Local and interurban passenger transport	8,881	63,709	8,088	71,561	7,165	87,838
Wholesale trade	1,708	325,343	2,212	664,052	3,651	858,584
Retail trade	27,691	1,397,012	31,741	1,994,224	63,237	2,560,659
General merchandise stores	971	35,200	887	47,854	977	31,079
Auto dealers and service stations	6,597	798,219	5,002	1,107,650	3,448	1,307,472
Other retail trade	20,123	563,593	25,852	838,720	58,812	1,222,108
Selected services	15,819	281,703	22,359	542,841	10,698	1,026,240
Business services	10,472	176,683	15,461	358,286	3,220	793,330
Auto repair services and garages	5,347	105,020	6,898	184,555	7,478	230,910
Sub-total	87,894	3,377,548	102,728	5,088,858	122,087	6,189,404
Other industries	14,340	44,053	14,751	671,408	105,928	2,111,635
Total: all industries	187,602	5,534,109	231,203	8,645,200	339,239	12,443,572

Source: Prepared by Brimmer & Company. Data from US Bureau of the Census, *Survey of Black-owned Businesses, 1972, 1977, 1982*

increases recorded were (per cent): insurance carriers (27.6); eating and drinking places (54.4); food stores (54.7); hotel and other lodging places (57.1); and personal services (75.2).

Firms in those industries which have concentrated on the black consumer market – but which achieved above average growth – also made noticeable strides in the general market. They included (per cent): health services (867.4); chemicals (356.5); banking (287.0); motion pictures (223.7); printing and publishing (219.1); and real estate (133.7).

Black-owned firms operating in the general open market also had a mixed growth experience. Their total sales rose by 83.3 per cent during the period 1972–82. The weakest performances were turned in by (per cent): general merchandise stores (–11.7); fabricated metals (29.0); and local transportation (37.9). The most striking gains (per cent) were: transportation equipment (1,601.6); business services (349.0); wholesale trade (163.9); and food manufacturing (159.0).

The continued diversification of black-owned firms into the general market is shown even more dramatically by changes in the industry pattern of activity between 1982 and 1987. The figures are presented in Table 2.10.

Table 2.10 Number and receipts of black-owned firms, 1982 and 1987 ($ thousands)

Market segment and industry	Level				Percentage distribution				Percentage change 1982–87	
	1982$_R$[1]		1987		1982		1987			
	Number	Receipts	Number	Receipts	Number	Amount	Number	Amount	Number	Receipt
Black consumer market										
Manufacturing	903	68,063	1,459	183,956	0.29	0.71	0.34	0.93	61.6	170.3
Printing and publishing	882	37,966	1,394	126,488	0.29	0.39	0.33	0.64	58.0	233.2
Chemicals and allied products	21	30,097	65	57,468	0.01	0.31	0.02	0.29	209.5	90.1
Retail trade	20,562	1,439,248	20,786	2,085,930	6.67	14.96	4.90	10.55	1.1	44.9
Food stores	9,156	820,155	8,952	1,001,462	2.97	8.53	2.11	5.07	–2.2	22.1
Eating and drinking places	11,406	619,093	11,834	1,084,468	3.70	6.44	2.79	5.49	3.8	75.2
Finance, insurance and real estate	12,957	280,305	26,989	804,252	4.20	2.91	6.36	4.07	108.3	186.9
Insurance carriers	10	–	36	6,220	–	–	0.01	0.03	260.0	–
Insurance agents, etc.	4,599	166,286	7,956	188,690	1.49	1.73	1.88	0.95	73.0	13.5
Banking	263	8,268	35	17,402	0.09	0.09	0.01	0.09	–86.3	110.5
Real estate	7,910	195,318	15,552	505,936	2.57	2.03	3.67	2.56	96.6	159.0
Selected services	69,746	1,509,627	124,206	3,628,216	22.64	15.69	29.28	18.36	78.1	140.3
Hotel and other lodging places	1,260	77,026	1,734	128,256	0.41	0.80	0.41	0.64	37.6	66.5
Personal services	38,709	551,099	56,772	959,696	12.56	5.73	13.38	4.86	46.7	74.1
Health services	16,772	568,296	30,026	1,350,606	5.44	5.91	7.08	6.83	79.0	137.7
Amusement and recreation services	6,869	121,059	13,250	502,847	2.23	1.26	3.12	2.54	92.9	315.4
Legal services	3,286	127,141	4,920	336,218	1.07	1.32	1.16	1.70	49.7	164.4
Motion pictures	271	7,315	733	61,911	0.09	0.08	0.17	0.31	170.5	746.4
Educational services	2,579	23,131	3,561	64,545	0.84	0.24	0.84	0.32	38.1	179.0
Social services	287	34,460	13,210	224,137	0.09	0.36	3.11	1.13	4500.0	550.4
Sub-total	104,168	3,297,243	173,440	6,702,354	33.79	34.28	40.89	33.91	66.5	103.3

General open market										
Construction	22,459	828,843	36,763	2,174,399	7.29	8.62	8.67	11.00	63.7	162.3
Manufacturing	4,525	437,804	11,082	1,410,467	1.47	4.50	2.61	7.14	144.9	225.9
Food and kindred products	59	28,005	286	60,595	0.02	0.29	0.07	0.31	348.8	116.4
Lumber and wood products	1,503	62,986	3,720	211,281	0.49	0.65	0.88	1.07	147.5	235.4
Electric and electronic equipment	55	16,638	136	113,567	0.02	0.17	0.08	0.57	147.3	582.6
Fabricated metal products	85	15,655	338	116,191	0.03	0.16	0.08	0.59	297.6	642.2
Transportation equipment	19	30,864	57	69,685	0.01	0.34	0.01	0.35	200.0	112.0
Other manufacturing	2,804	276,656	6,545	839,148	0.91	2.88	1.54	4.25	133.4	203.3
Transportation and public utilities	19,894	599,038	31,229	1,228,438	6.45	6.23	7.35	6.22	57.0	105.1
Trucking and warehousing	12,851	521,464	19,663	1,010,229	4.17	5.33	4.64	5.11	53.0	97.1
Local and interurban passenger transport	7,043	86,574	11,566	218,209	2.28	0.90	2.72	1.10	64.2	151.0
Wholesale trade	3,119	431,941	5,519	1,327,479	1.01	4.49	1.30	6.72	76.9	1433.3
Retail trade	50,249	2,041,821	45,443	3,803,724	16.30	21.23	10.71	19.25	-1.6	86.3
General merchandise stores	865	31,079	1,064	44,343	0.28	0.32	0.25	0.22	23.0	42.7
Auto dealers and service stations	3,298	901,231	3,690	2,155,680	1.07	9.37	0.87	10.91	11.9	139.2
Other retail trade	46,086	1,109,511	40,689	1,603,701	14.95	11.53	9.59	8.11	-0.9	44.5
Selected services	7,278	224,445	70,978	1,996,962	2.36	2.33	16.73	10.10	875.2	789.7
Business services	–	–	59,177	1,570,161	–	–	13.95	7.95	–	–
Auto repair services and garages	7,278	224,445	11,801	426,801	2.36	2.33	2.78	2.16	62.1	90.2
Sub-total	107,524	4,558,892	195,495	11,941,469	34.88	47.39	46.09	60.42	81.8	161.9
All other industries	96,568	1,762,920	55,230	1,119,053	31.33	18.33	13.02	5.66	-42.8	36.5
Total: all industries	308,260	9,619,055	424,165	19,762,876	100.00	100.00	100.00	100.00	37.6	105.5

Source: Prepared by Brimmer & Company. Data from US Bureau of the Census, *Survey of Black-owned Businesses,* 1987

Note: 1 Data for 1982 are revised

During this five-year period, the total receipts of those firms concentrating on the black consumer market expanded by 103.3 per cent. The industries whose growth rates lagged the most were (per cent): insurance agents (13.5) and food stores (22.1). Other slow-growth areas were: hotels (66.5); personal services (74.1); eating and drinking places (75.2); and chemicals (90.1). In contrast, the industries showing above-average growth rates were (per cent): banking (110.5); health services (137.7); real estate (159.0); legal services (164.4); educational services (179.0); printing and publishing (233.2); amusement and recreation (315.4); social services (550.4); and motion pictures (764.4).

In the general open market sector, the receipts of all black firms rose by 105.5 per cent. The most dramatic strides were made in industries where black firms have traditionally played modest roles. The growth rates were: (per cent): wholesale trade (1,433.3); fabricated metal products (642.2); and electric and electronic equipment (582.6). Significant gains were also recorded in several other industries (per cent): lumber and wool products (235.5); local transportation (151.0); auto dealers and service stations (139.2); food products (116.4); and transportation equipment (112.0).

In summary, over the period 1972–82, black-owned businesses did shift slightly away from reliance on the traditional black consumer market. The latter accounted for 37.9 per cent of their total receipts in 1972, and the fraction decreased to 33.3 per cent in 1982. Receipts of all other firms rose from 62.1 per cent to 66.3 per cent of the total. Between 1982 and 1987, the distribution of receipts between firms in the two market segments remained essentially unchanged at 33.9 per cent and 66.1 per cent, respectively. So, despite considerable diversification among black-owned firms in particular industries, the overall profile of black businesses changed only slightly over the last two decades.

Diversification among large firms

In contrast to the behavior of black-owned businesses as a group, diversification by the largest and most innovative firms has accelerated in recent years. The pattern of change can be seen in Table 2.11. The data show sales of BE-200 firms, by industry, in 1987 and 1993.

Several features stand out. A noticeable decrease occurred in the relative position of firms in food and beverages, whose share of total sales declined from 37.1 per cent to 25.4 per cent. The share of construction shrank from 6.3 per cent to 3.4 per cent, and the share of health care and beauty aids eased from 3.4 per cent to 2.5 per cent. In the opposite direction, manufacturing lifted its share of sales from 2.1 per cent to 5.4 per cent of the total. Strong gains were also registered by media/communications (from 5.5 per cent to 9.5 per cent).

Table 2.11 Sales of large black firms, by industry, 1987 and 1993
(Black Enterprise-200) (Amounts in thousands of dollars)

Industry	Sales: 1987		Sales: 1993	
	Amount	Percentage	Amount	Percentage
Food and beverages	$2,284,032	37.1	$2,616,311	25.4
Construction	389,221	6.3	345,506	3.4
Media/Communications	336,210	5.5	979,797	9.5
Computer/Information	281,300	4.6	–	–
Health care/Beauty aids	210,711	3.4	258,616	2.5
Entertainment	143,000	2.3	–	–
Technology	–	–	806,278	7.8
Manufacturing	129,315	2.1	556,006	5.4
Transportation	109,076	1.8	–	–
Petroleum	60,092	1.0	–	–
Security/Maintenance	49,662	0.8	–	–
Engineering	–	–	179,119	1.7
Other industries	126,280	2.1	415,188	4.0
Sub-total	4,118,899	66.9	6,156,821	59.9
Automobile dealers	2,037,435	33.1	4,123,980	40.1
Totals	6,156,334	100.0	10,280,801	100.0

Source: Prepared by Brimmer & Company. Data from *Black Enterprise* Magazine

Companies engaged in the high-technology industries also raised their share of total sales noticeably. These firms include those in computers/information, engineering, and technology. Their combined share of total sales climbed from 4.6 per cent in 1987 to 9.5 per cent in 1993.

Concluding observations

Finally, the foregoing analyses lead to a number of important conclusions:

- Over the last few years, black-owned businesses have significantly expanded their share of the nation's economy. This was a reversal of the trend which had prevailed since the end of official segregation in the mid-1960s.
- Historically, black firms concentrated on serving the essentially separate black consumer market which had grown up behind the wall of racial segregation. In recent years, a number of them have made significant strides in diversifying away from their traditional fields of activity and into the general open market.
- While black businesses never had the black consumer market exclusively to themselves, white-owned companies are competing more vigorously for the spending by black consumers. This has further constrained growth opportunities for black firms.
- Over the last two decades, black-owned businesses did shift slightly away from reliance on the traditional black consumer market. However,

many of the changes occurred in industries in which blacks had already
established small beachheads. As a result, the overall profile of black
businesses changed only moderately.

- In contrast, diversification by the largest and most energetic black firms
has accelerated in recent years. They have registered particularly noticeable gains in manufacturing and high-technology fields. To a considerable extent, they have been responding to opportunities opened up in the
private sector by large corporations and by government agencies.

THE BLACK BANKS

Assessments of performance and prospects

I have conducted a number of studies of the performance and progress of
black-owned banks. One of the primary goals was to determine the extent
to which they could contribute to the financing of economic development
in the black community. A common theme runs through the results from all
of these inquiries: the extensive and extremely high economic risks faced by
black businesses and households make it hazardous for banks to attempt to
meet their credit needs. Therefore, despite their best intentions, black banks
use a relatively small proportion of their resources to make loans to black
borrowers.

At the end of 1963, there were thirteen banks owned or controlled by
blacks. The latter also owned fifty life insurance companies and thirty-four
federally-insured savings and loan associations. These three groups of institutions had combined assets of $764 million, equal to only 0.12 per cent
of the total assets held by similar firms in the nation at large. Although a
number of individual banks had made major contributions, collectively they
had made only a modest impact.

The lack of progress cannot be attributed to the reluctance of blacks to
venture onto the financial terrain. Indeed, even before the Civil War, blacks
made numerous attempts to launch banks. Among these, the Freedmen's
Savings Bank and Trust Company sponsored by the Freedmen's Bureau was
the most ambitious. In its heyday, it had a network of branches in thirty-six
cities, and its deposits reached a peak of $57 million. While the bulk of its
deposits was backed by United States Government bonds, its reserve funds
apparently were not managed well. In any case, the failure of the bank in
the depression of 1874 greatly damaged the confidence of black depositors
in black-owned institutions. Yet, during each subsequent period of sustained prosperity, a new crop of black banks appeared. But again and again,
the end of prosperity brought another epidemic of bank failures and widespread losses to depositors. While this pattern was also typical of the
behavior of the banking system as a whole, the legacy in the poverty-
stricken black community was particularly discouraging.[9]

By the end of 1969, there were twenty-two banks owned or controlled primarily by blacks in the United States, and several others were in the process of formation. In 1963, there had been eleven black-owned banks, so almost one-half of these institutions had been started in the preceding six years.

These new banks were launched with the specific aim of fostering economic development in the black community. In a number of locations around the country, numerous groups were planning to establish similar institutions with the same objective. Charters were being sought from both State and Federal supervisors, and the movement was receiving strong support from large banks and other corporations as well as from many public officials. Moreover, a number of programs had been started to channel public deposits to the black banks to enable them to expand lending in urban areas.

Given the tempo of this movement and the enormously important economic development role which the black banks were expected to undertake, it appeared vital that an objective and systematic appraisal be made of the capacity of these institutions to perform this task. A comprehensive study, carried out in 1970, was devoted to such an assessment.[10] The main conclusions reached in the Study can be summarized briefly:

- Black banks trying to do business in urban ghettos appear to operate at a substantial disadvantage (even when compared with other banks of the same size) in terms of both operating costs and efficiency. For example, the margin of income over expenses in the black banks appears to be one-third to one-half that for banks in the country at large. The costs of handling a given volume of deposits in the black banks seem to run one-quarter to two-fifths higher than for other institutions.
- The black banks appear to be about one-quarter to one-third as profitable as the nation's banks generally. Aside from the high operating costs and low efficiency, the black banks experience substantially greater relative loan losses. In fact, loan loss rates at the black banks seem to be two to three times as high as at banks in the country as a whole.
- This experience, of course, is intimately related to the inherent risk of doing business in the urban ghetto: the high unemployment rates, low family incomes, the high failure rates among small businesses (compounded by high crime rates) make the ghetto an extremely risky place for small banks to lend money.
- At the same time, the black banks are handicapped by a severe shortage of management talent. The reason for this shortage is widely known: because of racial discrimination and segregation, blacks historically were kept out of the economic mainstream and thus lacked the incentives to acquire a mastery of skills in economics, finance, accounting, and business administration on which the management of banks depends.

- Because of this combination of handicaps, the black banks as a group appear to possess very little potential as instruments of urban economic development. A few of the banks have experienced noticeable success in tailoring their lending practices so as to lend a significant proportion of their resources to local borrowers – while keeping loss rates under reasonably good control. In contrast, a number of the banks have been aggressive lenders in their local communities, and virtually all of them have experienced sizable losses. In fact, several of the banks in this group have earned little or no net profit in the last four or five years; a few of them have just about exhausted their original capital – which had to be replaced at much higher cost and with much greater difficulty, including the necessity to seek capital funds outside the black community.
- On the whole, however, most of the black banks have found it wise to avoid concentrating their loans and investments in the ghetto. In general the proportion of their total resources represented by total loans is substantially below that for banks in the nation as a whole, and their relative holdings of US Government securities are much higher. In fact, the black banks as a group seem to channel as much as one-fifth of their total loans to borrowers outside their local communities; for several of them the proportion is in the one-third to two-fifths range – and for one fairly long-established bank it is as high as one-half. While part of this export of funds may be a reflection of the normal quest for diversification, it also seems to reflect the exceptionally high risks of lending in the ghetto.
- From this assessment of the performance and prospects for black banks, I am convinced that the multiplication of such institutions should not be encouraged in the belief that they can make a major contribution to the financing of economic development in the black community.

In 1990, I returned to the subject of black banks. The results of that analysis confirmed that the paradox black banks have faced historically still continues.[11] The study concluded that:

> Black bankers are confronted with a formidable problem: the more they try to meet the credit needs of the black community, the greater is the probability that their institutions will fail. This paradox arises from the exceptional risks which these lenders must assume when they extend credit to individuals who suffer from above-average instability of employment and income, or to black-owned businesses among which the rate of bankruptcy is quite high.

The record of growth and decline among black-owned banks over the last three decades documents this conclusion. Between 1963 and 1988, blacks started fifty-nine new banks, and thirty-three banks failed. Virtually all of the failures can be traced to aggressive lending practices, which reflected bankers' attempts to meet the credit needs of black consumers and black-owned businesses. The most dramatic example of the adverse consequences of pursuing fundamentally incompatible objectives is provided by the failure of Freedom National Bank of New York in November 1990.

Freedom National Bank, unlike the average black-owned bank in the country, took on far more risk in both its fund-raising and lending activities than its limited resources could support. The high cost of funds and losses resulting from these risky practices eroded its capital and drove it to the edge of bankruptcy. Yet, in the end, the narrow and insensitive approach of federal bank supervisors terminated its life. The latter's action wiped out a significant amount of wealth owned by uninsured black depositors in New York – who thought that by splitting their deposits into separate, insured accounts they would benefit by the insurance safety net provided by the federal government.

The experiences of black-owned banks discussed here hold a serious implication for these institutions: while they may want to be missionaries in serving the black community, they will have to exercise restraint in lending. Otherwise, they endanger their own survival.

NOTES

1 Andrew F. Brimmer, "Economic Development in the Black Community," *The Public Interest*, no. 34, Winter, 1975, pp. 146–63.
2 Andrew F. Brimmer, *Trends, Prospects, and Strategies for Black Economic Progress*, Joint Center for Political Studies, 1985.
3 Andrew F. Brimmer, "The Negro in the National Economy," in John P. Davis (ed.), *The American Negro Reference Book*, Prentice Hall, 1966, ch. 5, pp. 251–336, especially pp. 255–74.
4 Andrew F. Brimmer, "Income, Wealth, and Investment Behavior in the Black Community," *The American Economic Review*, vol. 78, no. 2, May, 1988, pp. 151–5.
5 Andrew F. Brimmer, "The Economic Cost of Discrimination Against Black Americans," in Margaret C. Simms (ed.), *Economic Perspectives on Affirmative Action*, Joint Center for Political and Economic Studies, 1995, pp. 9–29.
6 In 1987, the Bureau of the Census adopted a new methodology in its *Survey of Black-owned Businesses*. Essentially, firms organized as regular corporations were excluded. Data for 1982 were restated to conform to the new format, so revised sales for black firms were $9.6 billion in 1982. For consistency in comparison with early years, the pre-1987 methodology was used in the present analysis. Moreover, increasingly black firms are organized as regular corporations.
7 I first set forth this view of black business evolution in Andrew F. Brimmer, "The Negro in the National Economy," in John P. Davis (ed.), *The American Negro Reference Book*, 1966, ch. 5, pp. 251–336, especially pp. 251–5 and 291–7.
8 Andrew F. Brimmer and Henry S. Terrell, "The Economic Potential of Black Capitalism," *Public Policy*, vol. XIX, no. 2, Spring, 1971, pp. 289–308.
9 In two early studies, I also examined the performance of the black banks: 1 "The Negro in the National Economy," in John P. Davis (ed.), *The American Negro*

Reference Book, Prentice Hall, 1966, ch. 5, pp. 251–336, especially pp. 296–307.
2 "The Banking System and Urban Economic Development," presented before a joint session of the 1968 Annual Meetings of the American Real Estate and Urban Economics Association and the American Finance Association, Chicago, Illinois, 28 December 1968.
10 Andrew F. Brimmer, "The Black Banks: An Assessment of Performance and Prospects," *The Journal of Finance*, vol. XXVI, no. 2, May, 1971, pp. 379–405.
11 Andrew F. Brimmer, "The Dilemma of Black Banking: Lending Risks vs. Community Service," *The Review of Black Political Economy*, Winter, 1992, vol. 20, no. 3, pp. 5–29.

REFERENCES

Selected publications on economic development in the black community

"The Negro in the National Economy," in John P. Davis (ed.), *The American Negro Reference Book*, Englewood Cliffs: Prentice Hall, 1966, ch. 5, pp. 251–336.

"Desegregation and Negro Leadership," in Eli Ginzberg (ed.), *Business Leadership and the Negro Crisis*, New York: McGraw-Hill, 1968, ch. 3.

"The Negro in the National Economy," in John F. Kain (ed.), *Race and Poverty: The Economics of Discrimination*, Englewood Cliffs: Prentice Hall, 1969, pp. 89–99.

"The Black Revolution and the Economic Future of Negroes in the United States," *The American Scholar*, vol. 38, no. 4, Autumn, 1969, pp. 629–43.

"Economic Integration and the Progress of the Negro Community," *Ebony* (Special Issue), August, 1970, pp. 118–21.

"Economists' Perception of Minority Economic Problems," (with Harriet Harper), *Journal of Economic Literature*, September, 1970, pp. 783–806.

"Economic Agenda for Black Americans," *The Black Politician*, vol. 2, no. 3, Winter, 1971, pp. 12–14 and 32–7.

"The Economic Potential of Black Capitalism," (with Henry S. Terrell), *Public Policy*, vol. XIX, no. 2, Spring, 1971.

"The Black Banks: An Assessment of Performance and Prospects," *The Journal of Finance*, vol. XXVI, no. 2, May, 1971, pp. 379–405.

"The Economic Outlook and the Future of the Negro College," *Daedalus*, Summer, 1971, pp. 539–72.

"Economic Situation of Blacks in the United States," *The Review of Black Political Economy*, vol. II, 1972, pp. 34–54.

"Income and Welfare in the Black Community," *Ebony*, October, 1972, pp. 64–70.

"The Road Ahead: Outlook for Blacks in Business," *The Journal of Negro History*, vol. LVIII, no. 2, April, 1973, pp. 187–203.

"Economic Developments in the Black Community," in "The Great Society: Lessons for Future," *The Public Interest*, (Special Issue), No. 34, Winter, 1974, pp. 146–63.

"The Future of Black Business: Short-Run Problems Will Not Halt an Upward Trend," *Black Enterprise*, June, 1974, pp. 27–30.

"Widening Horizons: Prospects for Black Employment," *Labor Law Journal*, vol. 25, no. 6, June, 1974, pp. 323–5.

"The Outlook for Black Business," *Black Enterprise*, June, 1975, pp. 24–7, and 160.

"Economic Growth, Income Trends, and Prospects for Black-Owned Business," in *Minority Business Development*, Proceedings of a Conference Sponsored by the Federal Reserve Bank of Boston, November, 1976, pp. 19–35.

"Economic Growth and Employment and Income Trends Among Black Americans," ch. 6 in Eli Ginzberg (ed.), *Jobs for Americans*, Englewood Cliffs: Prentice Hall, 1976.

The Economic Position of Black Americans: 1976, (A Special Report of the National Commission for Manpower Policy), Special Report No. 9, July, 1976, 65 pp.

"Black Business in the 1980's," *Ebony*, January, 1980, p. 29.

"Blacks in American Economy in the Year 2000," *Ebony*, August, 1985, pp. 27–8.

Trends, Prospects, and Strategies for Black Economic Progress, Joint Center for Political Studies, 1985, 32 pp.

"Trends in Black–White Income Distribution,"*The Review of Black Political Economy*, Spring, 1986, vol. 14, no. 4, pp. 91–7.

"Income and Wealth of the Black Middle Class, *Ebony*, 1987, pp. 42–8.

"Income, Wealth, and Investment Behavior in the Black Community," *American Economic Review*, vol. 78, no. 2, May, 1988, pp. 151–5.

"45 Years in Business and Employment," *Ebony*, 45th Anniversary Edition, November, 1990, pp. 122–4.

"The Dilemma of Black Banking: Lending Risks vs. Community Service," *The Review of Black Political Economy*, Winter, 1992, vol. 20, no. 3, pp. 5–29.

"The Economic Costs of Discrimination Against Black Americans," in Margaret C. Simms (ed.), *Economic Perspectives on Affirmative Action*, Washington, DC: Joint Center for Political and Economic Studies, 1995, ch. II, pp. 9–29.

Part I

RACE, GENDER, AND ECONOMICS

3

THE AFRICAN AMERICAN AS SCHOLAR, ECONOMIST AND ACTIVIST

Robert S. Browne

As I look back over the fifty years of my adult life, more than forty of which were devoted to some form of activity affiliated with the economics profession, I think the foremost observation to be made is that the field of economics offered me an extremely broad range of activity within which to pursue my interests. The pervasiveness of economics in almost every aspect of human existence means that options for variety in the focus of one's work are plentiful – limited only by the degree of one's preference for skimming broadly across the surface as contrasted with selecting a restricted area and burrowing deeply into it.

I have been described as being non-traditional, or unconventional, and perhaps this is true. In any case, I have found that the discipline of economics has provided me a liberating, not a restricting, experience. It is a discipline of infinite applications in a world of infinite needs, which offers a menu containing options to suit every taste.

I'm often asked what led me to choose economics as my professional field. I certainly had no role models. Indeed, throughout my entire under-graduate studies I encountered only one other black person majoring in economics (Dunbar McLaurin, PhD, University of Illinois, circa 1943), and the picture changed little during the next twenty years.

So far as I can recall, my interest in the field had been kindled in my early childhood, when the newspapers and the radio periodically reported on unfathomable (to me) actions being taken by the government to deal with the great depression. At one point, the news reported on a massive stock of potatoes which the government was having dyed blue to ensure that they would not be used for human consumption; on another occasion, reports told of truckloads of food being deliberately destroyed by the government. All of this was taking place at a time when the press and the radio were reverberating with heart-rending accounts of the desperate plight of millions of unemployed people who were consistently unable to feed themselves and their families. When I asked my parents to explain these strange antics I was told that it was "economics." They really couldn't satisfy my

49

curiosity much beyond repeating that mysterious word – and I suspect that it was about then that I embarked upon an extensive journey to try to understand what "economics" meant and how it operated. Sixty years later, that journey is still in progress.

And what a marvelous journey it has been! Although effective agricultural economic policy remains as elusive today as it was during the New Deal (in my opinion, it is the most perplexing of all the economic policy areas), I cannot imagine a discipline which could have offered greater challenges or comparable variety. As with most of the social sciences, of course, the intellectual rewards in economics are considerably less than in the physical and biological fields, where both cause and effect are likely to be more unambiguously identifiable and attributable.

Although a need to understand what "economics" meant was the catalyst which drove me toward the discipline, there were other powerful factors which shaped what I would do with economics once I had acquired some mastery of it. As a young person I was subjected to the normal external conditioning which produced a mind set biased toward the desire to acquire great wealth. Internally, however, I was propelled by an extraordinarily powerful urge to ease the plight of poor people, and especially of blacks, reports of whose indignities and persecution I devoured with great emotion every week in the *Chicago Defender*.

With the arrival of adulthood, however, my urge for wealth gradually diminished in favor of more altruistic leanings, and my black nationalistic pride yielded to a more global outlook. As my professional career began to take shape, I vacillated widely between wanting to focus my efforts on addressing the problems of the black community and wanting to concentrate on aspects of economics such as Public Finance, Monetary Policy, and International Economic Affairs, which had relatively little to do with race.

This ambivalence expressed itself via an early academic focus on Labor Economics, followed by an MBA in Finance and then a subsequent graduate school focus on International Development. This intellectual evolution was heavily influenced by the experiences which I encountered. My first regular employment, and my first academic position, was at Dillard University. It was racism, however, which placed me in the classroom, not a desire for an academic career.

As I had approached the conclusion of my work on an MBA at the University of Chicago, I sought the placement officer's assistance in finding me a position. After several weeks of unresponsiveness, she finally called me into her office and stated quite frankly that she found it impossible to arrange a single interview for me – not with a bank, nor an insurance company, nor a brokerage firm, nor any other type of financial institution. There were no blacks in the finance industry, she said, and the thinking seemed to be that, hopefully, there never would be. With graduation only a few days away, she embarrassedly mentioned to me that she had a request for someone to fill a slot at a small Negro college in New Orleans. Thus began a totally unanticipated academic career for me, and perhaps also the first explicit shifting in my life objective, from the pursuit of wealth to the pursuit of service. Maturity was arriving.

The New Deal stimulus which had led me to seek the grail of economics may also have shaped the way in which I would utilize my learning, for the influencing of policy in the interest of the poor gradually emerged as the desired focus for my career efforts. I was not insensitive to the joy to be derived from sheer theoretical analysis and from the elegance of mathematical "proofs" of obscure theorems; but such scholarship, in isolation, had always struck me as an extravagance when there are so many genuine human problems crying out for our attention. And although the classroom became and remains a cherished venue for me, academic research has seemed important to me only if it had clear and immediate policy implications.

I have great admiration for faculty who can successfully pursue profound involvement in significant off-campus activity without penalizing and neglecting their students. For me, however, the tension between these two foci of attention was so great as to be ultimately unsustainable. Teaching never seemed to provide me with total fulfillment, but as my involvement with off-campus affairs inevitably made ever increasing demands on me, it was obviously my students' welfare which was being placed most at risk. Consequently, as these off-campus involvements became more demanding, I actively sought ways to reduce my obligations to students, ultimately largely abandoning the campus as my principal work place. Although I persist in perceiving of myself as an academician who has been intermittently absent from the classroom, the reality is that I have spent most of my career far removed from students.

Indeed, out of some forty years of adult civilian employment only ten have actually been spent on a university campus, and of these only seven were devoted to classroom teaching and three to research. Ten years were devoted to running the Black Economic Research Center and its affiliated organizations, eight years were spent working overseas for the US government (six in Southeast Asia and two in West Africa), and four and a half were spent on Capitol Hill. The remainder were committed to miscellaneous non-profit organizations such as the Phelps–Stokes Fund and the Urban League, and one year was devoted to the private corporate sector (a black life insurance company).

Sprinkled throughout this eclectic work history were a host of related and disparate activist involvements ranging from a highly influential role in the Vietnam anti-war movement to the position of chief advisor on economic policy for the first Jesse Jackson presidential campaign (1984). Membership on various official and unofficial commissions and on a variety of boards of directors (mostly non-profit organizations, but including one FORTUNE 500 corporation), plus the holding of equity positions in two or three black entrepreneurial ventures, filled out a rich menu of non-academic involvements. Some of them provided me ample opportunity to utilize my accounting talents, as well as the other skills which I had acquired in earning the MBA that racism had prevented me from directly capitalizing on in earlier years.

Leaving aside myriad other peripheral involvements, some of which were quite significant in terms of their linkage to national economic matters (most notably, membership on the Council of Economic Advisors to the Congressional Budget Office and on Governor Mario Cuomo's Commission on Trade and Competitiveness), I would like to discuss in somewhat greater detail the thinking which surrounded three major career involvements of my life: 1   the Black Economic Research Center and the ancillary activities linked to it; 2   my international involvements; and 3   my Congressional experience. In my opinion, these three involvements provide an ample overview of how one African American chose to use his economics training in the pursuit of a better world for himself, for black people, and for mankind in general. Although these three involvements collectively account for only a bit more than half of my forty years of participation in the civilian labor force, they constitute my most deliberate and prolonged attempts to put my economics training to use in the service of "the people". I view them as disparate facets of a coherent and unified effort to address the whole by addressing its parts. The linkages are clear and make sense to me, but they may be less apparent to others.

ABANDONING THE CLASSROOM

The ten years during which I directed the Black Economic Research Center (BERC) constituted the most sustained involvement of my career, spanning the entire decade of the seventies. As with most other seminal actions in my life, the creation of BERC occurred as much by chance as by design, although an increasingly felt need to make a drastic change in my work situation had already ripened me for BERC's emergence. In 1964 I had begun teaching at Fairleigh Dickinson University while completing the requirements for a doctorate degree at the City University of New York (a degree which was not conferred because I never got around to writing the dissertation). The five years which I taught there (1965–9) happened to coincide with a rising race consciousness among black students nationally, culminating in massive student-led efforts to expand the numbers of black faculty members and to introduce black studies programs as a part of the college curriculum. Meanwhile, newly empowered black community groups were emerging in both urban and rural areas as offshoots of President Johnson's extensive anti-poverty programs.

These were also the crucial years in the creation of the anti-war movement, a development in which I played a major role, and my contribution to which I view as the foremost achievement of my life. From 1955 to 1961 I had worked for the US economic assistance program in Cambodia and Vietnam, an experience which had afforded me unique and valuable insight and had rendered me highly critical of the US policy in that region long before the war had actually begun. Inasmuch as only a handful of Americans had ever been in this region, and none for so extended a time as myself, I was automatically awarded the status of "expert" once the US involvement there became critical. The mid- to late-sixties thus became for me a time of submersion in one of the two overpowering issues of the day, a submersion that eventually encompassed more than 150 major public talks, private consultations with key policy and opinion makers, dozens of published statements and radio and TV interviews, an abortive US Senatorial candidacy, and membership on the insurgent New Jersey delegation to the infamous 1968 Democratic National Convention. It also involved two fact-finding trips to Vietnam, the second of which led to the Vietnamese Buddhist community enlisting my support for an effort to persuade Dr. Martin Luther King to take a public stand against the Vietnam war.

Throughout this period I was subjected to an escalating sense of guilt arising from the fact that my heavy schedule of anti-war activities effectively precluded my devoting much time to the other seminal popular movement of the era: the exciting struggle for civil rights upon which the black community had embarked. Not surprisingly, I was more than a little relieved when, in 1967, Dr. King finally made a public denunciation of the war and eloquently linked the two crucial movements of the moment, perhaps partly as a result of efforts on my part. However, my racial conscience was being pricked by calls coming from newly formed groups of black militant students seeking to recruit black professors, and from newly emerging community economic development organizations seeking technical assistance which they felt I could provide. My employer, Fairleigh Dickinson University, had very few black students indeed, and during five years of teaching there I had never had more than two black students in any year, and frequently none at all. I was beginning to feel embarrassingly irrelevant insofar as my making any genuine contribution to the black student revolution.

I had, however, won for myself, almost innocently, a burgeoning national reputation for black militancy as a result of an article which I had been provoked to write on the highly contentious topic of black separatism. Under the title "The Case for Black Separatism," the piece had first appeared in the radical Catholic monthly, *Ramparts*, in November 1967, and was reprinted with only minor revisions in the *New York Times Magazine* (11 August 1968) and a few months later in *Ebony* magazine. In fact, it was the notoriety flowing from this article which inadvertently transformed me into a hero of sorts among militant black students, most of whom knew nothing of me beyond the fact that I had written a "cutting edge" article which was upsetting folks on both sides of the racial spectrum.

As my imagined irrelevancy became ever more intolerable to me, two alternatives seemed to present themselves: transfer to a black school, or transfer to a white school with a substantial black enrollment. Although the former promised to be the more comfortable alternative, the latter seemed to be the area of greater need, although the racial politics which were so much a part of the scene on major campuses at that time were not particularly appealing to me.

My first tentative step toward resolving this dilemma was to take a leave of absence from Fairleigh Dickinson in order to teach for one year at the (nearby) Newark campus of Rutgers, pursuant to an invitation which had its origins in black student unrest there. I had been summoned to Rutgers to mediate a tense student/administration confrontation, and upon achieving some success I was besieged by requests to come to Rutgers to teach, a career move which offered promise of easing my irrelevancy problem while avoiding the need to change my residence and otherwise disrupt my family. But at the very moment that I was commencing work on this visiting professorship, another vehicle for redressing my irrelevance was taking shape, to emerge almost abruptly in the Fall of 1969 as the Black Economic Research Center.

THE BLACK ECONOMIC RESEARCH CENTER

The dream of creating an institution where interested blacks could come and study the economics of the black community, and publish and possibly even implement their findings, was something which had entered and left my mind from time to time without ever establishing itself as a goal for serious consideration. I shared the frustration which most black scholars felt at the prevailing practice – pursued by all sectors of the society: the media, government, the corporate sector, and the non-profit sector – of relying almost exclusively on white institutions and economists as the "experts" on and the interpreters of the black economic condition. But the obstacles to finding the resources to create an institution which could mobilize black economic expertise were sufficiently daunting as to render it a totally unrealistic fantasy.

Nevertheless, in one of those inexplicable mysteries of the human experience, an unsolicited inquiry was directed to me asking if I might have an interest in launching an economic research center for blacks if funds were to be made available for such a purpose. (It was somewhat more complicated than this, involving a conference on black economic development and the famous Black Manifesto of James Forman, but essentially it was a spontaneous offer from someone who seemed to have been reading my mind.) My response was naturally an enthusiastic "yes!," and long before its creation had been assured I had turned my attention to how it should be structured and what its program should be. There is probably no better way to convey the motivation behind the launching of BERC than by quoting at length from its first Activity Report (1970–1):

> By the late nineteen-sixties, it was becoming clear that the high hopes which much of the black community had placed in the "poverty programs" were not to be realized. The failures and defects of the government programs, coupled with the growing disenchantment which the country was developing toward these minority-oriented programs, had demonstrated once again how vulnerable the black community is to the changing attitudes of the white majority. As the focus of the government's interest in the black community shifted from community development to black capitalism and from welfare to workfare, the universities and the "consulting firms" became the prime beneficiaries of the government's largess, conducting endless numbers of studies of the black community and its problems, of the poverty programs and their efforts, of the economic status of the black community and how it might be altered.
>
> A plethora of economic development programs conceived by whites for blacks, a burgeoning supply of white "experts" on black economic development, but very little in the way of measurable, visible im-provement of the black economic situation, was fast becoming the legacy of the highly publicized black economic assistance programs of the sixties. Indeed, the very term black economic development was beginning to be used as if it were a synonym for the narrower concept of black capitalism or black enterprise development, a shift in usage which accurately reflected the shift in focus which was beginning to take place at top levels of government.
>
> It was in response to this frustrating situation that a need began to be felt and articulated within the black community for a place where black scholarship, black expertise, and a black perspective could take a critical look at the economics of black America and hopefully bring to it some evaluative analysis as well as some sense of overall direction and of innovative assistance.
>
> To help meet this need, the Black Economic Research Center (BERC) was launched in the Fall of 1969 with the general objective of assisting and expediting the process of black economic development through the use of creativity, scholarship, and activism.

During the approximately ten years of BERC's existence, it managed to fulfill much of the mission which it had given itself. A splendid corps of young black economists spent varying amounts of time at BERC, either as regular staff or as student interns, and for several years BERC rendered serious service to a surprising number of black economic development undertakings of various sorts. BERC always perceived of itself as a center of applied research, so the studies it chose to perform were almost invariably linked to some concrete venture which was either underway or in the conceptualization stage. As BERC's reputation became better established, its staff members were in constant demand as resource persons at conferences, as witnesses for Congressional hearings, as "expert sources" for quotation in news stories, and for participation on radio and TV commentaries. Within the contemporary context, this was a revolutionary change, for the normal pattern had been to rely almost exclusively on whites for such purposes. An important by-product of this success in winning a voice for black economists was that the number of blacks demonstrating an interest in the study of economics increased substantially.

This is not to suggest that the mere creation of BERC somehow increased the number of black economists. There were also other factors at work at that moment, creating a marvelous synergy which inspired us all. Three months after BERC had opened its doors, the American Economic Association (AEA) held its annual meeting (December 1969) in New York City, and history was made when a trio of black AEA members from the west coast issued a call for all black AEA members to attend a meeting for the purpose of creating a black caucus. It was, of course, a fairly small gathering, but for the first time the scattering of black economists across the country became acquainted with one another and began to join forces for achieving common objectives.

Obtaining greater recognition for black economists as well as increasing our numbers were among the priority objectives set forth by the nascent Caucus of Black Economists (later renamed the National Economic Association). I naturally seized upon this meeting to announce the existence of BERC, and predictably the announcement was received with great excitement and enthusiasm. Indeed, swept up in the drama of the moment, I committed myself that evening to the launching of a scholarly, quarterly journal within the coming year, although my original plan had merely envisioned the creation of a periodical of some kind, to commence publication in some indefinite future, after BERC had established a track record of success in its activist undertakings. Having made the commitment, however, I honored it, and in the summer of 1970 we proudly published the first issue of *The Review of Black Political Economy*, one of BERC's most durable and tangible projects. Persons interested in the early years of *The Review* may wish to see the twenty year retrospective article on this topic in vol. 21, no. 3 of *The Review* (Winter, 1993).

Two other major projects spawned by BERC which still survive are the Emergency Land Fund (ELF) and the Twenty-First Century Foundation.

The Emergency Land Fund grew out of a study which BERC undertook looking into what was occurring with the ownership of land by blacks in the South. Some preliminary research had revealed that black land ownership had been at its maximum in about 1915 and had been on the decline ever since, with a considerable acceleration beginning in the fifties. Further exploration had uncovered a number of reasons for this, among which were some openly illegal as well as other only marginally legal practices widely utilized by sharp lawyers and tax officials in southern rural areas. The picture was so dismal, and the black community was so uncomprehending of what was taking place with their property, that we decided to create an organization for the specific purpose of fighting the problem. Thus was born the Emergency Land Fund, which quickly became a significant force in alerting and educating black rural landowners to their property rights. It also stimulated a number of black law students into focusing their attention on real estate and tax law, fields which had hitherto been grossly neglected by black law students in the South, and provided them with genuine cases upon which to cut their legal teeth. Because the retention of land is not a costless act, it gradually became necessary for ELF to immerse itself in a host of activities related to making land an economically viable asset, and ultimately the ELF merged its program with a sister organization, the Federation of Southern Cooperatives, where its work continues.

The Twenty-First Century Foundation was yet another child of BERC, created because of the felt need for permanent, self-financing sources of funds, under black control, for utilization on projects of importance to the black community. At the time of its creation it appears to have been one of only two endowed black grant-making foundations (the other being the Herndon Foundation, endowed by the Atlanta Life Insurance Co.). The Foundation opened its doors in 1971 with an endowment of one million dollars (provided by a non-black friend of mine), and while I had visions of expanding that endowment many-fold, such an expansion has not occurred. The million dollars remain intact, however, and over the past twenty years the Foundation has given away earnings of considerably more than one million dollars in the form of small grants to creative black undertakings. It was also hoped that the Foundation would serve as an example for others to follow, and in this it has not been disappointed. It can no longer claim uniqueness, for the emergence of a sizeable class of highly paid blacks in the entertainment, sports and business arenas has created conditions conducive to a flowering of black philanthropy. Entertainers such as Bill Cosby and business tycoons such as Reginald Lewis are among those who have created significant charities utilizing the foundation format. Although the surface has barely been scratched, there is a sound basis for predicting strong growth in this area. The Twenty-First Century Foundation expects to be a continuing catalyst in this growth.

INTERNATIONAL INVOLVEMENTS

Internationalism was apparently imbedded in my genes, for my fascination with foreign places and people goes back as far as my memory will carry me. As a draftee in the Second World War, I had eagerly looked forward to being sent abroad, but these hopes were not realized; so a few years after the war I took it upon myself to see what lay beyond the US shores. Liquidating such assets as I had, I arranged passage on a steamship sailing from New York City in 1952 and ultimately visited twenty-three countries in Europe, North Africa and the Middle East during a year of low budget, leisurely traveling. It was an extraordinary act in those days (irrational was the descriptive term favored by many of my friends and associates), but I view it as a watershed year in my life for a number of reasons. Whereas foreign travel and global thinking have now become commonplace, forty years ago this was not the case at all. Furthermore, my journey across North Africa was a particular rarity, for the western Maghreb was still under French control. Libya (then a monarchy) had just been afforded independence, with the United Nations predicting that it was destined to remain a permanent economic "basket case" inasmuch as its only known exportable resource was a crop known as "sparta grass."

This wonderful odyssey merely whetted my desire to see more of the world, and most especially to visit black Africa. That was not easily achievable, however, because black Africa was not then an area for tourist travel (except for the game parks). Visits to the colonies were generally permitted only for some identifiable and officially approved purpose. An unconnected African American such as myself, seeking to visit black Africa in the fifties simply to satisfy his curiosity, was not a likely candidate to be awarded a visa. One was considered "peculiar" even to entertain such ambitions. Furthermore, transport accommodations to such exotic places were not plentiful and were quite expensive. I was, therefore, obliged to put my projected Sub-Saharan Africa travel plans on indefinite hold.

My romance with places foreign was renewed a couple of years after my return from Europe, largely because of my having acquired some fluency in the French language. In a rush to recruit Americans to replace the French, who were being ousted from Indochina following their disastrous defeat at Dien Bien Phu, the US government offered me an appointment as a program economist with the US economic assistance program which was being established in Cambodia. I had been seeking a cheap way to resume my foreign travel rather than for any specific job, but good jobs in the foreign service did not fall readily into black hands in those days so I seized upon the opportunity with alacrity, planning to remain a year or so and then move on. In fact, I remained nearly six years, working both in Cambodia and Vietnam, and not only succumbing to the considerable charms of Asia and the seductiveness of the complex problems of assisting in the development of so-called "under developed" economies, but also occupying a box seat at the prologue to what became the most irrational and costly political and military venture in American history.

Just as I had earlier been thrust into a New Orleans classroom more by chance than by design, so did I now find myself working on "Third World" (a term which had not yet entered the global vocabulary) development by chance rather than by design. At that time, "economic development" was an applied activity but not yet a theoretical construct. The topic of development had not yet crept into elementary economics textbooks and its emergence as an organized study area within the economics discipline still lay in the future. W. Arthur Lewis was to publish his seminal *The Theory of Economic Growth* only in 1955, and the pioneering work of Nurkse, Bauer, Hirschman, Kindleberger and others had not yet appeared. Indeed, when I went to Indochina the World Bank was less than ten years old and its focus was still almost exclusively on the rebuilding of Europe and Japan. The Bank's soft loan window, the International Development Association (IDA), created specifically for lending to the Third World, had not yet been conceived, and the tidal wave of independence had yet to begin its sweep across Sub-Saharan Africa.

Although my return to the US (1961) after the six year sojourn in Southeast Asia inaugurated a nineteen year period of uninterrupted residence for me in the US, it was always my intention to one day reinvolve myself in Third World economic development work. The two decades of the 1960s and the 1970s constituted a period of domestically-based activity for me, but my work during that period was greatly enriched by the years which I had spent abroad. There can be no doubt that the particular focus which I brought to the issue of black economic development was strongly influenced by my experience in working closely with the government of Cambodia, a small, poor nation which was only beginning to exercise the right to make decisions for itself. Although the parallels between developing countries and the development efforts within the black community in the US are frequently exaggerated, there are certainly some similarities, and I feel certain that my work on domestic economic problems was greatly enhanced by my earlier work on international ones (although I am less certain that the reverse is also true.)

It was inevitable that my economic development experience in Southeast Asia would eventually link me to the emerging nations of Sub-Saharan Africa. After two decades of domestically focused activity, I was led back to the international arena with my recruitment as the first US Executive Director for the African Development Bank Group located in Abidjan, Cote d'Ivoire. The timing could not have been better. Raising money to keep BERC operating had become increasingly difficult and onerous for me. By the late 1970s I was devoting nearly 50 per cent of my time to such unpleasant activities. This caused me to become restless. One afternoon I received a call from Congressman Parren Mitchell's office inquiring as to my availability to fill this opening in West Africa. I had never heard of the African Development Bank Group, but after a brief researching of it I sent an enthusiastic affirmative response. It promised to be a golden opportunity for me to put to use both my economics and my business training, together with my previous experience in Third World development assistance. Because the African Development Bank was actively lending to all the African countries, I was afforded an excellent opportunity to acquire some limited familiarity with most of that enormous and varied continent. Particularly valuable to me was the chance to acquire some insight into the bureaucratic machinations which characterize the official and unofficial external relationships among the African countries, and especially their relationships with western governments and the multilateral financial institutions such as the World Bank and the International Monetary Fund (IMF).

The rationale supporting my job was that the US, as one of the major contributors to the African Development Bank Group, held a seat on the Executive Board from whence it could help shape policy and monitor administrative practices. Without in any way neglecting these responsibilities *vis-à-vis* Washington, I chose to use this position to urge the western countries to be more open-minded toward the Africans and to see problems from the perspective of the Third World rather than exclusively from the perspective of a developed country. I eventually felt that I had become so effective in that niche that it was with considerable regret that I relinquished it (in 1982, owing to US partisan politics) and returned to the US, where I was offered the position of Senior Research Fellow in the African Studies and Research Program at Howard University.

One involvement which I elected to undertake while at Howard was to mount a major campaign to give voice and interpretation to what I perceived to be a significant wave of fresh thinking about African economic development which was being articulated, without attracting much notice, by some astute African economists. They were calling on Africa to de-emphasize the export-led type of development which the continent had been pursuing since independence and to shift its emphasis toward a self-reliant development strategy (i.e., a modified form of import substitution). Unfortunately, the World Bank, which just happened to be preparing its first comprehensive report on African development at about that time, chose to ignore the work of these new-wave African economists. Instead, it chose to fire the opening salvoes of "structural adjustment lending," a new approach to lending which offered medium term but wholly inadequate programs for dealing with what was already emerging as a major continental crisis. (For an introduction to this debate, see Browne, Robert S., and Cummings, Robert J., *The Lagos Plan vs. The Berg Report*, Brunswick Publishing Co., Lawrenceville, VA, 1985.)

This confrontation, between the World Bank, the IMF and much of the donor community on the one hand, and the African economists on the other, continued unabated throughout the decade of the 1980s, reaching an accommodation of sorts by 1989, when the World Bank issued a second major report on Sub-Saharan African economic development in which it admitted and corrected some of its earlier errors, while clinging (but with considerably diminished certainty) to other of its inappropriate perspectives. The Africans, too, modified some of their original thinking, so that a tenuous working relationship prevailed as the decade of the 1990s opened, and the debate is still very much alive at the time of this writing.

The heart of this debate is whether Africa can better assure a sound economic future for itself by continuing its emphasis on export-led development or by shifting its priorities toward a more internally focused, self-reliant development strategy. In my opinion, the latter strategy, although far more difficult to achieve than the former, is the only one which offers real hope for Africa ever positioning itself on a path of self-sustaining growth. To what extent the opposition to this view (which has been widespread among the donor countries and in the World Bank) derives from honest differences in analyzing regional and global variables, as compared with differences in the role which various international actors wish Africa to play in future global arrangements, remains one of the great unanswered questions. But suspicions abound.

To enable me to further explore some of the problems and ramifications posed by Africa's nascent self-reliant development efforts, the Ford Foundation recently provided me a grant. The focus of the research will be on evaluating the actual progress which Africa has made in the development of viable sub-regional cooperation strategies and institutions for sub-regional economic integration, without which self-reliant development would remain an unreachable goal.

CAPITOL HILL

Working in the Congress occupied fewer than five years of my career but it proved to be such an instructive period for me that I rank it among the foremost of my work experiences. Indeed, I would go so far as to urge our younger black social scientists to give serious thought to working on Capitol Hill for a few years early in their work career. The jobs may not pay well (but then again, they can: Congressional staff salaries are set entirely at the caprice of the Congressman or Senator on whose staff or committee one is working) but there is no other work place where one is so intimately exposed to the way in which money, power, the public will and technical expertise interact to produce, not merely policy, but the very world as we know it.

The vast breadth of each Congressman's portfolio means that he must rely heavily on his staff for help and guidance on a vast array of issues, often including those of most importance to the country. The Congressman relies on his personal staff to recommend and defend positions that he takes on legislation which originates in committees for which he has no special responsibility (i.e., the bulk of the legislative agenda). Indeed, in some cases he may be inclined to follow the lead of a trusted and knowledgeable colleague if his staff have not been able to devote time to particular bills.

Even more crucial is the staff work performed by the dozens of committees and subcommittees of the House and Senate, for it is in these committees where the real work of the Congress is done. Responsibility for these committees is allocated on the basis of seniority, and the Congressmen and Senators who chair them are the real power barons of the Congress. Due to the low turnover which has characterized black Congressmen, a number of them rose to chair influential committees and subcommittees, on whose staffs they were strongly dependent.

Job tenure does not exist on Capitol Hill, and each incoming subcommittee and committee chairman has the opportunity to hire a staff of his choosing, tempered only by whatever sensitivities he may have in terms of wishing to preserve a degree of staff continuity or institutional memory for his committee. In a few committees, key staff have been held over through the administrations of several chairmen; the more usual pattern, however, is to replace the staff director and perhaps other key personnel by persons with known loyalty to the new chairman. This is understandable when one considers that the staff director may well become the key player in shaping that subcommittee – choosing the topics on which to hold hearings, selecting the witnesses to be invited to testify, requesting studies, drafting legislation, filtering lobbyists seeking access to the chairman and generally exerting enormous influence over the committee's work because of the chairman's necessary preoccupation with a vast array of other matters ranging from constituency affairs to fund raising to responsibilities on various other committees on which he may sit.

The number of blacks holding such positions is not great. Even the staffs of committees and subcommittees chaired by blacks are frequently headed by whites. This may be due to the fact that the committee's work is fairly technical, leading a newly chosen chairman to retain the incumbent staff director or to hire someone having previous Capitol Hill experience with the subject matter in question. This is quite understandable, because a novice can easily become mired in the anachronistic and anarchic procedures by which Congress rules itself. But a pool of experienced black Congressional staffers must be developed to fill more of these positions.

The Congress is too critical a pillar of our society for black Americans to rest content with merely the election of a growing number of black legislators. It is imperative that competent blacks with a genuine commitment to public policy be encouraged to bring their expertise to Capitol Hill in far greater numbers than is now the case. An internship on Capitol Hill is standard fare for the top social science graduates of several of the better colleges. Other young whites flock to the Hill upon completion of their Master's or law degrees, seeking Congressional employment as a capstone to their classroom studies, as a sort of finishing school for their liberal arts education. They are quite willing to accept low salaries in exchange for the Hill experience and contacts, both of which are priceless. A few remain on the Hill but the bulk seem to move smoothly from Capitol Hill to wherever their career interests carry them, including to academia. The range of specialties which the Hill offers can hardly be surpassed: health, technology, judicial affairs, taxation, housing, agriculture, military affairs, international affairs, budgetary issues, trade and commerce, the environment, employment, education, public works – and the list goes on. Almost any one of these areas would offer rich prospects for a young black economist to cut his teeth on.

My own sojourn on Capitol Hill materialized with the same serendipity as has characterized most other major engagements in my career. For some reason I had never focused on the Congress as a place of possible employment, and I was totally unaware of the rich potential which it held. During the months when I had been working with the Jesse Jackson presidential campaign, I had been thrown together with Congressman Walter Fauntroy in several strategy meetings. Apparently, he remembered me because some months later I received a call from him inquiring as to whether I would be interested in assuming the position of Staff Director of the House Banking Committee's Subcommittee on Domestic Monetary Policy, which he chaired. He had just fired his (non-black) Staff Director of several years' standing. At that time I had just completed my contract as a research fellow at Howard University, so I indicated to him that I was available but that it had been my intention to remain involved in international development activities. Nevertheless, I agreed to fill the job on a temporary basis while he sought a permanent replacement.

Again, fate played a surprising card, for a few days later, before I had yet moved into the new job, Congressman Fauntroy called to tell me that the chairman of the International Subcommittee of the House Banking Committee had just announced his intention to run for a state job, necessitating his relinquishing his Congressional seat. Congressman Fauntroy indicated that he had sufficient seniority to claim the International Subcommittee for himself, and that he was extremely interested in international affairs and would be willing to make the switch if I would agree to become Staff Director on a permanent basis. Nothing could have suited me better! Although I had never before even heard of that subcommittee (full name: Subcommittee on International Development, Finance, Trade and Monetary Policy), I quickly came to realize that this was the job for which I had been preparing all my life. The subcommittee portfolio included Congressional oversight of the Bretton Woods institutions (World Bank and International Monetary Fund) as well as oversight of the several regional development banks and the Export–Import Bank; international exchange rate policy; Third World debt (an especially hot topic at that moment); and a number of ancillary items dealing with international financial matters.

It was a portfolio that offered wide scope in addressing issues of considerable contemporary interest to me: the still raging debate between Africa and the World Bank over development strategy; the emerging global environmental debate in which I had developed some interest via earlier membership in the Club of Rome; the insufficiencies in the international monetary system, about which I had co-authored a major article just a few months earlier; the appropriateness of the IMF's stabilization policies in Africa, about which I had also recently published an article only a few months earlier; and alternative means for easing the Third World debt problem, which had been the focus of several conferences in which I had participated while at Howard. Not only was I to be well-paid for dealing with the very topics to which I had been voluntarily devoting myself, I was also being provided ready access to information and to key actors on these issues in a way that would never have been possible had I not been clothed with the authority of the US Congress.

It was a heady experience, but I quickly became acutely aware of its drawbacks – principally, the fast-track nature of the work. Whereas at the university I had become accustomed to moving at my own speed, and going public with my views only when I was reasonably assured that I had mastered the relevant data, on Capitol Hill I was immediately placed under constant pressure to come up with answers long before I fully understood what the question was. And what was worse, my answers mattered! At the university I had carried out research, reached conclusions, and published articles, which then collected dust on obscure shelves, sparsely read and hardly noticed. Now, suddenly, I found myself thrust into a situation where my opinions were listened to attentively, heeded, and promptly acted upon by persons of influence. But I had no time to think and ponder and reflect on what I was recommending. On Capitol Hill, everything is a priority and requires an answer yesterday! The contrast between the two work places could hardly be more stark.

Another negative aspect of working on Capitol Hill is the fact that so much of the work one does appears to be futile, either because it fails to win a serious hearing or is dropped for any one of a number of unrelated reasons. On the other hand, there is considerable satisfaction to be derived from witnessing the passage of legislation into which one has made substantial input and from observing the implementation of a policy which one has had a major role in shaping. Even when one's efforts come to nought, one can take encouragement from the historical evidence which shows that good ideas often die many deaths on Capitol Hill, only to win acceptance at a later time. My particular obsession in this regard is a proposal which I crafted urging the IMF to authorize a one-time issuance of a unique class of special drawing rights (SDRs, the IMF's international monetary units), as a means of bringing substantial relief to the most heavily debt-burdened of the less developed countries. I felt it to be a politically feasible and economically sound way to address a critical portion of the Third World debt problem as well as a useful catalyst for advancing the international monetary community a few steps toward a needed overall restructuring of itself. Treasury Secretary James Baker was hostile to the proposal, and because its technical complexity tended to spread a glaze over the eyes of potentially sympathetic Congressional supporters, the legislation was watered down to a mere request for a study/report, which meant its death of course. I am, however, hoping that the proposal will eventually be resurrected under more favorable circumstances. Such is life on Capitol Hill.

Unfortunately, jobs on Capitol Hill are very fragile, and in 1991 Congressman Fauntroy did not return to the Congress, resulting in my being displaced when the new subcommittee chairperson brought in her own staff director. I have been away from Capitol Hill for nearly five years now, and have returned to the more placid role of a research fellow in an academic surrounding. Naturally, I have asked myself many times which role I find more attractive: that of the thoughtful but perhaps ineffective scholar, or that of the less profound but more influential policy-shaper/activist? Both roles have much to recommend them, and thus far I have been unable to declare a preference. (Were I younger, however, I would almost certainly favor the latter.)

CONCLUDING REFLECTION

Economics certainly provided me the flexibility to practice my profession in widely disparate circumstances and according to my changing needs. It enabled me to do what I really *wanted* to do. Indeed, had I not needed an income for normal survival, I would have been content to do most of what I have done, at least in the last twenty-five years, even had I not been paid any salary for my efforts. I thoroughly enjoyed what I did and felt it to be important, which is why I did it. My own perspective on my career is well captured by the anonymous adage: the man who enjoys his job soon discovers that he never has to go to work.

4

THE INTERSECTIONALITY OF OPPRESSION AND ITS NEGATION OF COLOR BLIND REMEDIES

Race consciousness, race, class, and gender

Jerome McCristal Culp, Jr.*

Batson, in my view, depends upon this Nation's profound commitment to the ideal of racial equality, a commitment that refuses to permit the State to act on the premise that racial differences matter.... We ought not delude ourselves that the deep faith that race should never be relevant has completely triumphed over the painful social reality that, sometimes, it may be. That the Court will not tolerate prosecutors' racially discriminatory use of the peremptory challenge, in effect, is a special rule of relevance, a statement about what this Nation stands for, rather than a statement of fact.[1]

INTRODUCTION

One of the myths we tell children and law students is that the law is or can be color blind. In this myth, colorblindness poses as a moral requirement of all "right" thinking people and all good law. The truth is that colorblindness is always and everywhere a policy that is good or bad depending on the results which it produces. Racial justice and colorblindness are not, however, the same thing. No one thinks that economic efficiency[2] or the labor theory of value are moral requirements independent of their impact on the components of justice. In like manner, to assume that ignoring race in making decisions – colorblindness – will be justice is to create an imaginary legal situation that does not exist.

There are several reasons why people understand colorblindness as this mythic description of racial justice. Many people see the Civil Rights

* Thanks are owed to my colleagues H. Jefferson Powell, James Coleman, Sara Sun Beale, Christopher Schroeder, W. Kip Viscusi, and Kate Bartlett. I would also like to thank Derrick Bell, Paulette Caldwell, Angela Harris, Linda Greene, and Patricia Williams for helping me think through these issues over the years.

Movement[3] as having fought and sacrificed blood, sweat, and tears for colorblindness. This view of the Civil Rights Movement is embodied in the most quoted part of Martin Luther King, Jr.'s speech at the Lincoln Memorial, that people ought to be judged by the "content of their character not the color of their skin." If colorblindness was good enough for Rosa Parks and Martin Luther King, many argue, then it ought to be good enough for our society – a child of that very movement.

A second reason why people believe the myth of colorblindness as a moral requirement is because it permits the law and judges to consider moral issues without discussing what kind of moral system we aspire to, or how we get to that moral system. In a color blind world of mythic justice will black people be assimilated or remain distinct? Will a racial distinction be seen as interesting flavoring for society or as important components of an individual's personality? How are race and culture connected? Rather than providing answers to these important questions, colorblindness permits us to avoid any discussion of the morality or justice of assimilation, nationalism, or cultural difference. Instead, its proponents claim that justice and morality are imbedded in colorblindness. Finally, Americans do not have a concept of justice that can take account of racial difference; colorblindness is thought to be a description of racial justice.

In making the policy argument for the end of racial oppression, many black leaders and leaders of other civil rights movements also criticized the policy of racial separation for effectively allowing the covert use of race to limit the economic, legal, and social opportunities of black people. People turned that criticism into a claim that colorblindness is always and everywhere a moral system. But, the criticism of Jim Crow does not require an acceptance of colorblindness and, as our history shows, colorblindness is not a defense to adverse effects on black people.[4] Martin Luther King's work for civil rights lasted for almost fifteen years. Much of his work required the use of race consciousness on the part of black people to achieve change, and much also included the requirement of race conscious responses to existing evil.[5] Yet, people have created a mythic Martin Luther King, Jr. who is supposedly associated with a colorblindness that did not exist. In a similar fashion, the Supreme Court has declared colorblindness to be a legal watch word,[6] as it systematically continues to permit race awareness to limit access of blacks to jobs,[7] jury duty,[8] and subject blacks to over zealous police interrogation and investigation.[9]

Myths are often created to fill a necessary psychological space. Colorblindness has been created to help us get over the difficulty of race in a society where race is particularly powerful. Race is like the nakedness in the fairy tale of the emperor's new clothes.[10] In that fairy tale, the emperor was given a new set of clothes that was supposedly only visible to the virtuous. Only children were willing to laugh at the emperor's nakedness. Race shapes the often cold and stark reality of everyday life like the real nakedness in the fairy tale. But, the grownups tell us that in fact we are clothed with a nonracial reality which is not visible to those who are not part of the myth. Indeed, we are told by many that we too could see the colorblindness that clothes society, if only we were appropriately committed to individual achievement and liberal justice.[11]

The argument for racial blindness grew out of the abolitionist efforts to end slavery[12] and was effectively imported into constitutional discourse by Justice Harlan's powerful call for a color blind Constitution – or more correctly that our Constitution "is" color blind.[13] However, the earliest proponents understood that they were making an argument in favor of a particular legal policy and not creating a moral system. Many individuals also argue that we ought to extend similar principles of category blindness to all aspects of our private lives. They further claim if we did so, the issue of race would go away as an important legal and social phenomenon.[14] Some people would extend that principle to a whole array of concerns, from gender to questions of appearance.[15] However, this effort to make the private world color blind (or blind to any number of issues) has to confront the fact that, in general, we refuse to limit private actions. Thus blindness cannot avoid permitting some awareness and use of race.[16]

I would like to argue that this color blind principle is in fact a policy argument that makes several key assumptions which are not valid. In particular, I want to advance the seditious idea that we will not change the racial present until we adopt an effective program of race conscious policies, for only race conscious policies can alter the racial status quo in this country. Ultimately, I contend that the argument for colorblindness is part of the larger argument for keeping a racial status quo which leaves black people and other racial minorities in an unequal position.

Several other scholars and at least one Supreme Court justice have seemed to embrace, at least partially, the notion that race conscious policies are both moral and necessary, but they have not seen the full implications of understanding this policy truth.[17] For example, David Strauss has called colorblindness a "slogan" and "myth" and has argued powerfully that one cannot attack discrimination without hurting "innocent" people and drawing attention to race.[18] He argues persuasively that the antidiscrimination idea is a two edged sword and, properly understood, may require some color consciousness.[19] Similarly, Professor Strauss has called for race conscious hiring to get around the economic and legal difficulties of enforcing antidiscrimination legislation.[20] Additionally he argues that we ought to reorient race conscious policies to remedy the future inequalities that are likely to exist.[21] Professor Seidman has argued interestingly that Brown[22] and Miranda[23] are both examples of the Court enforcing a false sense of equality by suggesting that people have consented to their oppression.[24] Professor Gotanda has demonstrated that colorblindness is multifaceted when used by the courts, but that it cannot achieve the goals that it wants.[25]

However, none of these important and sensitive scholars has understood how much the notion of colorblindness is not a moral requirement. The problem is not that we cannot reach colorblindness because we are human and not perfect. Rather, the issue is that colorblindness is simply a policy goal which is good or bad depending on its circumstances. When Justice O'Connor laments that "[w]e ought not delude ourselves that the deep faith that race should never be relevant has triumphed over the painful social reality that, sometimes it may be,"[26] she is assuming both that colorblindness is the moral position that we ought to seek in the long run and that it is simply human foibles which prevent that glorious fact. Even though these assumptions are held across the political spectrum, I believe these conclusions concerning the moral status of colorblindness are wrong and remove whole questions from the legal discourse. In addition, I want to emphasize how racial oppression is a product of the array of oppressions that exist in our society – including gender, class, sexual orientation, and ethnicity – and that these oppressions intersect with race and each other to create a complicated reality which can never be addressed by a policy like colorblindness.

Accordingly, I will demonstrate in this chapter that colorblindness is not a moral principle or goal which ought to exist everywhere, and further that it is an unsuccessful policy prescription for altering the racial status quo. In Part I, I will describe the history of colorblindness and distinguish moral arguments from policy arguments. In Part II, I will distinguish between antidiscrimination and colorblindness and show that the moral claim which is being asserted by the policy argument of colorblindness actually maintains the racial status quo and thus leaves black people at the economic bottom. Part III will examine the major public policy argument made in defense of colorblindness in terms of the racial status quo. It will demonstrate that there are other ways of achieving racial justice. I will also argue that, for reasons that are understood but not applied to colorblindness, it is generally not possible to attack racism without dealing with race. In Part IV, I will show how the application of colorblindness in a voting rights case and antidiscrimination legislation demonstrates the procedural flaws inherent in colorblindness, especially the flaw of "peeking" and the flaw of not "peeking." Part V draws together my conclusions.

I A BRIEF HISTORY OF THE COLOR BLINDNESS PRINCIPLE

Kenneth Stampp created a good deal of controversy by suggesting that the question is simply how to create a legal system that considers blacks to be "white men with black skins, nothing more and nothing less."[27]

I would like to distinguish between policy arguments (arguments that make a particular claim based upon how a particular decision will impact concerns measurable in some particular way), and moral arguments (arguments that seek priority because of claims based on concerns connected to justice). The claim in the Declaration of Independence that all men are created equal is a moral claim based upon notions of justice embedded in the Jeffersonian language.[28] The argument for market economies in Eastern Europe is a policy argument based upon the "failure" of communism and the "success" of capitalism.[29] Policy arguments can be disproven by empirical evidence and challenged by showing that in some situations the policy does not work or has contrary results. To refute moral claims, however, first requires some agreement on the moral framework. Only then can one discuss whether the moral policy advocated conforms to the agreed upon framework. Of course, these two different claims are not completely unconnected. People do enhance their moral claim by making a policy argument about the social efficacy of a particular policy. In addition, policy arguments presume some implicit moral code for valuation. Those in favor of free markets argue that they have, and will produce, a more moral society in which individual economic freedom supports the general ability of individuals to be "complete" citizens.[30] The moral argument reinforces the policy claim for the efficacy of markets. It is because of the differences between these two types of argument that policy claims masquerading as moral claims can be so powerful. Since the only way to refute the moral claim is to question the framework of valuation, these policy claims tend to force their opponents to argue with, and lose to, strawmen. It, therefore, becomes important to distinguish between the moral arguments and the policy arguments imbedded in social discourse.

The color blind principle is a policy argument and not a moral principle. It is easy to demonstrate that fact, but harder for Americans to give up the long-held belief that the color blind principle is a moral requirement. It is easy to see that the notion of colorblindness is not sufficient to protect us from moral dilemmas if one examines the earliest efforts of our citizens to be color blind. Those who adopted the Constitution refused to put "race," "color," or "slavery" anywhere in the words of the Constitution.[31] The Constitution was blind to race, slavery and color. This conscious decision to be color blind, of course, did not prevent the creators of the American constitutional order from accepting the pernicious American form of slavery. The Constitution was, in modern constitutional parlance, facially neutral but color permissive towards private parties, and even governmental entities, so long as they did not state the racial grounds upon which their decisions were based. If they did, then they had to be stated in a situation where power did not exist to change them. The blindness implicit in the refusal to acknowledge the status quo of black people in America as both "free" and enslaved ignores the importance of black subordination in America. The morality in the notion of colorblindness simply denies the power of law to take account of, and, therefore, to be responsible for, enforcing the status quo. In the process, it sustains a racially subordinate present for African Americans.

The Constitution is color blind in a particularly unartful and improper way. Colorblindness in the Constitution makes a moral claim, but it is an extremely weak claim. Ultimately, the claim is simply to enforce the status quo. I want to acknowledge at this point that there are reasons for wanting to protect the status quo. For the white majority in this country, especially, the status quo may at least seem to represent important powerful property and status rights which are difficult to forsake.[32]

I should also admit at this point that I have some stake in the status quo as a tenured faculty member who owns a house and an automobile and is among the best paid in a highly regarded job. To the extent that I have some middle-class status, I too am invested in some form of the status quo. There is morality in protecting such claims, but it is hard to see the morality of such claims as representing some universal fairness. I want to emphasize that the moral claim of colorblindness is, in reality, an enforcement and defense of the status quo. In the United States, this status quo is one which leaves blacks permanently at the bottom of the economic ladder.

I should also note that when I speak of the status quo, I do not mean an absolutely fixed relationship between blacks and whites, but rather a range of positions responsive to the relative power of blacks and whites in American society. I would argue that historically there has been some small change in the relationship between black and white people over time, though not as much as some believe has occurred for African Americans. In addition, at various points, African Americans have made progress relative to whites in various ways. Their progress has been the largest when they have been associated with race conscious policies. These include the race conscious policies of the Freedman's Bureau and the race conscious policies of the government during the Second World War and Vietnam.[33] These public, race conscious efforts have been supplemented by the race conscious efforts of private groups, which have supported and supplanted the efforts of the government at various times.[34]

Also embedded in the color blind principle are several assumptions about social reality. The color blind principle assumes that policy changes will work on all individuals in the exact same way, irrespective of the race and culture of different groups. For example, a color blind policy which assumes white people do not have a culture that is distinct from American culture, but that black people do,[35] creates a situation where worrying about the existence of African Americans or other minorities in the ranks of ownership is color conscious. Yet giving all of the licenses to companies controlled by white people is not.[36] Similarly the color blind principle seems to assume that assimilation is the prescribed status quo that ought to be achieved. Such assumptions are produced by the power of the color blind principle to ignore the color of white people and, thus, to enforce the existing power relationships in society. Assimilation may or may not be a good thing. But, to the extent the color blind principle requires assimilation, it actually requires a genuflection by black people to white power and support for the status quo.

One final question to be asked is whether I have exaggerated the consequences of race conscious remedies and have minimized the advantages that color blind policies can produce. Take, for example, *Loving* v. *Virginia*,[37] the case where the Supreme Court found that the Virginia statute prohibiting interracial marriages violated the Constitution's equal protection standards of the Fourteenth Amendment. The supporters of the color blind principle would certainly contend that the advantages black citizens gained from the elimination of a race conscious statute prohibiting non-white people from marrying whites, with the exception of descendants of Pocohontas, grow directly from the implementation of the color blind principle. This view of the racial reality is stunted and inexact. The over-turning of the Virginia statute did not make Virginia safe for the Lovings (a black and white interracial couple), nor did it change the racial status quo that alters the status of participants in marriages because of the participants' race.[38] The Court could have adopted a racially conscious policy that protects the interests of people in racially mixed marriages, but the Court does not primarily because the color blindness principle does not mean to change the status quo as much as it means to simply assert that color blindness is morality. Black people who marry white people gain status, and some envy, before and after the constitutional change. Nothing that this color blind rule does alters the racial stereotypes associated with interracial dating and marriage. Those rules have changed, to the extent they have, primarily as a result of citizens' conscious effort to attack the racial stereotypes directly. The color blind principle does not eliminate the problems associated with racial subordination of African Americans in our society. Some proponents of colorblindness would contend that, in the allocation of power between the state and private individuals, a division of labor should be created between the government and the private sector. The government's job in this view is to do no harm, and the role of colorblindness is to prevent governmental harm both because the harm inflicted by governmental action is more pernicious and because the government has a hard time determining what is right or appropriate. In this division of labor the private sector is free to create a new and different racial status quo. The problem is that, like most evolutionary processes, the private sector can produce change and alter the status quo, but the change that is created need not produce justice for interracial couples. What colorblindness does in this situation is to enforce the racial status quo – a racial status quo that includes the right of private parties to discriminate against people in legal and illegal ways. This does not mean that colorblindness might not be the right policy in an appropriate situation, but in order to be certain of that result in terms of interracial marriage, the proponents of colorblindness have to convince us of that morality. The Court in *Loving* fails that test because it ultimately assumes that race neutrality is morality.

II COLORBLINDNESS AND THE ANTIDISCRIMINATION PRINCIPLE

In talking and thinking about how to deal with race, courts and commentators confuse the notion of colorblindness – the removal of race from the legal and governmental discourse – with the antidiscrimination principle – the elimination of decision making because of race, color, etc.[39] The antidiscrimination principle can be read in a color blind way, i.e., we could have written Title VII as requiring, for example, that people be hired on production and merit based grounds. The statute would not mention race, but would eliminate racial choices implicitly in the decisions that employers would make which were "meritorious" and "production" based.[40] However, this is not the choice that was adopted by the congress in the 14th Amendment or by the Congress in passing Title VII of the 1964 Civil Rights Act. The choice made by the 13th and 14th Amendments and by the Civil Rights Acts of modern times explicitly attempts to remove race from the social and economic discourse. This aspect of the antidiscrimination principle is color conscious. Race matters to the court in deciding whether the 13th or 14th Amendments apply and in interpreting the Constitution. Implicitly, the morality claims of the antidiscrimination principle are different from those for colorblindness. The antidiscrimination principle means to change the present by enforcing different norms on some decision makers. However, I would contend that the antidiscrimination principle has no such effect when it is color blind, precisely because it cannot see how to alter the racial present. It may be that a color blind antidiscrimination principle would prevent an increase in racial subordination, but it cannot change the racial present because it is invisible to its processes.[41] The antidiscrimination principle loses its power to change when it becomes color blind.

When courts and commentators argue for colorblindness, they implicitly are making a public policy claim and a morality claim. The public policy claim is that colorblindness will achieve the most efficacious society, and the morality claim is that the society so produced objectively will be good. However, if we understand that the public policy claim is ultimately to reinforce the status quo of society, including any implicit racial subordination, then it is clear that the morality claim being made is in defense of the status quo. Therefore, the claim of colorblindness is also one of white supremacy, to the extent white supremacy exists in the society as a whole, and that a color blind society would continue racial subordination of African Americans mandated by law. In such a world, subordination of black people becomes the natural state unchangeable by public policy or other efforts by governmental agents.[42] Indeed, the infusion of colorblindness into public policy makes it difficult for nongovernmental agents to change the status quo produced by color blind policies. Despite public/ private distinctions, colorblindness purposefully limits the ability of private agents to act race consciously.

Some of you who know your history better than the average law student and law professor will protest at this point that the color blind argument was most forcibly made before the Civil War by "free" blacks seeking to extend the rule of law to themselves and others.[43] I believe their claims support rather than defeat my point, for ultimately what they argue for and what they got – in those limited situations where they were successful – is a protection of the status quo for themselves. Racial subordination did not end in Massachusetts because blacks got the court to admit that it ought to be color blind about admission to the railway car.[44] Opposition to racial subordination did not create the right to vote everywhere for African Americans. In all of these situations, the most important rationale for these policies was the fact they were policy prescriptions which would help to alter the racial status quo. The status quo is not always bad, but it will not create a movement for change.

III COLORBLINDNESS AND MULTIOPPRESSIONS: THE PUBLIC POLICY ARGUMENT

The proponents of colorblindness have acknowledged implicitly that this policy may not change the status quo. Since this is true, the most important argument in defense of the color blind principle is that race is a poor proxy for change and that there is always a different – indeed better – proxy which will be color blind, but will permit the government or decision maker to make the appropriate choice. This view of the importance, power, and morality of colorblindness is held by a wide spectrum of people. Whenever the issue of race is raised as a way of altering the legal landscape, they contend that race is always a poor measure of other, more appropriate devices for discussing legal and social policy questions.

In making these claims, these commentators are acknowledging the policy aspects of colorblindness and comparing it to other policy programs. Richard Posner, for example, argues that race was the wrong measure in the DeFunis case. He argues, "Furthermore, the impact of eliminating racial preference is easily exaggerated. The preferred groups [who would benefit from forms of affirmative action] could be redefined as the underprivileged, the deprived, etc. – classifications not based upon race or ethnic origin. The constitutional objection to preferential treatment would thereby be removed, without substantial impairment of the purposes of such treatment."[45] Paul Brest, one of the leading liberal thinkers and scholars, argues in his seminal article on the antidiscrimination principle the following: "Race is, at best, a weak proxy for need; there are more direct and accurate ways of identifying needy people."[46] This is the route ultimately taken by the Supreme Court when it "solved" the problem of affirmative action in *University of Calif. v. Bakke*.[47]

This view was most recently taken by the Supreme Court in *City of Richmond v. J.A. Croson*.[48] Justice O'Connor said:

> Even in the absence of evidence of discrimination, the city has at its disposal a whole array of race-neutral devices to increase the accessibility of city contracting opportunities to small entrepreneurs of all races. Simplification of bidding procedures, relaxation of bonding requirements, and training and financial aid for disadvantaged entrepreneurs of all races would open the public contracting market to all those who have suffered the effects of past societal discrimination or neglect. Many of the formal barriers to new entrants may be the product of bureaucratic inertia more than actual necessity, and may have a disproportionate effect on the opportunities open to new minority firms. Their elimination or modification would have little detrimental effect on the city's interests and would serve to increase the opportunities available to minority business without classifying individuals on the basis of race. The city may also act to prohibit discrimination in the provision of credit or bonding by local suppliers and banks. Business as usual should not mean business pursuant to the unthinking exclusion of certain members of our society from its rewards [footnote omitted].[49]

Justice O'Connor assumes, as did Professors Posner and Brest, that race is an empty box into which other things, like poverty and oppression, are added and, if we take out those other things, there is no important difference connected to race. This assumption is overly simplistic for two reasons.

First, the issue of race is not easily encapsulated in other matters. To take just the most obvious one, being poor and black is very different in our society from being poor and white. Not only are the white poor likely to start with greater wealth – both human and nonhuman – but they are also not likely to remain in poverty as long as poor blacks.[50] Similar results emerge from the unemployment and other job-market experiences of workers.[51] This means that race is not a proxy for something else. Poverty, unemployment, and even social status are often not good measures of the costs imposed on blacks by differential treatment. Efforts to solve the problem of racism by ending poverty are bound to achieve some admirable goals, but almost never will such programs solve the issue of race. Racism can be destroyed only by attacking its causes.

Second, in trying to use something besides race to create change, the practitioners of colorblindness have assumed that all oppression is parallel to other oppressions, i.e., oppressions do not intersect to alter and change the nature of those with which there are intersections. However, we know from the empirical facts that this is not true. The interaction of race and poverty is so great that it creates a separate and distinct existence for many African Americans. This is particularly true of certain neighborhoods and sets of individuals, and it has produced a whole social science cottage industry of people who are concerned about the "truly disadvantaged" and the "underclass."[52] Worrying about class in such situations will not eliminate the intersections between race and class. In addition, even worrying about class as a subset of race may not be sufficient to deal with the subordination and oppression created by these intersections.

The claim made by the proponent of colorblindness ultimately becomes an argument about the relative worth of race and other categories of oppression. Those who believe that colorblindness will be effective are contending that these other categories (class, income, youth, being a small business, etc.) are better measures than race, of what we want to eliminate. But, I would contend that this is generally not true. If we eliminate poverty, we will not eliminate racism precisely because racism was not under attack. Indeed, we will not even eliminate the intersections between race and class in such situations, precisely because they are likely to resist purely class-based attacks. Programs to eliminate poverty, for example, reach "poor" people, but not the truly disadvantaged in the inner cities. Policy makers often complain of the difficulty of reaching the truly disadvantaged through school policies because of the externalities associated with the interaction of race and class. We see this same problem in the area of admissions, for example affirmative action plans often cream from the pool of black, and other minorities, people with the smallest class and race intersection. Educational institutions do this because it requires the least amount of investment in finding and preparing people to be students in their institutions. We could find students to admit to our schools from a much more diverse set of backgrounds, but we ultimately choose not to since it would require real investments in real race conscious policies. We prefer the mildly race conscious policy because it is cheap and likely to change us the least. I think such changes are important in breaking down the views about race and performance, but I do not want to suggest that such efforts will eliminate the intra-racial class differences.

Such polices of affirmative action are both blind to that intersection and support that status quo. Indeed, every time the Supreme Court has attempted to argue that a race conscious policy was incorrect, it has done so in ways that support the continuation of the racial status quo. When the Powell opinion became the opinion of the Court in *Bakke*, it enshrined into the Constitution the belief that the race conscious remedies adopted by the University of California were incorrect. However, the resulting change opens the opportunity of becoming a physician to precisely the kind of white person who, if he had been black, would have been described as undeserving, and certainly not the truly disadvantaged. A policy that adopted a Harvard kind of multiple factor analysis will only work to create changes in the status quo if the operators of the system are in fact race conscious. Because of the income and class factors, there are always a lot of white people who will appear disadvantaged by circumstances but who will not be "truly disadvantaged." Similarly, when the Court in *Wygant* v. *Jackson Board of Education*[53] permits white incumbent teachers to get seniority rights that had been given to black teachers, the person getting the rights will be representative of the status quo in the teaching profession.[54] The Supreme Court cannot prevent general disadvantage or color blind seniority from recreating the racial status quo, and their opinions have simply reinforced that racial present.

There is in general no proxy for race that does not become race itself. We see this also in the public debate about many programs that are in fact color blind – Pell grants, welfare eligibility, athletic scholarships – but that are perceived as somehow the products of race-conscious activity. People defending the colorblindness option have made their claims about the worth of other categories with little evidence to support that view. Take, for example, Justice O'Connor's assertion in *Croson* that the city could have attacked the problem of too few minority contractors by trying to help small business people get credit. Such a policy sounds like it will work, but such programs are likely to disproportionately help small white contractors who, for all of the reasons race matters, are better able to take advantage of such programs. Such contractors will be better connected to white contractors on average and, to the extent these contractors are able to use their right to make private choices unchecked by governmental policy, white contractors are likely to be advantaged.[55] Experience and economic constraints also suggest that many governmental programs will not be given the resources to influence enough black small businesses to create effective change. Like every other program that is possible, such programs have limited funds. The more money that is spent on white contractors, the smaller amounts that will be spent to change the racial circumstances. The colorblindness principle implicitly assumes that it will reinforce this status quo racially and, therefore, will not make changes in the relative position of blacks and whites. The program that Justice O'Connor urges will simply reinforce the status quo. Although those who oppose race conscious policies can see this point about race conscious policy, they contend that race conscious policies will not work because only the "wealthy" or "suburban" blacks will benefit from such programs, while those who are "truly disadvantaged" will be ignored.[56] These views about affirmative action are widely held but their implications for colorblindness are almost always ignored.

Almost all policies create change through imperfect instruments. This means that there is an error in measurement associated with their implementation. To the extent we care about eliminating the error of that measurement with respect to race, I would contend the error is almost always smaller with respect to race than it is with respect to other nonracial measures.[57]

IV PEEKING AND OTHER VICES OF BLINDNESS. NOT PEEKING AND THE TERROR OF COLORBLINDNESS

The most difficult problem of the color blind principle is the problem of "peeking," i.e., social actors are permitted to peek and covertly use race. If peeking is permitted, colorblindness becomes a sham to protect the existing structures and discretionary power in society. An important example from recent legal decisions raises this issue clearly.

It is not an accident that the nomination of Lani Guinier to be Assistant Attorney General for Civil Rights was blocked by a coalition of people concerned about voting rights issues.[58] A number of cases have created a stir about voting rights and black voters. But, the key concern seems to have been the 1982 Amendments to the Voting Rights Act[59] that eliminated the intent test required of voting rights cases in *Mobile* v. *Bolden*.[60] The Supreme Court required in *Thornburg* v. *Gingles*,[61] another North Carolina case, that black and other racial minorities be given the opportunity to challenge legislative decisions which improperly affect their ability to win. The reapportionment of congressional seats in 1990, in the wake of these legal developments, created the largest number of seats held by African Americans ever in the 1992 congressional elections, and had a similar impact on Hispanics elected to Congress in 1992.[62] The number of black congresspersons went from twenty-six to thirty-nine, and the number of Hispanic congressmen went up as well.[63] A number of the African American newly elected congresspersons were from districts which were created as a result of voting rights pressure on the reapportionment process. These districts were consciously chosen to produce African American majorities. Some of the districts created were oddly shaped in order to meet the requirements of *Baker* v. *Carr* and the other redistricting jurisprudence of the Supreme Court. Two of these seats are in North Carolina, and each elected an African American to Congress. When they took the oath of office in January 1993, they were the first African Americans to sit in Congress from North Carolina in almost a hundred years. One of the districts created in North Carolina is a district that stretches from Durham to Charlotte along I-85, the major highway in the region, and the other is a district that stretches across eastern North Carolina among rural districts.

The *Wall Street Journal* has described the congressional district where I vote, the one that stretches along I-85, as "political pornography."[64] I am tempted to suggest that the description proves that the *Wall Street Journal* does not understand politics and has never seen pornography. But, importantly, the attitude reflected in that quote demonstrates the poverty of the color blind principle. The Court's opinion in *Shaw* v. *Reno*[65] proves that a majority on the Supreme Court does not understand pornography, politics, or justice.

The 12th congressional district was the product of the redistricting of North Carolina after the 1990 census. The resulting district runs from Durham, along I-85, to Charlotte. In some places, it is the width of the highway. The Attorney General invoked his power under the Voting Rights Act to reject the first congressional redistricting plan. He suggested that the state ought to have produced two districts that were predominantly minority but had, in the original plan, produced only one. In response to his rejection, North Carolina decided not to appeal that use of federal power and produced the redistricting map that was, at least partially, successfully challenged by the five white residents of Durham.

Justice O'Connor, in perhaps the most fatuous racial decision this century, concludes that five white plaintiffs have been adversely and facially affected by North Carolina's use of race-conscious redistricting to create two black voter majorities.[66] Justice O'Connor tells us that these five white plaintiffs are not claiming to be white – just "citizens" adversely impacted by not being able "to participate in a 'color-blind' electoral process."[67] "Just citizens!" What is Justice O'Connor talking about? What angers my colleagues (two of the five plaintiffs teach law at Duke University School of Law) and led them to fight this case, long past the point when many might have been influenced by the cost, is not the shape of the district, but that race was taken into account.[68] The Court is caught in a box of its own making and does not understand the nature of the dilemma it has created. The Court has said that we can make no assumption about the nature of how people will vote, and it will not peek at the reality of the situation in North Carolina. If that is true, then these districts cannot violate the rights of these white plaintiffs because the decisions that will be produced are not discriminatory. If these citizens have no race, then how can race matter. The Court claims that it wants to make no invidious assumption about the way that black voters will vote. If indeed black voters will vote like everyone else, or at least that their vote will be just as appropriate, how have the rights of the five white plaintiffs been injured? What is the injury to these citizens who have no race? Is it being represented by an African American congressperson? The reason the Court wants to treat these five white plaintiffs as raceless is to avoid the difficulty of admitting that there is no injury.[69] The Court says these plaintiffs have a right to live in a color blind world, where redistricting does not upset their racial expectations. However, despite Justice O'Connor's effort to make the claim that such a world is possible, she does not, and cannot, suggest how the state could produce such a status, given the myriad of conscious policies that implicitly take account of race – policies that she admits are necessary parts of the redistricting process.[70] Indeed Justice O'Connor attempts to distinguish between permissible peeking and impermissible peeking. Justice O'Connor points to the redistricting in *Wright* v. *Rockefeller*[71] as an example of permissible peeking by the legislative process. In *Wright*, Justice O'Connor implies that the race neutral policies of compactness and contiguousness and the continuance of the integrity of political subdivisions are permissible racial peeking by the legislature.[72] But, somehow, the legislatures' peeking at race, so as to create black majority districts, is impermissible peeking. It is impermissible peeking because districts with irregular shapes give the appearance of unfairness and, therefore, appearance ought to matter. Appearance matters because "it reinforces the perception that members of the same racial group – regardless of their age, education, economic status, or the community in which they live – think alike, share the same political interests, and will prefer the same candidates at the polls." The danger that Justice O'Connor runs is, of course, that this view can be interpreted as the call for an enforced white supremacy. If white race does not count in this equation, as Justice O'Connor has suggested, then the enforcement of raceless neutral standards – like age, education and economic status – runs the risk of enforcing the existing racial circumstances. These racial circumstances have left black people without a congressional representative for over one hundred years, in a state which still has a significant number of counties covered by the Voting Rights Act and substantial racial block voting. Justice O'Connor understands the difficulty of her position with respect to this issue, and she responds in two different ways. First, she argues that, when we create such districts, we send the wrong message to congresspersons elected from those districts. We are saying that "their primary obligation is to represent only the members of that group, rather than their constituency as a whole." Second, she contends that the Court's prior precedent has applied a similar doctrine which prevents peeking to empower whites and thus exclude blacks in redistricting.[73] In essence, Justice O'Connor is arguing for the application of colorblindness to both peeking and redistricting cases. Both arguments are completely and utterly fatuous, and they show the way the Court still attempts to manipulate doctrine to avoid the racial implications of its decisions.

Justice O'Connor's theoretical argument about the impact of peeking is wrong on a number of grounds. She cannot support this argument with any empirical evidence to suggest that any congressperson elected from a district that has an odd shape will act this way. This is particularly true when, as is the case with both of the North Carolina districts and the other districts that may be at risk because of this opinion, the white minority has substantial control over who is chosen. Indeed, white candidates can win in these districts, since some white candidates ran in both of them. Justice O'Connor ignores the political power that superior wealth and political connections give to the white communities in these districts, and which continue to have disproportionate influence on the representatives who go to Congress. In at least one congressional election, the white voters were able to choose which black representative would represent an over-whelmingly minority district.[74] The Court's argument is an assumption about the dangers of using race. It ultimately assumes that, when whites are in power because of their majorities, it is constitutional. But, when those majorities are countered by racial consciousness, it is not. The Court, in essence, asserts the racial neutrality of any existing racial majority that is not the product of overwhelming conscious actions by the legislature. It is clear that a white candidate had a much better chance of winning, in either the new 12th or the new second district, than a black candidate did, in any of the other ten congressional seats in North Carolina. To Justice O'Con-nor, this is irrelevant because there is the possibility that race might matter to a representative. Justice O'Connor allows legislatures to peek as long as they do not violate the white supremacy existing in North Carolina. This is easy to see when we examine the nonracial examples she uses to create the possibility of race neutrality. She suggests that a neutral purpose might be to maintain political cohesiveness, but she, of course, assumes that the political subdivisions are achieved neutrally. In truth, Durham County is a product of the Reconstruction Era's opposition to black control of politics in Orange County, from which Durham was created. All five plaintiffs live in a racial atmosphere created by that non-neutral history. Similarly, the assertion that compactness or contiguousness are themselves race neutral, when a legislature may manipulate them in ways to create congressional majorities which happen to be white, assumes that the white majority is itself racially neutral. It may be. But, if it is, so is a black majority.

Similarly, Justice O'Connor's contention that she has adopted a racially neutral system regarding race consciousness is wrong. She reaches this result by distorting the Court's opinion in Gomillion v. Lightfoot. In Gomillion, the city of Tuskegee created an uncouth twenty-eight sided, municipal boundary that excluded all but four or five of the 400 black voters and none of the white voters. The purpose of the exclusion was to limit services and other benefits significantly to the white populace. This was no insignificant issue. By being excluded from the city, the residents of a largely rural county effectively lost city services. The effect was, in essence, to limit blacks' ability to enjoy the benefits that the Constitution requires. Justice O'Connor's use of Gomillion to create symmetry between her treatment of blacks and whites demonstrates her lack of understanding of Gomillion's reality. It reads as if it were created by law clerks out of hornbooks. The case is referred to in a lifeless manner – Justice O'Connor simply refers to Tuskegee as a municipality or "the city," and she misses the point that in Gomillion none of the white voters were excluded. Accord-ingly, Justice O'Connor misses the racial reality of Tuskegee that still haunts that city. In truth, the Court could have concluded that the actions in the city of Tuskegee were impermissible peeking precisely because there was an effort by a powerful and entrenched white power structure to deny blacks their right to participate in the political system. The plaintiffs in *Shaw* have a much closer connection to *Gomillion*'s defendants than to its plaintiffs. Like the defendants in *Gomillion*, the *Shaw* plaintiffs insist on being able to keep control of the political process. Justice O'Connor and a majority of her colleagues permit the white plaintiffs to make a case, without having to prove an injury. Unlike the plaintiffs in *Gomillion*, the *Shaw* plaintiffs have not been deprived of anything. Indeed, the *Shaw* plaintiffs are only required to participate in the process. This is a process which is not unfairly stacked against them.[75]

The Court's anxiety for the rights of my colleagues was not matched last term, when the real right to participate was altered by political theft.[76] In *Presley v. Etowah County Commission*, the Court refused to find a section five violation of the rights of black voters. These black voters successfully challenged the racial subordination in Alabama and had succeeded in electing a black representative.[77] In response to that election, the white-majority controlled commission changed the powers of the commissioner, and effectively denied the black representative any powers. The Court said that there was no need to preclear this change. Comparing the claims advanced by my colleagues and those by the black plaintiffs in *Presley*, it is difficult to see that the injury to these five white plaintiffs could be constitutionally more significant. After all, the constitutional interests in *Presley* require the least constitutional gamesmanship. They are a product of the Congress's power to create statutes, under the fourteenth and fifteenth amendments, preventing discrimination in voting. The Court found that the voting rights statute, which was meant to protect black voters from just such political theft, did not provide a meaningful avenue of attack. Here, "citizens" without a race and a party without any injury are found aggrieved by North Carolina's decision to be race conscious.[78]

In describing the 12th district of North Carolina, Justice O'Connor cites to the dissent in the district court case, the amicus brief of the Republican National Committee, and a comment by a state legislator reported in the *Washington Post* that "if you drove down the interstate with both car doors open, you'd kill most of the people in the district." The last is clearly a joke. But the Court is so intent on making fun of this district that it seems to miss the humor in the description and, instead, takes the statement seriously. The question of how to use race is an important one, and one that Justice O'Connor and I are likely to disagree about.[79] But, it deserves more serious attention from the Court than she gave it in *Shaw*. By not providing usable guidelines to lower courts on how to apply this decision, the Court does not deal with the real issues that might actually have concerned it. The Court takes the political musings[80] of the Federalist Society, as reported in the *Wall Street Journal*, and makes constitutional policy out of it.[81] Such actions might be dangerous if applied to economic or general social policy. When the Court applies it to race policy, however, it is really a little like putting the fox in charge of the proverbial chicken coop.[82]

The plaintiffs have attempted to argue that the use of race, or race consciousness, by the legislature is inappropriate if the result is to produce districts that would help black candidates. The Court accepts that argument and contends that race neutral policy must be applied.[83] However, it is clear here that the legislature can, and will, peek at race in making any redistricting policy. The only way that this would not happen is if all information about race and party were excluded from the deliberations. This is not required, and it will not occur. The race of the voters matters in North Carolina, precisely because the black voters have very consistently voted against the racial politics of North Carolina's Congressional Club[84] and Republican Party. Saying that the legislature has created racial division in North Carolina, given this history, is an insult to every black voter who has had to listen to vilification from the most serious antiblack statewide candidates in the country.[85] Indeed, the Court took *Shaw* because the case has almost nothing to do with race neutrality and everything to do with the fact that, despite the efforts of the Republican Party, the North Carolina legislature was able to create two districts that could elect a black congressperson without reducing the total number of districts in North Carolina likely, at least in the short run, to remain Democrat.

The problem with the Court's argument for race neutrality is that it is not possible for a redistricting plan to not consider issues that are very good proxies for race. For example, any plan in a state that looks at the likelihood that the district voted overwhelmingly Democratic can use that as a proxy for race. No procedure which uses any characteristics but perhaps geography is raceless.[86] There is no racially neutral way of creating congressional districts that do not become an enforcement of the status quo, where blacks can be elected to Congress only if they are able to convince white voters in disproportionately large numbers to vote for them. When the Supreme Court reverses a long jurisprudential policy and finds that race-conscious redistricting may be illegal, it seems to want to establish, for as long as white voters are hostile to black candidates, a policy where the congressional delegation from North Carolina will be all or almost all white.[87] Race consciousness does not of course require proportionality; after all, the black citizens of North Carolina are entitled to three representatives under that policy, not merely the two that were elected. The policy, as adopted by Justice O'Connor's opinion, has effectively concluded that a legislature trying to protect the constituencies of its white incumbents will not violate any cognizable right. But, any effort to affirmatively change that situation to potentially allow a black candidate or candidates to win runs afoul of constitutional strict scrutiny. Only in the mind of the current Supreme Court could one conclude that the latter situation is akin to an attempt at keeping white supremacy in the wake of the Civil War. The Court has lost all sense of history and purpose and has become a haven for the interests of white plaintiffs. The point is that in a world where race matters, as it does in North Carolina, it is not possible to ignore its intersections and impacts on our choices. Legislatures peek[88] when they redistrict and, as is becoming increasingly clear, this Supreme Court peeks when it decides what rights to protect.[89] This example from the voting rights cases is just one of many which have encompassed federal courts in recent years.[90]

The other side of the argument about colorblindness is that race matters in a number of situations where the proponents of colorblindness will not permit its use. The best example of this problem was the 1991 Civil Rights Act. In that act, Congress explicitly prohibited the use of race norming to change the racial composition of a workforce.[91] The purpose of this section was to eliminate race norming in examinations to permit the participation of black and other racial minorities in public sector jobs. The problem for those who believe in colorblindness and their successful effort to include race norming into the 1991 Civil Rights Act is that race matters. Tests, by their very nature can, and often are, changed to deal with different responses by ethnic groups and gender. This is easy to see if we look at tests not as neutral instruments of measuring the ability to do a job,[92] but as imperfect measures of people's ability to do jobs. In such situations, questions or tests which work for one group need not work for other groups. No one who creates these examinations would make the claim that they are the kind of neutral instruments suggested by some of their defenders. The color blind principle here prevents the Court from peeking at race to examine how the groups do differently with respect to the examination. If the courts give the widest support to this interpretation of Title VII it will make this kind of unconscious discrimination greater, not less, for people in public service jobs.

Not peeking is both unfair and decreases the usefulness of examinations to choose the most productive workers. Workers from gender or racial groups disfavoured by the examinations are likely to find themselves continuing to look in from the outside. As a hard and fast rule, colorblindness does not work to help us figure how or when to peek at race. Racial blindness is an inappropriate tool for conducting social policy.

Judge Peckham has suggested that some policies of color consciousness may survive the amendment of Title VII.[93] He has ruled that while the 1991 Civil Rights Act outlawed race norming, it did not outlaw banding.[94] Banding would permit the courts to examine what scores produced equivalent performance for different groups. However, what Judge Peckham does not understand is that the Court has been very explicit about the kind of peeking it will permit and what is inappropriate. It is hard to believe that this court will interpret the 1991 Civil Rights Act in a way that will permit banding precisely; to do so would upset the racial status quo. No current majority exists for permitting peeking outside racial blindness to alter the economic or social position of black Americans.

V CONCLUSION: RACE CONSCIOUSNESS IS NOT UNI-DIMENSIONAL

The proponents of racial blindness have often looked at race conscious policies as being uni-dimensional. Even those who make distinctions are often not consistent in making such distinctions when they write about race conscious remedies. The Supreme Court seems to have fallen into that trap as well. In a number of its cases involving race, the Court has written about race conscious policies without doing an adequate job of distinguishing their nature.[95] I want to debunk that claim by making it clear that there are many kinds of race conscious policies. As I have defined them, race conscious policies extend from antidiscrimination policy to fixed inflexible numerical requirements. All of these requirements, however, can, in some situations, help to alter the status quo. They use the best proxy we have – race – to try to alter its presence in the body politic. Of course, not all race conscious policies are born equal, and it is possible for race conscious policies to backfire. But it is not possible for change to occur without such policies. The question many of you must be asking is do we know how to use race consciousness to eliminate the status quo. The answer is that it depends on the circumstances. The appropriate race conscious policy will depend on how deeply entrenched racial subordination is in our society. The intersection of race and other issues of oppression, like gender and class, means that the appropriate race conscious policy will depend on how to eliminate the issue of race and the intersection. This makes the issue of how to eliminate the appropriate subordination more complicated, but it requires that policy makers and judges use practical policy instead of simple, bright line rules to try to eliminate the consequences of racial subordination.

Traditionally, courts and commentators have assumed that color blind policies were morally superior because the policy objectives of governmental agencies or actors could be reached by the use of color blind policies. If, as I have shown, such a view is incorrect and if indeed color blind policies cannot alter the status quo, then it is possible to understand the argument that Derrick Bell has made about race in American politics as a corollary of this point. Professor Bell has argued that race is permanently entrenched within the American body public and that our history has not shown a diminution of its power.[96] If Professor Bell is accurately describing the racial present, it is precisely because we have had such difficulty dealing with the fact that racial changes in our existence depend fundamentally on race conscious policies.

I should end by pointing out that not all race conscious policies need to occur through government action.[97] When black groups are able to form positive groups to create communities of influence to alter the existing structure of life, those communities are engaging in race conscious policies.[98] The eradication of the racial present ultimately requires a careful balancing of those race conscious policies. But, if I understand Professor Bell correctly, only by creating an appropriate array of race conscious policies can we deal with racial concerns. Such policies will require us to reject the policies of colorblindness so important to current dominant legal discourse. When we reject this colorblindness, courts will have to figure out an even more complicated and sophisticated program which does not rely on the formalism of colorblindness or the naivete of assuming that the status quo is easily remediable.

EPILOGUE

When my nephew visits me in the summer, I read to him a set of African folktales. One of his favorites is the story of the lizard and the turtle. This is an old African story about a lizard who believed in rules. The lizard saw a turtle dragging some fruit in the road attached to the turtle's tail. The lizard jumped on the fruit and claimed it because he had found it in the road. The turtle complained that, since he had harvested the fruit and dragged it along the road, it was his. The dispute was submitted to the legal authorities and the judges, a group of lizards, came back with the decision that the fruit should be divided in half and given to the two claimants. The turtle felt cheated but took his fruit home and thought. The next day the turtle waited by the side of the road and when the lizard came by, he jumped on his back. The turtle said, "Look what I found." The lizard complained that he could not belong to the turtle, but they submitted the complaint to the legal authorities. Based upon the previous adopted rule the authorities ordered that the lizard be divided in half with half to be given to each claimant. The turtle went home happy. The moral of the story is that formalistic blindness seldom leads to justice. The color blind principle is such a formal rule and the likelihood that its implementation will lead to justice is just as problematic and contingent. Adjusting color conscious policies to reflect justice and to achieve our policy goals has the potential to alter our present in appropriate ways.[99]

NOTES

1 *Brown* v. *North Carolina*, 479 U.S. 940 (1986) (O'Connor, J., concurring).
2 See Richard Posner, *The Economics of Justice* (1984) (Wealth maximization can describe a form of justice.) Posner does not assume that he can justify that position without showing that justice will result from choosing an economic efficiency system that maximizes wealth. Accordingly though, he thinks economics is justice and spends three hundred pages proving it. He seems to have rejected aspects of this view in a more recent book. Richard Posner, *Theory of Jurisprudence* (1991).

3 I capitalize the civil rights movement to distinguish its mythic structure in colorblindness from reality. The real civil rights movement is older than the one in the myth going back to abolition and being deeply involved in the larger struggle for gender and class justice and more complicated than the one in the colorblindness myth. See Aldon Morris, *The Origins of the Civil Rights Movement: Black Communities Organizing for Change* (1984) (The civil rights movement was not the accidental production of individuals for justice, but part of a larger structure of demands for racial justice.) The real civil rights movement also included women whose contributions are often left out of discussion of the Civil Rights Movement. See generally, *Women in the Civil Rights Movement: Trailblazers & Torchbearers 1941–1965* (Vicki L. Crawford, Anne Rouse, and Barbara Woods, 1990). See also Steven F. Lawson, *Running for Freedom: Civil Rights and Black Politics in America Since 1941*, pp. 1–31 (1991). The history of black people has been a history of struggle for racial justice so that one way of looking at the underground railroad is as part of a civil rights movement. See, e.g., Henrietta Buckmaster, *Let My People Go* (1992).

4 *McCleskey* v. *Kemp*, 481 U.S. 279 (1987).

5 Martin Luther King's Letter From the Birmingham Jail was addressed to the white clergy and asked them to think about their response to oppression. The Southern Christian Leadership Conference that Martin Luther King, Jr. helped to found and organize attempted to use the black church as a base for change. This effort though not exclusionary was clearly race conscious. See e.g., Adam Fairclough, *To Redeem the Soul of America: The Southern Christian Leadership Conference and Martin Luther King, Jr.* (1987) (The SCLC was a product of the black church and grew out of its demands for social justice and equality).

6 See *Brown* v. *North Carolina*, 479 U.S. 940 (1986).

7 See, e.g., Jerome McCristal Culp, Jr., "Neutrality, the Race Question, and the 1991 Civil Rights Act: The 'Impossibility' of Permanent Reform," 45 *Rutgers Law Review* 965 (1993); David Strauss, "The Law and Economics of Racial Discrimination in Employment: The Case for Numerical Standards," 79 *Geo. L.J.* 1619 (1991) (Courts' decisions leave no choice for change but fixed standards.); Paulette Caldwell, "A Hair Piece: Perspectives on the Intersection of Race and Gender," 1991 *Duke L.J.* 365. (The courts have ignored the intersection of race and gender and accordingly produced an antidiscrimination legal system that avoids protecting the legitimate interests of black women.)

8 See, e.g., Sheri Lynn Johnson, "Black Innocence and the White Jury," 83 *Mich. L. Rev.* 1611 (1985).

9 See, e.g., Dwight L. Greene, "Justice Scalia and Tonto, Judicial Pluralistic Ignorance, and the Myth of Colorless Individualism in *Bostick* v. *Florida*," 67 *Tul. L. Rev.* 1979 (1993); *Bostick* v. *Florida*, 111 S. Ct. 2382, 2384–85 (1991). See also Sheri Lynn Johnson, "Race and the Decision to Detain a Suspect," 93 *Yale L.J.* 214 (1983).

10 Lani Guinier, "Groups, Representation, and Race-Conscious Districting: A Case of the Emperor's Clothes," 71 *Tex. L. Rev.* 1589 (1993). (Professor Guinier independently thought this analogy applied.)

11 See, for e.g., Walter Williams, "False Civil Rights Vision and Contempt for Rule of Law," 79 *Geo. L.J.* 1777 (1991). (Noncolor blind legal systems destroy the very notion of law. People should adopt a liberal model of law and reject any resulting orient limitation on individual freedom that will rob us of our birthright to be appropriately color blind.); Shelby Steele, *The Content of Our Character* (1990). (Racism exists but it is possible for those in the black middle class to ignore the racism that they face and move on to help create that color blind system. Professor Steele seems to believe that the creation of a color blind system is only one wish away.)

12 See, e.g., Celeste Michelle Condit and John Louis Lucites, *Crafting Equality: America's Anglo-African Word*, pp. 69–100 (1993). (Abolitionist free blacks created the argument for colorblindness and help to make it a part of literary and eventually legal discourse.)

13 *Plessy v. Ferguson*, 163 U.S. 537, 559 (Harlan J. dissenting). ("Our constitution is color-blind, and neither knows nor tolerates classes among citizens. In respect of civil rights, all citizens are equal before the law.") See generally Neil Gotanda, A Critique of "Our Constitution is Color-Blind," 44 *Stan. L. Rev.* 1 (1991). (The notion of race is used in four different ways in constitutional discourse. These uses of race mask the extent to which the colour blind concept enforces white supremacy.) See also Andrew Kull, *The Color Blind Constitution* (1992). (The notion that certain issues should not sully the constitution goes back to its initial adoption and description. This notion of colorblindness has both positive and negative qualities to it.) Black leaders from Frederick Douglass to Martin Luther King have called for colorblindness. See, e.g., speech of Martin Luther King at the March on Washington on 25 August 1963. ("I have a dream that my four little children will one day live in a nation where they will not be judged by the color of their skin, but by the content of their character.") But see T. Alexander Aleinikoff, "*Plessy v. Ferguson*: Freedom, Antiracism, and Citizenship," 1992 *U. Ill. L. Rev.* 962. (Justice Harlan's dissent in *Plessy* has been misread in ways to support contemporary issues. His original intent was to make more modest claims about citizenship. I think that Professor Aleinikoff would agree with me that people have turned Justice Harlan's legal argument into a political claim masquerading as a moral claim.)

14 See, e.g., Lino A. Graglia, "Racial Preferences, Quotas, and the Civil Rights Act of 1991," 41 *DePaul L. Rev.* 1117 (1992). (Use of race conscious remedies is the adoption of the immoral for a good purpose.) Even when people urge that colorblindness ought to govern all our activities, they do not urge that we require colorblindness in private arenas. We are to voluntarily find racial blindness. See e.g., William Van Alstyne, "Rites of Passage: Race, the Supreme Court, and the Constitution," 46 *U. Chi. L. Rev.* 775, 808–09 (1979). But see Richard Delgado, "Norms and Normal Science: Toward a Critique of Normality in Legal Thought," 139 *U. Pa. L. Rev.* 933 (1991) (Traditional jurisprudence does not create justice or the possibility of change.) and Derrick Bell, *Faces at the Bottom of the Well: The Permanence of Racism* (1992) (Racism is endemic to American society.)

15 It is of course not possible to be neutral about everything. Most commentators stop at culture or some other limit that they would like to enforce. This raises the question how do we define particular categories like race or gender? Feminists have been raising the issue of this intersection in important and powerful ways. See e.g., Angela Harris, "Race and Essentialism in Feminist Legal Theory," 42 *Stan. L. Rev.* 581 (1990); Trina Grillo and Stephanie M. Wildman, "Obscuring the Importance of Race: The Implications of Making Comparisons Between Racism and Sexism, or other -Isms," 1991 *Duke L. J.* 397. Others have raised the question of intersection between race and culture and gender. These questions are raised in an interesting way in an article by Martha Chamallas, "Racial Segregation and Cultural Domination: A Rubin Trilogy on Title VII," 52 *Louisiana L. Rev.* 1457 (1992). (Judge Rubin was able to see the issue of segregation and oppression, but had a more difficult time seeing cultural oppression as race discrimination. Judge Rubin would find that culture is mutable but race is not, but Professor Chamallas shows that is a stilted and limited view of culture.) Professor Paulette Caldwell has raised similar questions about how we define race and gender in her path breaking article, "A Hair Piece: Perspectives on the Intersection of Race and Gender," 1991 *Duke L. J.* 365. (Professor Caldwell

demonstrates that courts and commentators have a difficult time understanding or dealing with the intersectionality of race and gender, but more importantly that intersection is important in ways not given credence by judges and the law.) One of the things that we can learn from this literature and other works in this area is that there are many possible intersections and that we cannot deal with them all, but that in looking at how oppression works it is important to know how they intersect.

16 See, e.g., Neil Gotanda, supra n. 13. Feminists have been among the earliest in the recent debates to raise the issue of the public/private distinction in the law. See, e.g., Nadine Taub and Elizabeth Schneider, "Women's Subordination and the role of Law," *The Politics of Law* 151–73 (Revised edn 1990); Ruth Gavison, "Feminism and the Public/Private Distinction," 45 *Stan. L. Rev.* 1 (1992). Katharine Bartlett, *Gender and the Law* (1993). But this issue has been raised before. See, e.g., Ira Nerken, "A New Deal for the Protection of Fourteenth Amendment Rights: Challenging the Doctrinal Basis of the Civil Rights Cases and State Action Theory," 12 *Harv. C.R.-C.L. L. Rev.* 297 (1978). (The constitutional distinction between public and private sphere, introduced in The Civil Rights Cases, is tied to outmoded notions of contract theory that ought to be rejected and replaced with an analysis that looks at the scope of the private power that the state actor is enforcing. The public/private distinction created by The Civil Rights Cases simply is the wrong one to enforce constitutionally.)

17 See *Regents of the University of California* v. *Bakke*, 438 U.S. 265, (1978) (Blackmun, J., concurring).

18 David Strauss, "The Myth of Colorblindness," 1986 *Supreme Ct. Rev.* 99, 100–1. Reduced to its simplest terms, my argument is as follows. The prohibition against racial discrimination prohibits – and must necessarily prohibit – the use of accurate racial generalizations that disadvantage blacks. But to prohibit accurate racial generalizations is to engage in something very much like affirmative action. Specifically, a principle prohibiting accurate racial generalizations has many of the same characteristics as affirmative action; and the various possible explanations of why accurate racial generalizations are unconstitutional lead to the conclusion that failure to engage in affirmative action may also sometimes be unconstitutional.... I am not suggesting at this point that it is impossible to draw a common sense distinction between affirmative action and nondiscrimination. But critics of affirmative action attack it on the ground that it causes innocent people to suffer, and that instead of enforcing colorblindness, it draws attention to race. Palmore shows that the prohibition against discrimination has precisely these characteristics as well.

19 David Strauss, supra n. 18, at 100, 118–34.

20 David Strauss, "The Law and Economics of Racial Discrimination in Employment: The Case for Numerical Standards," 79 *Geo. L.J.* 1619 (1991).

21 Kathleen Sullivan, "The Supreme Court, 1986 Term – Comment: Sins of Discrimination: Last Term's Affirmative Action Cases," 100 *Harv. L. Rev.* 78 (1986).

22 347 U.S. 483 (1954).

23 384 U.S. 436 (1966).

24 Michael Seidman, Brown and Miranda, 80 *Calif. L. Rev.* 673 (1992).

25 Neil Gotanda, supra n. 13.

26 *Brown* v. *North Carolina*, 479 U.S. 940 (1986).

27 Kenneth Stampp, *The Peculiar Institution*, p. viii (1956). This phrasing of the issue caused some controversy in the historical literature, but Stampp notes,

> I did not, of course, assume that there have been, or are today, no cultural differences between white and black Americans. Nor do I regard it as

flattery to call Negroes white men with black skins. It would serve my purpose as well to call Caucasians black men with white skins. I have simply found no convincing evidence that there are any significant differences between the innate emotional traits and intellectual capacities of Negroes and whites.

The Peculiar Institution, p. ix

See David Davis, "Slavery and the Post-World War II Historians," *Slavery, Colonialism and Racism*, pp. 1–10 (Sidney W. Mintz (ed.), 1974).

28 See generally Charles L. Griswold, Jr., "Rights and Wrongs: Jefferson, Slavery, and Philosophical Quandaries, A Culture of Rights," in Michael J. Lacey and Knud Haaksonssen (eds), (1991). (Professor Griswold examines the contradiction of the language of the declaration and the life and thought of Thomas Jefferson. He concludes that the practical political, and philosophical reasons advanced by Jefferson are rationalization of the greater theme of equality advanced by Jefferson in his writings.)

29 This is a comparison made of the relative worth of the two systems of government and economic activity. It is possible that both are failures or successes when measured against other systems.

30 See Friedrich A. von Hayek, *Road to Serfdom* (1976).

31 I of course exaggerate slightly here because the constitution does refer to Indians untaxed – by which of course they meant native Americans on tribal lands. See U.S. Const. art. II, +s 3 ("Representatives and direct Taxes shall be apportioned among the several States which may be included within this Union, according to their respective Numbers, which shall be determined by adding to the whole Number of free Persons, including those bound to Service for a Term of Years, and excluding Indians not Taxed, Three Fifths of all other Persons.") See also Jerome McCristal Culp, Jr., "Toward a Black Legal Scholarship: Race and Original Understandings," 1991 *Duke L. J.* 41; Anthony Cook, "Temptation and the Fall of Original Understanding," 1990 *Duke L. J.* 1163.

32 See generally, Derrick A. Bell, "Does Discrimination Make Economic Sense? For Some – it Did and Still Does," 15 *Hum. Rts.* 38 (Fall 1988); Derrick A. Bell, "Racism: A Prophecy for the Year 2000," 42 *Rutgers L. Rev.* 93 (1989); Jerome McCristal Culp, "Toward A Black Legal Scholarship: Race and Original Understandings," 1991 *Duke L. J.* 37; Cheryl I. Harris, "Whiteness As Property," 106 *Harv. L. Rev.* 1709 (1993), and Barbara J. Flagg, " 'Was Blind and now I See': White Race Consciousness and the Requirement of Discriminatory Intent," 91 *Mich. L. Rev.* 953 (1993). I believe that much of this property including the economic is illusory, and that if we were to end the power of racism in American life it would permit an increase in both the psychic and economic well being of "all" Americans. This is difficult to prove, but any other assumption suggests that the most pessimistic interpretation of Derrick Bell's thesis that racism is permanent, in *Faces at the Bottom of the Well*, is well founded.

33 See, e.g., Richard Freeman, "Black Economic Progress Since 1964: Who has Gained and Why?," *Studies in Labor Markets* (Sherwin Rosen (ed.), 1981). (Changes in relative position of blacks in the late 1960s attributable to demand changes partially wrought by government policy.) Black achievement gains in schooling were the greatest in the South where blacks were more likely to go to desegregated schools. See Thomas F. Pettigrew, "Advancing Racial Justice," *Opening Doors: Perspectives on Race Relations in Contemporary America* pp. 165 and 166 (Harry J. Knopke, Robert J. Norrell, and Ronald W. Rogers (eds), 1991). See also William Cohen, *At Freedom's Edge: Black Mobility and the Southern White Quest For Racial Control*, pp. 48–9 (1991).

34 By saying this I am contesting the largely unsupported history of racial progress included in a number of the works of Thomas Sowell. See, e.g., Thomas Sowell, *Markets and Minorities* (1981). I would contend that the market provides relatively narrow opportunities for economic progress outside of race conscious efforts of groups.

35 497 U.S. 547 (1990). See also Patricia Williams, *"Metro Broadcasting, Inc.* v. *F.C.C.:* Regrouping in Singular times," 104 *Harv. L. Rev.* 525 (1990).

36 For a similar view that white people do not have a race see the discussion of Justice O'Connor's opinion in *Shaw* v. *Reno*, 61 *U.S.L.W.* 4818 (1993), infra at n. 65, pp. 66–82.

37 388 U.S. 1 (1967).

38 See e.g., John F. Dovidio and Samuel L. Gaetner, "Changes in the Expression and Assessment of Racial Prejudice," in *Opening Doors: Perspectives on Race Relations in Contemporary America* (Harry J. Knopke, Robert J. Norrell, and Ronald W. Rogers (eds), 1991). Nationwide polls also indicate that personal acceptance of blacks is far from complete. Relatively high proportions of respondents continue to show racial biases on items involving some degree of intimacy between blacks and whites. A Harris Poll in 1978 revealed that only 35 per cent of whites favored full integration (another 42 per cent favored integration in some areas). In 1981, 31 per cent of whites surveyed preferred not to have blacks as neighbors; in 1988, one-third of white respondents preferred to live in "a neighborhood with mostly whites." *Although in 1982 the majority (66 per cent) of whites opposed laws prohibiting inter-racial marriage, in 1983, the majority of whites (60 per cent) personally did not approve of inter-racial marriage* (emphasis added).

39 See Paul Brest, "The Supreme Court 1975 Term: Foreword: In Defense of the Antidiscrimination Principle," 90 *Harv. L. Rev.* 1, 53 (1976); and Richard Epstein, *Forbidden Grounds* (1992).

40 This assumes by definition that such race neutral standards exist, and that there are no hidden racial concerns buried within the choices made through the use of production and merit.

41 See Jerome McCristal Culp, Jr., "Diversity, Affirmative Action, and Multiculturalism: Duke, the NAS, and Apartheid," 41 *Depaul L. Rev.* 1141, 1144–52 (1992).

42 The Supreme Court's creation of a jurisprudence of societal discrimination in its cases in *Bakke, Croson, Wygant*, etc. can only be understood as implementing this policy. See *City of Richmond* v. *J. A. Croson Co.*, 488 U.S. 469 (1989); *Wygant* v. *Jackson Board of Education*, 476 U.S. 267 (Plurality opinion 1986) ("[S]ocietal discrimination without more, is too amorphous a basis for imposing a racially classified remedy." Justice Powell also said, "This Court has never held that societal discrimination alone is sufficient to justify a racial classification."), and *University of California* v. *Bakke*, 438 U.S. 265, 274 (1978) (The court turned poor lawyering into an important constitutional principle that blocked effective discussion of where society is going.).

43 See, e.g., Celeste Michelle Condit and John Louis Lucites, *Crafting Equality: America's Anglo-African Word*, pp. 69–100 (1993). This of course is only part of the discourse of African Americans; some of the arguments for freedom were thought too radical to publish or when someone wrote them like David Walker they were killed. See Jane H. Pease and William H. Pease, *They Who Would Be Free: Blacks Search for Freedom, 1830–1861*, pp. 110–11. The assassinations of Martin Luther King, Malcolm X, Medgar Evers, and others suggests that speaking out even in our own time is not without political and personal risks. The political mugging of Lani Guinier by President William Jefferson Clinton over intellectual writing described as "radical" suggests that this principle works through today. To be too black and too outspoken is a risk too great for the

American political discourse. This difficulty permitted Senators on the Judiciary Committee to successfully argue that Professor Guinier did not deserve an opportunity to testify before the committee because the senators would have difficulty facing an articulate black woman so shortly after they had faced another articulate black woman law professor, Anita Hill, in the confirmation hearings of Clarence Thomas. As Patricia Williams has suggested her opponents finally resorted to the very weird statement that "She says she said." See Patricia J. Williams, "Lani We Hardly Knew Ye," *Village Voice* 25 (5 May 1993). Those making the argument evidently included the two women, one of them black, added to the committee to take account of the Anita Hill factor. See also Jerome McCristal Culp, Jr., "You Can Take Them to Water but You Can't Make Them Drink: Black Legal Scholarship and White Scholars," 1992 *U. Ill. L. Rev.* 1021.

44 See, e.g., Louis Ruchames, "Jim Crow railroads in Massachusetts," in *Blacks in White America Before 1865*, 395 (Robert Haynes (ed.), 1972).

45 See, e.g., Richard Posner, "The DeFunis Case and the Constitutionality of Preferential Treatment of Racial Minorities," 1974 *Sup. Ct. Rev.* 1, 32.

46 Paul Brest, supra n. 39.

47 438 U.S. 265 (1978) (Powell, J.).

48 488 U.S. 469 (1989).

49 Idem at 729–30.

50 See Jerome McCristal Culp and Glenn Loury, "The Impact of Affirmative Action on Equal Opportunity: A New Look, Bakke, Weber, and Affirmative Action," p. 124, in Rockefeller Foundation Working Papers (1979). (It is possible to define a permanent income, and comparing blacks and whites clearly demonstrates that blacks have lower permanent income than whites.)

51 See, e.g., Viscusi, "Race, Schooling and Employment Patterns: Log Linear Probability Models of Young Men," Report to Rockefeller Foundation (1979). (If low-income black youth were put in the same position as white workers, they would within three years return to original inferior economic position because of layoffs, quits, and job loss attributed to plant closing.)

52 See William Julius Wilson, *The Truly Disadvantaged* (1987).

53 476 U.S. 267 (plurality opinion 1986).

54 See also *Firefighters Local 1784* v. *Stotts*, 467 U.S. 561 (1984). In that case the Supreme Court required the city to enforce a seniority system that froze black workers into a vulnerable position based upon the flimsiest notions of justice.

55 Justice O'Connor assumes the opposite in *City of Richmond* v. *J. A. Croson*. [The set-aside of subcontracting dollars seemed to rest largely on] "the unsupported assumption that white prime contractors simply will not hire minority law firms." 488 U.S. 469, 502.

56 See William Julius Wilson, *The Truly Disadvantaged: The Inner City, The Underclass, And Public Policy* (1987). See also Thomas Sowell, *Civil Rights Rhetoric or Reality?* (1984) and Christopher Jencks, *Rethinking Social Policy: Race, Poverty and the Underclass*, pp. 64–7 (1992). (Black scholars are like Nobel prize winners. It is not possible to increase their numbers by doing affirmative action. The result of such efforts is to simply raise the wages of the few black scholars.) But see Michael R. Ransom, "Seniority and Monopsony in the Academic Labor Market," 83 *Am. Econ. Rev.* 221 (1993). (Academics pay a significant cost to staying in a particular institution. The tradeoff is between one and half a per cent a year.) Since black academics move more frequently they may be closer to the market wage, but may appear to be making more money than incumbent white academics.

57 This is an issue that can be thought of as a problem in measurement. Assume that as a court or legislature you want to know the value x, but that you cannot measure x directly. For example, it is difficult to measure disadvantage. In order to measure disadvantage we use things that tell us something about disadvantage. In this case income, wealth, social background, education, and a host of other factors enter into this equation, but there is no direct measure of disadvantage. The measures we do have will tell us a lot about disadvantage but we will not be perfect about measuring it. The more imperfect the indirect measures are the more imperfect our measurement will be of disadvantage or any other x. For the colorblindness to lead to the appropriate racial result the error associated with race would have to always and everywhere be larger and more important than the error associated with other possible alternative variables. This is an almost impossible assumption. In this situation race is what we are measuring and estimates of race, whether poverty or being a small business or being from a broken home, are always likely to have significant errors associated with their use. Errors that almost everywhere will be larger in terms of race than if we use something else. See generally Edward Leamer, *Specification Searches*, pp. 226–59 (1978).

58 See Patricia Williams, "Lani We Hardly Knew Ye," *The Village Voice* (June 44, 1993).

59 42 U.S.C. +s 1973.

60 446 U.S. 55 (1980).

61 478 U.S. 30. (Applying amended section 2 to vote-dilution claim involving multimember districts.)

62 One of the most interesting aspects of these cases is that they have the flavor of ignoring this history. No mention is made in Justice O'Connor's opinion that these are the first black representatives in Congress in almost a century or that the amendments to the Voting Rights Act had the desired result of increasing the opportunities of African Americans and Hispanics to seek and win congressional seats. The prior history of the real dearth of black representatives is ignored completely by the majority.

63 See Hamil Harris, "Congressman Mfume in fight to head Black Caucus," *Washington Afro-American* (28 November 1992).

64 Review and Outlook: "Political Pornography," *Wall St. J.*, 9 September 1991; "Political Pornography II," *Wall St. J.*, 4 February 1992. If they seek to find a useful definition of pornography they might look to James Lindgren, "Defining Pornography," 141 *University of Pa. L. Rev.* 1153 (1993). (The traditional strands of doctrinal definition of pornography were not applicable by students in a large midwestern law school in two professional responsibility classes. I am tempted to say that could be because of the students, the law school education, or because they are law students. How many law students does it take to find legal doctrine? The answer: Five law students and a Gilberts and a law exam.)

65 61 U.S.L.W. 4818 (1993).

66 The second most fatuous part of Justice O'Connor's decision is her failure to acknowledge that these districts could elect white candidates without the pattern of black and white voting changing. The two districts are only barely black majority districts. White candidates are likely to win in this district. The court treats this district and all race conscious activity as if it is homogeneous and has a similar impact on the voting process.

67 1993 U.S. LEXIS 4406, *22.

68 Indeed Robinson Everett, my Duke Law School colleague who argued this case, criticized the legislature for appropriating $500,000 to litigate this issue in state court. See *Durham Morning Herald* (27 July 1993).

69 Perhaps what Justice O'Connor is trying to do is similar to the standing argument articulated by Justice Thomas in *Northeastern Florida Chapter of the Associated Contractors of America* v. *Jacksonville*, Fla, 61 *Law Week* 4626 (1993):

> [T]hese cases stand for the following proposition: When the government erects a barrier that makes it more difficult for members of one group to obtain a benefit than it is for members of another group, a member of the former group seeking to challenge the barrier need not allege that he would have obtained the benefit but for the barrier in order to establish standing.

The problem with applying this standing argument to this case is that unlike a case of a contractor where there is something that could be gained from a different process, i.e., there is an exclusion and a different process, in this case no white candidate is excluded. Indeed if the court is right that there is no racial block voting white candidates have just as good a chance of winning as a black candidate. The injury to these five white plaintiffs is the same as if, for example, the state divided Durham into several districts thus reducing the chances that someone from Durham could be elected. Could a group of Durham people challenge the redistricting program because as a group they were adversely affected? I think not. The real injury that the Court refuses to acknowledge is to white supremacy.

70 Justice O'Connor writes:

> Despite their invocation of the ideal of a "color-blind" Constitution appellants appear to concede that race conscious redistricting is not always unconstitutional. That concession is wise: This Court never has held that race-conscious state decisionmaking is impermissible in all circumstances. What appellants object to is redistricting legislation that is so extremely irregular on its face that it rationally can be viewed only as an effort to segregate the race for purposes of voting, without regard for traditional districting principles and without sufficiently compelling justification....
>
> 113 S. Ct. at 2826. (Citations omitted. See also infra n.72.)

71 376 U.S. 52 (1964).

72 [R]edistricting differs from other kinds of state decisionmaking in that the legislature always is aware of race when it draws district line, just as it is aware of age, economic status, religious and political persuasion, and a variety of other demographic factors. That sort of race consciousness does not lead inevitably to impermissible race discrimination.... *The district lines may be drawn, for example, to provide for compact districts of contiguous territory, or to maintain the integrity of political subdivisions.*

> 113 S.Ct. at 2826. (Citations omitted and emphasis added.)

73 364 U.S. 339 (1968).

74 See voting patterns associated with the congressional election involving Julian Bond and John Lewis. Indeed some have suggested that the need to create cross racial coalitions has the potential to break down the racial divide. Thomas B. Edsall, "Whites Learn Minority Politics; Like Any Other Group's, Their Support Can Be Crucial in a Tight Race," *The Washington Post* (2 November 1986):

> While biracial coalitions are emerging in both parties, they are likely to have far more impact on the Democrats. The restored importance of whites in majority black districts and cities has the potential to ameliorate

the racial tensions that have severely undermined the Democratic Party coalition in the South and in urban centers of the North.

The resurgence of white voting strength is forcing politicians to adopt biracial elective strategies, lessening racial tensions. This, in turn, should have the effect of slowing the steady drift of whites in many southern communities to the Republican Party. "This brings whites back into the ball game," a Democratic consultant said. "When politics is all black, then the whites are going to move over to the Republican Party. This way, they get a piece of the action. It's black action, but still, whites have a piece of it."

In the Atlanta congressional fight between civil rights leaders John Lewis and Julian Bond, Lewis, who in the past had run on the local "Black Slate," this year pointedly ran on "the people's slate." *Lewis won because of the strong majorities he received in the white community.*

"It can be argued that blacks are not getting their premier choice," said Williams of the Joint Center, "but in a sense, it seems that whites are doing what blacks have done for years."

Luix Overbea, "Black Caucus hopes to increase its numbers in US House," *The Christian Science Monitor*, p. 5 (8 November 1988). (Black incumbents confident of victory but black candidates seeking new seats need white votes.); see also Paul Ruffins, "Interracial coalitions: 'new moderation' doesn't account for the dramatic gains that Black politicians made in the last elections," *The Atlantic* (June 1990):

The point is that there is no new, more moderate generation of black politicians. Most have been moderate all along. There have been angry civil-rights leaders and black activists, but the angry black politician is a stereotype of conservatives. "What I think happens," Congressman Ed Towns, of Brooklyn, recently told me, "is that people confuse black politicians with black civil-rights leaders such as Martin Luther King and Stokely Carmichael, most of whom never ran for anything."

75 See Lani Guinier, supra n. 10 at 1593:

By this definition, the majority in *Shaw* misuses the term gerrymandering to describe a 54 per cent black district that, as the majority concedes, was drawn to remedy a century of racial exclusion and that, as the majority also acknowledges, did not arbitrarily enhance or diminish the political power of any group.

76 See *Presley v. Etowah County Commission*, 112 S. Ct. 820 (1992).
77 *Presley*, 112 S.Ct. at 822.
78 I am waiting for this court to extend this policy to any issue that black plaintiffs might raise in constitutional discourse. I am willing to bet that as long as the current majority exists on this court no black plaintiff will ever find that they have been able to get standing to challenge a decision of a municipality or state based upon this principle of violation of constitutional right.
79 When I voted for Mel Watt, a black Yale graduate with impeccable credentials, it was the first opportunity in almost twenty years of voting that I had the opportunity to vote for a candidate who was black who had a chance to win a congressional seat. Justice O'Connor ignores or belittles the racial past of North Carolina. She cannot even see that for example Durham County exists because the people of Orange County feared political control by black voters. Only a jurist unacquainted or unwilling to be acquainted with the racial reality of

North Carolina could give credence to the fact that race does not matter in our voting.

80 To borrow a phrase from the description of Justice Thomas about several of his Federalist Society speeches.

81 You may think I exaggerate, but I would point to the political pornography columns in the *Wall Street Journal* noted above. The court simply adopts the view expressed by the *Journal*. One in fact suspects that this case was taken by the Court precisely because the Federalist Society has made this issue such a cause célèbre.

82 The *Wall Street Journal* is not known for its commitment to racial equality. See e.g., "Review and Outlook, An Immoral Law," *Wall Street Journal*, p. 14, col. 1 (22 March 1965):

> When President Johnson last Monday asked Congress for a new law to safeguard the voting rights of Negro citizens he rested his case on the Constitution and on a basic principle of morality.
> What he has now proposed that the congress do is enact a law which would violate that Constitution he asks us not to flout and, more, which is itself immoral.

Review and Outlook, "The Ways of Good Men," *Wall Street Journal*, p. 18, col. 1 (28 April 1964):

> Thus one lesson is that the "law" merely by its existence has no power to change men's views or to guarantee that all men will abide by the law.
> Consequently it seems clear that the Federal civil rights bill [what became the 1964 Civil Rights Act], even if it were passed in its extreme form, will not accomplish what is promised. It will not open all doors for the Negroes...

Review and Outlook, "Tension and Tolerance," *Wall Street Journal*, p. 8, col. 1 (12 February 1964). The editorial pats itself on the back for the house passage of the Civil Rights Act, notes that many question its constitutionality and its strength in creating a federal antidiscrimination agency and in extending public accommodations to "every hotel, restaurant, theater and the like in the country," and says that a "well-disposed majority deserve a rest." In addition it said:

> The civil-rights leaders, we suspect, could make a highly favorable impression on public attitudes if they showed less interest in demonstrations and more interest in helping Negroes adapt, as many have, to a society trying to more fully accept them. Better race relations requires an effort on the part of the Negroes as well as the whites.

83 The difficulty in understanding race-neutral policy is enhanced once you drop the notion that somehow I have more in common with someone who lives in Northern Durham where I have seldom been than I have in common with the largest and most extensive transportation system in the region. In fact I have spent a lot more time with people along that route than I have with people in parts of Durham.

84 The Congressional Club is a political action network in North Carolina that has been the principal support for Senator Jesse Helms.

85 It is difficult to not see this challenge to the congressional redistricting plan by five white citizens of Durham as part of a larger scheme to "take back" political power in the City of Durham. Just last October as part of a larger scheme the city defeated the first black mayor as a part of a conservative largely white-led program of attack on the political integrity and savvy of the first black mayor of

Durham. Despite the fact that Durham is 45 per cent black it has been a city where blacks have been involved but controlled little historically. The Committee for the Affairs of Black People, the political organizing group that has led the concerns of black people, has chosen historically to vote for the white candidate who is marginally better than his opponent. This has created a situation where it has been very difficult to move the political landscape. This effort to require "race neutrality" is part of a plan to return black people to that failed program.

86 However, even geography is problematic if, as is the case in North Carolina, black voters are concentrated in some towns and neighborhoods. Racial segregation in the United States makes not peeking at race particularly difficult.

87 The last black representative from North Carolina before the application of the voting rights act in 1990 was in 1898.

88 A similar concern can be raised in a slightly different context about homosexuality and the 1991 Civil Rights Act. The proponents of protection for homosexuals were unsuccessful in passing a provision for that purpose in the 1991 Civil Rights Act. In the rhetoric of this article the 1991 Civil Rights Act is homosexually blind. The question is what does that blindness mean in the context of employment discrimination. Some of the opponents of the explicit provision would like to interpret that to mean that an employer can do anything to an employee as long as the claim is made that the decision was based upon the employee's sexual orientation. This view would turn the absence of a provision in the 1991 Civil Rights Act into positive legislation that homosexuality may be discriminated against. Such a view seems inappropriate with respect to homosexuality blindness and the law. Indeed, what this suggests is that given the general failure to explicitly exclude homosexuality the 1991 Civil Rights Act requires judges to figure out what being blind to homosexuality is. My colleague, William Van Alstyne, has suggested that an employer who discriminated against a lesbian but not a male homosexual would be violating Title VII's provisions against sexual discrimination. Such an argument illustrates the difficulty that peeking permits and colorblindness does not solve. The 1991 Civil Rights Act permits employers to peek at homosexuality, but does not tell the courts and juries when they may peek and how they may peek at homosexuality. The 1991 Civil Rights Act has been interpreted as requiring employers to be blind to race but it permits them to peek at race and to use the evidence so gathered to make choices.

89 See *Patterson* v. *Mclean Credit Union*, 491 U.S. 164 (1989). (A black woman claiming racial harassment had no right to protection under 42 USC 1981 because that statute, despite much conflicting judicial opinion, does not cover post contract activities.); *Wards Cove Packing Co.* v. *Atonio*, 490 U.S. 642 (1989). (Claims of racial segregation by nonwhite plaintiffs not covered by Title VII.); *J.A. Croson Co.* v. *City of Richmond*, 488 U.S. 469 (1989). (A white contractor who was asked to seek black subcontractors successfully challenged the city council of Richmond to make such a requirement despite the fact that there were essentially no black subcontractors.); *R.A.V.* v. *City of St. Paul*, 112 S. Ct. 2538 (1992). (A white defendant's conviction of violation of municipal statute that prohibited cross burning overturned because the ordinance discriminated against speech because of its content. It is not permissible to discriminate against racially derogatory speech without also choosing to discriminate against other content neutral offensive activity.); *Wisconsin* v. *Mitchell* (upheld the enhancement of a penalty against a black defendant convicted of engaging in an assault for racial reasons. *R.A.V.* was not applicable because the Wisconsin statute involved only conduct while the activity addressed in *R.A.V.* was directed at speech.); *Northeastern Florida Chapter of the Associated Contractors of America* v. *Jacksonville*,

Fla, 61 Law Week 4626 (1993) (White contractors have standing to sue without alleging that they would have been awarded the contract in the absence of the challenged ordinance.) Justice Thomas describes the injury this way:

> [T]hese cases stand for the following proposition: When the government erects a barrier that makes it more difficult for members of one group to obtain a benefit than it is for members of another group, a member of the former group seeking to challenge the barrier need not allege that he would have obtained the benefit but for the barrier in order to establish standing.

As one reads these cases it is hard to believe anything but that Chief Justice Taney's famous dictum in Dred Scot is right: "Black people have no rights that a white man need respect." The Court seems to go out of its way to limit statutes and read the constitution so as not to protect the interests of black individuals and to go out of its way to protect the interests of white plaintiffs. Certainly, law schools ought to teach in our constitutional law courses that race matters to who will win cases before this Court.

90 Another example of peeking with disastrous results is *Batson* v. *Kentucky*, 476 U.S. 79 (1986) and its progeny. Take for example, *U.S.* v. *Uwaezhoke*, 1993 W.L. 142050 (3rd Cir. 1993). In that case the third circuit permits the trial judges' ruling that a black woman postal worker who is the single mother of two be excused on a peremptory challenge despite the evidence that the challenge was racially based. The court quotes this colloquy in support of its decision:

> The prosecutors, at the time they exercised the peremptory challenge, knew that Ms. Lucas was a single parent of two children who was making the salary of a postal worker with four years of seniority and renting an apartment in Newark, New Jersey. It is, we believe, fair to infer that the prosecutors, in the absence of any more detailed information concerning Ms. Lucas, speculated that she might live in low income housing in Newark. Having so speculated, the prosecutors inferred that Ms. Lucas was more likely to have had direct exposure to drug trafficking than someone who did not live in low-income housing in Newark. While this conclusion may or may not be empirically correct, we cannot say that it exhibits racially discriminatory intent as a matter of law. Finally, the prosecutors concluded that if they had their preference (as they did so long as they retained a peremptory challenge), they would rather not have jurors who have had personal experience with drug trafficking. While neither the district court nor the defense attorney pressed the prosecutors to spell out their reasoning, it is possible that the prosecutors may have wanted to avoid jurors with direct drug experience for any number of legally legitimate reasons, the most likely of which is a concern that a personal experience may have left a strong impression on the juror, thus influencing her evaluation of the evidence in a way difficult for the prosecutors to predict. (n5)
>
> We do not, of course, suggest that the information available to the government would support a finding that Ms. Lucas, more probably than not, would be an unqualified juror, or even an undesirable juror from the government's point of view. But that is not what peremptory challenges are all about. A primary reason for their existence is that it is not feasible for lawyers to know much about individual jurors. Counsel must rely on educated guesses about probabilities based on their limited

knowledge of a particular juror and their own life experiences. If a lawyer can show some specific conflict between information about a particular juror and the particular case to be tried, he or she is in a position to make a challenge for cause. Peremptory challenges are intended for those situations in which counsel cannot demonstrate such a specific conflict, but has some reason to believe a prospective juror may be less desirable from his or her perspective as contrasted with other jurors likely to be called in the event of a peremptory challenge.

n5 A prosecutor may rationally believe, for example, that a juror living in a neighborhood with a drug problem may fear retaliation from dealers there if she votes to convict an alleged drug trafficker or may have had an unpleasant contact with the police in the context of drug trafficking.

As the dissent points out of course the alleged racial neutral standard permits the prosecutor to peek at race and claim something else is involved. Here the peeking amounts to excluding all black people from a jury involving a black alleged drug trafficker. Such exclusions are bound in the long run to lead to notions of exclusion and noninvolvement. If a black postal worker cannot be seated then no black person from this neighborhood can. If the court does not want racial peeking then they should require at least for some level of the screening that the person's face and accent not be obvious to the lawyers. However, the whole point of the peremptory challenge is to peek. When people peek they will use race. For a further discussion of colorblindness and peremptory challenges see Kenneth B. Nunn, "Rights Held Hostage: Race, Ideology and the Peremptory Challenge," 28 *Har. C.R.-C.L. L. Rev.* 63, 70–81 (1993).

91 See 42 U.S.C. 2000e-2(J). ([It is unlawful] for a respondent, in connection with the selection or referral of applicants or candidates for employment or promotion, to adjust the scores of, use different cutoff scores for, or otherwise alter the results of, employment related tests on the basis of race, color, religion, sex or national origin.)

92 See, e.g., *Billish* v. *Daley*, 962 F.2d 1269, 1302 (J. Posner dissenting 7th Cir. 1992). ("So the fact that blacks and Hispanics didn't do as well as whites on the engineers' exam – 44 per cent of the white firefighters who took the exam passed, compared to 32 per cent of the blacks and Hispanics – is hardly evidence of persisting discrimination that might warrant remedial action. On the contrary, the exam results supply a noninvidious reason why there is a smaller fraction of black and Hispanic engineers than of black and Hispanic firefighters.")

93 Officers for *Justice* v. *City and County of San Francisco*, 1992 U.S. Dist. Lexis 3098.

94 Citing *Bridgeport Guardians, Inc.* v. *City of Bridgeport*, 933 F.2d 1140 (2d Cir. 1991), and suggesting that the legislative history of 42 U.S.C. 2000e-2(J) seems to cite *Bridgeport Guardians* with approval.

95 See discussion of *City of Richmond* v. *J. A. Croson* supra.

96 See Derrick Bell, *Faces at the Bottom of the Well: The Permanence of Racism* (1992).

97 Indeed it is the very existence of the positive race conscious policy that is partially responding to negative racial and ethnic stereotypes that makes clear that race conscious policy is still required. When groups no longer defend and enhance group status and people stop seeing groups in stereotypical ways, race no longer matters.

98 Richard Epstein's call to outlaw public race consciousness and to leave private parties free to make decisions, only chastened by private tastes and market

pressures, would at least be consistent about the racial reality of America. I do not believe that such a bright line policy can deal with the subtleties of race in America and therefore even if this is the appropriate policy in some places, something I gravely doubt, it is not the appropriate policy everywhere. Richard Epstein, *Forbidden Grounds* (1992).

99 If we were to analogize this story to the current supreme court jurisprudence, the results would have been different. If the turtle was black and the lizard white, the court would have ruled for the lizard in the first action to divide the fruit, and would have said in the second action that of course we will adhere to our formally adopted rule. However, the court would also conclude that the formal rule's application to a situation where two citizens are involved has to be left to the sound neutral discretion of a local board of lizards who should take into account the appropriate prior precedents and policy concerns including the fact that lizards lie in the road. Indeed, the court might have concluded with language something like this in upholding the lower court decision on remand to not divide the lizard in half,

> Nothing this court does today should be construed to indicate that we have at any point failed to adhere to our policy of species neutrality crucial to the just application of the law and the dissent's suggestion today that somehow we have failed to adhere to the requirement that the law be fair to turtles simply ignores our long and successful effort to rid our society of every aspect of discrimination.

5

BLACK WOMEN IN THE HISTORY OF AFRICAN AMERICAN ECONOMIC THOUGHT

A critical essay

Lynn C. Burbridge

ABSTRACT

This chapter argues that the research on African American women is inadequate and fragmentary. There are three primary reasons for this. One is the shortage of black economists, who probably are more likely to focus on issues affecting African American women. But there also appears to be a reluctance to raise gender issues among African American scholars. Further, the fragmentation of social science into smaller and smaller sub-specialties, often precludes an analysis of issues affecting the black woman that is sufficiently integrated to provide an overall picture of her economic status. The author argues for analyses that combine micro-level and macro-level variables, and that incorporate work and family issues.

INTRODUCTION

A common theme found among those discussing the research on black women is its inadequacy (e.g. Conrad 1986; Malson *et al.* 1988; and Wallace 1980). This has been expressed regarding black women in the labor market and in other areas of life. But some disciplines – such as history and sociology – have been more successful than others – notably economics – in highlighting issues facing African American women. One only needs to make note of Darlene Clark Hine's sixteen volume anthology, *Black Women in United States History* (1990), to be aware of the larger volume of work conducted by historians in comparison to economists.

The lack of attention to black women in the literature is evident from a review of titles listed in *The Journal of Economic Literature (JEL)*. The *JEL*

101

is published quarterly, listing all journal articles in economics. In 1993, among 7,041 articles listed, only 19 (0.3 per cent) had titles indicating an examination of differences by race and sex (and only three of these specifically referred to black women).[1] Many articles may present information about African American women, however, without direct reference to them in the title. This would include articles focusing on race or ethnicity in general (79 articles or 1.1 per cent) or on women and family issues in general (123 articles or 1.7 per cent) or on issues of poverty and inequality in general (42 articles or 0.6 per cent).[2] Thus, as many as 3.7 per cent of the articles in 1993 may make some reference to African American women.[3]

Of the 1685 books abstracted in the *JEL* in 1993, only one (0.0006 per cent) had a specific reference to black women, while nine (0.005 per cent) focused on race or ethnicity, fifteen (0.009 per cent) focused on women and family issues, and sixteen (0.009 per cent) focused on poverty and inequality. Thus, as many as 0.024 per cent of new books on economics in 1993 may contain information on African American women.[4]

Of course, there is a tremendous breadth of subject matter contained within the economics profession: finance, trade, economic development, industrial organization, and so on. There is no clear way of knowing how much *should* focus on black women or on people of color, in general. Nevertheless, in the "real world" key policy decisions are being made that will have important repercussions for black women. For example, health reform and welfare reform are the cornerstones of President Clinton's domestic agenda. Unemployed black women are disproportionately dependent on the welfare rolls, employed black women depend disproportionately on the health care sector for jobs and are disproportionately represented in jobs that offer few health care benefits (e.g. see articles by Burbridge 1993a and 1994c). Many other policies under consideration, from revamping the training system to macroeconomic policies encouraging expansion of the economy, can have an impact on African American women in both positive and negative ways. Yet relatively little attention has focused on possible impacts.

Research on black women has been considered inadequate in another respect, however. In one of the final chapters of *Slipping Through the Cracks: The Status of Black Women*, edited by Simms and Malveaux (1986), Phyllis Wallace notes that much of the literature on black women is often too narrow in scope, leaving the reader without a total sense of the circumstances of African American women and therefore inhibiting useful policy analysis focusing on them. For example, one can read one paper on black women and discover that they have made tremendous employment and earnings gains since the Second World War; another paper will show how black women are disproportionately poor and dependent on welfare (Burbridge 1993b).

In part, these differences reflect the heterogeneity of African American women. But the overall well-being of most women also depends upon resources and wealth within the family, not their individual achievements alone. Black males and females are also vulnerable to major policy and macro-economic shifts. All the many variables affecting women and all of those affecting African Americans, impinge on African American women. Bringing these variables together to form a coherent analysis of the status of African American women has not been a priority in the economics literature.

There are three reasons for gaps in the scholarship on black women in the economics profession. First, there is a shortage of African American scholars in the economics profession, especially African American women. Second, the dominant paradigm in economics does not adequately address issues relevant to minorities or women. Third, the fragmentation of the profession into a variety of specialties and sub-specialties inhibits the possibility of providing a "holistic" perspective, as discussed by Wallace.

In the long run, this last reason may be the hardest to overcome since the more comprehensive approaches in social science, such as those undertaken by DuBois and other social scientists early in this century, are generally considered a thing of the past. Success in the profession militates against an integrated and multi-disciplinary approach.

Nevertheless, this paper argues that a comprehensive view of the status of African American women requires the incorporation of many variables: family as well as labor market variables; wealth and resources, as well as income variables; macro-economic as well as micro-economic variables. The discussion that follows examines the reasons for gaps in the literature on African American women, some of the analyses that have been undertaken, and the issues that need to be addressed in discussing the economic status of black women.

REASONS FOR GAPS IN THE LITERATURE

Shortage of black economists

Probably the most obvious reason for gaps in the literature is the relative shortage of African Americans in the economics profession in comparison to other academic fields. African Americans received less than 2 per cent of all PhD degrees awarded in Economics in the 1970s (Simms and Swinton 1988). African American women represented less than a quarter of these. Data from the early 1990s indicate that African Americans represent approximately 3 per cent of new PhDs in economics, with black women representing a little more than a third of these (Table 5.1).[5]

Interestingly, the low proportion of new black male PhDs in economics primarily reflects the small number of black male PhDs overall; of those

Table 5.1 New black doctorates as a percentage of all new doctorates, by sex, 1990 and 1991

Field	1990		1991		1990 and 1991	
	Male	Female	Male	Female	Male	Female
Anthropology	0.4	0.4	0.7	1.1	0.6	0.7
Economics	2.1	1.3	2.4	0.3	2.2	0.8
Psychology	1.5	2.4	1.4	2.7	1.4	2.5
Political Science	3.7	1.1	3.5	0.9	3.6	1.0
Sociology	2.8	3.5	1.6	4.5	2.2	4.0
Other Social Science	1.6	2.3	3.9	3.4	2.8	2.9
History	3.2	0.6	2.4	2.2	2.8	1.4
Education	2.3	5.4	2.5	5.0	2.4	5.2

Sources: Thurgood, D. H. and Weinman, J. M. (1991); Ries, P. and Thurgood, D. H. (1993)
Note: Data are for US citizens only

black males who obtained doctorates in the early 1990s, PhDs in economics were a slightly higher proportion of all new black male doctorates than was the case for all men. (Doctorates in economics were 2.4 per cent of all new black male doctorates and 2 per cent of all new male doctorates, for 1990 and 1991.) Black women, however, obtained economics PhDs at a lower rate than was the case for all women (0.6 per cent of all new doctorates earned by black women were in economics compared to 0.9 per cent for all female new doctorates in economics).

In addition to the shortage of African American scholars, important black scholars are often neglected or forgotten; for example, see Darity's (1989) book on Abram Harris. Among black women economists, only Phyllis Wallace is ranked among the top-twenty African Americans most often cited in the economics literature (Medoff 1989).

Of course, non-black scholars can make and have made important contributions to the literature on black women; an excellent example is *Labor of Love, Labor of Sorrow* by Jacqueline Jones (1985), another historian. But African American scholars have been important in raising issues that often go unrecognized in the literature.

Collins (1990) has noted, however, that within the black community of scholars, a focus on feminist issues is sometimes considered divisive or as detracting from the importance of race. White feminists, alternately, have been criticized for glossing over differences among women, as if "women's issues" are the same for all women (Malveaux 1986). Thus, it has often been left to a relatively small number of black feminist scholars (such as Collins and Malveaux cited above) to insist on a multi-dimensional approach to issues affecting black women.

It is argued here, however, that it is not the shortage of black scholars alone that explains the shortcomings in the literature on black women in economics. Even among black scholars there have been gaps in the treatment of black women in economic thought. This reflects, in part, problems in how the economics profession, in general, has approached issues that are relevant to women and to excluded minority groups. Given that the shortage of African American scholars is a fact that we must live with in the short run, this chapter will focus on these other issues.

The dominant paradigm

The neo-classical paradigm in economics has been critiqued by black and female scholars for an inadequate treatment of discrimination and group power dynamics in affecting economic outcomes for minorities and women (e.g. Boston 1988; Darity 1984; Folbre 1993; Folbre and Hartmann 1988). This reflects biases in the paradigm which views the world as consisting of atomistic individuals whose placement and choices in the world are determined by their preferences, endowments, and whatever "exchanges" are made with other individuals. That one's preferences, endowments, and exchanges may, in turn, be determined by external pressures imposed differentially by race or sex, is often not incorporated into economic models.

Nevertheless, in spite of important work by black and feminist scholars, relatively little attention has focused on differences that exist by race *and* sex. This may, in part, reflect the time and energy expended by a small number of black and feminist scholars to gain recognition for specific issues of race *or* sex, without adding the complexity of an analysis by race *and* sex.

Further, even with an increasing recognition of race and gender issues, there are many subject areas that often are not perceived as being particularly amenable to a gender focus, but which may have tremendous implications for women.

Another characteristic of the economics profession that may affect the volume and scope of studies conducted on black women is the fragmentation of the literature into a number of specialties.

Fragmentation

The majority of economic studies focusing on race or gender issues are incorporated under the general heading of labor economics. However, many black economists have invested considerable research effort in the economic development literature as well, particularly literature which focuses on urban or community economic development. This literature rarely examines development issues as they are relevant to women. Yet, in an urban central city where most of the households are headed by single women and where the road out of poverty requires that women work as many hours as men, any community development strategy that does not consider the particular issues of women – such as the need for equitable wages and child care – is often incomplete.

Further, with the exception of the above-mentioned community development literature, macro-economists generally have devoted little attention to issues affecting minorities or women; they have primarily been issues discussed within labor economics, within micro-economics. Nevertheless, the dynamic of the macro-economy has a tremendous effect on blacks and women (Gottschalk and Danziger 1984; Okun 1973). Even within labor economics, labor market issues are often discussed separately from family issues, although women make their labor market decisions simultaneously with, or in lieu of, important family decisions. In addition, the focus in labor market analyses is often on income, with little attention given to differences in family wealth and resources.[6] A woman's access to wealth, however, affects her relationship to the labor market, her overall economic well-being and her family's overall well-being.

THE EXISTING LITERATURE

This section examines key elements of the existing literature on black women. While the discussion is generally relevant to the research of black and white authors, it focuses particularly on the economic thought of black scholars. While some of the issues raised are relevant to blacks in general and women in general, the paper will emphasize the specificity of research on black women in the US economy. Finally, in analyzing African American economic thought, one cannot overlook the fact that black scholars in other disciplines – notably sociology – have had an important influence on economic thought. In the following discussion, important contributions to the literature are highlighted, regardless of the discipline of the authors.

The early scholars

Some of the earliest black scholars actually gave a great deal of attention to black women. In *The Philadelphia Negro* (1967) which W. E. B. Du Bois first published as a young man in 1899, considerable attention was given to the work and family problems faced by black women. Another seminal work, containing an exhaustive analysis is St. Clair Drake and Horace R. Cayton's *Black Metropolis* (1945), first published in 1945. Both books are case studies of African Americans in a specific city, Philadelphia and Chicago respectively, and both examined all aspects of black life in those areas. Issues affecting men and women are discussed separately and together, and special attention is given to domestic work, the primary occupation of black women in cities. The similarities between these two works were not coincidental; Drake and Cayton deliberately followed in the footsteps of Du Bois, whom they greatly admired (Harrison, 1992).

This can be sharply contrasted to two other books written in the first half of this century: *The Black Worker* (1974), first published by Sterling Spero and Abram Harris in 1931, and *The Negro Ghetto* (1948), first published by Robert Weaver in 1948. In these two books there is little or no discussion of black women. In the case of Spero and Harris this may reflect their focus on the black proletarian. Black women – who were still primarily domestic workers – were excluded because they were a very small part of the industrial work force. Collins (1990) has observed that scholars interested in a class analysis, sometimes focus so heavily on industrial labor to the exclusion of the service economy, that – by default – they leave out black women almost entirely (although this was not the case with Drake and Cayton). In the case of Weaver, the exclusion of black women may reflect his focus on housing and other economic development issues. As noted earlier, scholars in certain subject areas generally do not incorporate a discussion of women into their analyses.

Falling in between Du Bois and Drake and Cayton on one side, and Spero and Harris and Weaver on the other, is Greene and Woodson's *The Negro Wage Earner* (1930). Greene and Woodson are unlike the latter in that they pay a great deal of attention to all forms of employment, including women in the domestic economy; they are unlike the former in that they *only* focus on employment and make no attempt to incorporate issues of family into their analysis. Probably the inductive sociological and anthropological methodology used by Du Bois and Drake and Cayton made them more comfortable taking a broader approach than the other authors.[7] Nevertheless, their influence on the history of economic thought cannot be ignored.

In addition to these seminal books are those focusing more specifically on the black family, including Du Bois's *The Negro American Family* (1969a) first published in 1908 and E. Franklin Frazier's *The Negro Family in the United States* (1940), first published in 1939. While not focusing specifically on women, both books speak with great concern about the disproportionate number of female-headed families among blacks, in comparison to the larger society, a theme that continues today. Unlike some recent authors, both Du Bois and Frazier attributed the "social disorganization" found among black poor families to the socio-economic conditions that surround them rather than suggesting that social disorganization is a cause of economic poverty.

There are important differences between Frazier and Du Bois, however, that are directly relevant to perceptions about black women. Frazier was obsessed with what he felt was the dominance of black women within the black family. An examination of the chapters of his book reveal that of twenty-two chapters overall, seven have titles specifically referring to women in the family: Motherhood in Bondage, Hagar and Her Children, Unfettered Motherhood, The Matriarchate, Granny: The Guardian of the

Generations, The Downfall of the Matriarchate, and Outlawed Mother-hood. Not that these are all unflattering portrayals – Frazier writes sym-pathetically about the strong bond between mothers and their children – but Frazier's emphasis on the black matriarch has no parallel in Du Bois's work. Nor does Frazier's approach seem to issue from concerns about the women themselves. Rather Frazier is driven by his concern that blacks need to assimilate dominant American cultural values about what the family should be like (Stewart 1991; Sudarkasa 1988).

Du Bois was not an assimilationist to the degree that Frazier was; he did not put the same negative emphasis on female-headed households, although it was a concern. As one of the most outstanding advocates of his time for women's rights, Du Bois described the greater commitment of black wo-men to labor market work as an important step in the eventual economic liberation of all women (even though, at the time, it largely reflected the greater economic need for African American women to engage in paid labor) (Davis 1983; Stewart 1991). And as an essayist, Du Bois spoke eloquently of an often romanticized black woman struggling to make a place for herself in a hostile environment (Du Bois 1969b).

There are two important issues that Du Bois and Frazier agreed upon, however. Both recognized the imbalance of the sex ratio between black men and women as a problem for black women and their families. It is humbling to realize that the recent popular literature on the shortage of black males which was seemingly discovered in the 1980s as an important issue for the black family, was identified by Du Bois as an issue in 1899. Both Du Bois and Frazier – along with Drake and Cayton – also repeatedly pointed to the de-stabilizing effects of urbanization on blacks and black families, another theme of the 1980s.

The later scholars

While some of the early black scholars paid considerable attention to issues affecting black women, these observations were few and far between. Until the 1970s, when the number of black scholars increased dramatically, schol-arly contributions were dominated by a few giants. As noted earlier, the ranks of history and sociology were particularly expanded with new black scholars. The new sociologists paid considerable attention to black family issues raised by Du Bois and Frazier, particularly following the intense controversy created by Daniel Moynihan's report which draws on Frazier's work (Moynihan 1965). That literature developed a greater understanding of the importance of the extended family and family networks in providing support to black families, including single parent families, and argues for an examination of black families on their own terms rather than in comparison to a "norm" as set by the dominant society (Allen 1978; Billingsley 1968; Hatchett et al. 1991).

In the economics literature, much of the discussion on female-headed households centered on whether welfare benefits were responsible for their dramatic rise, particularly among blacks.[8] Many black scholars rejected this literature as inconclusive, arguing that the primary explanation rests with the low male-to-female sex ratio as well as the low marriageability of young black men because of their poor job prospects (Darity and Myers 1984; Wilson 1987). Wilson and others, who focus on the loss of job opportunities for young black males, are often like Spero and Harris in that they focus almost exclusively on industrial employment, such that the service jobs where black women are employed scarcely receive any attention (e.g. Johnson and Oliver 1990). And while this probably reflects the desire of the authors to enhance our understanding of the specific issue of black male joblessness, the reality of black women having to support their families on the low wages earned in service sector jobs is missed.

As with the discussion of low male-to-female sex ratios, current discussion of black male joblessness has echoes from the past. Much earlier in this century, both Du Bois (1967) and Greene and Woodson (1930) discussed the greater ease black women in urban areas had in finding jobs, primarily domestic employment, often leaving them as primary family breadwinners. While the jobs they often hold now are non-household service jobs, they are service jobs nevertheless. The recent loss of industrial jobs, while devastating to the employment opportunities of young black men, should not obscure the historical precedent – at least in urban areas – of black women carrying the weight of family income because of their access to the service economy (and black men's lack of access to employment opportunities available to other men).

To try and get a handle on the extent to which black women are given consideration among black economists currently, a content analysis of *The Review of Black Political Economy* was conducted. This journal was chosen as it is the only one in the country solely focusing on economic issues facing people of African descent. Since it was not always possible to distinguish between white and black contributors, all articles written between Fall of 1971 (the earliest date the journal is available on microfiche) and Spring of 1992 (the last journal available at the time the content analysis was conducted) are included. Since *The Review of Black Political Economy* depends heavily on contributions and editorial comment from black scholars, it was felt that the inclusion of some white authors did not invalidate the content analysis as representing black economic thought. Articles focusing on international issues or that were biographies, were not read.

As Table 5.2 indicates, only 4.8 per cent of articles in the journal focused specifically on black women and only 4.8 per cent of articles focused specifically on black men. Interestingly, these percentages include a special issue on black women and a special issue on crime (which focused almost

Table 5.2 Content analysis of *The Review of Black Political Economy*,
Fall 1971–Spring 1992 (sample size 503)

Type of article	Percentage
Articles with a gender focus:	*9.6*
Black females	4.8
Black males	4.8
Articles making gender comparisons	*9.9*
Excluded articles:	*15.7*
International	14.1
Biographical	1.6
Remaining articles	*64.8*

Note: The main (italicized) categories are mutually exclusive and
sum to 100%

entirely on black men). Without these special issues, then, the number of articles focusing specifically on women or on men would be considerably less. This result indicates no particular bias towards men in the journal (although there were a couple of articles with titles indicating a focus on blacks in general but which only presented data on black men).

While the content analysis does not indicate a bias against black women, it does reveal unwillingness to discuss gender differences of any kind, however. About 10 per cent of the articles discussed differences between black men and women, or made some reference to gender differences among blacks, but there was little discussion of sex differences in the remaining articles. In other words, 20 per cent of the articles focused on black men or on black women, or made some reference to sex differences among blacks.

Another 16 per cent of the articles were excluded because they focused on international issues or were biographies. The remainder, 65 per cent of the articles, never touched on gender differences at all. Of these, roughly a third focused on economic or business development, fields which traditionally do not encompass gender analysis (although, as indicated earlier, there is no a priori reason why this has to be the case). Yet, even with this caveat, it is clear that there has been a general reticence either to write articles about, or to include articles focusing on, sex differences in the black community.

The Review of Black Political Economy is not totally representative of work done by black economists, however, and may reflect several biases. For example, since black male joblessness is a "sexy" issue in mainstream economics, those writing on this issue may have an easier time getting into more prestigious journals. Similarly, since black female-headed households have also received a lot of attention in mainstream economics, those writing on this aspect of black women's lives may also end up more easily in the higher status journals. The analysis of titles in the *Journal of Economic*

Literature presented earlier suggests, however, that the number of articles focusing on issues relevant to black women in the general literature is quite small.

Other than journal articles, there have been important books on black women, such as Phyllis Wallace's *Black Women in the Labor Force* (1980) which includes, as DuBois did, a special section on domestic workers written by Julianne Malveaux. *Slipping Through the Cracks: The Status of Black Women*, edited by Simms and Malveaux (1986) also deserves mention although it represents the special issue on black women from *The Review of Black Political Economy*, discussed above. There is also more work appearing on black women in the services sector (Burbridge 1994b; Malveaux 1988; Woody 1992). And of course, historians and sociologists continue to write on black women from their vantage points.

Several recent books examining economic (and other) issues affecting African Americans in general have also been careful to provide separate information on black men and women, such as *A Common Destiny* (1989), edited by Gerald Jaynes and Robin Williams, *The Color Line and the Quality of Life in America* (1989) by Reynolds Farley and Walter Allen, and *Life in Black America* (1991), edited by James Jackson. These books are problematic, however, in that the information presented on black women is scattered and fragmented, making it difficult to obtain a total picture of the condition of black women. In fairness to these authors, it was never their intent to focus on black women in particular; nevertheless these books call attention to the need for more holistic analyses of black women in the labor market.

ECONOMIC STATUS OF BLACK WOMEN

It is argued in this paper that an understanding of the economic status of African American women relies on knowing three things: 1 how well black women do in the labor market based on their own abilities and endowments and the receptivity of employers to black women as actual or potential employees; 2 the nature and characteristics of the labor market, including long-run economic growth and sectoral differences in economic growth; and 3 the family situation of African American women, including the characteristics of the family and the wealth and resources contained within the family. Any one of these issues, taken alone, does not provide the necessary information to furnish an understanding of the economic status of black women. That few analyses are available with this level of complexity is not the fault of African American scholars. Economics, and other social sciences, have become so divided and sub-divided into specialty areas that there is little encouragement to pursue a more holistic approach.

In the 1993 *JEL*, for example, eighteen specialties are identified, with 626 sub-specialties. As indicated earlier, this is not all negative but reflects the tremendous range of modern economics. Further, some of the emerging, new fields in economics actually represent attempts to deepen the study of economics or to be more multi-disciplinary (e.g. socio-economics, psychological economics, cultural economics, and so on). Yet the high degree of specialization in economics has caused one critic to despair that the typical graduate program in economics "takes intelligent young people and makes them into idiot savants" (McCloskey 1994: 173).[9]

There are some good reasons for this. More can be written about a narrowly defined topic in a given space of time and even small topics can be full of complexities that need to be understood; a holistic analysis requires a tremendous amount of energy, time, and resources. Without this approach, however, the economic well-being of black women often appears to be more positively depicted than is warranted. This is not to diminish the great gains made by many African American women in recent decades, but to emphasize that many of these gains have not extended to all black women, particularly those who are less skilled, and they have occurred in an adverse environment for black families overall. The importance of combining a micro-economic and a macro-economic perspective, and then bringing in family variables is discussed below.

Micro and macro perspectives

All the evidence indicates that although black women started out the second half of this century with the lowest earnings – when compared to black men, white women, and white men – they have made the greatest gains (Jaynes and Williams 1989). While still having the lowest earnings in comparison to the latter three groups, the gap in their earnings relative to the others has narrowed substantially. But this is not the entire picture. While African American women who work still make less than African American men who work, African American women are now more likely to work in the civilian labor force, a trend that is expected to continue. Table 5.3 presents recent data from the Bureau of Labor Statistics on the civilian labor force in 1990 and the projected civilian labor force in 2005. In 1990 there were 84,000 more black women working than black men working and in 2005 it is projected there will be 350,000 more black women working than black men. While the differences are still small in percentage terms (and projections can be notoriously unreliable) they suggest something that is almost unheard of in modern, Western, industrial societies: a higher civilian employment rate among a group of women than for their male counterparts.

Several writers have discussed how sectoral changes in the decades since the Second World War have dramatically changed the employment situation of women in general and African American women in particular (Burbridge 1994b and 1994c; Wallace 1980; Woody 1992). Of particular importance has been the rise of the service sector which draws largely on female labor. A

Table 5.3 Civilian labor force, 1990, and projection to 2005

	Labor force 1990		Projected labor force 2005	
	Number (thousands)	Percentage	Number (thousands)	Percentage
Black				
Men	6,628	5.3	8,537	5.7
Women	6,712	5.4	8,910	5.9
Hispanic				
Men	5,756	4.6	9,902	6.6
Women	3,822	3.1	6,888	4.6
White (non-Hispanic)				
Men	53,784	43.1	57,545	38.2
Women	44,229	35.4	52,470	34.8

Source: US Department of Labor, Bureau of Labor Statistics, *Outlook: 1990–2005*, Washington, DC: Government Printing Office, 1992

study by Burbridge (1994c), using 1990 census data, found that half of all African American women work in government or in non-governmental human service fields (referred to as the Third Sector, or nonprofit sector). There are dramatic differences by occupation, however: 89 per cent of black female professionals, 74 per cent of black female technicians, 60 per cent of black female service workers, and 50 per cent of black female managers work for government or the Third Sector. Most of these jobs are in health, education and social services. Most of these jobs, even those staffed by non-government employees, rely heavily on government funding (e.g. Medicare and Medicaid).

While the numbers are high for all women, the reliance on government and the Third Sector is higher for African American women than for any other group (although American Indian women are a close second). Without the expansion of health services, education services and social services, therefore, it is unlikely that African American women would have experienced the gains they have since they are more dependent on these industries than any other group defined by race or ethnicity and sex. What this means is that any major government initiative – such as health care reform or comparable worth – has a large potential impact on African American women (Burbridge 1993a, 1994a; Malveaux 1986).

It is important to emphasize these points since some authors attribute the gains made by black women to micro-level variables exclusively, such as the greater human capital attainments of black women or a preference for black women on the part of employers. There is some truth to this. Black women have made tremendous gains in education. And although it is unlikely that employers are generally choosing black women over black men for jobs – primarily because black women are largely in female-intensive occupations (Burbridge 1994c) – it may be that black women have had more success competing with white women for jobs in the sectors where women are confined than black men have had success competing with white men for jobs in the sectors where men are confined. But, as the study by Burbridge (1994c) indicates, the success of black females has been dependent on their absorption into sectors characterized by high labor demand; black men have been falling out of the labor market as they have borne a disproportionate share of male job losses resulting from economic restructuring. Thus, while education and employer preferences may be an issue, in a much broader context, structural changes are driving the changing fortunes of black men *and* women.

This is not to suggest that black women have achieved any parity with white women, however. Although black and white women are close to parity in earnings, this partly reflects the longer hours and greater job tenure of African American women in the labor market (Boston 1988; Jaynes and Williams 1989). Further, there continue to be significant occupational differences between black and white women, even within female-intensive occupations (Malveaux 1988). Table 5.4 presents the occupations in which black and white women are largely concentrated, based on 1990 census data. A group is considered over-represented if the percentage in the occupation divided by the percentage in the labor force is greater than one (the index of representation). In other words, if a group (e.g. black women) has a higher percentage in the occupation than their percentage in the labor force, the index is greater than one; if the percentage in the occupation is the same as the percentage in the labor force the index is equal to one; and if the percentage in the occupation is less than the percentage in the labor force the index is less than one.[10]

Table 5.4 indicates several occupations in which white women are over-represented and in which black women are not (column 1). Most of these are professional and technical occupations, remunerative sales occupations, or skilled craft occupations. The next column shows occupations in which the representation of black women is similar to or less than that of white women, but in which both black and white women are over-represented. This column includes, not surprisingly, managers or administrators in health or education, teachers and nurses, and a variety of administrative support and predominantly-female blue collar jobs. Columns 3 and 4 show occupations in which black women have a higher over-representation than white women (Column 3) or where black women are over-represented and white women are not. With the exception of dieticians, counselors, social workers, and public administrators, most of these are low-paying jobs in comparison to their counterparts in Columns 1 and 2. All of the occupations in Table 5.4, with the exception of the last two in column 4, are predominantly female. Thus, to say that black and white women share a concentration in female-intensive occupations, and to say that both groups have benefitted from the expansion in female-intensive occupations, is not to say that they have shared equally in this expansion.

Table 5.4 Occupations of importance to black women and white women, 1990

White women over-represented	Both over-represented BFI ≤ WFI	Both over-represented BFI > WFI	Black women over-represented

Managers
  finance
  food
  personnel
  property
  service
Management related
Postmasters
Therapists
Teachers
  art
  business
  foreign language
  health specialties
  secondary
Librarians
Social scientists
Religious workers
Writers and artists
Legal assistants
Physician assistants
Real estate sales
Advertising sales
Financial records processing
Animal caretakers
Optical goods workers
Food batchmakers
Photographic process machine operators
Typesetters
Misc. printing machine operators
	Administrators, education
	Managers, medical/health
	Registered nurses
	Teachers
	  elementary
	  special education
	  social work
	  physical education
	Recreation workers
	Sales, retail
	Supervisors, administrative support
	Secretaries
	Information clerks
	Food preparation workers
	Personal service workers
	Precision workers, textiles
	Precision workers, assorted materials
	Solderers
		Dieticians
		Teachers
		  home economics
		  kindergarten
		  pre-kindergarten
		Counselors
		Social workers
		Health technologists and technicians
		Computer equipment operators
		Records processing workers
		Duplicating, mail, and other office machine workers
		Communications equipment operators
		Adjusters and investigators
		Misc. administrative support
		Private household workers
		Health service workers
		Maids and housemen
		Graders and sorters
		Bookbinders
		Electrical equipment assemblers
		Textile operatives
		Packaging operatives
		Folding machine operatives
		Production inspectors
			Administrators and officials, public
			Mail and message distributing workers
			Machine operators, assorted materials

Source: US Bureau of the Census, Detailed Occupation and Other Characteristics from the EEO File for the United States, 1990 Census of Population Supplementary Reports, CP-S-1-1, Washington, DC: Government Printing Office, 1992
Note: BFI and WFI are black female and white female index of representation, respectively

Work and family issues

The issues in comparing black and white women do not end with these comparisons. The economic well-being of black and white women depends on work and family variables. And it is in this context that the differences between the two groups become stark and the gains of black women relative to black men lose their dramatic impact.

Most people live in families, and their economic success in the labor market (or lack thereof) is shared with all members of the family. In spite of the gains in the earnings of black women, total black family income has shown no improvement (Cotton 1989). One reason for this has been the economic losses of black males. There has also been a large decline in marriage among African Americans and a dramatic rise in female-headed households that has been attributed to the poor economic prospects of black men (Jaynes and Williams 1989; Mitchell-Kernan and Tucker (forthcoming); Wilson 1987). Thus, more and more black women are the sole support of their families, often with little or no support from absent fathers. In spite of gains in the labor market, therefore, the true economic well-being of black women may not have improved at all and, for low-income black women, their situation has worsened.

White women have faced similar issues. The wages of white men have also declined and there are increasing white female-headed households as well. But the magnitude of the differences between black and white families is large. The great majority of white families with children are two-parent families, while the majority of black families with children are now single-parent families. White males contribute more to white family income than black males can contribute to black family income (Burbridge 1993b). And in addition, white women have higher earnings and better jobs as mentioned above.

In addition to the income contributions made to families by men and women, wealth holdings are an extremely important component of total family well-being. In this respect, blacks are significantly more disadvantaged in comparison to whites than when only incomes are compared (Cotton 1989; Jaynes and Williams 1989). Studies indicate that an important reason why black wives work more than their white counterparts is that there is less non-labor income in black families (Fosu 1993; Wallace 1980). A study of black and white female-headed households finds that white, female, single parents are much more likely to receive financial support from their parents and other family members than are black, female, single parents. Thus the strain of being a sole family earner is lessened by the greater wealth within the extended family among whites (Okongwu 1993).

This is not to diminish the importance of black extended family networks which, if they cannot provide cash, still contribute greatly in terms of in-kind support to struggling nuclear and single-parent families (Billingsley

1968; Okongwu 1993). One of the important contributions of black socio-logists has been in highlighting the importance of kin networks in black families.

It is a mistake, however, to consider black female-headed households as a homogeneous group; some are "wealthier" than others in family support (McAdoo 1988). This is an important issue when evaluating the economic well-being of black women. For the support a woman receives from family members will often determine the extent to which she is "time poor."

Time poverty is a concept that evolved out of the concerns of feminist economists who argue that the unpaid contributions made by women to the family should be included in calculations of economic well-being. In particular, the contribution that a woman makes to her family in paid and unpaid work is much higher than what a simple measure of her labor market earnings would suggest. Women work much more than most labor market models – focusing on paid work – would suggest.

As women contribute more to the labor market, however, they become increasingly time poor. In other words, as more and more women work a "double day," first in the office and then at home, they have considerably less leisure time.[11] The more of their time that goes to paid and unpaid work, the less leisure time they have, the more time poverty they experience.

In this respect, black women who are in the labor market may be increasingly time poor and significantly more disadvantaged with respect to either white women or to black males than is reflected in data only focusing on incomes. In a world where black women are working more and have less support from a spouse, they may be increasingly time poor. The one mitigating factor may be the support received from extended family networks, which is available to many but not all female-headed households (Hatchett, *et al.* 1991). While white women are also working more and may be increasingly time poor, they are more likely to reside in families with two adults to share in family responsibilities and to have more wealth in their family to help them defray the costs of purchasing support (e.g. child care, housekeepers, and so on).

This is an area where little research is available. Black scholars need to put more effort into assessing paid and unpaid work being performed in black families; in making comparisons to white families in this regard; and in assessing the time poverty of black women in particular (Collins 1990). Unfortunately, given the expense in mounting a project that examines and measures unpaid work, an examination of these issues may not occur for many years yet.

SUMMARY AND CONCLUSIONS

This chapter has argued that the research that has been conducted on the economic status of black women – by blacks and whites – has been insubstantial and fragmentary. This is not to diminish the good work that has been done by scholars from Du Bois to the present. In fact, one of the tragedies of the situation is the lack of continuity through the years in some of the ideas put forward. It is unfortunate, for example, that the discussion of the de-stabilizing effects of the unequal sex ratio between black men and women essentially had to be re-discovered after being identified as a significant issue earlier in the century by W. E. B. Du Bois.

The shortage of black scholars, particularly economists, is certainly an important reason for this lack of continuity and for the persistence of gaps in the literature. Black scholars have been much more likely to focus on these issues and are also more likely to raise concerns – like the inequality in the sex ratio – that were not considered by non-black scholars. Black scholars have also been more likely to challenge aspects of the dominant paradigm that precludes a better understanding of issues facing African Americans.

Nevertheless, even within the economic literature of black scholars, the discussion of African American women in particular seems lacking. A content analysis of *The Review of Black Political Economy* suggests that little attention has been given to gender issues generally. This is not to say that this journal does worse than others. While a content analysis of other journals was outside the scope of this paper, it would not surprise the author if *The Review of Black Political Economy* did decidedly better in raising these issues. Nevertheless, feminist economists have been struggling for years to bring greater attention in the economics profession to specific issues affecting women, and similar attention needs to be given by those focusing on issues relevant to African Americans, as well.

Including attention on gender not only benefits the research focusing on black women; this paper has tried to show how black families have been affected by the disproportionate impact economic restructuring has had on black men and women. Thus, it is difficult to have a complete understanding of economic issues in the black community in general, without bringing a gender lens to the analysis. Recent research on joblessness among black males recognizes this, but often ignores how black women may be affected, not only in terms of employment, but in terms of the total burden of responsibilities that they have to carry.

An understanding of this burden of responsibilities requires an understanding of how work and family variables together define the economic status of African American women. Without bringing attention to work and family, one is sometimes left with the impression that black women are in better economic shape than they really are. Much more research is needed to increase our understanding and awareness of the economic status of black women, incorporating both work and family variables.

Finally, it has been frequently noted that, in many respects, the fragmentary nature of the research on African American women reflects the fragmentation of the economics profession. Social scientists in general have become so specialized that the left hand does not always know what the right hand is doing; one aspect of black life is focused on at the expense of another, related sphere of life. This affects many aspects of research on African Americans, women, and a variety of other issues. For the African American woman it is particularly problematic, given the contradictions in, and complexities of, her situation.

Thus, above all else, this paper is a call for a more integrated and holistic understanding of the economic status of African American women. This is not the first call for such a treatment. Unfortunately, it is probably not the last.

NOTES

1 Journals not in English and journals specifically focusing on countries outside of the US were excluded from the analysis. The analysis is based on titles only; time and resources did not permit a content analysis of all journal articles in the year.
2 Titles were sorted into mutually exclusive categories: race or ethnicity in general, analyses by sex and race, women and family in general, and poverty and inequality in general.
3 Based on my analysis of *JEL* titles, it is highly unlikely that the number of articles referring to black women comes even close to 3.7 per cent of all articles, even when taking into account the possibility of underestimating the number of titles focusing on the four subject areas identified. (For example, some of the articles classified as focusing on race or ethnicity in general pertained to non-black minority groups.) Thus, 3.7 per cent represents an upward bound estimate.
4 Books were classified in the same way as articles. Since there is more room in books to discuss a variety of subjects, reference to black women may be more likely even when not referred to in the title.
5 Due to low response rates to the National Academy of Sciences surveys in the 1980s, data in the 1980s under-reported African Americans. For this reason, no data for the 1980s are included. (For discussion, see Thurgood and Weinman 1991.)
6 This may reflect, in part, the dearth of good data on wealth holdings, however.
7 Harrison (1992) provides a more detailed discussion of the methodological concerns of these authors.
8 A review of this literature can be found in Wilson (1987).
9 This comment was made with respect to a survey of economic graduate students in which only 3.4 per cent of respondents indicated that it was very important to have a thorough understanding of the economy to achieve academic success in economics.
10 This is similar to the indices developed by a variety of scholars, such as Broom and Glen (1969) and Sokoloff (1992).
11 Most studies indicate that men are increasing their family responsibilities, as more women enter the labor market, but that contributions of men are still far from comparable to those of women (Pleck 1993).

REFERENCES

Allen, W. R. (1978) "The Search for Applicable Theories of Black Family Life," *Journal of Marriage and the Family*, 40 (4): 117–29.

Billingsley, A. (1968) *Black Families in White America*, New York: Simon and Schuster.

Boston, T. D. (1988) *Race, Class and Conservatism*, Boston, MA: Unwin Hyman.

Broom, L. and Glenn, N. D. (1969) "The Occupations and Income of Black Americans," in N. D. Glenn and C. M. Bonjean (eds), *Blacks in the United States*, San Francisco: Chandler Publishing Co.

Burbridge, L. C. (1993a) "The Labor Market for Home Care Workers: Demand, Supply, and Institutional Barriers." *The Gerontologist*, 3 (1): 41–6.

——(1993b) "Toward Economic Self-Sufficiency: Independence Without Poverty," in B. J. Tidwell (ed.), *The State of Black America 1993*, Washington, D.C.: National Urban League, Inc.

——(1994a) "The Occupational Structure of Nonprofit Industries: Implications for Women," in T. Odendahl and M. O'Neill (eds), *Women, Power, and Status in the Nonprofit Sector*, San Francisco, CA: Jossey-Bass.

——(1994b) "The Reliance of African American Women on Government and Third Sector Employment," *American Economic Review*, 84 (2): 103–7.

——(1994c) "Government, For-Profit, and Third Sector Employment: Differences by Race and Sex," report to The Aspen Institute Nonprofit Research Fund, Wellesley, MA: Center for Research on Women.

Conrad, C. A. (1986) "Book Reviews: When and Where I Enter and Labor of Love, Labor of Sorrow," in M. C. Simms and J. M. Malveaux (eds), *Slipping Through the Cracks: The Status of Black Women*, New Brunswick, NJ: Transaction Books.

Collins, P. H. (1990) *Black Feminist Thought: Knowledge, Consciousness, and the Politics of Empowerment*, New York: Routledge.

Cotton, J. (1989) "The Declining Relative Economic Status of Black Families," *The Review of Black Political Economy*, 18 (1): 75–86.

Darity, W. A., Jr. (ed.) (1984) *Labor Economics: Modern Views*, Boston, MA: Kluwer-Nijhoff Publishing.

——(1989) "Introduction: The Odyssey of Abram Harris from Howard to Chicago," in W. A. Darity, Jr. (ed.), *Race, Radicalism, and Reform: Selected Papers of Abram Harris*, New Brunswick, NJ: Transaction Publishers.

——and Myers, S. L., Jr. (1984) "Changes in Black Family Structure: Implications for Welfare Dependency," *Journal of Marriage and the Family*, 46: 765–79.

Davis, A. Y. (1983) *Women, Race, and Class*, New York: Vintage Books.

Du Bois, W. E. B. (1967) *The Philadelphia Negro: A Social Study*, New York: Schocken Books.

——(1969a) *The Negro American Family*, Westport, CT: Negro Universities Press.

——(1969b) *Darkwater: Voices from Within The Veil*, New York: Schocken Books.

Drake, S. and Cayton, H. (1945) *Black Metropolis: A Study of Negro Life in a Northern City*, New York: Harcourt, Brace and Company.

Farley, R. and Allen, W. A. (1989) *The Color Line and the Quality of Life in America*, New York: Oxford University Press.

Folbre, N. (1993) "How Does She Know? Feminist Theories of Gender Bias in Economics," *History of Political Economy*, 25 (1): 167–84.

Folbre, N. and Hartmann, H. (1988) "The Rhetoric of Self-Interest: Ideology of Gender in Economic Theory" in Klamer, A., McCloskey, D. N., and Solow, R. M. (eds), *The Consequences of Economic Rhetoric*, Cambridge: Cambridge University Press.

Fosu, A. K. (1993) "Differences in the Labor Force Participation of Black and White Married Women: Evidence From Urban Labor Markets," paper presented at the American Economic Association Meetings, Anaheim, CA.

Frazier, E. F. (1940) *The Negro Family in the United States*, Chicago: University of Chicago Press.

Gottschalk, P. and Danziger, S. (1984) "Macroeconomic Conditions, Income Transfers, and the Trend in Poverty," in D. L. Bawden (ed.), *The Social Contract Revisited*, Washington, DC: Urban Institute Press.

Greene, L. J. and Woodson, C. G. (1930) *The Negro Wage Earner*, New York City: Van Rees Press.

Harrison, F. V. (1992) "The Du Boisian Legacy in Anthropology," *Critique of Anthropology*, 12 (3): 239–60.

Hatchett, S. J., Cochran, D. L., and Jackson, J. S. (1991) "Family Life," in J. S. Jackson (ed.), *Life in Black America*, Newbury Park: Sage Publications.

Hine, D. C. (1990) *Black Women in American History*, Brooklyn: Carlson Publishing, Inc.

Jackson, J. S. (ed.) (1991) *Life in Black America*, Newbury Park: Sage Publications.

Jaynes, G. D. and Williams, R. M., Jr. (eds) (1989) *Common Destiny: Blacks and American Society*, Washington, DC: National Academy Press, 1989.

Johnson, J. H., Jr. and Oliver, M. L. (1990) "Economic Restructuring and Black Male Joblessness in U.S. Metropolitan Areas," UCLA Center for the Study of Urban Poverty Occasional Working Paper Series, Los Angeles, CA: Institute for Social Science Research, University of California, Los Angeles.

Jones, J. (1985) *Labor of Love, Labor of Sorrow: Black Women, Work and the Family, From Slavery to the Present*, New York: Vintage Books.

Malson, M. R., Mudimbe-Boye, E., O'Barr, J. F. and Wyer, M. (1988) *Black Women in America: Social Science Perspectives*, Chicago: University of Chicago Press.

Malveaux, J. M. (1986) "Comparable Worth and Its Impact on Black Women," in M. C. Simms and J. M. Malveaux (eds), *Slipping Through the Cracks: The Status of Black Women*, New Brunswick, NJ: Transaction Books.

Malveaux, J. M. (1988) "The Economic Status of Black Families," in H. P. McAdoo (ed.), *Black Families*, Newbury Park: Sage Publications.

McAdoo, H. P. (1988) "Changes in the Formation and Structure of Black Families: The Impact of Black Women," Working Paper No. 182, Wellesley, MA: Wellesley College Center for Research on Women.

McCloskey, D. N. (1994) *Knowledge and Persuasion in Economics*, Cambridge: Cambridge University Press.

Medoff, M. H. (1989) "The Relative Quality of Black Economists," *The Review of Black Political Economy*, 18 (2): 81–6.

Mitchell-Kernan, C. and Tucker, M. B. (forthcoming) *The Decline in Marriage Among African Americans: Causes, Consequences, and Policy Implications*, Newbury Park: Sage Publications, Inc.

Moynihan, D. H. (1965) *The Negro Family: The Case for National Action*, Washington, DC: Office of Policy Planning and Research, United States Department of Labor.

Okongwu, A. F. (1993) "Some Conceptual Issues: Female Single-Parent Families in the United States," in J. Mencher and A. Okongwu (eds), *Where Did the Men Go? Female-Headed Households in Cross Cultural Perspective*, Boulder, CO: Westview Press.

Okun, A. (1973) "Upward Mobility in a High-pressure Economy," *Brookings Papers on Economic Activity*, 1: 207–52.

Pleck, J. H. (1993) "Are 'Family-Supportive' Employer Policies Relevant to Men?," in J. C. Hood (ed.), *Men, Work, and Family*, Newbury Park: Sage Publications, Inc.

Ries, P. and Thurgood, D. H. (1993) *Summary Report 1991: Doctorate Recipients from United States Universities*, Washington, DC: National Academic Press.

Simms, M. C. and Malveaux, J. M. (eds) (1986) *Slipping Through the Cracks: The Status of Black Women*, New Brunswick, NJ: Transaction Books.

Simms, M. C. and Swinton, D. H. (1988) "A Report on the Supply of Black Economists," *The Review of Black Political Economy*, 17 (1): 67–88.

Sokoloff, N. J. (1992) *Black Women and White Women in the Professions*, New York: Routledge.

Spero, S. and Harris, A. L. (1974) *The Black Worker: The Negro and the Labor Movement*, New York: Atheneum.

Spriggs, W. E. and Williams, R. (1993) "A Logit Decomposition Analysis of Occupational Segregation: Results for the 1970's and 1980's," paper presented at the American Economic Association Meetings.

Stewart, J. B. (1991) "Back to Basics: The Significance of Du Bois's and Frazier's Contributions for Contemporary Research on Black Families," in H. E. Cheatham and J. B. Stewart (eds), *Black Families: Interdisciplinary Perspectives*, New Brunswick, NJ: Transaction Publishers.

Sudarkasa, N. (1988) "Interpreting the African Heritage in Afro-American Family Organization," in H. P. McAdoo (ed.), *Black Families*, Newbury Park: Sage Publications.

Thurgood, D. H. and Weinman, J. M. (1991) *Summary Report 1990: Doctorate Recipients from United States Universities*, Washington, DC: National Academy Press.

Wallace, P. (1980) *The Black Woman in the Labor Force*, Cambridge, MA: The MIT Press.

Weaver, R. C. (1948) *The Negro Ghetto*, New York: Harcourt, Brace, and Company.

Wilson, W. J. (1987) *The Truly Disadvantaged: the Inner City, the Underclass, and Public Policy*, Chicago: University of Chicago Press.

Woody, B. (1992) *Black Women in the Workplace: Impacts of Structural Change in the Economy*, New York: Greenwood Press.

6

MISSED OPPORTUNITY
Sadie Tanner Mossell Alexander and the economics profession*

Julianne Malveaux

Sadie Tanner Mossell Alexander (1898–1989) was the first black woman in the United States to receive a PhD (Thomas Potterfield, 1990). She earned her degree in economics from the University of Pennsylvania in 1921. Her dissertation, "The Standard of Living Among One Hundred Negro Migrant Families in Philadelphia," was, in her words, "an attempt to arrive at conclusions concerning the migrants to Philadelphia, through an intensive analysis of the budgets of a small number of their group" (Mossell 1921). When she finished her graduate work in 1921, Mossell was unable to find employment in the economics profession in Philadelphia or in the surrounding areas (Potterfield). This is not surprising, since the only academic employment available to African Americans in the early 1920s was at the black colleges, and black women faced barriers to employment at some of those colleges.

In any case, Mossell worked as an assistant actuary at the black-owned North Carolina Mutual Life Insurance Company from 1921 to 1923. She returned to Philadelphia to marry Raymond Alexander in 1923, and entered the University of Pennsylvania Law School in 1924. She was the first African American woman to graduate from Penn's Law Schools in 1927, and the first black woman admitted to the Pennsylvania bar in the same year (Potterfield).

Given her family background, Alexander's academic and career achievements are not surprising. Her grandfather was a bishop in the African Methodist Episcopal Church. Her uncle, Henry O. Tanner, was a noted artist. Nontraditional occupations and employment were not unusual for the Tanner women – an aunt, Hallie Tanner Johnson, was a physician and founder of the nurses' school and hospital at Tuskegee Institute (Potterfield).

During her career, Alexander distinguished herself as a lawyer in both the public and private sectors, working as Assistant City Solicitor in the City of

* Reprinted, with permission, from the *American Economic Review*, May 1991, *(Papers and Proceedings)*, *81*(2), pp. 307-10

Philadelphia in 1928–30 and 1930–4, and serving as a Truman appointee to the Committee on Human Rights (Gerald Fraser 1989), a Kennedy appointee to the Lawyers' Committee on Civil Rights, and the Carter-appointed Chair of the White House Conference on Aging (Fraser). She was also active in civic affairs, serving as the Secretary of the National Urban League for twenty-five years, and as a member of the National Advisory Council of the American Civil Liberties Union. She was the first national president of Delta Sigma Theta Sorority (currently the largest black women's public service organization; see Paula Giddings 1988), and its legal advisor for thirty-five years.

Alexander's household seems similar to the modern two-career household. Her husband was a lawyer, a member of the Philadelphia City Council (1951–9), and a distinguished jurist on the Philadelphia Court of Common Pleas. They had two daughters, Mary Elizabeth Alexander Brown (born 1934) and Rae Pace Alexander-Minter (born 1936). Alexander successfully juggled household, family, career, and civic responsibilities. The achievements of her life touch areas that range from the law, government, civil rights, education, and aging, to women's rights (Potterfield).

A striking aspect of Alexander's career was the longevity of her interest in the topics she identified as important – serving as Secretary of the Urban League for twenty-five years, and as the Legal Advisor to Delta Sigma Theta for thirty-five years. Her involvement in the economics profession, on the other hand, seems fleeting. Alexander earned a PhD degree, sought employment in economics but did not find it, and worked as an actuary for a short time before pursuing legal studies. The Alexander papers suggest that Alexander all but abandoned the economics profession after 1923,[1] although at least one of the books in the Alexander collection suggests that thirty years after obtaining the PhD, she maintained at least a passing interest in economic issues.[2]

Why did Alexander abandon economics? According to her daughter, Rae Alexander-Minter, "there was no way for her to make a living in the profession." Alexander-Minter indicates that her mother did not look back and expressed no regrets about her career, but worked hard at her law practice and at maintaining her family. Indeed, at her peak, Alexander had one of the largest divorce practices in Philadelphia.[3]

While her withdrawal from the economics profession may not have been a personal tragedy for Alexander, the fact that she did not continue her work in economics seems a missed opportunity for her, for the economics profession, and for the body of economic knowledge that pertains to African Americans. My goal in this essay is to probe the nature of that missed opportunity, both through discussion of the major example of her economics work, the doctoral dissertation, and through speculation about ways she may have followed up on the dissertation, given her interests.

BLACK MIGRATION AND CONSUMPTION IN PHILADELPHIA, 1916–18

According to Philip Foner and Ronald Lewis (1989), the "machinery of segregation" had been installed in the South by the beginning of the twentieth century. "Economic intimidation, violence, and lynching" suggested to blacks that the South had no future for them. In addition, the early twentieth century was an economically devastating period in the South, with agriculture plagued by flooding, an epidemic of boll weevils, and other hardships. As the South declined, the North and Middle West developed industrially, especially with demand stimulated by the production needs of the First World War. As white men went to war, black men moved north to replace them in industry. "The Great Migration," a significant exodus of black workers from the South, took place in the second decade of the twentieth century, triggered both by hardship in the South and by new opportunities in the North.

Between 1890 and 1915 in Chicago, for example, the black population grew from less than 15,000 to more than 50,000 (Allan Spear 1967). Similar population jumps took place in other industrial centers, including Philadelphia. Alexander's dissertation, "The Standard of Living of Negro Families in Philadelphia" (henceforth referred to as NMF), looks in detail at this migration in Philadelphia, both from a macro and a micro perspective.

Alexander documents the labor shortage in Philadelphia, and discusses industrial efforts to attract black workers to manufacturing sites. NMF discusses the living conditions for migrant families, conditions Alexander describes as deplorable. She goes on to detail the civic response to poor housing conditions, on the part of the black church, the black middle class, and whites. Some of the racial conflicts that took place because of migration are detailed by Alexander, mainly to place the issue of migration into a socio-political context, and to develop research questions and pose hypotheses for her dissertation.

"Was the migrant to Philadelphia able to adapt himself to the environment of an industrial economy?" she asks. "Did his presence help or hinder the racial condition of the city?" Alexander asserts that the standard of living maintained by a people is an index of the extent to which they have adapted themselves to a given environment. She proposes to analyze the incomes and expenditures of a group of migrant families to measure standards of living and "judge the degree of adaptation."

Thus, Alexander set the tone for doing a cross-sectional consumption survey of black migrant families. Over a two-month period, Alexander visited 100 families in Philadelphia's twenty-ninth ward. Using a detailed questionnaire, she asked about origin, family structure, labor market status, unemployment, and household expenses, including rent, utilities, church, insurance, tobacco, alcohol, carfare, and savings. In a manner reminiscent of contemporary dissertations, Alexander discusses both her research methodology and the accuracy of her data before analyzing results.

The results of Alexander's dissertation provide fascinating information about expenditure patterns, and also reveal her familiarity with federal and municipal data on household incomes and consumption patterns, and theories of consumption and spending. NMF also reveals Alexander's penchant for detail and accuracy, as well as a good eye for reporting of the minute aspects of migrant lives. Discussing expenditures on heat, for example, Alexander expanded the discussion to deal with families who rented rooms where landlords provided heat and ventilation and health aspects of these rentals. She concluded that many of these dwellings "were unfit for families."

NMF reports many of the economic inefficiencies that migrant families were forced to endure. "The average price paid for renting one room was $163 per year, $6.05 less than average price of renting a house of four rooms," writes Alexander. She adds that renting a home increased income earning potential since so many renters took in lodgers. Noticeably absent from this discussion, however, was an acknowledgement of the institutional forces that forced black migrant families into inefficient economic arrangements.

Alexander's discussion of migrant spending provided information about the culture and lifestyles of black migrants. She details information about health and the use of free clinics, the financial ties among extended families, and savings patterns, including participation in benevolent societies and church thrift clubs. Alexander concludes the discussion of expenditures by comparing black migrant expenditure patterns with those posited by consumption theorists and those measured by the war labor board. Essentially, she found that black migrant families behaved in the same way Engel theorized they would. The percentage of income spent on food fell as income increased. The percentage of income spent on clothing stayed the same with increasing income. The percentage of income spent on sundries increased as income increased. In a result that differed from Engel's theory, expenditures on rent, fuel, and light decreased as income rose.

After analyzing black migrant budgets and expenditures, Alexander developed a suggested budget. In the context of this discussion, especially as it relates to housing, she dealt with supply and segregation issues and indicated that "a two story brick house, fitted with tub, washstand, and toilet" might be scarce for blacks because "the Negro population of Philadelphia increased without an equal increase in housing." Alexander put off issues of housing availability for the concluding chapter of her dissertation.

Armed with data about actual and suggested spending, Alexander asks two questions. "Do black migrant families earn enough to have fair standards of living, as defined by published reports?" "Do black migrant families choose to spend their money in ways to attain a fair standard of living?" She notes that 64 per cent of all families had a sufficient income to provide a fair standard of living, though the primary breadwinner's earnings were enough to provide a fair standard in only 41 per cent of cases. She further indicates that some of the families able to afford a fair standard of living do not attain such standards because of "unwise" spending.

In this context, Alexander deals with issues of class and migration in distinguishing segments of the black community from each other. She notes that family size, "ignorance resulting from unwise spending" (insurance spending is especially targeted here), and racial prejudice were all factors preventing black migrant families from attaining a fair standard of living. She deals with both institutional barriers to fair living standards ("Recreation appeared seldom in his budget, for the Negro was admitted to few places where it was offered"), and individual barriers (such as lack of education). Alexander concludes by suggesting that the status of the black migrant can be improved by the "Negro businessman," the black church, and the city, which she says "[have] the responsibility of seeing that at least adequate housing is secured."

MISSED OPPORTUNITY: BEYOND NEGRO MIGRANT FAMILIES

Alexander's doctoral dissertation illustrates the perception, sensitivity, racial concern, and ability of a young upper middle-class black woman to use her professional skills to tackle a contemporary racial issue. Her dissertation is a case study that reveals institutional aspects of racial segregation in Philadelphia, as well as confirming the consumption theories of the time. It also reveals Alexander's middle-class biases, for example, in her use of terms like "unwise purchases" and her remark that she does not advocate the consumption of alcohol, Prohibition or not. On the other hand, in her concluding chapter Alexander reveals herself both as an advocate for black self-help ("churches could help to alleviate the housing problem by building houses instead of expensive church edifices") and as an advocate of government economic involvement in the housing market.

In thinking of the missed opportunity revealed by Alexander's dissertation, I think about the work that Abram Harris did on black business development, Oliver Cox's work on class, the W. E. B. Du Bois Atlanta University studies, and D. Parke Gibson's books on black consumer patterns. Given her interest and ability, Alexander might have followed in any of those directions or, indeed, continued to look at black family and migration patterns both through further case studies and from a macroeconomic perspective. Because Alexander discussed so many possible areas for further research in her dissertation, one can posit that, given the opportunity, she would have had a productive and significant research career.

Indeed, it is possible to speculate that had Alexander pursued her research interests, given her long involvement with the Urban League, we might have seen the earlier production of titles like "The State of Black America," which was first produced in 1975 (John Jacob 1991). And, given the opportunity to teach, what kinds of students might Alexander have nurtured, and how many other economists would have tackled socioeconomic issues of migration, consumption, housing availability, health care access, and insurance availability?

Alexander's dissertation suggests that the young economist might have taken quite a different career path after she earned her PhD had there only been opportunities for her in her profession of first choice. While the economics profession's loss was the legal profession's gain, Alexander might well have made a significant contribution to economics, given the opportunity.

NOTES

1 Telephone conversation between Mark Lloyd, Director of University of Pennsylvania Archives and Records center and myself, 21 September 1990.
2 According to Potterfield (p. 229): Among the twenty-two miscellaneous books included in the joint papers of Raymond Pace Alexander and Sadie T. M. Alexander was *Away From Freedom: The Revolt of the College Economists*, edited by Orval Watts in 1952.
3 Personal interview with Rae Alexander-Minter, 10 December 1990.

REFERENCES

Alexander, Sadie Tanner Mossell, Vitae, 1982.
Foner, Philip S. and Lewis, Ronald L. *Black Workers: A Documentary History from Colonial Times to the Present*, Philadelphia: Temple University Press, 1989.
Fraser, Gerald, "Sadie T. M. Alexander, 91, Dies; Lawyer and Civil Rights Advocate," *New York Times*, 3 November 1989.
Giddings, Paula, *In Search of Sisterhood: Delta Sigma Theta and the Challenge of the Black Sorority Movement*, New York: William Morrow, 1988.
Jacob, John, "Urban League Releases State of Black America 1991 Report," *Urban League News*, 8 January 1991.
Mossell, Sadie Tanner, "The Standard of Living Among One Hundred Negro Migrant Families in Philadelphia," in *Annals of the American Academy of Social and Political Science*, November 1921.
Potterfield, Thomas G., "Guide to the Alexander Papers," University of Pennsylvania Archives and Records Center, 1990.
Spear, Allan, *Black Chicago: The Making of A Negro Ghetto*, Chicago: University of Chicago Press, 1967.

7

TILTING AGAINST THE WIND

Reflections on the life and work of
Dr Phyllis Ann Wallace*

Julianne Malveaux

Most contemporary scholars with an interest in the labor market knew about the life and work of Phyllis Ann Wallace. Her research on the AT&T case (*Women, Minorities, and Employment Discrimination*, 1977), the career aspirations of young girls in Harlem (*Pathways to Work: Unemployment Among Black Teenage Females*, 1974), her edited volume on women's work choices (*Women in the Workplace*, 1982), or black women's work (*Black Women in the Labor Force*, 1980), or her book on the career patterns of Sloan School graduates (*MBAs on the Fast Track*, 1989), are all pulled together by the thread of Wallace's interest in the workplace and the way that those who are "other" move through the workplace.

If one were to summarize the Wallace career, though, it would be a mistake to limit one's focus to her research and scholarship on the workplace. Instead, the theme of Wallace's academic and civic work, of her scholarship and her mentorship, is the theme of tilting against the wind, shattering stereotypes, choosing the road less traveled. Wallace did not travel along nontraditional paths simply because they were there, but because she was convinced that the directions would be interesting. She was not discouraged by the notion that "blacks" or "women" or "black women" did not trek along a certain course. Instead, with quiet confidence, she focused on the path, often cleared it of debris, and walked along it with dignity and determination. Further, she encouraged those in her orbit, those who she mentored and nurtured in business, economics, science, and the arts, to do the same. From her choice to major in economics at NYU, to her leadership of the Museum of Fine Arts Committee for New Audiences, Wallace's chosen path was that of myth-buster, of one who shattered stereotypes and opened doors.

This essay is a work in progress about the life of Phyllis Wallace. When she lived, Wallace encouraged me to query her about her past with the hope that I might write her biography. A few days before her death on 10

* Reprinted, with permission, from the *American Economic Review*, May 1994, *(Papers and Proceedings)*, 84(2), pp. 93-7.

January 1993, we had scheduled time to tape a session at the end of that month. Having missed the opportunity to ask Wallace a set of questions directly, I have pulled together some combination of recollections and secondary source data for this essay. My continuing effort to write more fully about Phyllis Wallace's life and career will include interviews with her friends and colleagues.

PHYLLIS WALLACE'S EARLY CAREER, 1944–57

Phyllis Wallace wrote that she chose the economics major because she wanted to leave Maryland, and because the peculiarities of the law offered her a window of opportunity to leave the state and pursue a broader range of educational opportunities. State law prevented her from attending the all-white University of Maryland because of her race, but provided out-of-state educational expenses for those black students whose chosen major was not offered at all-black Morgan State College. Wallace chuckled when she spoke of comparing the Morgan catalogue with that at the University of Maryland, and choosing economics as a major because it was available at Maryland but not Morgan. Phyllis Wallace majored in economics at New York University, graduating magna cum laude and Phi Beta Kappa in 1943.

At NYU, and later at Yale, Wallace was known to be serious, studious, and interested in conversation and the arts. Her sisters and friends laugh that she would bring books to parties because she was less interested in some social aspects of undergraduate life than she was in the scholarly aspects. Initially, she planned to teach in the Baltimore high schools upon graduation from NYU, but a professor encouraged her to apply to Yale, where she received the master's degree in 1944, and the doctorate in 1948. According to her application to the National Register of Scientific and Technical Personnel (1962), she had proficiency in four foreign languages: German, Russian, Spanish, and French.

Those who knew Phyllis Wallace often commented on her lack of racial bitterness. This should not be construed to suggest that she did not experience racial discrimination. At Yale, department regulations prevented her from holding traditional graduate-student employment as a teaching assistant. However, employment opportunities as a research assistant, as well as fellowship support from the Rosenwald Foundation and the Sterling Fund made it possible for her to complete her course of study. Later, as a professor and researcher, she had difficulty attending the American Economics Association meetings when they were held in cities that restricted African American access to public accommodations. In response to her written protest, she received a letter in 1958 from NBER's Solomon Fabricant that indicated "Nobody on the Executive Committee wants to hold the meetings in a city that will make it unpleasant for any of our members. As far as I know, the meetings will therefore not be held in New Orleans."

While Wallace later became known for her work on race, during this period her research largely revolved around issues of international trade. She wrote her dissertation on commodity trade relationships, focusing on international sugar agreements. After earning the PhD at Yale, Wallace lived in New York, teaching at City College of New York and doing research at the National Bureau of Economic Research, focusing on international trade and productivity issues. Her graduate international work also included a research stint with "a defense-related federal agency" (as she described her work for the National Register of Scientific and Technical Personnel, 1962), very possibly an intelligence agency, in the late 1940s and early 1950s.

While Phyllis Wallace did not say why she left her research career in New York to move to Atlanta in 1953, one can speculate on the possibilities. Her position at NYU was not a tenure-track position (she was a part-time lecturer in economics and statistics), and it seems that much of her time was spent doing research at NBER. In private conversations, she alluded to the limitations she might face because of race matters, though she never spoke explicitly of discrimination in those early years. It is my impression that Wallace was interested in the contribution she could make as a full-time teacher in the 1950s, and that may have contributed to her decision to consider a move to the Atlanta University, where she served on the economics faculty from 1953 to 1957. These years were also among the most personally rewarding of her life, as she met lifelong friends and colleagues like M. Carl Holman, Nice and Ves Harper, Whitney Young, and others. In an application for 1956 summer support from the Southern Fellowships Fund, she spoke of the nexus between teaching and research and why she found the two important. From the application, it is clear that she maintained her connection with NBER, and that she planned to use a data base there for her summer work.

PHYLLIS WALLACE AND GOVERNMENT INTELLIGENCE, 1957–65

I met Phyllis Wallace when I was a first year graduate student at MIT in 1974. At the time, other students whispered that she had been a member of the CIA or another intelligence agency. Wallace's résumé from that period refers to her 1957–65 employment quite unspecifically as "government economist." When the issue was raised with her at the time she asked whether her former employment mattered, or replied, simply, that she worked "for the government."

Lamond Godwin was a Rutgers PhD student when he went to work for Wallace in the early 1970s. He recalls that when the two of them traveled to a Chicago manpower meeting, they were met by protesters who talked about repelling the CIA. Godwin notes that he was stunned and attempted to correct the protesters, but when he and Wallace left the site by cab, he asked her why they would think such a thing of her, and she responded in a deadpan voice, "because it's true."

Phyllis Wallace seemed increasingly ready to talk about her government intelligence involvement as the Cold War ended. I wrote a 1990 biographical sketch about her, and, following her CV, referred to her work in the 1957–65 period as "research in international economics for a government agency." She hand-corrected the manuscript to read that she worked "as an economic analyst in intelligence." During the period between 1957 and 1965, she was coauthor of an *American Economic Review* article, "Industrial Growth in the Soviet Union" (1959), and gave testimony before the Joint Economic Committee, "Dimensions of Soviet Economic Power" (1962).

In 1992, Wallace indicated that she was willing to talk about "her Agency years" in more detail. Although we never spoke directly about the work she did, she talked about the way her work affected her quality of life. Already relatively isolated as an African American woman economist, she was further isolated because her intelligence work made it impossible for her to talk about the work she did to friends and family. Indeed, she indicated that this forced her to limit her social circle during her early Washington years, since people had to understand that she was not free to talk about her work. In some ways, her focus on the terms and conditions of work in the 1972–92 period seems to reflect some of the stresses she felt in her "Agency" years, and the relationship between work and identity.

FROM INTELLIGENCE TO EQUAL-OPPORTUNITY RESEARCH, 1965–72

The atmosphere of social change that infused the years before the passage of the Civil Rights Act of 1965 made Phyllis Wallace consider a shift in her research focus. The Equal Employment Opportunity Commission set up operations in July 1965; Wallace began working as its Chief of Technical Studies a few months later. She was a pioneer in research on the economics of discrimination and distinguished herself by stretching scarce resources to get research results by providing government data to academicians for analysis. Lester Thurow, Orley Ashenfelter, James Heckman, Ray Marshall, and Robert McKersie were among the economists who worked closely with Wallace on early EEOC data sets.

Wallace also worked to coordinate hearings for EEOC about racial employment patterns in many industries including the textile industry, the drug industry, and other industries. Her research focused on the status of African Americans in urban-poverty neighborhoods and on patterns of employment in private industry. Another of her key contributions was the development of interdisciplinary teams that focused on issues of discrimination and employment testing. Her group of legal scholars such as

Rutgers University's Albert Blumrosen and industrial psychologists such as Patricia Gurin developed the first EEOC guidelines on employee testing. This work influenced the outcome of the *Griggs* v. *Duke Power Company* case.

When Wallace left EEOC in 1968, she was fully committed to continuing research in the area of racial employment discrimination and equal employment opportunity. She joined the Metropolitan Applied Research Center to work on issues affecting urban youth in labor markets and focused on the issues affecting young black women, an area that had been unexplored to that point. She participated actively in EEOC and other government advisory commissions on work issues and published extensively on race and gender discrimination in the labor market, including an *AER (Papers and Proceedings)* article with Bernard Anderson (1975) on black economic progress, and an invited paper on measurement and societal values for the Employment Testing Service.

MIT SCHOLAR-ACTIVIST, 1972–93

In 1972, Phyllis Wallace joined MIT's faculty as a visiting professor. She was tenured as full professor in 1974 and continued her research on employment discrimination, which resulted in several publications. She also participated fully in professional and government review panels on issues of employment policy. During her years as professor at MIT, she was involved in the Boston business community as a board member of State Street Bank and Stop and Shop stores, as a trustee of the Museum of Fine Arts, and on several government boards.

Her colleague Alice Rivlin says that "she applied the skills of a well-trained scholar activist to some of the most important and intractable problems of our time, especially the problems of alleviating poverty and the damage of racial and sexual discrimination." Without subscribing to the notion that "the personal is political," Wallace turned the disadvantage of the discrimination she experienced into a powerful theme for the research she did during her MIT years.

Among her most powerful work is her book *MBAs on the Fast Track*. A longitudinal study of Sloan School graduates that was completed only through painstaking research, the MBA study shows gaps between men's and women's pay, and between pay of black and white MBAs. Wallace was also able to document trends that have only recently been distilled into jargon: "dinks" (i.e., double incomes, no kids), "glass ceilings," and commuter marriages were all trends that she captured in the early days of compiling her data.

Often the "first" or only African American woman in a particular role, Wallace never relished that role or basked in it. "You do your work and that's it," she said, viewing hurdles only in retrospect. As the first African

American and first woman President of the Industrial Relations Research Association, she focused on moving her colleagues to expand their view of industrial-relations research, encouraging labor economists, trade unionists, and corporate human-relations specialists to deconstruct the barriers to advancement of minorities and women in internal labor markets. She noted that employment and training programs may serve as the critical factor in helping the US economy maintain its competitive edge in many global market-places. Wallace also noted that development and maintenance of human capital will be central in the emerging information technology where boundaries between blue-collar and white-collar jobs may gradually disappear. Her comments about internal labor markets reflected points she made when she accepted the National Economic Association's Westerfield Award in 1981. In making both sets of remarks she spoke of the importance of case studies, of the participant–observer mode of data collection. Speaking to groups of researchers, she noted that "research is only part of the task."

Wallace's tendency was to challenge in a way that was gentle, probing, and unthreatening. Completely convinced that her approach was the right one, she did not acknowledge that blinders might rise or ears might close. Indeed, sometimes she indicated that she saw hurdles not as obstacles, but simply something that needed to be dealt with. Her attitude enabled the dozens of students she mentored, predominantly African Americans, other minorities, and women, in economics and the arts, to accept challenges with the same grace and dignity that she accepted them. Those she helped include, beyond economists and managers, banking professionals, fledgling artists, elementary-school teachers, and others.

Indeed, the work that occupied the last year of her life speaks volumes about the way that Phyllis Wallace went about her life, work, and commitment. As a member of the Museum of Fine Arts Board of Trustees, she was informed that the museum owned a large collection of Nubian artifacts. With the help of the professional staff at the museum, she worked to establish the Nubian Gallery there. Then, she raised funds to bring Boston elementary- and secondary-school children, especially African Americans, to the museum to see the collection. Finally, she chaired a museum committee on "new audiences" to reach out to find new museum members and supporters in the community. As she spent a year working in an unfamiliar system, she learned more about museum bureaucracy and arts boards of directors than she perhaps cared to know. But she maneuvered her course with the same quiet dignity that took her from Baltimore's Frederick Douglas High School to NYU to Yale University to EEOC to MIT. Weeks before her death, she was circulating brochures to her friends, asking for contributions to the museum.

This very short essay simply scratches the surface of Phyllis Wallace's life. I did not talk much about the many awards she received, from the National

Economic Association (1981), Yale (1980), Brown University (1986), and other universities and organizations. I did not talk much about the dozens of working papers she wrote about affirmative action and equal employment opportunity, some presented as MIT working papers, many that remain unpublished. It would take volumes to talk about the hundreds that she mentored and nurtured, the calls she made to help secure careers or to shore up flagging egos. Nor have I talked about Wallace's civic presence, her behind-the-scenes participation in national women's organizations, and her support of politicians and political issues that she cared about.

All of these are important aspects of Wallace's life and work, but most important is the fact that Phyllis Wallace was a woman who refused to be defined by her race, gender, or occupation. Those who knew her well defined her by her compassion, by her willingness to make space for outsiders in an inside world. She did this by her scholarship, through her quiet activism, in the leadership roles she accepted, in the work that she did. Her academic work in the post-1965 period is distinguished by her efforts to deconstruct exclusion and to make it obsolete. Fortunately, her efforts to banish exclusion transcended her academic work. We are all better off for her efforts.

REFERENCES

Greenslade, R. V. and Wallace, Phyllis Ann, "Industrial Growth in the Soviet Union: Comment," *American Economic Review*, September 1959, *49*(4), pp. 687–95.

Wallace, Phyllis Ann, *Dimensions of Soviet economic power*, Testimony before the Joint Economic Committee, US Congress, Washington, DC: US Government Printing Office, 1962.

——, *Pathways to work: Unemployment among black teenage females*, Lexington, MA: Lexington Books, 1974.

——, *Women, minorities, and employment discrimination*, Lexington, MA: Lexington Books, 1977.

——, *Black women in the labor force*, Cambridge, MA: MIT Press, 1980.

——, (ed.) *Women in the workplace*, Boston, MA: Auburn House, 1982.

——, *MBAs on the fast track*, New York: Harper and Row, 1989.

Wallace, Phyllis Ann and Anderson, Bernard E., "Public Policy and Black Economic Progress: A Review of the Evidence." *American Economic Review*, May 1975, *(Papers and Proceedings)*, *65*(2), pp. 47–52.

8

PROLEGOMENON INTO RACE AND ECONOMICS*

Leonard Harris

Oliver Cox meticulously distinguished a class from a caste and a race from an ethnic group – each stood for a different kind of cohesive social entity. Cox rejected the idea that the social position of blacks was best understood as a caste.[1] One reason for his rejection was that blacks did not form a distinct religious, geographical, and linguistic community. The racial segregation and identity of blacks distinguished them from other Americans, not religion, geography, language or basic class structures. The social position of blacks, for Cox, and the discrimination they faced, were a function of deep class conflicts and historical prejudices. Blacks formed, for Cox, a separate racial community or a quasi-society; on occasion, blacks formed a group similar to Andrew Hacker's view of the black community in *Two Nations*, a quasi-nation within a nation.[2]

Marcus Singer, in a curious article on ethnogenesis, noted that neither Cox, in *Caste, Class and Race*, nor Myrdal in *The American Dilemma*, "...tells us the position of the Negroes in the structure of Negro–white relations. They do not indicate *what* the Negroes are, *what* they constitute as a social entity."[3] Singer argued that blacks are co-jointly a race and an ethnic group in the process of developing toward an ethnic reality rather than an already well-formed static racial entity with neatly defined boundaries. Possibly because Singer was ambivalent about the cogency of categories in social explanations, he does not tell us "what" blacks are; possibly he does not answer the question because he considered the "Negro" culturally inclined to be an ethnic group without the shackles of racial identity.

Tommy Lott draws our attention, when evaluating debates over whether W. E. B. Du Bois in the "The Conservation of Races" is committed to defining "race" as biology or "race" as a socio-historical entity, to what Singer avoids: "What is at issue...is whether the rigid dichotomy between race and ethnicity is tenable."[4] Lott doubts whether it is tenable. The debate

* I am indebted to Felmon Davis, Union College; Vernon Williams, Purdue University; Jeff Crawford, Central State University; and Patricia Knox, University of Kentucky for critical comments on earlier versions.

over the "what" has a very long history, one that I will draw on, but I offer a different description of the "what."[5] The dichotomy between race and ethnicity is, I believe, simply not tenable.

One way to see the import of defining the "what" and denying that the dichotomy between race and ethnicity is tenable, is by considering the following questions: What does the "Black" in "Black Economics" mean? What on earth was the Department of Labor doing with an Office of Negro Economics directed by the stalwart scholar George Edmund Hayes?[6] What is it that economists are explaining when they explain the difference between black and white incomes – incomes that belong to what sort of group? What economic solutions follow from an explanation of income differences if the "what" is a race?; what solutions if an ethnic group?

Assume that the objective of explaining income differences is not to prove that white workers with lower incomes than black workers are biologically inferior, nor vice versa, but that the objective is to uncover the variables that function to create black exclusion and differential incomes. In order to uncover such variables and depict relative positions, it must be the case that the entity upon which income differences are predicated can be said to exist – the "what" is taken as already answered. The uncovering will focus on variables relevant to race, ethnicity, or some combination, depending on how the existing "what" has been defined. The implication of denying the dichotomy between race and ethnicity suggests, I argue, stark confrontation with a Calvinist dilemma and a Faustian predicament, neither of which may be understood, nor a workable solution recommended, by traditional approaches.

APORIA: RACIATED ETHNICITY

I will use "raciated ethnicity" to stand for a form of life – the "what" type of social entity that best describes African Americans. In an admittedly tentative way, "raciated ethnicity" is intended to allow us to collapse the distinction between race and ethnicity. A "raciated ethnicity" is to be understood as a social construction, similar to the way in which Charles Wagley refers to social race as a construction: "The term 'social race' is used because these groups or categories (for example, Negroes in America, mulattoes in Brazil, mestizoes in Mexico) are socially, not biologically, defined in all of our American societies; although the terms by which they are labeled may have originally referred to biological characteristics."[7] The guiding idea behind "social race," and thereby behind "raciated ethnicity," is that actual biological categories have little or nothing to do with the way social races are defined – by ancestry, appearance, or status – as biological races.

No particular social race exists because of any general feature of human nature, i.e., mulattoes do not exist because humans are nepotistic and inclined to favor familiars. Family histories, as "biologized" kinds, and self and other recognitions define social races.

Social races are like sets with ethnic groups as subsets. It is a cohesive group, irreducible to any particular individual member.[8] "White America," for example, includes a collection of ethnic groups.[9] "White" subsumes Irish, German, English, and French. Moreover, white allows non-ethnically specific persons to live and be perceived, whether or not they actively promote the rubric of whiteness, if they can establish or be perceived as having the requisite background and phenotype. If individuals can live as if there is no sub-Saharan ancestry in their family history in America, they can possibly count as white or some exotic ethnic.

Black is exorcised from the history of European ethnic groups the way that lynching was used to symbolically exorcise black from the morally defective white community – as if black is the defect.[10] Black functions as degenerative in a world of antiblack racism. That is why, among other reasons, one drop of black blood makes a person black and actual biological categories are irrelevant to defining social races. Whether one agrees with Etienne Balibar that nationalism is rooted in racist formations; whether one agrees with Michael Omi and Howard Winant that racial formations define the character of modern exploitation, biologized kinds are often, if not always, amorphously associated with how ethnicity is defined.[11]

The classical definition of ethnocentricism by William G. Sumner, the "view of things in which one's own group is the centre of everything and all others are scaled and rated with reference to it,"[12] remains paradigmatic of how ethnic groups are understood. At least common religion, language, and imagined or real place of group origin help define ethnic groups. There must be integrative social structures such as family structures, marriage patterns, stressed values, consumer habits, etc. which help dictate the ethnic group's cohesion over time. Like social races, ethnic group members feel pride and shame if harm befalls other members and they treat the lives of group members as morally more important than those of non-group members.

The marked difference between ethnic groups and races, for our purposes, is that the latter is always biologized as a categorical physical kind; membership is never voluntary, escape is never possible. Categorization without choice is imposed. Even if there are no integrative structures between blacks in America and blacks in Brazil, the world of racial identity is imposed, forced, and pressed upon them; experiences of discrimination are binding experiences even when integrative structures are absent.

Race can refer to a category of individuals without those individuals necessarily having integrative structures of family, business, religion, language, class or geographical ties. One way to understand this is by noting various explanations for discrimination. Marxist models usually consider racial discrimination to be a consequence of class conflict or at least a condition, the resolution of which requires the resolution of class conflicts.[13] Accounts from liberal traditions such as Gary Becker's *The Economics of Discrimination* or Lester Thurow's *Poverty and Discrimination*, explain racial discrimination in terms of interests, rational choice, and group behavior.[14] Thus, according to Thurow, white workers benefit from discrimination although perpetuating discrimination for competing investors is not beneficial.

One common feature of such accounts is the racial character of the economic unit under discussion. The black is not simply a worker, investor, or consumer – blacks exist independent of whether they act or live out their lives in any racial enclave. "Black" defines their being regardless of their life's station. Blacks function, in the analysis of such works, as a race. Personal structures such as strong or weak family ties or dedication to a particular geographic community are irrelevant to why blacks face discrimination. Internationally, a black community in Peru, for example, may have no relationships with any other black community and thus lack any integrative structures with other blacks. However, they fit in the category of "blacks" in the world and thereby fit any explanation of the relative position of all blacks in the world. The cultural properties that define black identity internationally are hardly biological race properties but social–cultural goods and features. Yet, blacks also function, depending on the existence of integrative structures, as an ethnic group.

It might be argued, against my view, that stereotyping, categorizing, and overgeneralizing are essential to human nature. Races, it might be held, are a direct consequence of such traits and are thereby natural entities – natural in the sense that race typing is a necessary feature of society which gives rise to fairly well-defined cohesive social units of racial groups. However, I contend, nothing about stereotyping, categorizing, and overgeneralizing can be said to cause the belief in the existence of races or the constitution of existing social races. These beliefs, and many more, may make it possible for race thinking to exist; they may equally make it possible for millions of other modes of thinking to exist. In addition, biological races are completely disjoined from socially defined races. In America, for example, one drop of Sub-Saharan African ancestry makes a person black.[15] Actual biologies have nothing to do with social race membership. The existence of racial differentiations are simply not somehow "there" because of the kind of species we happen to be, even if something like race is necessitated.

What, I suspect, Du Bois understood in "The Conservation of Races" and Alain Locke in "The Contribution of Race to Culture" is that social races lack properties important for the existence or flourishing of social life.[16] Dedication to familiars, development of productive forces, or the evolution of the species can all occur and continue without the inimical idea of race. The fact that social race categories are without properties important to social life does not mean that social races do not cause events, i.e., social races can be causal group agents, albeit, unwarranted. Races were not considered warranted agents by Du Bois or Locke, yet ethnic groups were considered warranted agents because ethnic groups have integrative structures and are not, like races, sheer fabrications and necessarily heinous forms of differentiation. Thus Locke and Du Bois use race to mean civilization, cultural traits, character type, spiritual inclinations, etc. Paradoxically, they also use race to refer to the experiences of persons with a certain phenotype. That is why Du Bois's "The Conservation of Races" and Alain Locke's "The Contribution of Race to Culture" are so curious – race as strictly biological is rejected, yet race as culture is considered a positive good. Du Bois and Locke are trapped by trying to use well-defined categories to account for a raciated ethnicity. It is the same trap that ensnarled Oliver Cox in *Caste, Class and Race*.

Du Bois and Locke found appealing the ethnic spirit, cultural expressivity, and the history of African civilizations encoded in the social reality of black life. Yet, the reality of racial identity had become a feature of black social life that was inescapable. The possibility of self-esteem as a cultured people was thus contingent, in a Faustian fashion, on the ascendancy of the race.

The cost of knowledge for Faust was death and eternal damnation; analogously, the cost of self-esteem for blacks is the death of race, as a good, and empowerment of the raciated. The perplexing demand of Alexander Crummell, the Cambridge educated Platonist and promoter of African American migration to Africa, for an African civilization even at the cost of black exploitation of blacks, or the Student Non-Violent Coordinating Committee's perplexing demand for Black Power as separate power in America *and* equal rights regardless of race are perplexing because they demand the empowerment of the race while simultaneously demanding the negation of the race as a condition of its being. Black Power, in its best formation, is the empowerment of black people that would allow the control, ownership, and transgenerational transfer of wealth by black people. A free and empowered black people in America, with sufficient separate power to protect themselves from malicious whites, would thus allow blacks to live according to their wills; not as tokens of a type, but as persons empowered to live a wide range of life types. The moral worth of black lives would thus count whether the system were an African socialist one or a reformed benevolent capitalist American system. The moral worth of black lives, however, would be ironically contingent on the end of black identity as a stereotypical type and simultaneously the empowerment of black people as a people whether or not they had integrative structures.

The economic interest shared by those exploited by social race, exploited by virtue of sharing a certain phenotype, includes an interest in the negation of their racial being as objects of property and exclusion. Those exploited by race want to escape raciation as a condition of their being. The interest of a race, I have argued elsewhere, is absolute negation.[17] There is nothing redeeming about being a member of a despised race; nothing redeeming about being a token of any racial type. Redemption is in overcoming being despised; pride can be reasonably held in the value of the despised progressive culture, ethnic group accomplishments, and empowerment of the previously abject. Successfully accomplishing the negation of race, and thereby affirming one's humanity, is arguably a good in itself, but perpetuating racial identification as a good in itself is not. There is nothing to redeem from having been identified as a race, other than one's humanity as not being a token of a race.

One way to see this is by considering the following question: How is it possible for a people to be cohesive when a central feature of the definition of that people is an object of their own active negation? That is, how is it possible for black people to function as a cohesive group when the idea of race is a definitive feature of black identity and yet that feature is actively argued against as a relevant feature of a person's being? Fanon noted that black identity exists in relationship to white identity. Independent of the idea of race as a marker, the idea of there being black and white people is empty. Thus while entities with enriching integrative structures arguably have living interests, social races cannot be shown to have such interests.

If race is the intended unit, that is, if race is the unit of which the author understands the object to be analyzed, then concerns relevant to biologically conjoined groups are relevant. The social Darwinist contention, for example, that racial groups are competing for scarce resources is at least plausible. Racial groups would be constantly created, redefined, and evolving. The continual redefinition of such groups, and the addition or extinction of raciated groups, is to be expected. Nepotistic behavior exists and functions on a social Darwinist level to help maximize a race's chances for survival; however, if races as biological kinds do not exist, then nepotistic behavior exists and functions to maximize the survival chances of familiars, but not because people are categorized into races.

This is why M. F. Ashley Montagu's argument against the idea of race as a scientific or biological category is so compelling: what entities and how and why they are created, redefined, or evolve is not explained by biological race. Races, as biological kinds matching social kinds, do not exist and therefore cannot cause social behavior. Without race as an explanadum, social Darwinist explanations become implausible. However, the obvious – social race nepotism – had to be explained even by Montagu in some fashion other than race as any sort of entity. Montagu's *Man's Most Dangerous Myth* depicted black Americans as an ethnic group. Having decentered biological race, and knowing that social race as a construction in no way represents causal properties endemic to social life, Montagu, like many other scholars, decided that blacks were an ethnic group. This allowed social race nepotism to be understood as aberrant behavior because races lack any biological or structural social basis. The glaring reality of social race is simply dissipated on such an approach. The interests of those exploited by race have also curiously dissipated. These unacceptable anomalies occur if we fail to see that blacks are a raciated ethnicity – the dichotomy between race and ethnicity is simply untenable – yet it makes sense not to erase the reality of race and ethnicity as operative variables in explanations.

Richard F. America's *The Wealth of Races* considered the history of maldistribution between races and across generations and thereby established the existence of American racism.[18] Yet, racial groups as biological kinds do not have coherent histories, transgenerationally transferred wealth, or bonds requiring the exclusion of others because race cannot count as a cause. We can, however, analyze transgenerationally transferred wealth of social races *even when the transfers were not intended for racial reasons, even if a social race is not an entity that embodies causal properties essential to their natures, traits necessary for flourishing, and even if it exists without integrative structures.* That is why St. Clair Drake's two volume *Black Folks* and Martin Bernal's *Black Athena* are so compelling – most of the history of racial formation had little to do with maniacal intentions or established integrative social and economic structures.[19] That is also why Robert W. July's classic, *A History of the African People,* can almost never mention race and constitute an excellent history of Africa.[20] It does not matter, even if V. Y. Mudimbe is right in the *Invention of Africa,* that African identity is, like European identity, a construction of eighteenth and nineteenth century anthropology, because the reality of Africa's rape by European colonists remains the most important external incursion in Africa – as a new social construction that now has real material internal links and a real world position.[21]

The "black" exists as a function of all Africans counting as "black" by Irish, German, French, Spanish, etc. who count themselves as "white". No intellectual deconstruction replaces the real existence of who lives, who dies, and who suffers as a function of their raciated ethnicity.

The first American census in 1787 used white male, white female, Indian, slave, and all others. Coloured and free coloured were added in 1830; Negro, mulatto, and quadroon used in 1890, Jews and Bantus have never been racial census categories, Hindus were once a racial category and Chinese and Aleut were once ethnic categories, now dropped. The only stable category since the founding of America has been "white male, white female." The only socially constituted race formally treated as an undiluted, uncorrupted, and unalterable natural social entity in America has been "white" – America proceeds as if "white" is a biological race, and all other races are aberrations, defective, polluted, and subject to the travels of evolution – "white" remains uniform. Racial reasoning erroneously puts together socially constructed categories with categories substantively important to social life.[22] The perpetuation of "white", as a completely, socially fabricated array of identities used to legitimate the super-exploitation and social alienation of blacks, is in no way a natural distinction. Who counts as "white" is not only contested territory, but it does not embody any traits endemic to human nature any more than the Hindu, Jew, Alor, Tiopia, Cheyenne, Bedouin, Lapp, Gypsy, and Australian Aborigine embody racial or ethnic natures.

Stephen Steinberg, in *The Ethnic Myth*, persuasively argued that the idea of cultural pluralism, particularly its praise of ethnic diversity and valorization of ethnic group economic success, "has its origins in conquest, slavery, and exploitation of foreign labor."[23] Racial distance was romanticized and surreptitiously legitimated by cultural pluralism. Ethnic groups have failed to be economically successful, according to Steinberg, and cultural pluralism simply functions to legitimate racist and ethnocentric exclusions.

Contrary to the idea that ethnics fail to be successful, Joel Kotkin in *Tribes* argues that some ethnic "global tribes are today's quintessential cosmopolitans." They are, for Kotkin, the most successful tribes, and define a good deal of the material reality for all others.[24] The most successful global tribes for Kotkin are British, Chinese, Japanese, Jews and Indians. Other global tribes are also important, for example, the Italians, Dutch, Portuguese, Spanish and Germans and more recently, Armenians, Palestinians, Greeks, Ibos, Cubans, and Koreans. Racial unity may be a feature of the mythology enlivening different groups for Kotkin, but it is hardly substantive. "The great revolutionary leader Sun Yat-sen might have sought to define the Chinese as a 'single race with common blood,' but in reality this is no more true for them than for the English, the Jews, or the Japanese; their diversity of racial ancestry can be seen in how Chinese differ markedly from region to region in height, color and bone structure."[25] Kotkin considers such traits as a belief in a common origin, integrative family structures, geographic dispersion, the practice of subterfuge, control over particular markets, and a strong belief in scientific progress as crucial determinants of success.

Whether or not Steinberg or Kotkin are right in their judgments of ethnic group success, what is important here is that it is the ethnicity of their reality which functions as the entity under explanation; race is its trope. Conversely, race can be a reality under analysis and ethnicity can function as a trope.

In the best of all possible worlds, it is arguable that ethnic groups as open, cooperative, and culturally fluid entities should exist. It is not arguable that social races should exist.

APORIA: EXPLAINING BLACK AND WHITE INCOMES

The miseries that black people suffer across lines of class, gender, and geography in America help make the "Black" in "Black Economics" meaningful as an entity. The differences in net worth, ownership, poverty rates, gender differences in opportunities, and rates of income and asset growth define the contours of black life, even if the "what" is not neatly answered except as a function of racial identity markers in government and research reports. The measurable differences and miseries explored in Jeremiah Cotton's "Towards a Theory and Strategy for Black Economic Development," Julianne Malveaux's "The Political Economy of Black Women," and Jennifer L. Hochschild's "Race, Class, Power, and Equal Opportunity," depict the position of blacks relative to whites.[26] It is reasonable on these accounts to assume a fairly common income between blacks and whites, failing discriminatory influences. That is, the best explanation for differences, in the absence of contrary evidence, is to assume the existence of discrimination when all other variables are identical. If members of the black middle class, for example, are in every relevant way identical to their white counterparts – even without personal reports of discrimination – the best explanation for income differences is to assume the influence of discrimination.[27] However, as an ethnic group, this background assumption is of weaker merit. As an ethnic group, maintaining segregated geographic communities, effective control over inheritances to ascending generations, links to an original homeland in the form of providing business and employment opportunities, and adaptability to adversity by the ethnic culture become very important variables in assessing why differences exist. For ethnic groups, these variables are never identical. Consequently, an assumption of discrimination as a cause of differences cannot be readily made when blacks are compared to other ethnic groups.

Conservatives such as Thomas Sowell are fond of comparing how well European ethnic groups have performed in America and how poorly blacks have performed.[28] According to conservative accounts, discrimination cannot be the cause so often considered the reason for black income differences because there are hundreds of other ethnic groups that have done well regardless of the veracity of discrimination. It must be, or so the conservative culture of poverty explanation goes, the intrinsically immoral and invirtuous character of the black, or the black's pathetic culture, or the black's knowledge of how to avoid work during slavery carried forward in some amorphous consciousness, or misguided leaders etc., that cause income differences. Conservatives may be right in contending that discrimination cannot carry the weight for explaining differences. However, one reason that such comparisons are notoriously misguided is that spillover benefits from foreign links must be surreptitiously discounted as important and racial discrimination surreptitiously excluded. The "what" of the entity shifts in such comparisons from being a social race, the specificities of which are defined by the social context of America to an ethnicity, the specificities of which are defined by world positions. Even if an assumption of discrimination is not warranted, and the conservatives are right on this issue, it does not follow that equally egregious forms of exclusion such as nationalism or colonialism are not causal variables.

Imagine that an explanation provides sufficient reason to believe that white workers in a Pennsylvania coal mine have higher incomes than black coal mine workers and white workers are often racists because racism provides them with relative economic advantage and a sense of honor, although their racism in general is disadvantageous. If the explanation for why the Pennsylvania white coal miners are racist excludes variables related to the relationship of the whites to lands of real or imagined origin, the explanation would lack an important variable. The advantages that white Americans have over black Americans because of their trading relationships with citizens of various European countries – relationships that exclude almost all blacks if for no other reason than that they are not family members – are important variables. The "spillover" benefits of biologized family links with Africa are not enjoyed by black Americans because Africa is itself a site of super exploitation. The relative positions of blacks and what blacks are as a people is thus integrally linked.

Economic explanations intended to account for the difference between blacks and whites have also had the burden of providing suggested solutions, presumably implied by the explanation. That is, explanations are often assumed to provide a basis for solutions. Abram L. Harris' critique of "buy Black" programs, for example, reflects his deep understanding of the relationship of explanation and solutions as explored by Darity.[29] Even if blacks were impoverished in America because of white selfishness, for example, the solution was not one requiring blacks to only buy from blacks, even if the solution does require greater black internal cooperation. In a similar way, ethnic groups can arguably form nation states, but, even if Balibar is right and all forms of nationalism and ethnocentricity are grounded on conceptions of racial purity, it does not follow that racial groups have the same potential to form separate enclaves or nation states.[30]

Explanations of black impoverishment and differential standing as a race, if followed by ethnic solutions, bespeak the problem of explaining a raciated ethnic group. Imagine that labor market discrimination is the major cause of not only income differences but all other major economic differences (assets, ownership, rates of growth, etc.). It does not follow that ending labor market discrimination will significantly impact economic standing. What if black control of crucial industries such as plastics, trucking, gold production, or government securities would have more impact on equalizing incomes in other non-black controlled industries than doing anything about labor market discrimination? If so, this would not follow from an analysis that established labor market discrimination caused income differences. Labor market discrimination might even persist with greater force, but no longer have dominant influence over incomes if blacks had strategic control over key industries. If labor market discrimination is the cause of income disparities, solutions to reduce income disparities may have nothing to do with ending labor market discrimination. Drawing solutions from explanations in this way without further arguments is erroneous whether offered by conservatives, liberals, or radicals.

APORIA: EXPLANATIONS AND SOLUTIONS

The relationship between an explanation of black and white income differences and solutions drawn from such explanations returns us to considering the status of the "what". One way to see why the solutions we draw from explanations heavily depend on whether the "what" we have explained is considered an unnecessary social construction, such as a social race, God ordained communities, or a naturally evolving group is by considering the role cohesive social entities play in several intellectual traditions.

Classical economists such as Adam Smith, David Ricardo, and Thomas R. Malthus believed objective reality consisted of natural social entities. *The Wealth of Nations, The Principles of Political Economy and Taxation* and *An Essay on the Principle of Population*, for example, make little sense unless we take nations, investors, and classes to represent cohesive social entities, some of which represent natural groups, i.e., the "what's" are "there" because of some feature of our human nature which gives rise to them. The explanation of such entities used, among other things, general traits of human anthropology, psychology, and biology as embodied in one way or another in social entities. "Up until the 1930's the dominant view of theory appraisal in economics was that economics proceeds by deducing the consequences of well-established generalizations about human behavior and technology when these are conjoined with premises concerning specific circumstances."[31] Explanations, as Hausman aptly notes, hardly need to be matched with generalized human behavior to be appraised as meaningful. Nonetheless, solutions are drawn from, or are correlative to, explanations by reference to the character of the "what" sort of social entity has been explained.

In the similar intellectual stream as classical economists, Oliver Cox, Abram L. Harris, Phyllis Wallace, Max Weber, Karl Marx, John Stuart Mill, and W. E. B. Du Bois share an important idea: social entities can be adequately explained by scientific laws, rules, and methods without recourse to providential design or teleologies. Marx provides a convenient example.

Classes embody real properties of human nature for Marx.[32] Classes embody the methods by which labor transforms nature. The working class, for Marx, has the potential of embodying human nature in its most unalienated form. If Marx is right and humans are naturally workers and transformers of nature, the solution to class conflict will at least include the negation of alienation and the establishment of a classless society. If

146

classes cause racial conflict and alienation, the negation of the existence of classes conceivably solves the problem – not simply, if at all, because the cause of misery has been removed – but because the entity as such is unnecessary, morally odious, disadvantageous and dysfunctional.

G. W. F. Hegel, Werner Sombart, Herbert Spencer, and Alexander Crummell share at least one important idea relevant to my argument: they believed that races were natural entities which embodied causal properties and behaved according to a providential design. Social entities are caused, on their accounts, to exist and behave in certain ways because of God's design. Social entities are explainable if we understand God's design, i.e., providence defined the "what" and determined its ultimate behavior. Hegel, for example, considered nations, normally coterminous with races, as the embodiment of modes of consciousness invested in the Absolute Spirit; ethnic groups embodied a people's spirit in Werner Sombart's latter works; and species as well as races were the original issue of the ultimate unknowable for Herbert Spencer, the famed social Darwinist, although for Spencer the explanation of such entities should rely on scientific investigation of evolution.

Alexander Crummell joined providential and evolutionary explanations.[33] Nepotistic behavior, for Crummell, enhances the ability of a species to reproduce itself more than does random or extrinsic cooperation. Nepotistic behavior, however, can be dysfunctional for any given species if variability is too restrictive. Nepotistic behavior in such cases would be dysfunctional in relationship to the natural inclination for a group to survive through procreation. Evolutionary progress tends to be irreversible, cumulative, and gradual. Revolutions are at best stellar moments of transition in processes of gradual adjustment to exigencies faced by evolving groups. Social groups are expected by Crummell to substantively change – become more endogamous, disappear, or mutate.

Crummell explained the endurance of races by depicting their character, mission, and historical circumstances – all ultimately in accord with providence. The African race, according to Crummell, has a common interest, forced on it by slavery, and a common mission, bequeathed by a racial being. For Crummell, Africans were enslaved not primarily because of racial antipathy, but because they were incapable of stopping the rapacious pursuit of profit by foreign civilizations. For Crummell, it is in the material interest of whites to keep blacks enslaved, or close to it, thereby making freedom for blacks impossible in America.

Moreover, for Crummell there is a compelling mission to Christianize Africa, which the black in the Americas is best suited to accomplish. Why the African race had endured, and will be able to endure in the future, is explained not only by its history but by its useful nepotism, e.g., the race has primarily avoided, and should in the future avoid, having its spirit corrupted by cross-racial breeding. The ideal for Crummell was a coterminous match between the biology of the race and its social standing, an ideal of which evolution was so inclined, given transitional phases of interracial procreation. Crummell explained the endurance of Africans by describing how races performed their assigned roles in God's design for human development. A renewed and modern African civilization which appropriately embodied the race spirit therefore offers for Crummell the solution to income differences and other disparities between civilizations.

Booker T. Washington, as Vernon Williams aptly portrays, considered the African heritage bankrupt. God, for Washington, had different plans for the race spirit of blacks than the one imagined by Crummell. The potential for racial uplift in America was possible for Washington. The possibility of racial endurance was conditioned in important ways for Washington by adjustment to the Americas. Washington considered slavery, as unfortunate as it was, a "school" preparing the race for a potentially bright future. The race is, for Washington and Crummell, an entity subject to external influence in conjunction with its internal path of constant reformation and adjustment; although the teleology and therefore solution to racial disparities differed between Washington and Crummell because of different judgments about the status and mission of the race.

Consider the import of the following: if race discrimination is in the interest of workers but stymies economic growth, is its solution in changing how workers gain job security? If God and evolution ordained race spirits to be embodied in nations, is the solution to racial dissatisfactions the successful establishment of such nations? Elites, ethnic groups, and nations embody a variety of interests for Max Weber; not explained by divine ordinance but by human nature, history, and circumstance. Whether nations, investors, institutions, classes or elites turn out to embody these propensities in one form or another is less central to the point here, namely, that something crucial about solutions is contingent on how entities are defined. Defining nations, investors, institutions, classes or elites as embodying properties important to social life is pivotal in explanations and what sort of solutions are reasonably drawn from explanations. Causal agents which are social constructions, if considered unnecessary because not God ordained or God condemned, non-natural, dysfunctional, morally odious or otherwise disadvantageous, are likely candidates for a recommendation of negation.

Unlike a God ordained race spirit, alienated worker, or self-interested groups of investors and employees, raciated ethnic groups simply are not things with neat integrative structures. The "what" is inherently ambiguous.

APORIA: INJUSTICE AGAINST SOCIAL CONSTRUCTIONS PAYS

Boxill is right – injustice pays.[34] Martha C. Nussbaum is right in *The Fragility of Goodness* – accident and luck exit and goodness is fragile even if it is earnestly sought. Sissela Bok in *Lying* is right, lying, or at least withholding vital information in order to gain an advantage, can be very profitable.[35] The practice of subterfuge is as least as important in controlling markets as it is in controlling personal relations. The undeserving may gain and the innocent may suffer, thereby allowing injustice to pay – not only for the agents of injustice, but for those who inherit ill-gotten wealth through transgenerational transfers.

Darwin, Malthus, Marx, and Crummell share an important similarity – they provide interesting accounts for why slavery, misery, starvation, war, barbarity, cruelty, and domination have functioned in various ways to create democracy and development. It does little good to argue that rape, child abuse, or torture are morally unjust; nor does it do much good to argue that human development could have existed or can exist without such atrocities. Assuming that only unreasonable individuals find these pleasurable, reasonable individuals are hardly the engine of experience – on almost any account of reasonableness, the history of humanity is not the history of individuals believing or acting as reasonable agents.

Absolute fabrications and completely imagined entities with no substance have functioned exceedingly well in human history. Licentious women, the Oriental threat, or homosexual devils, have been used to justify tremendous horrors on people imaged to be tokens of these types; embodied representatives of a defective, impure, and corrupting social kind. The oppression of people, categorized as natural entities, when the categories are in no way a natural entity, pays.

Have black Americans considered another race sufficiently degenerate, barbaric, and inferior to egregiously exploit? Where is the black hero who killed large numbers of whites while they were praying; where is the black hero who embezzled from white people, remained free, and passed the wealth onto the next generation? What black capitalists have had a sufficient network of trusting lenders, technical employees, dedicated accountants, slave traders, and social honors to pursue colonial activities? What blacks have married and confiscated the wealth of a family and then left, like Frenchmen leaving their Polynesian families after collecting bags of precious pearls? One possible reason blacks have not enjoyed the advantages of holding the inheritances of ill-begotten wealth nearly as much as whites is because "blacks" have not formed a "people" the way the Yoruba, Anglo-British, or Welsh constitute a people nor sufficiently formed the link between a race and a nation, where a race forms the subtle archetypal symbol of a nation, e.g., the German Aryan, British Anglos, Japanese Yamamoto descendants, French Gauls, Israel as Jewish, or American as caucasian. There are certainly individuals, small groups, bourgeoisie of new national formations, and African tribal groups that are, or function as, maniacal agents. The point is that none functions with a black identity as its racial archetypal being. Economically effective ethnic enclaves hardly require territorial cohesion or even self employment of the ethnic kind.[36] They do, however, require a good deal of internal trust and consciousness of imagined ethnic kind.

A Spanish galleon, the *San Diego,* sank in 1600. It contained over 3,000 pieces of blue and white Ming Dynasty china, Philippine pottery, Japanese swords, Spanish cannons and muskets, astrolabes, Spanish silver coins, hazel nuts, and bones of wild pig and cows. It may be some arrangement of assets, imperial motivations, and systems of legitimation for domination which drive forces behind the relentless march of disjointed human societies toward civilization. If so, aberrant behavior is not to be explained away as transient effects from the wayward movement of a few misguided souls.

What if blacks are trapped in what I shall term a Calvinist dilemma, namely, that no matter whether they focus on self help schemes (for example, the sort recommended by Booker T. Washington, Thomas Sowell, or Alexander Crummell) or whether they focus on structural changes (for example, the sort recommended by Oliver Cox, Abram Harris or William J. Wilson) it turns out that they are still *Faces at the Bottom of the Well*?[37] Calvinists believed that no matter what behavior, beliefs, or practices a person followed, it was always possible for an omnipotent, omnipresent and omniscient God to justly condemn them to eternal damnation. Consequently, righteous or sinful beliefs and actions could, from a consequentialist standpoint, net the same result. Moreover, Calvinists, as a group, are subject to collective damnation, even if they have the right religion.

In a chronically racist society, every institution and every arrangement of networks is arraigned against the oppressed. If honor, for example, demands that the dominant group is treated as worthy, even if any particular member or group of the despised gains in status – like rich eunuchs or mulatto mistresses in rich households – it is still not possible for them to overcome being degraded as a token of a despised group.[38] Eunuchs and mistresses, no matter how rich, were always subject to degradation by the poorest Brahman and mulatto mistresses; even if they were the mistress of an American President, they were always subject to degradation by members of the honored group. Individual members of generally dishonored groups, of course, have good reason to be free riders. If an individual from such groups can gain by betraying the group, that individual can be said to have acted as reasonably as someone with an altruistic attachment to the group (as if they were its total instantiation) or someone with an ideal of progress of which they are its representative. It is ridiculous for a group to seek the kingdom of heaven when so doing, in terms of the consequences, leaves them as likely to be eternally condemned to hell as raised to heaven – unless they hold some belief in the intrinsic goodness of the "seeking" process or associated beliefs and practices, i.e., unless they are Calvinist.

There is no solution to the Calvinist dilemma. However, the dilemma does not exist, if its terms are rejected.

What if there is only the earthly kingdom, the one where injustice pays, social constructions are active agents destroying native Americans and inhabiting the land, atheist socialist revolutionaries defeat Christian feudalist/capitalists in various sundry countries before they became autocratic oppressors, and theoretical abstractions explain?[39]

What if race and ethnicity are theoretically polluting tropes, infesting and bifurcating well defined cohesive social entities, making explanations, predictions, and solutions based on the use of such entities defective?

What if explaining why racialism is unnecessary for human flourishing, why it is dysfunctional, morally odious or otherwise disadvantageous, by showing that income differences exist because of prejudices which rely on the belief in the existence of distinct racial types, nonetheless do not yield workable solutions?

What if slavery, colonialism, and class exploitation are "schooling" locations in an evolutionary movement toward an uncertain future – and "this" is that bestial future – then the schooling can be said to continue, dressed in the structural clothes of the underclass, the under-developed nation state, the tribalism romanticized by postmodern intellectuals living comfortably in France, and the underemployed service worker living on the fringes of modernity. If schooling is going to end, then the terms which sustain the dilemma and the solutions used to create transgenerationally transferred wealth, may need to be refigured.

No one likes Faustian predicaments: trying to explain race – as that which is unnecessary – while also trying to explain in a way that allows one to draw out a solution for the uplift of the race as a cultured people – may be simply too much to expect from an explanation. (Theoretical abstractions which are social constructions, unnecessary social groupings, dysfunctional collectives, disadvantageous categories, and morally odious distinctions may explain when the use of well-defined cohesive social entities fails – even if no neat solutions conveniently follow.)

PROLEGOMENON INTO RACE AND ECONOMICS

Explanations for why there are income and asset differences between blacks and whites in America are bedeviled by a lacuna: If blacks and whites are understood as a race, then explanatory causes, variables, and solutions relevant to race fail to capture ethnic features; if blacks and whites are understood as ethnics, then explanatory causes, variables, and solutions relevant to ethnics fail to capture racial features. It is not that raciated ethnic groups are hard to explain; it is that they cannot be adequately explained if the explanation is strictly contingent on the use of a strict dichotomy between race and ethnicity. As raciated ethnics, drawing solutions from explanations is complicated by the ambiguous character of the "what". It does not follow, however, that a solution to the problem of income differences is invariably illusive. The solution, however, cannot be a function of a causal explanatory account in which well defined cohesive social entities dominate as variables. That is why this is a prolegomenon into race and economics.

No one likes entrapment in Calvinist dilemmas, peppered with Faustian choices and predicaments.

With the help of our explanations but without assuming that they provide neat deductively certain guidance, we must confront what Du Bois perceived well as the most important problem bedeviling our world – the color line.

NOTES

1 Cox, Oliver, *Caste, Class, and Race*, New York: Doubleday, 1948. Also see Vernon Williams, *From a Caste to a Minority*: New York: Greenwood Press, 1989.

2 Hacker, Andrew, *Two Nations*, New York: Scribner, 1992. Also see Vernon Williams, *From a Caste to a Minority*.

3 Singer, Marcus, "Ethnogenesis and Negro-Americans Today," *Social Research*, 29: 4, Winter 1962, p. 419.

4 Lott, Tommy, "Du Bois on the Invention of Race," *The Philosophical Forum*, XXIV: 1–3, Fall–Spring, 1992–3, p. 176.

5 Two fairly recent discussions give some hint to the extensive literature on this topic: Bill E. Lawson, "Individuals and Groups in the American Democracy: Group interest and Civil Rights," *Logos*, 6: 1985, pp. 73–115. Doris Y. Wilkinson and Gary King, "Conceptual and Methodological Issues in the Use of Race as a Variable: Policy Implications," *The Milbank Quarterly*, 65: 1, 1987, pp. 546–71.

6 See James B. Stewart, "George Edmund Hayes and the Office of Negro Economics," Chapter 12, this volume.

7 Wagley, Charles, "On the Concept of Social Race in the Americas," in *Contemporary Cultures and Societies of Latin America*, Dwight B. Health and Richard N. Adams (eds), New York: Random House, p. 531.

8 See for a discussion of the ontological status of social entities, a matter of great importance to my argument, such works as David-Hillen Ruben, "The Existence of Social Entities," *Philosophical Quarterly*, 34: 129 (October 1982) 295–310; Anthony Quinton, "Social Objects," *Aristotelian Society*, 76, 1975–6, pp. 1–27.

   See also J. L. Thompson, "What is the Problem Concerning Social Entities," *International Journal of Moral and Social Studies*, 6: 14, 1991, pp. 77–90.

9 Fredrickson, George M., *The Black Image in the White Mind*, New York: Harper and Row, 1971.

10 See Trudier Harris, *Exorcising Blackness*, Bloomington: Indiana University Press, 1984.

11 See Etienne Balibar, Immanuel Wallerstein, *Race, Nation, Classe*, Paris: La Decouverte, 1988.

   See also Michael Omi, Howard Winant, *Racial Formation in the United States*, New York: Routledge & Kegan Paul, 1986.

12 Sumner, William G., *Folkways*, Boston: Ginn, 1906, p. 13. Also see William Petersen, Michael Novak, Philip Gleason, *Concepts of Ethnicity*, Cambridge, MA.: The Belknap Press of Harvard University, 1982.

13 Mason, Patrick L., "Some Heterodox Models of Inequality in the Market for Labor Power," Chapter 16, Volume 2 of this work. Also see Jo Freeman, "The Tyranny of Structurelessness," *Berkeley Journal of Sociology*, XVII, 1972–3, 118–49.

14 Becker, Gary, *The Economics of Discrimination*, Chicago: University of Chicago Press, 1957. Lester Thurow, *Poverty and Discrimination*, Washington, DC: Brookings Institute Press, 1969.

15 See James F. Davis, *Who is Black*, Pennsylvania: Pennsylvania State University Press, 1991.

16 See Alain Locke, "The Contribution of Race to Culture," in Leonard Harris, *The Philosophy of Alain Locke*, Philadelphia: Temple University Press, 1989, pp. 201–6; W. E. B. Du Bois, "The Conservation of 'Races'" in Howard Brotz (ed.), *Negro Social and Political Thought, 1850–1920*, New York: Basic Books, 1966.

17 See Leonard Harris, "Postmodernism and Racism: An Unholy Alliance," in Michael Cross (ed.), *Racism, the City and the State*, London: Hans Zell Pub. Co., 1992. "The Horror of Tradition or How to Burn Babylon and Build Benin While Reading *A Preface to a Twenty Volume Suicide Note*," *Philosophical Forum*, XXIV: 1–3 (Fall–Spring 1992–3) 94–119. "Historical Subjects and Interests: Race, Class, and Conflict," Michael Sprinkler *et al.* (eds), *The Year Left*, New York: Verso, 1986, pp. 75–106.

18 America, Richard F., *The Wealth of Races*, New York: Greenwood Press, 1990.

19 Drake, St. Clair, *Black Folks*, Los Angeles: Center for Afro-American Studies, 1987; Bernal, Martin, *Black Athena*, New Jersey: Rutgers University Press, 1987.

20 See Robert W. July, *A History of the African People*, New York: Scribner, 1970.

21 Mudimbe, V. Y., *The Invention of Africa*, Bloomington: Indiana University Press, 1988.

22 See David T. Goldberg, *Racist Culture*, Cambridge, MA: Blackwell, 1993; Cornel West, *Race Matters*, Boston, MA: Beacon Press, 1993.

23 Steinberg, Stephen, *The Ethnic Myth*, Boston, MA: Beacon Press, 1981, p. 6.

24 See Joel Kotkin, *Tribes*, New York: Random House, 1992.

25 ibid., p. 174.

26 Cotton, Jeremiah, "Towards a Theory and Strategy for Black Economic Development," in James Jennings, *Race, Politics, and Economic Development*, New York: Verso, 1992, pp. 11–32; Julianne Malveaux, "The Political Economy of Black Women," in James Jennings, *Race, Politics, and Economic Development*, New York: Verso, 1992, pp. 33–52; Jennifer L. Hochschild, "Race, Class, Power, and Equal Opportunity," in *Equal Opportunity*, Norman Bowie (ed.), Westview, CO: Westview Press, 1988, pp. 75–111.

27 See Ellis Cose, *Rage of the Privileged Class*, New York: Harpers, Collings, 1993.

28 See Thomas Sowell, *Race and Economics*, New York: D. McKay Company, 1975.

29 See Abram L. Harris, *Race, Radicalism, and Reform*, William Darity, Jr. (ed.), New Brunswick, NJ: Transaction Publishers, 1989.

30 See Balibar, Wallerstein, *Race, Nation, and Class*.

31 Hausman, Daniel M., *Essays on Philosophy and Economic Methodology*, New York: Cambridge University Press, 1992, p. 3. Hausman focuses on the methodological strengths of Mill's philosophy of economics. Certainly, Mill can be understood for both his contributions to the science of economics as well as his more cosmological or metaphysical views. Samuel Hollander, *The Economics of John Stuart Mill*, vol. I, II, London: Blackwell, 1985.

32 See for example Allen W. Wood, "Marx's Critical Anthropology: Three Recent Interpretations," *The Review of Metaphysics*, XXVI: 1, September 1972, 118–39.

33 See for examples of these concerns Wilson Moses, *The Golden Age of Black Nationalism, 1880–1915*, New York: Oxford University Press, 1978. See the

problem emigration creates for Booker T. Washington in Vernon J. Williams, Jr., "Booker T. Washington: Myth Maker," Chapter 11, this volume.

34 See Bernard Boxill, "How Injustice Pays," *Philosophy & Public Affairs*, 9:4 (Summer 1980) 359–71.

35 See Martha Nussbaum, *The fragility of goodness*, Cambridge: Cambridge University Press, 1986. Sissela Bok, *Lying*, New York: Pantheon Books, 1978.

36 I. Light, G. Sabagh, M. Bozorgmehr, and C. Der-Martirosian, "Beyond the Ethnic Enclave Economy," *Social Problems*, 41:1, February 1994, 65–80.

37 See Derrick Bell, *Faces at the Bottom of the Well*, New York: Basic Books, 1992.

38 See for the issue of honor, Holy, Ladislav, *Kinship, Honour and Solidarity*, Manchester: Manchester University Press, 1989; Bertram Wyatt-Brown, *Southern Honor: Ethics and Behavior in the Old South*, Oxford: London, 1982. Honor was an important variable shaping the cohesion of southerners and later, the regard of northerners against blacks who fought with the north. Also see Pitt-Rivers, Julian, *Mediterranean Countrymen*, p. 80. Also see J. Pitt-Rivers and J. G. Peristiany, *Honor and Grace in Anthropology*, Cambridge: Cambridge University Press, 1992.

39 See Pierre Bourdieu, "What Makes a Social Class? On the Theoretical and Practical Existence of Groups," *Berkeley Journal of Sociology*, XXXII, 1987, pp. 1–18 for a discussion of classes as theoretical abstractions representing potential groups rather than actual groups. Also see Bracken, H., "Essence, Accident and Race," *Hermathena*, 116 (1973) 91–6; Harris, L., "Historical Subjects and Interests: Race, Class, and Conflict," Michael Sprinkler *et al.* (eds), *The Year Left*, New York: Verso, 1986, pp. 91–106.

Part II

THE ECONOMIC PHILOSOPHERS AND THEIR VISION

9

BOOKER T. WASHINGTON AND THE POLITICAL ECONOMY OF BLACK EDUCATION IN THE UNITED STATES, 1880–1915

Manning Marable

Booker T. Washington was the most influential black American educator in the early twentieth century. Born as a slave in 1856, he attended Hampton Institute, an industrial and agricultural school for blacks and American Indians. At the age of twenty-five, in 1881, he was appointed Principal of Tuskegee Institute, an industrial school which had recently been created by the Alabama state legislature. Washington developed a comprehensive economic and social program for black development within the capitalist system during the period 1880–1915. His achievements, and those of black educators who accepted his ideas, were substantial. Black schools were largely successful in improving literacy, health standards, and in promoting black land tenure and capital formation. The limitations and problems inherent within Washington's political strategy, however, helped to establish a rigid system of racial inequality and segregation – termed "Jim Crow" – across the US South. Many contemporary social dilemmas confronting black American universities and educators are rooted in the conceptual and programmatic contradictions of Washington's educational and economic paradigms.

The social forces which produced Booker T. Washington and an entire generation of conservative black educators were the result of the American Civil War and the collapse of the Reconstruction period (1865–77), which extended the electoral franchise to black males and abolished slavery. During Reconstruction, the newly freed black laborers articulated two political demands above all others – the right to universal education, including the creation of black colleges and vocational institutes, and 'the acquisition of the land they had tilled and developed and learned to think of as their own.'[1] These central concerns were closely linked: capital accumulation and a higher standard of living in a rural society was not possible without land tenure, and an educated black community could develop its own resources for credit and to finance economic and social institutions.

The black college, as Benjamin E. Mays, former President of Morehouse College, has written, was the social product of an "era of change."[2] Only twenty-eight Afro-Americans graduated with baccalaureate degrees from white colleges before 1860.[3] As the "social forces" which "precipitated the Civil War" emerged, as Mays noted, Lincoln University in Pennsylvania was founded in 1854.[4] Seventeen black colleges were established between 1854 and 1890, including Morehouse College, Howard University, Hampton Institute, Atlanta University, and Tuskegee Institute. Most were private teachers' training schools or focused primarily on industrial and agricultural education. The growth of black institutions was retarded by the US government's decision to exclude blacks from funding under the Morrill Act of 1862, which created land-grant colleges with direct Federal subsidies. In the 1890s, however, this policy was reversed, and a second group of state-supported but racially segregated institutions was created in most southern states. It is frequently and conveniently forgotten today that millions of white southerners vehemently opposed the creation of higher educational institutions for blacks, even behind the barriers of Jim Crow. Daniel C. Thompson notes:

> almost everything was done to discourage the founding of Black schools. State legislatures and local school boards tended to ignore Blacks' efforts to establish schools. The white masses often took drastic steps to squash the school movement sponsored by the Federal government, missionary groups, and a few private philanthropists; teachers were beaten, schools were burned, the Black students and their parents were frequently intimidated.[5]

Such opposition was usually expressed in explicitly racist terms, yet at its core was the white South's determination to suppress the entire labor force, and to maintain blacks as a subordinate stratum beneath white workers. As Thompson explains, "Underneath these apologies was the white employers' perennial belief that educated Blacks are largely unfit for the dirty, menial, low-paying jobs traditionally assigned to them."

By 1899, a total of eighty-one Negro colleges, agricultural and vocational institutions had been created: seventy-five of these were located in the South. The severe limitations of these schools can only be understood against the harsh environment of black Southern economic and social life immediately after Reconstruction. Over 90 per cent of the Negro population lived in the South, and 80 per cent of the population resided in rural areas. The vast majority of black farmers, 82 per cent in 1890, rented their homes and property – compared to only 47 per cent for whites that same year. Less than three million acres of land had been purchased or redistributed to black freedmen at the end of the Reconstruction period. The rural black peasantry was caught in an almost impossible cycle of penury. Sixty-five per cent of them were illiterate in 1890. They had scant knowledge of modern agricultural techniques, such as soil erosion prevention, crop rotation, and the use of complex farm machinery. Barely one-fifth of them could even afford fertilizers. As sharecroppers, they were forced to give half of their annual crop to their landlords. But most had accumulated little capital after selling their cotton and corn crops. Black farmers required credit for canned goods, farm equipment, seeds and other supplies from rural merchants. And according to economists Roger Ransom and Richard Sutch, white merchants lent credit in the 1880s at an average annual rate of 35 to 60 per cent. Merchants usually refused to give credit to farmers who were not producing cotton or corn. Consequently only 3.7 per cent of all black farms produced any other cash crops. This economic dependency on the cotton market and credit had several social effects. The per capita production of sheep and swine dropped steadily on black-owned farms; and diets of black sharecropping families suffered as a result. Although the data is not conclusive, there is even some evidence that black life expectancy at birth actually fell slightly, from an average of 35 years in 1850 to less than 34 years in 1900. During the same period, whites' life expectancies increased from forty to about fifty years.[6]

Black oppression in the South was an essential component of class exploitation throughout the region. The dominant Southern classes of the period may be roughly subdivided into two major groups. The older elites were located in the South's "Black Belt", an agricultural region nearly one thousand miles in length from eastern North Carolina to Texas, noted for its black fertile soil and high percentage of black rural workers. About 50,000 white planters, only 2.5 per cent of all Southern farmers, comprised this rural elite. White planters usually owned farms which varied in size from three hundred to three thousand acres, and hired poor black and white tenants, sharecroppers or wage laborers to do their work.[7] A second group, which emerged only after the Civil War period, were the new industrialists – owners and managers of the South's growing textile mills, railroads, iron, coal and timber resources. These fractions of the South's capitalist class were frequently in conflict over matters of electoral politics and regional economic policies, yet they expressed common objectives regarding the black worker. Both required a steady supply of workers, and used state governments and the court systems to procure their labor quotas. The most infamous method in this regard was the "convict leasing" system, wherein prisoners would be leased by the state and local authorities to a private contractor for a fee. As the demand for labor increased, states complied by passing more repressive legislation: in Mississippi, for example, the theft of a pig was defined as "grand larceny", punishable by up to five years imprisonment. Many white politicians became wealthy from bonuses they received by leasing convicts; the state of Georgia alone netted over $350,000 in 1906 from its convict leasing system.[8] Both ruling class tendencies vigorously opposed the development of labor unions, and were fearful of any signs of black–white worker coalitions which might threaten the status quo. And both groups usually favored the creation of the black agricultural and trade schools in the 1880–90s. As Sterling D. Spero and Abram L. Harris observed in their classic study, *The Black Worker*:

> To the proponents of Negro industrial education, an efficient worker was one who was reliable, capable of giving the maximum return for his wages, and loyal to his employer. Enlightenment on the problems peculiar to the wage earner in modern industry had no part in the education which the industrial schools gave to the future Black workers.[9]

This was the socio-economic background which challenged the resources of most black educators in the United States a century ago. Booker T. Washington advanced a strategy of black economic development through the resources of black state-supported and private institutions. Washington understood that economic growth in per capita income for blacks was possible only under several conditions. Increased productivity was possible when labor was reorganized along more efficient lines. The development and utilization of new technologies, and the reeducation of the labor force would also increase productivity. Nevertheless, sustained economic growth could not occur without increased capital investment – that is, the acceleration of the ratio of capital to labor. How could the black colleges assist the process of black savings, reinvestment and the general formation of capital?

The Tuskegee Institute

The Tuskegee Institute approach to black development rested on four key points. First, a major responsibility for black educational institutions was the social and cultural transformation of the black Southern labor force. Through the creation of extension programs, rural training centers and colloquia, the schools attempted to retrain the black peasantry. Farmers were taught soil conservation techniques, crop rotation, and the importance of agricultural diversification. Students at Tuskegee were sent to staff rural primary and secondary schools, in a concerted effort to reduce the level of black illiteracy. Great emphasis was placed on personal hygiene, diet, and the improvement of residential quarters. Black farmers were encouraged to break from their dependency on landlords by gradually purchasing their own lands. This became essentially a problem of credit. So long as black farmers relied on white merchants for working capital at exorbitant interest rates, the growth of black land tenure would be minimal. To provide an alternative credit source, Tuskegee started a savings department which functioned as a local bank. Tuskegee graduates used these funds to initiate "social settlements" in rural areas, and after purchasing former plantation properties, resold them to black sharecroppers. Other black colleges and churches initiated similar lending establishments. By 1911, there were two black-owned banks in Georgia, eleven in Mississippi, and seven in Alabama. These banks and other black-owned lending institutions in the US did $22 million worth of business by 1910.[10]

Second, Washington and the Tuskegee Institute staff attempted to make their school a 'model' for all black educational institutions in the South. The student population, drawn primarily from the rural black peasantry of Alabama, Georgia and Mississippi, was taught to respect authority without debate. "We are not a college," Washington informed students in an 1896 campus convocation, "and if there are any of you here who expect to get a college training, you will be disappointed." Washington reluctantly permitted courses in sociology and psychology at the Institute, but immediately halted faculty efforts to start classes in Latin and Greek. Male students scheduled rigorous courses in carpentry, printing, agricultural economics and other technical training, while females were given skills in laundry, sewing, and kitchen duties. Male students were even responsible for producing clay bricks from the Institute's kiln, and constructing all classroom buildings, dormitories and faculty houses. Every aspect of their work fell under Washington's constant scrutiny. At mandatory religious exercises, all students had to pass him for inspection. "His keen, piercing eyes were sure to detect any grease-spots that were on the students' clothes or any buttons that by chance were conspicuous by their absence from the students' clothing." Every day, Washington received extensive faculty reports on the smallest aspects of campus life: the "daily poultry report," the "daily swine herd report," the state of the latrines, the "condition of the kitchens."

Faculty who seemed to shirk their duties were strongly censured. Washington checked with the campus librarian to learn which teachers had not checked out books; the campus' assistant principal, Warren Logan, maintained a list of those "teachers who were conspicuously irregular in their attendance upon prayers..." Louis R. Harlan, Washington's biographer, comments: "(Washington) was paternalistic and even dictatorial in the manner of the planters and business tycoons for whom he always reserved his highest public flattery." Despite these measures, the Institute acquired a notable reputation. By 1901, the school had 109 full-time faculty, 1,095 pupils, and owned property valued at nearly $330,000. Many of black America's leading researchers and scholars found employment at the Institute: gifted agricultural chemist George Washington Carver; architect Robert R. Taylor; dramatist Charles Winter Wood; and Monroe N. Work, director of records and research and the editor of the *Negro Year Book*.[11]

The third component in Washington's strategy was the development of a black middle class, and in particular, a black entrepreneurial stratum which was highly organized. According to the US Bureau of the Census records, there were only a total of 431 black lawyers, 909 black physicians and 15,000 black college, secondary and elementary school teachers in 1890, out of a total black population of 7.5 million. Barely one per cent of the black labour force was employed in clerical, professional or business-related activities. In 1893, there were only 17,000 black-owned businesses in the United States, and well over 80 per cent did not have a single paid employee. Washington and other black educators (such as W. E. B. Du Bois) believed that Negro college-trained students could form the core of an entrepreneurial class, based on the domination of the black consumer market. In 1900, Washington initiated the National Negro Business League, a black version of the Chamber of Commerce, in order to promote black private enterprise and cooperative activities between black businessmen. The 'Tuskegee spirit' was subsequently expressed in the creation of other black professional societies: the National Bar Association in 1903, the National Negro Bankers' Association in 1906, the National Association of Funeral Directors in 1907, and the National Negro Retail Merchants' Association in 1913. The close cooperation between black educational institutions and the black private sector in providing business and managerial skills and modest access to capital to thousands of young entrepreneurs was largely responsible for the creation of a new black elite in the early twentieth century. In these years, the number of black-owned drug stores rose from 250 to 695; black undertakers from 450 to one thousand; black retail merchants from 10,000 to 25,000; and black-owned banks, from four to fifty-one.[12]

The fourth aspect of the Tuskegee strategy was the cultivation of white financial support for Negro education. During Reconstruction, several Northern philanthropies had begun to make modest subsidies available to black trade schools and colleges. Tuskegee's first outside grant, amounting to $1,000, was donated by the Peabody Education Fund in 1883. Most of these funding sources were rather small, and usually permitted the continuation of existing programs rather than the development of new projects. Booker T. Washington recognized that the conservative leaders of the newly emerging industrial and commercial enterprises were potentially a much greater funding base for black vocational education than the older liberal philanthropic agencies with ties to the abolitionist tradition of the Northeastern United States. Washington's relationships with camera manufacturer George Eastman and steel industrialist Andrew Carnegie are illustrative. After reading Washington's Horatio Alger-styled autobiography, *Up From Slavery*, Eastman promptly sent $5,000 to Tuskegee Institute. From 1910 to 1915 Eastman gave $10,000 annually to Tuskegee, and upon Washington's death he sent the school $250,000. After Carnegie heard Washington speak at a public forum, he handed the Negro educator ten one-thousand dollar bills as a "secret gift". In the spring of 1903, Carnegie gave Tuskegee

Institute $600,000 in United States Steel Company bonds, stipulating that one-quarter of that amount was for Washington's personal use. Washington used these funds to build Tuskegee, but also channeled many funds to subsidize other ventures, e.g. expanding the Negro Business League; and purchasing controlling shares of major black newspapers.[13]

The apparent successes of this strategy of educational–political economy – the development of black-owned commercial establishments, the initiation of black private farms and small banks, and the dependence upon funding from conservative capitalists – were difficult to refute. In Macon County, Alabama, the location of Tuskegee, the number of black land-owners increased from 157 in 1900 to 507 by 1910.[14] There were, of course, many other parallel examples of educational institutions which promoted black self-help. In the early 1890s, R. L. Smith, a graduate of Atlanta University and principal of the Oakland, Texas, Normal School for Negroes, established the Farmers' Improvement Society of Texas. The Society engaged in several activities: urging blacks to grow their own food supplies and to sell their produce on a cooperative basis; improving their homes; teaching farmers the latest methods in agricultural production; and providing insurance to black families. By 1909 the Society had 21,000 members in Arkansas, Texas and Oklahoma, and had created a bank and a rural vocational college. Hampton Institute initiated the Negro Organization Society in 1909, which was soon joined by local organizations representing 85 per cent of the state's black population. The Virginia Society stressed the Tuskegee and Hampton Institute philosophy of capital accumulation, land-ownership, patronization of black-owned businesses, and initiated programs in family hygiene, health care and literacy.[15]

The Tuskegee approach to the political economy of black education was not confined to the United States. In 1899, during a London visit, Washington promoted a proposed Pan-African conference organized by Trinidadian lawyer Henry Sylvester-Williams as a "most effective and far reaching event." The product of this 1900 conference was the modern Pan-Africanist movement, which was later led by W. E. B. Du Bois and George Padmore.[16] Henry Sylvester-Williams corresponded with Washington in 1899 and 1900, and had asked him to distribute materials on the "proposed conference...as widely as is possible."[17] Washington established an economic partnership with a private German firm which held concessions in Germany's African colonies, and in January 1900, three Tuskegee graduates and one faculty member initiated an agricultural project in Togo. Tuskegee graduates were employed in the Sudan, Nigeria and the Congo Free State. Inspired by Washington, Zulu minister John Langalibalele Dube spoke at Tuskegee's commencement in 1897, and four years later started the Zulu Christian Industrial School in Natal, South Africa.[18] The sage of Pan-Africanism, Edward Wilmot Blyden, also endorsed Washington's leadership. After reading a speech by Tuskegee Institute's Principal, Blyden declared that

Washington's "words" and "work will tend to free two races with prejudice and false views of life."[19]

Washington and racial "accommodation"

The political linchpin of the Tuskegee educational and economic agenda was Washington's philosophy of racial "accommodation." His real rise to national attention came in September 1895, when he delivered a speech at Atlanta's Cotton States and International Exposition. Washington observed that one third of the South's population was black, and that an "enterprise seeking the material, civil or moral welfare" of the region could not disregard the Negro. Blacks should remain in the South – "Cast down your bucket where you are" – and participate in the capitalist economic development of that area. During the Reconstruction era, blacks had erred in their priorities. "Ignorant and inexperienced" blacks had tried to start "at the top instead of at the bottom," a Congressional seat "was more sought than real estate or industrial skill." To the white South, Washington pledged the fidelity of his race, "the most patient, law-abiding, and unresentful people that the world has seen." And on the sensitive issue of racial integration and the protection of blacks' political rights, Washington made a dramatic concession: "In all things that are purely social we can be as separate as the fingers, yet one as the hand in all things essential to mutual progress...The wisest among my race understand that the agitation of questions of social equality is the extremest folly...."[20] Washington's social policy "compromise" was this: blacks would disavow open agitation for desegregation and the political franchise; in return, they would be permitted to develop their own parallel economic, educational and social institutions within the framework of expanding Southern capitalism. Obscured by accommodationist rhetoric, Washington's statement was the expression of the nascent black entrepreneurial elite, many black landholders and some educators.

White America responded to Washington's address with universal acclaim. President Grover Cleveland remarked that the speech was the foundation for "new hope" for black Americans. More accurate was the editorial of the Atlanta *Constitution*: "The speech stamps Booker T. Washington as a wise counselor and a safe leader."[21] Within several years after the "Atlanta Compromise" address, Washington had become the nation's preeminent black leader. Through his patronage, black and white supporters were able to secure Federal government posts. Washington's influence with white philanthropists largely determined which Negro colleges would receive funds.

The "Tuskegee Machine" never acquiesced to the complete political disfranchisement of blacks, and behind the scenes Washington used his resources to fight for civil rights. In 1900 he requested funds from white philanthropists to lobby against racist election provisions in Louisiana's state constitution. He privately opposed Alabama's racial disfranchisement laws in Federal courts, and in 1903–4 personally spent "at least four thousand dollars in cash" to advance "the rights of the Black man."[22] Nevertheless, Washington's entire public approach to racial policies in the US implied to whites that blacks were no longer interested in political power or civil rights.

Washington cemented his alliance with white capitalists by making polemical attacks on organized labor. Even before his rise to prominence, Washington professed anti-labor opinions. Strikes were caused by "professional labor agitators," he commented critically in his autobiography. Striking workers must spend "all that they have saved" during their protests, and must later "return to work in debt at the same wages..."[23] Organized opposition to the demands of capital seemed foolish, and even criminal to Washington. He encouraged the Negro to seize the "opportunity to work at his trade" by "taking the place" of striking white workers. "The average Negro does not understand the necessity or advantage of a labor organization which stands between him and his employer and aims apparently to make a monopoly of the opportunity for labor," Washington wrote in 1913. Black laborers were "more accustomed to work for persons than for wages." The capitalist was the best friend of the unemployed Negro, not an enemy. The black worker should "not like an organization which seems to be founded on a sort of impersonal enmity to the man by whom he is employed." The black man's labor "is law-abiding, peaceable, teachable... labor that has never been tempted to follow the red flag of anarchy."[24]

The most controversial incident which tested Washington's economic strategy occurred in 1908, during the Alabama coalminers' strike. The Alabama United Mineworkers' Union (UMW) had 12,000 members, including 6,000 black miners. When United States Steel refused to renew workers' contracts and ordered substantial wage cuts, the miners announced a strike. The state government of Alabama assisted the company by sending convicts to work in the mines. The conflict soon escalated: miners dynamited the homes of nonunion strike breakers; police and company security guards shot and physically assaulted UMW leaders; the governor of Alabama ordered the state militia to destroy the tent encampments of black and white strikers, and hundreds of labor leaders were imprisoned. Washington did not hesitate to choose sides in the class struggle. Negroes must not be "given to strikers" Washington declared. The collective bargaining process of unionism must be avoided as a "form of slavery." As thousands of white miners lost their jobs, nonunion black laborers replaced them at lower wages. Following the collapse of the UMW strike, the companies worked with Tuskegee Institute to initiate a form of nonunion "welfare capitalism." United States Steel hired Tuskegee graduate John W. Oveltree as its "efficiency social agent" to monitor the work habits of 15,000 black laborers. The De Bardeleben Coal Company of Alabama employed another Tuskegee alumnus, R. W. Taylor, as its supervisor of black coalminers. The De Bardeleben Company, in gratitude, gave its black employees several scholarships per year for their children to attend Tuskegee Institute. The reaction of white miners to the strikebreaking tactics of Tuskegee was predictable. By 1910, less than 600 blacks were members of UMW, and even these had no access to positions of union leadership. Nonunion blacks now comprised 75 per cent of all miners in Alabama, but their reduced wages left them only marginally above poverty.[25]

Washington's open alliance with white capitalists and public acceptance of racial segregation could be justified to the small black petty bourgeoisie in economic terms. "No race that has anything to contribute to the markets of the world is long in any degree ostracized," Washington observed.[26] As white firms retreated from black sections of towns and rural areas, the graduates of Tuskegee Institute and other industrial schools were fully prepared to assume their roles as entrepreneurs in the private enterprise system. Black consumers were poor, but collectively their market was sufficiently large to maintain the development of a black petty bourgeois stratum. In Montgomery, Alabama, a town with only 2,000 blacks in 1900, black entrepreneurs had established twenty restaurants, twenty-three grocery stores, and three drugstores. Blacks in Montgomery also had twelve building contractors, fifteen blacksmith shops, five physicians, and two funeral establishments.[27] By 1913, fifty years after the abolition of slavery, a substantial black entrepreneurial, professional and landholding elite had been created. Black Americans owned 550,000 homes, and had accumulated $700 million in wealth. The number of black-owned businesses had doubled in only 13 years, from 20,000 to 40,000. Afro-Americans owned 15.7 million acres of land across the South, and the total number of black farm owners had reached 200,000 out of 848,000 black farmers in all. As economic historian Gilbert C. Fite has noted:

> When it is considered that Blacks started out without capital or independent business experience and faced severe racial discrimination...the record of Black ownership by the early twentieth century was remarkable.[28]

Contradictions in the Tuskegee approach

Afro-American intellectuals, journalists and college teachers were largely alarmed by Washington's immense influence. With some exceptions, they did not reject Tuskegee's economic strategy, but they did question its emphasis on rural development at the expense of the urban petty bourgeoisie. Nor were they opposed to industrial and agricultural education for the vast majority of Southern Negroes. Their principal objection was Washington's social policy of accommodation. They believed that the abandonment of electoral politics and the acceptance of racial segregation in all public accommodations and civic life would make black advancement in economic and educational fields extremely difficult, if not impossible. They also perceived that the "Tuskegee Machine" had developed such influence over national educational policy that non-vocational schools for Blacks were in serious jeopardy. The most articulate representative of the anti-Washington tendency in Negro higher education was W. E. B. Du Bois, who in 1910 founded the National Association for the Advancement of Colored People (NAACP). Du Bois argued that only the black liberal arts colleges, not schools based on the Hampton–Tuskegee Institute model, were able to produce a stable, educated black middle class, or what he termed the "Talented Tenth." Indeed, "to attempt to establish any sort of a system of common and industrial school training, without *first* (and I say *first* advisedly) without *first* providing for the higher training of the very best teachers, is simply throwing your money away to the winds," Du Bois argued in 1903. Black America would only be "saved by its exceptional men," those who possessed "intelligence, broad sympathy, knowledge of the world that was and is, and of the relation of men to it." The Talented Tenth must "guide the Mass away from the contamination and death of the Worst, in their own and other races."[29] Du Bois believed that industrial and agricultural education was "a splendid thing. But when it is coupled by sneers at Negro colleges whose work made industrial schools possible, when it is accompanied by the exaltation of men's bellies and depreciation of their brains," Du Bois declared, "then it becomes a movement you must choke to death or it will choke you."[30]

Washington was totally unscrupulous in his attacks against Du Bois and other black liberal critics. The Negro press aligned with Tuskegee printed personal and political attacks against Du Bois. Black ministers and educators who favored an aggressive approach to civil rights were dismissed or demoted by Washington's surrogates. Spies were placed inside civil rights organizations, and black colleges whose faculty or administrators opposed the Tuskegee philosophy were denied funds from white philanthropists and corporations. Even within his own ranks, Washington cautiously looked for signs of insubordination. One Tuskegee Institute instructor expressed misgivings about Washington's authoritarian behavior to his pastor in Boston. Washington's aides managed to steal these personal letters, and the teacher in question was promptly humiliated for actions which "were disloyal to the Institution."[31] Washington's many efforts to suppress free speech and civil rights reveal his determination to play an aggressive role as "collaborator" with white corporations, the state and segregationists in controlling the status of the Negro. As sociologist Oliver C. Cox suggested, "the term 'Uncle Tom' does not seem to describe the role of the leadership of

Washington. The 'Uncle Tom' is a passive figure; he is so thoroughly inured to his condition of subordination that he has become tame and obsequious." Washington, by contrast, projected himself as a mass leader, but his effective power was obtained from the white ruling class. Washington was "an intercessor between his group and the dominant class," Cox noted. He was "given wide publicity as a phenomenal leader" precisely because "he demanded less for the Negro people than that which the ruling class had already conceded."[32]

The contradictions in the Tuskegee approach to black development only became apparent over several years. A public policy of compromise and appeasement to white racism, for example, permitted white legislatures to dismantle much of the black educational system which had been built a generation earlier. In 1900, the average black child received about one-fourth as much funding as a white child attending public schools in Georgia; in North Carolina, the figure for black children was approximately one-third, and in South Carolina, about one-sixth. In Georgia, there were 108 black children per teacher compared to fifty-one students per teacher in white schools; black teachers' salaries were roughly one half that of whites. By 1915, the educational gap between blacks and whites had widened dramatically. The number of Southern, four-year high schools had increased from 123 to 509, but the ratio of white to black secondary school students was twenty-nine to one. In 1917, North Carolina had 285 public high schools with a total enrollment of 15,469 students. In a state which had a black population of 32 per cent at that time, the *total* enrollment of black high school students throughout North Carolina was nineteen. The ratio of school expenditures per child between black and white students had also soared. In South Carolina, for example, the average white child received $13.98 annually, and the black child obtained $1.13 – only about 8.1 per cent of the amount received by whites. Student–teacher ratios in Southern black public schools were down slightly to 95 to 1; but in white schools, the figure was 44.6 to one.[33]

This educational underdevelopment was replicated at the university level. Southern whites of most social classes placed little value on higher education generally, and allocated marginal resources for the advanced training of their own young adults. As historian C. Vann Woodward notes, white Southern colleges were "pitifully" endowed. In 1901, the combined endowments of all Southern colleges in eleven states were "less than half of the funds held by the colleges of New York State alone." Harvard University alone had a larger annual income in 1901 than the combined sums of "the sixty-six colleges and universities of Virginia, North Carolina, South Carolina, Georgia, Alabama, Mississippi, and Arkansas." Few white technical schools and graduate schools were genuinely capable of doing research, and standards at the bachelor's degree level were barely above secondary school levels in the North.[34] Given the poverty of white higher education, it is not surprising that black colleges and industrial schools fared poorly during the flood of white supremacy. White critics complained that college and technical training had made blacks "uppish" and "bumptious", and had prompted them "to despise work."[35] State legislatures sharply cut into the budgets of black state-supported schools. In 1916, the segregated Negro Agricultural and Technical College at Greensboro, North Carolina, received only one-thirteenth of the amount appropriated to white state schools. Also in 1916, the black public colleges in Virginia, Georgia, and the Carolinas "received from their states less than one-eighth of the amount for whites in Virginia alone."[36]

Washington's public position of accommodation to racial inequality prepared the ideological ground for a series of repressive laws governing race relations. Washington had hoped that a conservative social order would respect the civil and political rights of Negro Americans. This was unfortunately not the case. In Alabama, for example, there were 180,000 black adult males of voting age in 1900. After the ratification of Alabama's white supremacist state constitution in 1901, black voters almost disappeared. In 1908, only 3,700 black males in Alabama were registered voters; two decades later, the figure had fallen to 1,500. Other states carried out similar measures. In Louisiana, the black electorate declined from 130,000 in 1896 to below 5,000 in less than a decade. In Virginia, black voters dropped to 21,000, out of a black adult male population of 150,000. It is important to note that these restrictions were aimed at poor and working class whites, as well as blacks. Nearly half of all white Mississippi voters were barred from elections by literacy tests and poll taxes.

The demand for white supremacy was extended to public accommodations. Georgia had racially segregated all public streetcars in 1891, and within a decade all other Southern states had similar codes. In 1905 the "Separate Park Law" was approved by the Georgia state assembly, which restricted Blacks from public parks. By 1908 Atlanta's major public buildings had racially segregated elevators. In later years Jim Crow restrictions tightened. In 1922 Mississippi adopted a state Jim Crow law for all taxicabs. Texas banned whites and "Africans" from boxing or wrestling together in 1933. Oklahoma barred interracial fishing and boating in 1935. And Birmingham's city council outlawed blacks and whites from playing dominoes or checkers together in 1930. Such city ordinances and state-wide legislation inevitably gave sanction to racist violence. Alabama had 246 lynchings of Negroes between 1885 and 1918, well behind the national leader, Georgia, with 381 lynchings. Although the rate of lynchings declined gradually after 1900, these vigilante crimes persisted. In 1915, the year of Washington's death, Georgia recorded eighteen lynchings, including some blacks who had been burned alive, and Alabama had nine lynchings.[37]

The critical weakness of Washington's economic strategy was his failure to comprehend the negative effects of rigid segregation on all sectors of the black labor force. Although the barriers of Jim Crow helped to generate a black consumer market which was exploited by Negro entrepreneurs and professionals, the reality was that black workers suffered severe income losses in other ways. First, racial segregation permitted white employers to lower the general rates of wages to all workers. White laborers were protected from higher unemployment rates by the rule of whites-first in all vocational hirings, yet they also suffered a reduction in wages. White union members frequently accepted poor contracts with companies just to maintain the color line in their industry.[38] Second, the anti-union philosophy of Tuskegee provided a justification for racists inside organized labor to expel black members. In the early 1900s, there were forty-three national unions which did not have a single black member. By 1912, thousands of additional black trade unionists had been removed: the national printers' union had only 250 black members, the Lithographers' one, the potters' union none, the glass bottle blowers' none, the hatters' union none, and the Iron, Steel and Tin Workers' Union, only two or three blacks.[39] Thirdly, thousands of black artisans and entrepreneurs who depended solely or primarily upon white clients were displaced with the imposition of Jim Crow. Many positions which had been defined as "Negro jobs" were seized by whites. In 1870, according to Woodward, New Orleans "had listed 3,460 Negroes as carpenters, cigar makers, painters, clerks, shoemakers, coopers, tailors, bakers, blacksmiths, and foundry hands, (but) not 10 per cent of that number were employed in the same trades in 1904. Yet the Negro population had gained more than 50 per cent."[40] On balance, Washington's policies of accommodation and anti-unionism retarded the accumulation of capital within black working class households, and helped to liquidate thousands of skilled black artisans from the marketplace.

Tuskegee Institute's curriculum did not adequately respond to the rapidly changing status of black workers in the labor force. Vocational schools continued to train black students as blacksmiths, wheelwrights, masons, plumbers, and dozens of other positions which either became nonexistent with the development of new technologies, or in which blacks were eliminated (as in brickmasonry) due to the expansion of racial segregation in organized labor. With the rise in cotton prices in 1900–14, black farmers trained by Tuskegee's methods still had not adequately diversified their crop production. The closure of the European markets in 1914–16 due to the First World War sharply reduced cotton prices, leading to a chain reaction of default. Black rural tenants and landholders were unable to sell their crops at any price, and thousands went bankrupt. By 1918, only one black-owned bank was left in Alabama, the savings firm at Tuskegee Institute. The number of Mississippi black banks declined to only two. As credit disappeared or became more costly, many black farm families trekked north, where the prospect of higher wages and life without rigid Jim Crow barriers was a more attractive alternative. The black exodus in 1900–10 was 170,000;

by 1920–30, it amounted to 749,000. The steady deterioration of the inter-racial environment, the absence of effective legal rights and the continuation of vigilante violence combined with economic factors which pushed many Afro-Americans from the rural South into Northern ghettoes.[41]

What was Washington's legacy to the educational and economic development of Black America? Writing in 1936, Du Bois suggested a partial answer:

> Washington was an opportunist, slow but keen-witted, with high ideals...He knew that the Negro needed civil and social rights. But he believed that if the Negroes showed that they could advance despite discrimination, that the inherent justice in the nation would gradually extend to deserving Negroes the rights that they merited...He expected that the Black owners of property would thus gain recognition from other property-holders and gradually rise in the scale of society.[42]

Washington was wrong – on his economic policies, on his authoritarian measures of instruction at the Institute, on his blind faith in petty capital accumulation for Negroes, and on his public capitulation to racism. Yet his school still exists in Tuskegee, Alabama; his National Negro Business League provides the leadership for today's black American petty capitalists; and his tactics of political accommodation with white corporations to generate funding for black social institutions is taken as normative behaviour among broad sectors of the black educational community. Booker T. Washington's economic and educational insights remain, with their respective strengths and contradictions, a permanent feature of Afro-American social organizations and leaders.

NOTES AND REFERENCES

1 Holt, Thomas, *Black over White: Negro Political Leadership in South Carolina during Reconstruction* (Urbana: University of Illinois Press, 1977), p. 68.
2 Mays, Benjamin E., "Black Colleges: Past, Present and Future," *Black Scholar*, vol. 6 (September 1974), p. 32.
3 Harris, J. John, Figgures, Cleopatra, and Carter, David G., "A Historical Perspective of the Emergence of Higher Education in Black Colleges," *Journal of Black Studies*, vol. 6 (September 1975), p. 56.
4 Mays, "Black Colleges: Past, Present and Future," p. 32.
5 Thompson, Daniel C., "Black Colleges: Continuing Challenges," *Phylon*, vol. 40 (June 1979), p. 185.
6 Bureau of the Census, *The Social and Economic Status of the Black Population in the United States: An Historical View, 1790–1978* (Washington, DC: Government Printing Office, 1979) pp. 13, 92, 96, 120, 138; Fogel, Robert William, and Engerman, Stanley M., *Time on the Cross: The Economics of American Negro Slavery* (Boston: Little, Brown, 1974), p. 125; and Ramson, Roger, and Sutch, Richard, *One Kind of Freedom: The Economic Consequences of Emancipation* (New York: Cambridge University Press, 1977), pp. 150–4, 182–5.

7 Fite, Gilbert C., *Cotton Fields No More: Southern Agriculture, 1865–1980* (Lexington: University of Kentucky Press, 1984), p. 32.

8 Henri, Furette, *Black Migration: Movement North 1900–1920* (Garden City, New York: Anchor Books, 1976), pp. 39–40; and Woodward, C. Vann, *Origins of the New South, 1877–1913* (Baton Rouge: Louisiana State University Press, 1951), pp. 213. The average annual death rate of black prisoners leased to private contractors was 11 per cent in Mississippi in 1880–5. In Arkansas, the death rate was 25 per cent in 1881.

9 Spero, Sterling D., and Harris, Abram L., *The Black Worker: The Negro and the Labor Movement* (New York: Atheneum, 1968), pp. 49–50.

10 Work, Monroe, *Negro Year Book and Annual Encyclopedia of the Negro* (Tuskegee Institute: Tuskegee Institute Press, 1912), pp. 22, 168, 176–8.

11 Harlan, Louis R., *Booker T. Washington: The Making of a Black Leader, 1856–1901* (New York: Oxford University Press, 1972), pp. 144–6, 255, 272–3, 278–80.

12 Bureau of the Census, *The Social and Economic Status of the Black Population in the United States*, pp. 14, 72, 73, 76, 78; and Meier, August, *Negro Thought in America, 1880–1915* (Ann Arbor: University of Michigan Press, 1963), p. 127.

13 Harlan, Louis R., *Booker T. Washington: The Making of a Black Leader, 1856–1901*, p. 141; and Harlan, Louis R., *Booker T. Washington: The Wizard of Tuskegee, 1901–15* (New York: Oxford University Press, 1983), pp. 130–1, 135.

14 Kirby, Jack T., *Darkness at the Dawning: Race and Reform in the Progressive South* (Philadelphia: Lippincott, 1972), p. 171.

15 Meier, August, *Negro Thought in America, 1880–1915*, pp. 123–4, 253.

16 Marable, Manning, "Booker T. Washington and African Nationalism," *Phylon*, vol. 35 (December 1974), p. 398.

17 Esedebe, P. Olisanwuche, *Pan-Africanism: The Idea and Movement, 1776–1963* (Washington, DC: Howard University Press, 1982), p. 48.

18 Harlan, Louis R., *Booker T. Washington: The Wizard of Tuskegee, 1901–1915*, pp. 267–9; and Marable, Manning, "A Black School in South Africa," *Negro History Bulletin*, vol. 37 (June–July 1974), pp. 258–61.

19 Harlan, Louis R., *Booker T. Washington: The Making of a Black Leader 1856–1901*, p. 227.

20 Washington, Booker T., *Up From Slavery* (1901), in *Three Negro Classics* (New York: Avon, 1965), pp. 146–50.

21 Harlan, Louis R., *Booker T. Washington: The Making of a Black Leader, 1856–1901*, pp. 222, 224.

22 Meier, August, *Negro Thought in America, 1880–1915*, p. 111.

23 Harlan, Louis R., *Booker T. Washington: The Making of a Black Leader, 1856–1901*, pp. 90–1.

24 Spero, S. D., and Harris, A. L., *The Black Worker*, pp. 129, 131; and Foner, Philip S., *Organized Labor and the Black Worker, 1619–1973* (New York: International Publishers, 1974), p. 79.

25 Foner, Philip S., *Organized Labor and the Black Worker, 1619–1973*, p. 99; Woodward, *Origins of the New South 1877–1913*, pp. 363–4; and Spero, S. D., and Harris, A. L., *The Black Worker*, pp. 359, 363–6.

26 Meier, August, *Negro Thought in America, 1880–1915*, p. 101.

27 Henri, Furette, *Black Migration*, p. 33.

28 Woodward, *Origins of the New South, 1877–1913*, p. 368; and Fite, *Cotton Fields No More*, p. 21.

29 Du Bois, W. E. B., "The Talented Tenth," in Booker T. Washington, *et al.* (eds), *The Negro Problem* (New York: Arno, 1969), pp. 31–75.

30 Du Bois, W. E. B., 'Lecture in Baltimore', (December 1903), in Aptheker, Herbert (ed.) *Against Racism: Unpublished Essays, Papers, Addresses, 1887–1961 by W. E. B. Du Bois* (Amherst: University of Massachusetts Press, 1985), pp. 75–7.

31 Harlan, Louis R., *Booker T. Washington: The Wizard of Tuskegee, 1901–1915*, pp. 153–5.

32 Cox, Oliver Cromwell, "The Leadership of Booker T. Washington," *Social Forces*, vol. 30 (1951), pp. 91–7.

33 Harlan, Louis R., *Separate and Unequal: Public School Campaigns and Racism in the Southern Seaboard States, 1901–1915* (New York: Atheneum, 1969), pp. 12, 13, 250, 255–8; and Bureau of the Census, *The Social and Economic Status of the Black Population in the United States*, p. 17.

34 Woodward, Vann, *Origins of the New South, 1877–1913*, pp. 437–9.

35 Henri, Furette, *Black Migration*, p. 37.

36 Harlan, Louis R., *Separate and Unequal*, pp. 134, 256.

37 Woodward, C. Vann, *Origins of the New South, 1877–1913*, pp. 351–5; Woodward, C. Vann, *The Strange Career of Jim Crow* (New York: Oxford University Press, 1974), pp. 99, 116–18; and Work, Monroe N., *Negro Year Book, 1918–1919* (Tuskegee Institute: Tuskegee Institute Press, 1919), p. 374.

38 See Reich, Michael, *Racial Inequality: A Political-Economic Analysis* (Princeton: Princeton University Press, 1981), p. 269.

39 Foner, Philip S., *Organized Labor and the Black Worker, 1619–1973*, pp. 74, 102.

40 Woodward, C. Vann, *Origins of the New South, 1877–1973*, p. 361.

41 Marable, Manning, "The Land Question in Historical Perspective: The Economics of Poverty in the Blackbelt South, 1865–1920," in McGee, Leo and Boone, Robert (eds) *The Black Rural Landowner – Endangered Species: Social, Political and Economic Implications* (Westport, CN: Greenwood Press, 1979), pp. 15–19; and Bureau of Census, *The Social and Economic Status of the Black Population in the United States*, p. 15.

42 Du Bois, W. E. B., "The Negro and Social Reconstruction," in Aptheker, Herbert (ed.), *Against Racism*, p. 114.

10

WHY BOOKER T. WASHINGTON WAS RIGHT

A reconsideration of the economics of race

John Sibley Butler

It has been over sixty years since Booker T. Washington burst upon the national scene with a single program for the economic "advancement of black America." The program was economic specific in a very hostile racial atmosphere. Scholars have debated the work of Washington, correctly criticized him for his public stand on the issue of civil rights, and debated his overall "philosophy" of economic development. The purpose of this paper is not to debate his ideas on the importance of civil rights, nor is it to engage in a critical review of the debate between Washington and Du Bois. These issues have been debated many times in the literature. The purpose of this paper is to show that in terms of Washington's program for the future of the race, he was simply right.

In order to understand the logic of my argument, it is necessary to engage in comparative theoretical analysis, with consideration given to the relevant data that fit such an approach. Such an approach will allow us to move away from what I refer to as "dream" theories of economic development to those that are grounded in data. This comparative analysis will take us through important theoretical developments and models that allow us to examine the relationship between race, ethnicity, and success in American society.

When one stops to examine the data on black Americans since the turn of the century, one thing becomes clear. Those blacks that are grounded in the tradition of enterprise, regardless of size and type, have developed a strong tradition of the education of children and success within America that most white groups cannot match. Put differently, in the midst of racism and discrimination, both legal and personal, they have been able to develop a sense of economic stability. As a group, they have developed a set of values and strategies that have been passed from generation to generation; this value structure still influences the present day offspring of this group.

Over the years, scholars have not understood what to do with this segment of black society. They have been called the black elite, the black

174

middle class and black Brahmans. But the group that can trace their development back to entrepreneurship are none of the above. Rather, they bear a striking resemblance to what have been called middleman minorities throughout the centuries.[1] Because they bear this resemblance, they can be distinguished from today's black middle class. As a result, the ideas of Booker T. Washington bear a frightening similarity to the ideals that are instrumental in making middleman minorities successful.

In order to move us through the analysis, we must first develop an understanding of middleman theory, and the groups that provide the data for the development of the theory. We then ground portions of the black experience into that tradition. Because of the importance of legal segregation, and using the framework found in my earlier work, we develop the concept of truncated middleman minority. We then ground the ideas of Washington into middleman theory and show how theoretical frameworks have misinterpreted the experience of blacks in America.

I

In *The Protestant Ethic and the Spirit of Capitalism*, a turn of the century work that was concerned with explaining the philosophical roots of capitalistic economic behavior, Max Weber observed that there was a relationship between the exclusion of a group and entrepreneurial behavior.[2] In fact, Weber wrote his treatise because Catholics, a group that had experienced discrimination and exclusion, had not turned entrepreneurial. They were not following a pattern that had been observed for hundreds of years:

> The smaller participation of Catholics in the modern business life of Germany is all the more striking because it runs counter to a tendency which has been observed at all times, including the present. National or religious minorities which are in a position of subordination to a group of rulers are likely, through their voluntary or involuntary exclusion from positions of political influence, to be driven with peculiar force into economic activity. Their ablest members seek to satisfy the desire for recognition of their abilities in this field, since there is no opportunity in the service of the State. This has undoubtedly been true of the Poles in Russia and Eastern Prussia, who have without question been undergoing a more rapid economic advance than in Galicia, where they have been in the ascendant. It has in earlier times been true of the Huguenots in France under Louis XIV, the Nonconformists and Quakers in England, and, last but not least, the Jews for two thousand years.[3]

Weber solved this problem by arguing that the philosophical ideas of Catholicism did not encourage the spirit of capitalism because it was concerned with riches in the heavenly world. On the other hand, he argued that the philosophical ideas of Protestantism were used by non-religious people for the justification of what he called "the spirit of capitalism." In fact, he argues that these ideas were the religious justification for the practice of capitalism throughout the world.

Our major concern is not with the specific religious preoccupations of Weber[4] *vis-à-vis* capitalism, but his observation that groups of people who are excluded from society are driven into economic activity, or what we would call small enterprise. This idea is also present in the work of scholars such as Georg Simmel, who called them strangers in society. To Simmel, the stranger was a social type or immigrant who never fully belonged to a society, and was always on the move. Simmel noted that "throughout the history of economics the stranger everywhere appears as the trader, or the trader the stranger."[5] They enter the market place as business people and develop enterprises in order to develop economic stability.

Strangers, or groups that depend on business enterprise for their survival are documented throughout the literature, which is conclusive and systematic. In the classic work *On the Theory of Social Change*, Everett E. Hagen describes them as follows:

> The trade they conduct is importing and exporting and domestic trade divorced from production. Their loans may be to peasants and to princes. In spite of their economic power, almost nowhere are the trader-financiers accepted by other elite groups as equal in worth or as occupying a natural and proper place in the society. Napoleon's sneering reference to the English as a nation of shopkeepers, the attitude of the German Junkers toward money-grubbing upstarts, and the desire of Jesus to drive the money-changers from the temple are repeated the world around.... In Asia, Africa, and Latin America the great traders are often aliens – Chinese, Indians, persons from the Near East, Jews, and so on. In many countries they come from the trading group of their home country; in others they pursue in an alien society an occupation they would not pursue where their own folkways prevail. The local trader too ... is typically set apart from the rest of the community.... In India he is usually separate, and low, caste; in Japan, before industrialization, he was of a separate group forbidden to turn to other occupations...[6]

In the seventeenth century, the literature is clear about the observation of Weber, and later Hagen, on the relationship between exclusion and business enterprise. Throughout the European continent, the Jewish group was persecuted and known as a group that was interested in business enterprise. So influential was the group that when anti-semitism developed, non-Jewish merchants of a city feared that if the Jews were expelled, the local economy would suffer. Consider the following quotation:

It is the same tale in Hamburg. In the 17th century the importance of the Jews had grown to such an extent that they were regarded as indispensable to the growth of Hamburg's prosperity. On one occasion the Senate asked that permission should be given for synagogues to be built, otherwise, they feared, the Jews would leave Hamburg, and the city might then be in danger of sinking to a mere village. On another occasion, in 1697, when it was suggested that the Jews should be expelled, the merchants earnestly entreated the Senate for help, in order to prevent the serious endangering of Hamburg's commerce.[7]

Throughout Europe, the persecution of Jews resulted in their placing a strong emphasis on business enterprise in order to survive. Persecution, which led to the dispersion of the group in different countries for centuries, meant that the group was for years without an official "homeland" and had to depend on business enterprise. As noted by Sombart, "Israel passes over Europe like the sun: at its coming new life bursts forth; at its going all falls into decay."[8]

Connected to this emphasis on business enterprise for excluded groups is the importance of education, especially for future generations. With hostility a part of their history, and the fear of being excluded from a city ever present, education, like enterprise, was seen as something that was portable. Chaim Bermant, writing in *The Jews*, notes the following:

> The effect of this doctrine [reading the Torah] was to establish a tradition of near universal literacy so that even if not all were equipped to study, nearly all felt compelled to try. There were great academics in Palestine long before the birth of Christ, but the greatest centres of learning were in the cities of Sura, Pumpeditha and Nehardea in Babylon, which flourished from about the third century until the eleventh century AD. As Jews migrated westwards other academies were established in North Africa, Spain and the Rhine Valley, and then, after the sixteenth century, Poland and Lithuania became the main centres of Jewish learning.[9]

This relationship between exclusion and the importance of education became a trade mark of "strangers" or trader groups throughout the world.

On the African continent, the Ibo has experienced hostility and business enterprise throughout the centuries. Early research noted that the origins of this group might relate to the "lost tribe of Judah," a theory which draws similarities between the Ibo and the Jews. Indeed, this literature often refers to the Ibo as the "Jews of Africa" or the "Jews of West Africa." This comparison developed because some Ibo claim that the word "Hebrew" must have been mutilated to "Ubru" or "Ibru," then to "Uburu," and later to "Ibo."[10] But the comparison with the Jews relates to similar patterns of business enterprise and the importance of education that characterize the two groups.

Research has not documented the origins of the Ibo people. Some theories argue that the Ibo were of Egyptian origin. Some scholars have argued that they were the founders of ancient Egypt. Drawing upon what we know about Judaism, it is argued that the Jews learned the idea of statehood from the ancient Egyptians. This is one of the major arguments that is used to draw similarities between the two groups. Some have also theorized that the ancient Egyptian art of embalming disappeared because the Ibo were defeated and chased out of Egypt. As they wandered to their new land, they were not able to find the herbs that were necessary to recreate the art of embalming. The Arabs who took over Egypt were ignorant of the art. As they traveled, the older generations died off, leaving behind no evidence of their massive knowledge except for pride in past achievements. It is this pride, or achievement orientation, that explains why the average Ibo is motivated to do well today.[11] As noted by one author, the Ibo lived quite differently than other groups in Africa, they had neither states nor empires, and therefore used totally different institutions.[12]

What we do know about the Ibo is that they have been very instrumental in business in West Africa, especially Nigeria. Whatever their origin, there is little evidence that they engaged in warfare in order to make their way around the African continent. Their methods of expansion were peaceful and can be identified as penetration, attraction of relatives and absorption. In study after study, it has been documented that the Ibo, through conflict and mobility, have been very successful in enterprise. Indeed, a major study argued that the Ibo have a very high need for achievement in the business world. Still another study showed that the majority of entrepreneurs in the sample were Ibo.[13]

Throughout history, the Ibo have faced hostility and survived on the back of business enterprise. The Aro, the main trading people of the Ibo, found themselves always in search of business activity. This was also true of the slave trade, a situation in which the Ibo were both middlemen for slave traders and members of the African slave groups who made the dreadful journey to America:

> The virile commerce practiced by the Aro and the powerful organization built by them to conduct it certainly brought an economic unifying factor to the Ibo. Yet, at the same time, the commerce also led many Ibo to the slave ships and a life of slavery on the other side of the Atlantic, for the lucrative slave trade was a crucial part of the Aro commercial mastery, while the small-scale nature of Ibo government left clans, villages, and families constantly exposed to the raiders, traders, and extortion of the oracles.[14]

This author points out that the fact that these people survived such depredations is an indication of the strength of their culture and the stamina of their institutions. Although about sixteen thousand Ibo were sold into slavery, they remained closely populated and maintained the spiritual strength and determination to rebuild their depopulated villages and to maintain, against great odds, the social order of enterprise on which their survival depended.[15]

Although it is not the purpose of this paper to explore the Ibo and their culture,[16] especially the conflicts in which they have been engaged, it is necessary to point out that the Ibo have produced a strong emphasis on the importance of education:

> Motivated by the desire for "progress," Ibo unions worked to recruit their talented "sons" for leadership in the emerging nation of Nigeria. The phrase "catching up" became crucial in the goal of building educational institutions and offering educational scholarships. The [Ibo unions] believe education to be the greatest single benefit they could offer to their people; so they taxed themselves to raise money to award scholarships to their "deserving youth" to acquire secondary and overseas education. The constitutions of various unions were specific in their aims and objectives regarding education.[17]

But, like the Jews of Europe, the Ibo have had to endure intense societal hostility against them for generations. Perhaps the most recent hostility occurred in the 1960s, when the final solution to the "Ibo problem" was instituted. It was during a time when Nigeria was going through political change, and old ethnic stereotypes were resurfacing. Hatch explains what happened during a conference of leaders from across the country:

> At this stage of the conference the ulcers of poisoned emotions in Nigerian society suddenly burst.... Resentment against Ibo economic, educational, and technical superiority had simmered for years. It was the familiar case of an alien minority economically dominating a larger community beside which it is living.... The program in the north whatever its immediate cause, produced a trauma that will affect Nigerian life for a generation. It has been variously estimated that between ten thousand and thirty thousand Ibo...lost their lives during the holocaust of September, 1966; perhaps another million fled back to the eastern region.... The killings were accompanied by mass looting as the northerners gave vent to their jealousy of Ibo wealth. Many Ibo found succor in the palace of the Emir of Kano; but nothing could halt the northern fury.[18]

It is clear that Max Weber's observations about hostility, exclusion, business enterprise, and education have been observed throughout the world. Today, middleman theory takes its intellectual model from the work of scholars such as Weber and Simmel. It is this model that is guiding work in this area, an area which throws light upon the experiences of groups in other countries as well as across the world.

Middleman theory is dedicated to understanding how groups carve out a sense of economic security within societies in which they are excluded.[19] Sometimes this exclusion is based on race, religion or the inability of the group to speak the language. Edna Bonacich utilized the works of scholars such as Becker, Blalock, Schermerhorn and Stryker to develop the theory systematically.[20] The theory began to take form in the work of Turner and Bonacich.[21] The major questions remain the same as those posed by Weber at the turn of the century, but with variations in where they are posed: How do ethnic groups "succeed" in America in the face of systematic discrimination and prejudice? How is a degree of economic security carved out of a society which is hostile to the group?[22]

As can be seen from our discussion of the Jewish experience in Europe and the Ibo experience in Africa, scholars have documented the fact that some groups play an unexpected role in the economic structure. Unlike most ethnic and minority groups in a society who sink to the bottom of the economic structure, they develop economic security by playing the "middleman" position within the economic system.

In advanced capitalist societies, the middleman is found in occupations such as labor contractor, rent collector, money lender, and broker. Playing the middleman position means that they negotiate between producer and consumer, owner and renter, elite and masses and employer and employee.[23] European Jews, Asians in East Africa, Japanese in the United States in the early 1900s, and Chinese in Southeast Asia are examples from the literature of middlemen in capitalist societies. Although trade and commerce are their "bread and butter," they are also found in bureaucratic organizations. Bonacich notes that even here they act as middlemen, interposed as they are between the consumer and his economic purpose. Put simply, minorities conceptualized as middlemen are less likely to be primary producers of goods and services; their major purpose is to generate the flow of goods and services through the economy.[24] Because of this, middleman minorities are viewed as petit bourgeoisie rather than members of the classic capitalist class.

Bonacich notes that early treatment of middleman minorities in the literature has produced two significant themes. The first emphasis is on the relationship between hostility directed toward the middleman minority and the loss of occupations and economic security, as they are pushed out of good occupations and are forced to develop economic security on the fringes of the economic system. Another theme of the early sociological literature stresses the relationship between elites, masses, and middleman minorities. Here the concentration is on the type of society in which middlemen are found. Where there is a significant gap between elite and masses, middleman minorities "plug" this status gap by acting as go-betweens. Because elites feel that they may lose status by dealing with the masses, middleman minorities do it for them. These minorities are not concerned with status considerations, and they feel free to trade with any-one: thus, they negotiate the economic relationships between elites and masses.[25]

II

The ideas of Booker T. Washington cannot be viewed in an intellectual or historical period vacuum. His ideas must also be divorced from the cele-brated debate that took place between him and W. E. B. Du Bois. Although this debate is important for historical evaluations, and we will briefly review it, we must look to a broader field of ideas and real experiences in order to understand Washington. More importantly, we must look at the data and see which groups have been successful in following the ideas of Washington. Put simply, we must screw our wigs on tight and ask different kinds of questions in order to understand Washington.

It is important to understand that when the ideas of Washington are grounded in the experiences of groups that have received hostility in host societies for centuries, they are not new at all. As a matter of fact, his ideas bear a strong resemblance to those that are grounded in middleman theory; they could have guided the experiences of the Ibo in Africa, or the Jews in Europe. More importantly, we can look to the experiences of free blacks in America prior to slavery and the experiences of blacks after slavery to provide data as to the "rightness" of Washington's ideas. We define "right-ness" as the ability of groups to live and prosper under hostile conditions. For purposes of exposition, after a cursory review of Washington, we will concentrate on the black American experience.

The ideas of Washington, and the debate between him and W. E. B. Du Bois, developed in an atmosphere of rigid segregation following the period of reconstruction.[26] Within the context of segregation and disenfranchise-ment, W. E. B. Du Bois saw the destruction of democracy and constitutional rights of black Americans, rights which were exercised during the period of reconstruction. His major concern was to re-establish these rights that were so necessary for a group to live in a civil society. Booker T. Washington also saw these evils in segregation and disenfranchisement. But he also saw a captured black market and the possibility of black American economic stability through business development.

Because of Washington's "compromise" on civil rights, most scholarly treatments of his ideas relegate him to the status of "uncle Tom." Although his ideas on civil rights were conservative, he laid the foundation for economic community development, the analog of today's ethnic middleman theory, within the black community. As a matter of fact, there is hardly any idea within the ethnic middleman theory which is not nested within the writings of Washington. Of course, scholars within this tradition do not recognize the contributions of Washington.

Washington's ideas rested on a three-way deal between the "new South's" white, leading class, black Americans, and northern capitalists. Put simply, he offered to trade black Americans' demand for equal rights, or the maintenance of segregation, in return for a promise by whites to allow black Americans to share in the economic growth of the South.[27] In Washington's scheme, small business enterprises, which took advantage of the skills that were developed during slavery, were to be the projectiles of this growth.

Before 1895, Washington was not a national figure; all of his energies were geared toward the development of the Tuskegee Institution. But in Atlanta, at the Atlanta Exposition in 1895, Washington spoke the words that have been quoted by all scholars interested in placing him in a tradition of black economic thought. He noted that

> [The] opportunity afforded will awaken among us a new era of industrial progress. Ignorant and inexperienced, it is not strange that in the first years of our new life we began at the top instead of at the bottom; that a seat in Congress or the state legislature was more sought than real estate or industrial skill; that the political convention or stump speaking had more attractions than starting a dairy farm or truck garden.... Our greatest danger is that in the great leap from slavery to freedom we may overlook the fact that the masses of us are to live by the productions of our hands, and fail to keep in mind that we shall prosper in proportion as we learn to draw the line between the superficial and substantial.... No race can prosper till it learns that there is as much dignity in tilling a field as in writing a poem. *In all things that are purely social we can be separate as the fingers, yet one as the hand in all things essential to mutual progress* (emphasis added).[28]

Washington believed that civil rights would develop when economic stability within the race developed. In the same speech he noted:

> The wisest among my race understand that the agitation of questions of social equality is the extremist folly, and that progress in the enjoyment of all the privileges that will come to us must be the result of severe and constant struggle rather than of artificial forcing. No race that has anything to contribute to the markets of the world is long in any degree ostracized. It is important and right that all privileges of law be ours, but it is vastly more important that we be prepared for the exercise of these privileges. The opportunity to earn a dollar in a factory just now is worth infinitely more than the opportunity to spend a dollar in an opera house.[29]

Washington's major goal was to develop a substantial propertied class of black American businessmen and landowners. These "captains of industry," as he envisioned them, would not have to be subordinate to white business-men in the economy. This belief was based on two key assumptions: 1 since black Americans were not protesting for Civil Rights, there would be little hostility toward them; and 2 black Americans would be wel-comed if their business talents were directed in certain salient areas.[30]

The first assumption has been reiterated in the work on middleman minorities, which stresses the idea that they are not actively engaged in politics unless they relate directly to the community in which they live. But Washington missed the fact that it is the business success of middleman groups that creates hostility against them. Although black Americans were forced to give up the ballot and could not pay attention to issues pertaining to their community, Washington incorporated the idea that the group could develop enterprise in areas where whites were not active. This would afford them an economic niche. Washington believed this because, as he wrote,

> The Negro was also fortunate enough to find that while his abilities in certain directions were opposed by the white South, in business he was not only undisturbed but even favored and encouraged. I have been repeatedly informed by Negro merchants in the South that they have as many white patrons as black, and the cordial business relations which are almost universal between the races in the South—proved... *there is little race prejudice in the American dollar.*[31] ... A merchant, unlike a physician, for example, is not patronized because he is white or because he is black; but because he has known how to put brains into his work, to make his store clean and inviting... and to foresee and provide the commodities which his patrons are likely to desire. I am convinced that in business a man's mettle is tried as it is not, perhaps, in any other profession.[32]

One can assume that Washington drew ideas from the experiences of black American businessmen who had already attained a certain degree of success. Stories of successful businesses run by free black Americans in both the North and South since the 1700s had been passed down through the decades. Although many scholars view Washington as the guiding force behind Black American business, he simply took an old experience and added an element of national organization. Because of this, it is important to briefly review the experiences of this group.

The experience of free blacks during the period prior to the Civil War was in the tradition of oppressed groups everywhere.[33] But it was also difficult for free Afro-Americans to engage in business because they actu-ally had only a half-free status. The fear of being captured and enslaved was also with them. Wherever they resided, states passed laws to restrict their movement and thus, their possible business success:

There was a mass of legislation designed to insure the white community against threats or dangers from the free Negroes. Virginia, Maryland, and North Carolina were among the states forbidding free Negroes to possess or carry arms without a license.... By 1835 the right of assembly had been taken away from all free Negroes in the South... Benevolent societies and similar organizations were not allowed to convene.... A number of proscriptions made it especially difficult for free Negroes to make a living.[34]

These kinds of governmental restrictions continued to hinder the development of Afro-American business[35] as the country developed, but despite these hardships, wherever there were free Afro-Americans, a business tradition was developed. Because historical Afro-American scholars studied this development, we have excellent documentation of its existence.

One of the earliest documents regarding the business of free blacks under hostile situations is a pamphlet entitled "A Register of Trades of Colored People in the City of Philadelphia and Districts." This work listed 656 persons engaged in fifty-seven different occupations.[36] Included in the enterprises were eight Bakers, twenty-three Blacksmiths, three Brass Founders, fifteen Cabinet Makers and Carpenters, and five Confectioners. There were also two Caulkers and two Chairbottomers and fifteen Tayloring enterprises. The register also lists thirty-one Tanners, five Weavers, and six Wheelwrights.[37]

Although most of the enterprises listed were in the tradition of middleman groups, or service enterprises, manufacturing enterprises were also present. For example, nineteen sail makers were recorded in the business register of 1838. Indeed, this enterprise provided the foundation for one of the most successful black entrepreneurs in the period prior to the Civil War. James Forten, who lived between 1766 and 1841, ran a major manufacturing firm that made sails and, in 1829, employed some forty black and white employees.[38]

Matching Forten's entrepreneurial spirit in manufacturing was Stephen Smith of Philadelphia, who lived between 1796 and 1873. Smith was a lumber merchant, who by the 1850s was grossing over $100,000 annually in sales, a sum which was viewed as the "magic" number that earned one the status of "wealthy." In fact, when Moses Beach published, between 1842 and 1855, a series of twelve handbooks on New York's wealthy citizens, he set $100,000 as the lower limit of wealth.[39] By 1864 Smith's net worth was placed at $500,000. An indication of his wealth and race can be seen in an 1857 credit entry in which he was described as the "King of the Darkies w. 100m."

Although several individuals succeeded in manufacturing trades, the business which brought "prosperity" to the largest number of Afro-Americans in Philadelphia was catering. Robert Bolge, a black waiter, conceived the idea of contracting formal dinners for those who entertained in their homes. Catering spread rapidly across the newly developing country, but it was in the city of its birth that it was king.

The historical record of material progress of blacks in Philadelphia is also documented in the pamphlet previously mentioned. "They owned fifteen meeting houses and burial grounds adjacent, and one public hall. Their real estate holdings were estimated at $600,000 and their personal property at more than $667,000 dollars."[40] But this was all accomplished within an atmosphere permeated with racial hostility. There are records which show that, as early as 1789, Afro-Americans found it difficult to borrow money in order to establish business establishments. Nevertheless, through hard work and thrift, many were able to do so. For example, it is recorded that in 1771, Sara Noblitt was refused a licence to keep a public house.[41] In addition to service businesses, there were also those engaged in entertainment. The Walnut Street theatre was opened in 1808 and served as one of the focal points for "night life" in the city.[42]

In addition to Philadelphia, Cincinnati was the center of enterprise for the free black population of the Middle West. In 1835, this city's black population was 2,500; of these, 1,195 or about 48 per cent had been slaves. But by 1840 the free blacks had accumulated, not including personal and church property valued at $19,000, a total of $209,000 in real property. (In addition other cities in Ohio had significant black enterprises.) By 1852 their property holdings had increased to more than half a million dollars. "Of a population of 3,500 at the time, 200 were owners of real estate.... There were...300 Negroes in Cleveland in 1895, twenty of whom owned real estate valued at $36,000. Eight years prior to this date, 1837, Columbus had twenty-three free Negroes whose real estate investments amounted to $17,000, while that of twenty Negroes living in Lancaster amounted to $17,000 in 1840."[43]

Free blacks also dominated the restaurant business before the Civil War. They were famous for their ability to prepare a meal and serve it in the "right" way. Their clientele in the North were leading white citizens. In 1769, Emanuel, an emancipated slave, established the first oyster and ale house in Providence, Rhode Island. In 1800 Thomas Downing opened a restaurant near Wall Street in New York. He was successful for thirty years at this location, serving members of New York's professional and commercial classes. George Bell and George Alexander also operated a successful restaurant business near Wall Street.[44] Throughout the North, the restaurant business was a significant source of income for black business people.

In the South, free blacks also built a business tradition despite the presence of slavery. The state of Louisiana, which had large numbers of "free" blacks, was one of the places where Afro-Americans generated economic stability that resulted from slavery. In this state

there were large numbers of wealthy colored families many of whom owned plantations and slaves....Recaud, head of one of these families, purchased in 1851 an estate in Iberville Parish stocked with ninety-one slaves. Marie Metoyer of Nacogdoches Parish left an estate of two thousand acres of land and fifty-eight slaves in 1840. Charles Rogues of the same parish left forty-seven slaves and a thousand acres at his death in 1854, and Martin Donate of Saint Landry owned his wife and seven children at his death in 1848, and also eighty-nine other slaves, 4,500 acres of land, and notes and mortgages valued at $46,000. Nowhere in America was there a black planter aristocracy comparable with that of Louisiana. However, there had been in Saint Paul's Parish, South Carolina, a black planter who was reported before the close of the eighteenth century to have two hundred slaves, as well as a white wife and son-in-law and the returns of the first federal census appear to corroborate it. Such persons were also to be found infrequently in North Carolina, Virginia and Maryland.[45]

In addition to wealthy families, the state of Louisiana had the largest number of successful businessmen during this period, and they were involved in almost all phases of business activity. For example, between 1850 and 1857 Pierre Cazanave, a merchant and commission broker, increased his income from $100,000 to $400,000; by 1857 he was worth $100,000,000.[46]

But it was in the skilled trades that free southern blacks established themselves as businessmen in the South. Afro-Americans were denied the possibilities of formal education (which is also true of white southerners). The slaves' main work was confined to agriculture on the plantations, and they were forced to accomplish all other tasks for their master. Therefore, every kind of craft was open to a slave; he learned trades and crafts so that masters would not have to pay white labor to perform certain duties. As Kinzer and Sagarin note, "The Negro in the South was not only proficient as a carpenter, blacksmith, shoemaker, barber, tailor, and cook, but as a result of almost two and a half centuries of slavery, up to the outbreak of the Civil War, the knowledge of these skills was concentrated almost exclusively in the hands of the Negroes, free and slave."[47] One of the interesting comments made on the development of Afro-American business in general, and this time period in particular, is that they did not have the skills to run a business. As has been pointed out, a knowledge of reading and writing was not needed by businessmen during this period:

A knowledge of reading, writing, and elementary arithmetic was not as important to the conduct of a small business a century ago as it would be today [1950]. If one were able to count the money, and knew how to give the proper change, the mathematics problem was frequently solved. Few of the smaller businessmen, Negro or white, kept books or records of any kind to aid them in the conduct of their businesses.[48]

186

In North Carolina there was a free black boat builder who employed both white and black labor in his plant. In the state of South Carolina two mulattos owned one of the finest factories for the manufacture of agricultural machinery, and Anthony Weston was a famous millwright for thirty years prior to the Civil War. His wealth was generated by perfecting a thrashing machine. In Alabama, the most enterprising black contractor and bridge builder was deemed so essential to the welfare of the state that the Legislature passed a special enactment to allow him to practice his business unmolested.[49]

The stories of success are numerous and varied. In New Orleans, in 1852, a Mr. Cordovall was the leading mercer and tailor, and the styles created by him were very popular among the white elite. Albert and Freeman Morris were respected tailors in New Berne, North Carolina. Of particular interest is the story of Robert Gordon, who began in the South but ended up in Cincinnati. Gordon's history is worth putting into narrative form because it captures the spirit of entrepreneurship among free Afro-Americans before the Civil War:

> As a slave in Richmond, Virginia, Gordon had charge of his master's coal yard. He was given the privilege of keeping the profits from the sale of coal slack. By 1846 he had saved several thousand dollars. He purchased his freedom and moved to Ohio where he invested $15,000 in a coal yard and built a private dock on the waterfront. White coal merchants attempted to force him to the wall by ruthless price-cutting. Gordon craftily filled all of his orders from his competitors' suppliers by hiring light mulattos to act as his agents. When he retired from business in 1865 he invested his profits in real estate. His fortune passed eventually into the hands of his daughter.[50]

As noted earlier, capitalism allows for entrepreneurship even under extreme conditions such as slavery. Slave entrepreneurs before the Civil War were bondsmen who purchased or hired their own time. They depended on ingenuity, resourcefulness, and business sense in order to run successful enterprises. The profits generated by these enterprises were first utilized to pay slave owners for allowing the slave to hire his own time. Remaining profits were used as venture capital to purchase freedom for family members, friends and themselves.[51]

Other examples of slave entrepreneurship include Free Frank, a bondsman who, in 1812, hired his own time from his master and developed a saltpeter manufactory in Kentucky. Saltpeter was the major ingredient in the manufacture of gunpowder. As a result of Frank's enterprising, he was able to purchase his wife's freedom in 1817 and his own in 1819, at a total cost of $1,600. Historically, this reflects the fact that the purchase of freedom occurred primarily among slave entrepreneurs. For example, in the state of Ohio in 1839, over one-third (476 out of 1,129) of Afro-Americans who had been slaves had purchased their freedom for a total amount of $215,522. In Philadelphia in 1847, of the 1,077 former slaves, 275 bought their freedom at a total cost of $60,000.[52]

Because slaves often ran their owners' businesses, there existed a phenomenon known as entrepreneurship; this arose when a slave was given decision-making authority in the management of the owner's business in industry, commerce, or agriculture. A spin-off of such an arrangement was, at times, the development by the slave of a separate enterprise – as described in the case of Robert Gordon above.[53] The literature on Afro-American entrepreneurship, both slave and free, is systematic testimony to the spirit of enterprise even under troublesome conditions. It is also testimony to the fact that Afro-Americans began early to build a tradition of business enterprise.[54]

Although our discussion of Afro-American business before the Civil War merely scratches the surface, it is clear that historical documents show that a very impressive business class evolved wherever there were free Afro-Americans. In the North and South their clients were of both races. Whenever they became very successful, however, Euro-Americans tried to disrupt their businesses. There were laws passed by some states which made it very difficult to make black enterprises successful. As suggested by many scholars who studied Afro-American business, and later included in Bonacich's theory of middleman minorities, "The lines of business in which Negroes met with greatest success were those which whites did not wish to operate. [As can be seen from the above discussion] these were mainly of the labor and service types. Negro barbers, mechanics, artisans, and restaurant and hotel operators could be found in most southern cities."[55] The growth of these businesses was limited by capital and by the fact that the Afro-American market was not strong.

In terms of economic stability, Washington's motto was that there is "No Job-Hunting For Those Who Are Able To Do Something Useful." In his writings he notes that you rarely see a man idle who knows all about house-building, who knows how to draw plans, or how to test the strength of materials that enter into the making of a first-class building. He asks, "Did you ever see such a man out of a job? Did you ever see such a man as that writing letters to this place and that place, applying for work?" He notes that "people are wanted all over the world who can do work well; men and women are wanted who understand the preparation of food – not in the small menial sense – but people who know all about it."[56] Put simply, Washington believed that business activity was the key to economic stability and independence. Racial integration was not as important as the right to establish business enterprises, no matter how small, and to have them be successful.

It is very clear that in his original conceptualization, Washington was banking on an integrated clientele for black American business development. After all, this had been the case for black American business in the pre-Civil War, North and South. But the system of complete segregation, which we will call complete governmental control of black Americans, ultimately doomed Washington's economic plans for the South.

The self-help group of African Americans developed a strong emphasis on education for their children. My research reveals that offspring of the black entrepreneurial, self-help tradition are more likely to be professionals. This pattern began to develop strongly during the period of the 1920s and continues today. Thus, it is not uncommon for African Americans today who are in the self-help tradition to rise from poverty and become second, third, and, indeed, fourth generation college graduates. The importance of education has been passed from generation to generation among blacks who adjusted to America through self-help. Also, like the Japanese and Jews, descendants of this group are less likely to be found in unemployment lines in America.

Another interesting value developed by this self-help group is an absolute respect for black institutions. After all, it was their foreparents who built, maintained, and cherished these institutions. Evidence shows that they never considered these institutions inferior in any way. This phenomenon, which is mostly southern, accounts for the fact that many offspring of this self-help black group still proudly attend African American universities and colleges. For example, in my present ongoing work, entitled *The Truly Advantaged of the Disadvantaged*, I examine the families who have been attending these colleges for four generations. It is quite clear that up until the 1960s most professionals such as doctors and lawyers were produced from this self-help group of African Americans. It is also clear that, for continuing generations, role models have been family members and other important members of the community.

These people trace their historical rise from poverty to small enterprises developed in the African American community, professional experiences in one-race settings (hospitals, schools, etc.), and to the strong value placed on education. Put simply, the roots of their success in America, through the generations, have been "home-grown." Atlanta, Chicago, and Durham are still vital black business enclaves because of the continued momentum from turn-of-the-century successes in such areas as insurance, banking, and newspaper, magazine and book publishing.

The vast majority of African Americans who adjusted to America in the larger economy worked hard to develop economic stability. But like European ethnic groups, as a collective group they did not develop the same kind of attitude toward self-help and education. Like the Irish and Italians in larger American cities, their lot was affected by the twists and turns of the American economy. Because their offspring were repeatedly told that excellent jobs were available after a high school education, they were not as prepared academically as those African Americans who adjusted by self-help. This is not to say that college education has not become important to this group of blacks. But unlike their self-help counterparts who have a strong tradition of education, those who adjusted to America by entering the larger society just began attending colleges in "large" numbers in the 1960s. What is interesting is that this group owes its educational "success" more to the dynamics of change in society than to the dynamics of its own community.

One of the major propositions coming out of this exploration of adjustment to American society is that the effects of economic stability can be passed down to future generations when people faced with poverty add a significant dimension of self-help (community building, importance of education, etc.) to their development. Comparative research helps to illuminate the reasons for this phenomenon and can serve as a stepping stone to solving some of our nation's most intractable problems.

III

Booker T. Washington was right because he understood the relationship between business enterprise, education, and the success of future generations. Indeed, one can say that every idea found in the literature on ethnic entrepreneurship in America, or the experiences of groups such as the historical Jews in America and the present Asians, can be found in the work of Washington. Indeed, if Booker T. Washington had been Japanese American or Jewish American he would be held as a national economic hero. His philosophy, rather than representing a new mode of thought at the turn of the century, was followed by free blacks prior to the Civil War. The Ibo in Africa have also followed a similar path.

Without a doubt Washington was very "soft" on protesting for the right to vote. This was especially devastating because the right of the ballot was taken away from blacks. But it is interesting that a trademark of middleman groups around the world is that they pay very little attention to political behavior, except when it relates to their own communities.[57] This does not mean that political behavior is not important, but it does mean that there is not necessarily a relationship between political participation and the economic stability of a group.

What we are learning is that blacks in the tradition of business enterprise in America have, as a group, lived a life of economic stability for generations. Over the years, scholars have not understood this group of blacks. They have been called the black bourgeoisie, black Brahmans, black elite, and the black upper class. Whatever they are called, their adjustment to America bears a striking resemblance to middleman minorities throughout the history of the world. Today, as we prepare to turn the century mark, their children are better educated than most Americans, and this education has been a part of their family for two to three generations.

NOTES

1 John Sibley Butler, *Entrepreneurship and Self-Help Among Black Americans: A Reconsideration of Race and Economics* (New York: State University of New York Press: 1991).

2 Max Weber, *The Protestant Ethic and the Spirit of Capitalism.*

3 *ibid.*, p. 35.

4 For a discussion of the impact of Weber on the theory of capitalism see Gordon Marshall, *In Search of the Spirit of Capitalism* (New York: Columbia University Press, 1982) and Alan MacFarlane, *The Culture of Capitalism* (Oxford and Cambridge: Blackwell, 1987).

5 Georg Simmel, "The Stranger," in *The Sociology of Georg Simmel*, edited by Kurt H. Wolff, pp. 402–8 (Glencoe, ILL: Free Press, 1950). See also, *ibid.*, p. 402. Quoted from Edna Bonacich and John Modell, *The Economic Basis of Ethnic Solidarity: Small Business in the Japanese American Community* (Berkeley: University of California Press, 1980, p. 29). For an excellent discussion of the place of the stranger in historical societies see Bonacich and Modell. See also Herbert Blalock, *Toward a Theory of Minority Group Relations* (New York: John Wiley, 1967); Lloyd A. Fallers (ed.), *Immigrants and Associations* (The Hague: Mouton, 1967).

6 Everett E. Hagen, *On The Theory of Social Change* (Homewood, Illinois: The Dorsey Press, Inc., 1962, p. 60).

7 Werner Sombart, *The Jews and Modern Capitalism* (New Brunswick, N.J.: Transaction Books, 1982 – reprint of 1951 edition, p. 20).

8 *ibid.*, p. 12.

9 Chaim Bermant, *The Jews* (New York: Times Books, 1977, p. 109).

10 *Independent Nigeria: The People of Nigeria* (Lagos: Government Printer, 1960, p. 13). See also Ngwuru Njaka and Umunna Dimewere, *Ibo Political Culture* (Evanston, ILL, 1974).

11 Ngwuru Njaka and Umunna Dimewere, *Ibo Political Culture* (Evanston: Northwestern University Press), p. 18.

12 John Hatch, *Nigeria: A History* (London: Secker & Warburg, 1971, p. 62) and *ibid.*, p. 20.

13 Robert A. LeVine, *Dreams and Deeds: Achievement Motivation in Nigeria* (Chicago: University of Chicago Press, 1966, pp. 71–5); see also Phoebe Ottenberg, "The Afikpo Ibo of Eastern Nigeria," in *Peoples of Africa*, James L. Gibbs, Jr. (ed.), (New York: Holt Rinehart and Winston, Inc., 1965, p. 6); and E. Wayne Nafzier, *African Capitalism: A Case Study in Nigerian Entrepreneurship* (Stanford, California: Hoover Institution Press, 1977).

14 John Hatch, *Nigeria: A History*, p. 68.

15 *ibid.*

16 For those who are interested in exploring this group see Audrey C. Smock, *Ibo Politics: The Role of Ethnic Unions in Eastern Nigeria* (Cambridge, Massachusetts: Harvard University Press, 1977); J. W. Lieber, *Ibo Village Communities* (Nigeria: Institute of Education, 1971); Don C. Ohadike, *Western Ibo Resistance to the British Conquest of Nigeria, 1883–1914* (Athens: Ohio University Press, 1991).

17 Boniface I. Obichere (ed.), *Studies in Southern Nigerian History* (Great Britain: Frank Cass and Company Limited, 1982, p. 164).

18 John Hatch, *Nigeria: A History*, p. 241.

19 This discussion follows the discussion of the development of middleman minority by Butler. For a full discussion of the relationship between middleman minority and scholars such as Weber see John Sibley Butler, *Entrepreneurship*

and Self-Help Among Black Americans: A Reconsideration of Race and Economics (New York: State University of New York Press, 1991), especially chapter 1.

20 Howard Becker, *Man in Reciprocity* (New York: Praeger, 1956); Hubert M. Blalock, Jr., *Toward A Theory of Minority Group Relations* (New York: John Wiley & Sons, 1967); R. A. Schermerhorn, *Comparative and Ethnic Relations* (New York: Random House, 1970); Sheldon Stryker, "Structures and Prejudice," *Social Problems* 6 Spring 1959; 340–54.

21 Jonathan H. Turner and Edna Bonacich, "Toward a Composite Theory of Middleman Minorities," *Ethnicity* 7: 144–58.

22 Edna Bonacich, "A Theory of Middleman Minorities," *America Sociological Review* 38 October 1972: 583–94.

23 Bonacich, *op. cit.*, p. 583.

24 For an exposition on this point see Walter P. Zenner, "Middleman Minorities in The Syrian Mosaic," *Sociological Perspectives* 30: 400–21, October, 1987.

25 *ibid.*, p. 584.

26 This discussion follows that by John Sibley Butler's *Entrepreneurship and Self-Help Among Black Americans: A Reconstruction of Race and Economics* (New York: SUNY Press, 1991, pp. 64–71).

27 Louis R. Harlan, *Booker T. Washington: The Wizard of Tuskegee* (New York: Oxford University Press, 1983).

28 Booker T. Washington, "The Atlanta Exposition Address," in John Hope Franklin and Isidore Starr (eds), *The American Negro America* (New York: Vintage Books, 1967, pp. 85–7).

29 *ibid.*, p. 88.

30 John Sibley Butler, *Entrepreneurship and Self-Help Among Black Americans: A Reconsideration of Race and Economics* (New York: State University of New York Press: 1991), p. 66.

31 Author's emphasis.

32 Booker T. Washington, *The Negro in Business* (Chicago: Hertel, Jenkins & Co. 1907, pp. 14–15).

33 For an excellent analysis of enterprises by blacks prior to the Civil War see Juliet E. K. Walker, "Racism, Slavery, and Free Enterprise: Black Entrepreneurship in the United States Before the Civil War," in *Business History Review* 60 (Autumn 1986) p. 333.

34 John Hope Franklin, *From Slavery to Freedom* (New York: Alfred A. Knopf, 1948). Quotation taken from Robert Kinzer and Edward Sagarin, *The Negro in American Business* (New York: Greenberg Press, 1950, p. 32).

35 For a discussion of the experiences of free Afro-Americans see Leonard P. Curry, *The Free Black in Urban America 1800–1865* (Chicago: The University of Chicago Press, 1981); Ira Berlin, *Slaves Without Masters* (New York: Pantheon Books, 1974); Kenneth G. Goode, *California's Black Pioneers* (Santa Barbara: McNally & Loftin, Publishers, 1974).

36 Henry M. Minton, "Early History of Negroes in Business in Philadelphia", read before the American Historical Society, March 1913.

37 *ibid.*, pp. 8–10.

38 Walker, *op. cit.*, p. 252.

39 *ibid.*, p. 349.

40 *ibid.*, p. 8.

41 *ibid.*, pp. 8–9.

42 *ibid.*

43 Abram L. Harris, *The Negro As Capitalist* (College Park, MD: McGrath Publishing Company, 1936, pp. 6–7).

44 *ibid.*, pp. 11–12.

45 *ibid.*, pp. 4–5.
46 Walker, *op. cit.*, p. 354.
47 Kinzer and Sagarin, *op. cit.*, p. 36.
48 *ibid.*, p. 36.
49 Harris, *op. cit.*, p. 17.
50 *ibid.*, p. 17.
51 Walker, *op. cit.*, p. 364.
52 *ibid.*, p. 365.
53 *ibid.*, p. 366.
54 Most of this literature has been produced by historians. See especially Juliet E. K. Walker, *Free Frank: A Black Pioneer on the Antebellum Frontiers* (Lexington, KY: University of Kentucky Press, 1983); Gary B. Mills, *The Forgotten People: Cane River's Creoles of Color* (Baton Rouge: Louisiana State University Press, 1977); Leonard P. Curry, *The Free Black in Urban America, 1880–1850: The Shadow of A Dream* (Chicago: The University of Chicago Press, 1981).
55 Joseph A. Pierce, *Negro Business and Business Education* (New York: Harper Brothers Publishers, 1947).
56 *ibid.*, p. 347.
57 Edna Bonacich and John Modell, *The Economic Basis of Ethnic Solidarity: Small Business In The Japanese American Community* (Berkeley: University of California Press, 1980, p. 16).

11

BOOKER T. WASHINGTON
Myth Maker
Vernon J. Williams, Jr.

On 18 September 1895, Booker T. Washington, the young Principal of Tuskegee Normal and Industrial Institute, delivered an address to a mixed audience at the opening of the Atlanta Cotton States and International Exposition. Thirty-nine years old, the Tuskegeean had spent nine years as a slave and had witnessed the demise of slavery. Washington had also lived through the period when the North attempted to reconstruct the South and had seen the reconciliation between two great sections take place in 1877. Furthermore, he bore witness to the subordination of blacks in the South after Reconstruction. Disfranchisement by amended state constitutions had taken place in Mississippi in 1890 and was taking place in South Carolina at the time of Washington's address in 1895. Through the gradual proliferation of Jim Crow laws, extra-legal violence, and the removal of blacks from positions in skilled labor – all aided and abetted by the unethical political climate in the South – whites, at the time of Washington's address, had consolidated their higher caste positions over blacks.

Although he did not mention any specific names, Washington began by scolding black emigrationists "who depend on bettering their condition in a foreign land," and those militant blacks "who underestimate the importance of cultivating friendly relations with the Southern white man as his next-door neighbor" (Washington (1901) 1986: 219). The ex-slave's interpretation of black history stressed the idea that blacks had been loyal servants "nursing your children, watching by the sick bed of your mothers and fathers, and often following them with tear-dimmed eyes to their graves" (Washington (1901) 1986: 221). Revealing his nativist thought, Washington argued that whites "who look to the incoming of those of foreign birth and strange tongue and habits for the prosperity of the South" (Washington (1901) 1986: 220) had a limited knowledge of the black contribution to Southern history. For blacks "without strikes and labour wars, tilled your fields, cleared your forests, built your railroads and brought forth treasures from the bowels of the earth..." (Washington (1901) 1986: 220). Despite-Washington's emphasis on the monumental role blacks had played in whatever achievements the South made during the antebellum period, he argued that blacks were not prepared for the coming of industrialization.

During Reconstruction, Washington asserted, "ignorant and inexperienced" blacks "began at the top instead of at the bottom" (Washington (1901) 1986: 218). For those blacks "a seat in Congress or the state legislature was more sought than real estate or industrial skill...the convention of stump speaking had more attractions than starting a dairy farm or truck garden" (Washington (1901) 1986: 218–19). In effect, Washington exonerated white Southerners of any responsibility for the so-called Negro problem, and placed it squarely on the shoulders of blacks. Learning the virtues of common labor, he believed, would yield far more gains than politics. In regard to the role of blacks in the South's economy, he suggested that some would find a place in the professions. For the overwhelming number of blacks, however, Washington asserted: "It is at the bottom of life we must begin, and not at the top" (Washington (1901) 1986: 220). Sociologically speaking, he envisioned a South where there would be great social distance between blacks and whites – "In all things that are purely social we can be as separate as the fingers" – yet considerable intergroup collaboration – "one as the hand in all things essential to mutual progress" (Washington (1901) 1986: 221–2). Projecting the social Darwinist mind-set with its emphasis on the "survival of the fittest," and a buoyant spirit of optimism, the Tuskegee Wizard argued that African Americans would eventually achieve equality – not by agitation for social equality, but by a "severe and constant struggle" in the market place (Washington (1901) 1986: 223).

Historical interpretations implying that Washington's Atlanta Exposition address either soothed the consciences of the justices of the Supreme Court that legitimized Jim Crow laws in the *Plessy* v. *Ferguson* case in 1896, or was an expedient strategy, have generated heated scholarly debates. Those debates, however, seem unresolvable – especially when the adversaries take into account the virulent racism that pervaded the nation and Washington's surreptitious struggle against the forces of reaction in the South (Meier 1963: 110–14; Harlan 1972: 298–9). Nevertheless, Washington's ideas deserve close scrutiny; for Washington was more than a mere "man of action". He was a consummate mythmaker. When "history" eventually discredited Washington's mythology, this thoughtful, reflective man modified some of his myths; yet left others intact. Part of this essay is an examination of that process.

I

On 19 May 1931, in a lecture before his sociology course entitled "The Negro" at the University of Chicago, Robert Ezra Park outlined the social philosophy of Washington. Park, who had served as a ghostwriter for Washington during the years between 1905 and 1913 and was the most distinguished student of race relations in the country, asserted: Washington "really represented" the freedman who wanted to attain first class citizenship. Unlike the aristocratic W. E. B. Du Bois, who represented educated blacks and in the tradition of the abolitionists appealed to "'rights'" in the Fourteenth and Fifteenth Amendments to the Constitution in an attempt to make laws which existed operative, Washington thought that whites believed it was their "right and duty to keep" the African American "in his place" (Park, 19 May 1931: 31–2). Drawing on the conservative social Darwinist William Graham Sumner, whose concept of "the mores" encouraged what the late Swedish political economist Gunnar Myrdal called a "laissez faire, do-nothing" approach to white–black relations, Park argued that Washington knew that the subordination of African Americans "was deep in the mores of the South" (Park, 19 May 1931: 31). Furthermore, Park suggested, Washington "realized and knew" that effective laws "must rest" on mores and customs; and, as a consequence, "in order to make laws operative," both whites and blacks would have to be "reeducated – particularly the whites" (Park, 19 May 1931: 32). By changing the "sound, natural conditions which made the mores what they were," one could "then change the mores" (Park, 19 May 1931: 31). Thus, Washington's philosophy of gradual economic uplift through industrial education was, according to Park, set up to "reeducate" African Americans in the South for a new system of labor, in which, unlike slavery, the black masses were supposed to "find work dignifying…a privilege." In reference to the positive aspects of Washington's program for African Americans, Park asserted that the "purpose of Washington's education was to convince [the] negro that he could do things. Start him on *his own*" (Park, 19 May 1931: 32). According to Park, Washington believed that providing African Americans in the South with an industrial education could provide the impetus for transforming the mores of whites. In *agape*-like terms, Park interpreted Washington's philosophy of community in the following manner:

> Washington [was] always saying that both white and black have a community of interest. [Washington] didn't appeal to mores, or law, but to the individual. If [the blacks] don't get justice, it reacts back on the whole community.… His appeal [was] that interests of negro and white were alike [and] would lead to laws that protect both alike.
>
> (Park, 19 May 1931: 31)

Despite what seemed like a sane social philosophy, at the height of his influence, it should be stressed that Washington publicly adumbrated the political mythology most frequently promulgated to justify turn-of-the century race relations in order to rationalize his program of the gradual economic advance of African Americans in the South through industrial education. In his autobiography, *Up From Slavery*, which sold 30,000 copies between its initial publication by Doubleday, Page and Company in 1901 and September 1903, Washington implied that African Americans were the descendants of barbarous peoples, and as a result only capable of progress under the Christian and civilizing influences of whites. He then enjoined the themes of African primitiveness and the civilizing effects of slavery when he wrote:

> Then, when we rid ourselves of prejudice, or racial feeling, and look facts in the face, we must acknowledge that, not withstanding the cruelty and moral wrong of slavery, the ten million Negroes inhabiting this country, who themselves or whose ancestors went through the school of American slavery, are in a stronger and more hopeful condition materially, intellectually, morally, and religiously than is true of an equal number of black people in any portion of the globe. This is to such an extent that Negroes in this country, who themselves or whose forefathers went through the school of slavery, are constantly returning to Africa to enlighten those who remain in the fatherland.
>
> (Washington (1901) 1986: 16)

Washington's ghostwriter, S. Laing Williams, a prominent African American who practiced law in Chicago, was even more emphatic about the progressiveness of Anglo-Americans and the primitiveness of African blacks when he wrote in a biography of Frederick Douglass in 1907:

> The chance or destiny which brought to this land of ours, and placed in the midst of the most progressive and most enlightened race that Christian civilization has produced, some three or four millions of primitive black people from Africa and their descendants, has created one of the most interesting and difficult social problems which any modern people has had to face.
>
> (Washington (1907) 1968: 5)

Although Washington's and Williams's statements to the contemporary reader seem to be little more than a rationalization for the status quo in white–black relations, it must be remembered that their defense of the institution of slavery and the limited progress of African Americans was a moderate position. Other intellectuals such as General Francis A. Walker, James Bryce, Joseph Le Conte, Eugene Rollin Carson, Joseph A. Tillinghast, Paul B. Barringer, Frederick L. Hoffman, and Walter F. Willcox argued that African Americans were degenerating and predicted that they would become extinct. These spokesmen for black degeneracy, as Professor George M. Fredrickson has correctly pointed out, were Darwinians. Fredrickson has asserted that it logically followed from their position that:

> If the blacks were a degenerating race with no future, the problem ceased to be one of how to prepare them for citizenship or even how

to make them more productive and useful members of the community. The new prognosis pointed rather to the need to segregate or quarantine a race liable to be a source of contamination and social danger to the white community, as it sank even deeper into the slough of disease, vice, and criminality.

(Fredrickson 1971: 255)

It is true that Washington was a social Darwinist of a sort – insofar as his philosophy was primarily materialistic. Washington, however, did not exclude moral or religious forces in accounting for the evolution of humans. For example, he wrote in *The Negro in the South* in 1907:

I sometimes fear that in our great anxiety to push forward we lay too much stress upon our former condition. We should think less of our former growth and more of the present and of the things which go to retard or hinder that growth. In one of his letters to the Galatians, St. Paul says: "But the fruit of the spirit is love, joy, peace, long-suffering, gentleness, goodness, faith, temperance; against such there is no law."

I believe that it is possible for a race, as it is for an individual, to learn to live up in such a high atmosphere that there is no human law that can prevail against it. There is no man who can pass a law to affect the Negro in relation to his singing, his peace, and his self-control. Wherever I go I would enter St. Paul's atmosphere and, living through and in that spirit, we will grow and make progress and, notwithstanding discouragements and mistakes we will become an increasingly strong part of the Christian citizenship of this republic.

(Washington (1907) 1970: 74–5)

In addition to disagreeing with the Darwinians concerning a Supreme Being or purpose in the universe, Washington also disagreed with them on the issue of the potency of human beings' agency or will. His embracement of Neo-Lamarckianism suggested that will or purpose could and was bringing about evolutionary change. In other words, the idea of the inheritance of acquired characteristics suggested that not only bad behavior, but also good behaviour could be transmitted from one generation to another. Washington used the principle to demonstrate that the purported differences between the races were not permanent. "It is only through struggle and the surmounting of difficulties that races, like individuals," Washington asserted in 1907, "are made strong, powerful, and useful" (Washington (1907) 1970: 40). As early as 1899, in *The Future of the American Negro* Washington clearly drew a distinction between his position and that of those intellectuals who believed in the impending extinction of blacks:

A few people predicted that freedom would result disastrously to the Negro, as far as numerical increase was concerned; but so far as the census figures have failed to bear out this prediction.... It is my

198

opinion that the rate of increase in the future will be still greater than it has been from the close of the war of the Rebellion up to the present time, for the reason that the very sudden changes which took place in the life of the Negro because of his freedom, plunged him into many excesses that were detrimental to his physical well-being.

(Washington (1899) 1968: 6–7)

Although it is clear that Washington drew a distinction between his moderate liberal position and that of the prognosticators of the impending extinction of African Americans, he did, however, cast grave doubts about the viability of Reconstruction. The period of Reconstruction, in Washington's view, was one in which "two ideas were constantly agitating the minds of colored people, or, at least, the minds of the larger part of the race. One of these was the craze for Greek and Latin learning, and the other was a desire to hold office." The fascination of African Americans with such status and power symbols, Washington argued, should have been expected from "a people who had spent generations in slavery and generations before that in the darkest heathenism" (Washington (1901) 1986: 80).

Yet, the desires of African Americans to learn the classical languages and to hold political office were not the most serious flaws that Washington detected in the defunct Reconstruction period. Washington's major grievance centered on the maternal relationship between the government and the African American wards of that government. Thus he wrote:

During the whole of the Reconstruction period our people throughout the South looked to the Federal Government for everything, very much as a child looks to its mother. This was not unnatural. The central government gave them freedom, and the whole Nation had been enriched for more than two centuries by the labour of the Negro. Even as a youth, and later in manhood, I had the feeling that it was cruelly wrong in the central government, at the beginning of our freedom, to fail to make provision for the general education of our people in addition to what the states might do, so that the people would be the better prepared for the duties of citizenship.

(Washington (1901) 1986: 83)

It would be a mistake to argue that Washington was wholly critical of Reconstruction. In fact, as early as 1899 he wrote in *The Future of the American Negro* that: "The period of reconstruction served at least to show the world that with proper preparation and with a sufficient foundation the Negro possesses the elements out of which men of the highest character and usefulness can be developed" (Washington (1899) 1903: 13–14). Two years later in *Up From Slavery*, Washington stated emphatically that "not all coloured people who were in office during Reconstruction were unworthy of their positions by any means. Some of them, like the late Senator

B. K. Bruce, Governor Pinchback, and many others, were strong, upright, useful men." The problem, according to Washington, was not race but education and experience. Therefore, Washington recommended the disfranchisement of both blacks and whites through the use of property and educational qualifications. These "tests," he suggested, "should be made to apply honestly and squarely to both the white and black races" (Washington (1901) 1986: 85–6).

In short, Washington in 1901 viewed the vast majority of Africans and some African Americans as barbarous underachievers who, in his days, were unable to attain the heights of civilization of Anglo-Americans. His solution to the problems of African Americans was industrial education. Through this "education of the hand, head, and heart," – in other words, by becoming acculturated – Washington believed African Americans could eventually contribute to the markets of the world and become prepared for the exercise of first-class citizenship.

In order to fully comprehend the essence of Washington's philosophy of gradual uplift through industrial education, I think it is necessary to examine the social and intellectual influences that produced the idea that the concept was a positive good and therefore a solution to problems centering around the economic arrangements that differentiated most blacks from most whites in the South. The concept of industrial education had its origins in the educational theories of Europeans such as Pestalozzi and Fellenberg. Yet, despite its European origins, the concept with its emphases on morality, thrift, industry, economic independence, and material success, according to August Meier, took hold in the United States as early as the 1820s (Meier (1963) 1968: 85). The idea that some youth should acquire a trade or mechanical skill later arose during the Negro Convention movement as a result of the exclusion of blacks from the skilled trades. As early as 1831, the Philadelphia convention drew up a plan which stated "that a college be established at New Haven as soon as $20,000 are obtained, and to be on the Manual Labour System, by which in connexion with a scientific education they [Young Men of Colour] may also obtain a useful Mechanical or Agricultural progression" (Moses (1978) 1988: 93). The conventions during the 1830s and 1840s continued to adopt plans for potential manual trade schools; to no avail, however. In fact, at a convention in 1848 a committee of five which included Frederick Douglass stated that

> every blow of the sledge hammer, wielded by a sable arm, is a powerful blow in support of our cause. Every colored mechanic, is by virtue of circumstances an elevator of his race....Trades are important. Whenever a man may be thrown by misfortune, if he has in his hands a useful trade, he is useful to his fellow man, and will be esteemed accordingly....
>
> (Moses (1978) 1988: 93)

The fallacious idea that a black man or woman with a useful trade would be esteemed and treated accordingly was sustained from 1860 through the 1890s by the Freedman's Bureau commissioners, missionary school teachers, the Methodists, and the American Missionary Association. The latter organization helped to create the most successful agricultural and industrial school for blacks before 1890: Hampton Institute. It was under General Samuel Chapman Armstrong at Hampton, who believed industrial education was a moral force, that Booker T. Washington was trained. In his last address, delivered before the American Missionary Association and the National Council of Congregational Churches in New Haven, Connecticut, on 25 October 1915, Washington celebrated "a transformation" that had been "wrought to my race since the landing at Jamestown and the landing of the last slaves at Mobile!" (Washington 1932: 277). "This transformation involves," he continued, "growth in numbers, mental awakening, self-support, securing of property, moral and religious development, and adjustment of relations between relations. To what in a single generation are we more indebted for this transformation in the direction of a higher civilization than the American Missionary Association?" (Washington 1932: 277).

Although, as Meier has astutely pointed out, industrial education could be viewed as either "a means for helping the laboring classes to rise in the world," or "as a type of instruction suitable for adjusting them to their social role," it is not clear which function Washington truly believed it served (Meier (1963) 1968: 86). Yet, despite Washington's optimism, historical hindsight has demonstrated that Washington had sustained a myth with a greater degree of falsity than truth. "The fact remains," wrote C. Vann Woodward in 1951, "that Washington's training school, and the many schools he inspired taught crafts and attitudes more congenial to the premachine age than to the twentieth century...." (Thornborough 1969: 157).

By publicly embracing the myth of African inferiority and the "positive good" of slavery, Washington could but would not admit that his program of gradual uplift through industrial education was a sham. At the end of this period in Washington's development, he wrote in 1907:

In his native country, owing to climatic conditions, and also because of his few simple and crude wants, the Negro, before coming to America, had little necessity to labor. You have, perhaps, read the story, that it is said might be true in certain portions of Africa, of how the native simply lies down on his back under a banana-tree and falls asleep with his mouth open. The banana falls into his mouth while he is asleep and he wakes up and finds that all he has to do is to chew it – he has his meal already served.

Notwithstanding the fact that, in most cases, the element of compulsion entered into the labor of the slave, and the main object sought was the enrichment of the owner, the American Negro had, under the regime of slavery, his first lesson in anything like continuous progressive, systematic labor.

(Washington (1907) 1970: 20–1)

Washington's myth of African inferiority attracted most social scientists in "history." And although the Boasian position of equipotentiality in reference to West and Central Africans surfaced in 1904 and would influence most prominent sociologists and anthropologists in the field of race relations by 1929, the myth of African inferiority in history proper sustained itself for forty more years.

II

It should be noted here, however, that the myth of Africans of some blacks and whites was not static. Louis R. Harlan has correctly pointed out that Washington's myth, in particular, of the African was dynamic, "due to growing knowledge of African history and the new ideas of anthropology, sociology, and archaeology." Washington, influenced by Franz Boas, Monroe N. Work, Robert E. Park, and James H. Breasted, was not, however, merely "a man of action", but a thoughtful, reflective person who slowly modified his views until they conformed to the most recent and authoritative findings in the social sciences.

In 1904, Boas contacted Washington. Seeking to diversify the racial composition of students in American anthropology, he solicited Booker T. Washington's advice concerning the admission of James Emman Kwegyr Aggrey, a Fanti born in the Gold Coast, to graduate study in anthropology at Columbia University. Of Aggrey who had received a BA at Livingston College in 1902, Boas wrote: "He [Aggrey] is a full-blood negro and so far as I can learn, his standing is such that he will require at least one year of undergraduate work before he can be admitted to university...From what I hear from my colleagues who made his acquaintance at the session of the summer school, he is a very bright man. He is, however, without means, and will require support in order to complete his studies. I do not know whether it would be possible to obtain this support here in the city, but I do not think it is unlikely" (Boas Correspondence: 30 November 1904). Nevertheless, Boas clearly labored when he considered the dismal career prospects that Aggrey would face once he had satisfactorily completed the requirements for an advanced degree. "I very much hesitate to advise the young man to take up this work, because I fear that it would be very difficult after he has completed his studies to find a place," Washington wrote. "On the other hand, it might perhaps be possible for him to study for two or three years and to take his degree of master of arts, and then to obtain a position in one of the higher schools established for his race. I feel that the matter is a rather delicate one, and I do not wish to advise the young man or to assist him in beginning a study which may ultimately put him in a most unfortunate position" (Boas Correspondence: 30 November 1904). At the end of the letter, Boas was extremely pessimistic about the employment prospects of Aggrey and suggested they might be solved through Aggrey's participation in the Colonial service of one of the European powers: "It is of course evident that if he developed into a good scientist," Boas argued, "he could do excellent work particularly in Africa, which would be of the greatest service to science. This is a consideration which makes me desirous of assisting him. On the other hand, I am very much afraid that it would be almost impossible to find a place for him even in this field. Perhaps by proper application, and if he were the right man, it might be possible to get him into Colonial service of one of the European countries that have colonies in Africa" (Boas Correspondence: 30 November 1904). Indicative of the fact that Boas's liberalism, when Boas initiated their correspondence in 1904, was far too progressive for the leading black spokesman of the period is Booker T. Washington's response to Boas's letter. Washington, who believed blacks needed to enter the practical vocations, told Boas:

> Judging by what you state in your letter and knowing what I do, I can not rid myself of the feeling that the course which he is planning to take will be of little value to him. At the present time I know of so many cases where young colored men and women would have done well had they thoroughly prepared themselves for teachers, some kind of work in the industries, or in the applied sciences, but instead, they have made the mistake of taking a course that had no practical bearing on the needs of the race; the result being they ended up as hotel-waiters or Pullman car porters.
>
> (Boas Correspondence: 9 December 1904)

As Boas would later learn, the Tuskegee "Wizard" was no man's fool. Although Aggrey went on to receive an MA at Livingston College in 1912, a DD degree from Hood Theological Seminary, an MA from Columbia University in 1922, became a member of the Phelps-Stokes Committee on Education in Africa during the early 1920s, and eventually served as Vice-Principal of Achimota Prince of Wales College and School in present-day Ghana, Washington's statements had some basis in empirical reality – especially when one considers the career of Zora Neale Hurston almost three decades later. Hurston's biographer, Robert E. Hemenway, has described how Boas did not hesitate to direct her studies in 1934. But even Boas, who had helped Hurston draw up a plan for the Rosenwald Foundation for her doctoral program, was unable to gain long-term support for her – despite the fact that Hurston was the author of a novel and a book of folklore (Hemenway 1977: 206–14).

On 8 November 1906, Boas wrote a letter to Booker T. Washington, seeking to speak with him when he came to the Carl Schurz Memorial Meeting in New York City. Boas indicated that he was "endeavoring to organize certain scientific work on the Negro race which" he believed would "be of great practical value in modifying the views of our people in regard to the Negro Problem." He was "particularly anxious to bring home to the American people the fact that the African race in its own continent has achieved advancements which have been of importance in the development of civilization of the human race." As an afterword, Boas insisted that he wanted to "talk over the possibilities of practical steps in this direction" (Boas Correspondence: 8 November 1906). The Tuskegee "Wizard" did not respond to Boas' letter, but would later extend an invitation to him on 17 June 1912 to serve on the executive committee of the International Conference on the Negro (Boas Correspondence: 17 June 1912).

There are clear indications, nonetheless, that Boas modified Washington's image of Africans, due to the influences of his ghostwriters, Robert Ezra Park and Monroe Nathan Work. As early as the winter of 1903–4, Washington had begun writing a two-volume history of the Negro in Africa and America for Doubleday, Page and Company. In 1906, he assigned the writing of the work to Park. Yet when work of higher priority flooded Park's desk, it was put aside. Two years later, after the insistence of the publisher, the writing of the volumes was assigned to Alvis Octavius Stafford, a teacher at the Institute for Colored Youth in Cheyney, Pennsylvania. The drafts that Stafford sent back were so poor that Work, the new Director of Records and Research, was called in to salvage the project. Writing to Washington concerning Work's contribution to the project, Park stated:

> I think I ought, now as "The Story of the Negro" is off our hands, to say something of the way in which Mr. Work has helped me during this long, tedious, and often very discouraging task. From the very first, although the work I was doing was not anything he felt responsible for and although the demands I made upon him often interfered with his own work, he has never shirked or complained. He has met every demand I made upon him in perfect cheerfulness, and has done the work I asked him to do, as faithfully as if he were working at some task of his own choosing, and according to his own methods and ideas.
>
> (McMurray 1985: 60)

In addition to Park's rather lengthy remarks concerning Work's diligence, some background information on Work is necessary in order to clarify why he was able to play such a monumental role in writing *The Story of the Negro*, a work – to use Harlan's words – "significant for its consciousness of Africa" (Harlan 1972: xxxvii).

Work, the son of former slaves, was born in Iredell County, North Carolina, in 1866. He was raised in Cairo, Illinois, and rural Kansas. Like many men who formed the ranks of the early sociologists, he embarked on a ministerial career, joining the African Methodist Episcopal Church. Describing his career from 1897 until 1903, Work recalled that he was studying at Chicago Theological Seminary on the city's west side to become a preacher. Graham Taylor, who taught what was called "Christian Sociology," became interested in a paper that Work had completed on black crime in Chicago. When Work changed his career aspiration from the ministry to sociology in 1898, he brought his paper with him. After he had made some revisions when he entered the University of Chicago to study under William I. Thomas, the article was published in the *American Journal of Sociology* later in 1900, the first one published by an African American in that journal (Jessie P. Guzman Papers: n.d.). After receiving his Master of Arts degree from the University of Chicago, Work accepted a position at Georgia State Industrial College in Savannah in order to be near W. E. B. Du Bois. (Work considered Du Bois, along with himself, Richard R. Wright, Jr., and Kelly Miller "the four originals," Negroes in the newly-formed discipline of sociology.) Work was confident that DuBois, through his pioneering Atlanta series, held the key to a truly meaningful uplift of blacks. So closely was Work allied to Du Bois that he even joined the short-lived Niagara movement (Jessie P. Guzman Papers: n.d.).

Nevertheless, in 1908 Du Bois's arch rival, Booker T. Washington, invited Work to come to Tuskegee Institute. Work told the story about his departure from Georgia in the following manner in 1908:

> Mr. Washington wrote to me and said he wanted to establish a department of history at Tuskegee in which there would be an opportunity for the study of the Negro. He had been urged to have a study made of graduates of Tuskegee. He wrote me that he wanted to see me and said that he was coming through Savannah. He was in his private car going to Beaufort, South Carolina to make a speech. I met him and said to him, "I have your letter." He said, "Yes, come over to Tuskegee and we'll talk it over." The conversation was just a minute and didn't consume as much time as it takes me to tell you about it.
>
> (Jessie P. Guzman Papers: n.d.)

However, in an "Autobiographical Sketch" written in 1940, Work portrayed himself as taking a more assertive role in the negotiations with Washington. When the latter asked him "to establish a department of Negro history," Work indicated that in his "opinion it would be more important and valuable to have a department specializing in the compiling of current data relating to the Negro. My suggestion was accepted and at Tuskegee Institute was established the first department, in a Negro Educational Institution, devoted to compiling from all available sources data relating to every phase of Negro life and history" (Monroe N. Work Papers: 7 February 1940).

Work stated that when he came to Tuskegee many persons who were involved in black uplift were asking questions such as: "What has the Negro accomplished? What can he do? Does it pay to educate him? Morally and physically, is he not deteriorating? Has his emancipation been justified?" He noted that Frederick Hoffman's *Race Traits and Tendencies of the Negro* (1896) "had presented a more or less hopeless view." Furthermore, Work argued that, "to the indictment by this publication there was at hand no effective answer." A person who believed that all generalizations about blacks should be based on concrete, universally verifiable data – "You can't argue with facts," as he once put it – Work from 1908 on "was compiling a day by day record of what was taking place with reference to the Negro." "Thus it became possible," he believed, "to answer in a factual manner questions relating to all matters concerning him" [the Negro] (Monroe N. Work Papers: 7 February 1940). As a result of answering questions concerning blacks, Work began to publish a biennial with a worldwide circulation. Entitled *Negro Yearbook*, it was "a standard reference on all matters pertaining to the Race" (Monroe N. Work Papers: 7 February 1940).

Work's fascination with Africa had begun in graduate school, while studying under William I. Thomas – a scholar influenced significantly by Franz Boas. Before the publication of *The Story of the Negro* in 1909, Work, who would later become a distinguished Africanist, had published three articles treating Africans in the *Southern Workman*. Furthermore, in *The Story*, Work quoted Boas extensively on the art of smelting ores by Africans; the artistic industries of Africa; the agriculture of Africans; native African culture; African law; and the character of African states (Washington (1909) 1940, 1: 32, 47, 50, 58, 59, 71, 74, 75). In sum, Work was the conduit between Boasian anthropology and the Tuskegee machine.

Robert E. Park also helped to ghostwrite the early chapters of *The Story*. Park was born on 14 February 1864, on a farm six miles from Schickshinny, Luzerene County, Pennsylvania. His mother – Theodosia Warner – was a school teacher; his father – Hiram Asa Park – was a soldier in the Union Army. After the end of the Civil War, the elder Park moved his family to Red Wing, Minnesota, a town located on the Mississippi River forty miles south of Minneapolis, where he established a wholesale grocery. Park spent eighteen years in Red Wing, a town whose population was mainly composed of Norwegian and Swedish immigrants. After graduating from high school in 1882, the young Park attended the University of Minnesota for one year before transferring to the University of Michigan, where he graduated with a PhD in philology in 1887 (Raushenbush 1975: 1–62).

From 1887 to 1898, Park worked for various newspapers in the midwest and New York City; attempted (unsuccessfully) to publish a novel; tried (again unsuccessfully) to publish a new type of newspaper with Franklin

Ford and John Dewey, his undergraduate professor in philosophy, who, along with the Germanist, Calvin Thomas, had influenced him significantly during his college years; and in 1894, Park married Clara Cahill, the daughter of a Michigan State supreme court justice. In 1898 Park entered Harvard, intending to earn an MA in philosophy. Studying under William James, George Santayana, and Hugo Münsterberg, Park was, as his biographer Fred H. Matthews has pointed out, "particularly impressed by William James" who "turned him away from philosophy. He reinforced not only Park's distaste for reductionist science, but more broadly his revulsion from all abstract, categorizing thought" (Matthews 1977: 32–3). As a consequence, in 1899 Park moved his family to Berlin, where he entered Frederich Wilhelm University. Park studied under Georg Simmel, whom he later referred to as "the greatest of all sociologists," during his second year in Berlin. Later, under the direction of Wilhelm Windelband, he wrote his dissertation, entitled *Masse und Publikum: eine methodologische und sociologische Untersuchung* at the University of Heidelberg, and was awarded the doctorate in 1903. Park returned to the United States in 1903 and worked as an assistant to William James at Harvard. In 1904, he became the secretary of the Congo Reform Association, an organization dedicated to protesting the atrocities perpetrated against the indigenous population in Belgian King Leopold's Congo Free State, and organized the American chapter through the Massachusetts Commission of Justice. Park wrote four articles on the Congo between 1904 and 1907 which appeared in *Outlook*, *The World To-Day* and in *Everybody's Magazine*. In these articles, as Stanford Lyman pointed out in 1992, Park made a transition from "Germanic romantic philosophy...toward...the rational and excessively positivistic social science that is represented today by its mainstream professionals" (Lyman 1992: xvii). Disillusioned with the reformers with whom he had come in contact within the Congo Reform Association, Park left that organization in 1905. Yet, still interested in narrating the details of the atrocities perpetrated against the indigenous peoples of the Belgian Congo, Park was preparing to go to Africa to study the situation when he met Booker T. Washington. The Tuskegeean suggested to Park that he should "visit Tuskegee and start his studies of Africa in the southern states" (Johnson 1944: 355). Park, who was financially insecure, was appointed press secretary for Tuskegee Institute by Booker T. Washington for the sum of $150.00 per month, "with traveling expenses (railway fare and sleeping car, but not hotel)." In return, Park pledged "all that I earn by writing or any other means whatever, whether more or less than $1,800 per year, unless by special arrangement, shall be either turned over to the funds of the school or charged against the $150 per month guaranteed me in this agreement" (Washington Papers: 2 June 1905).

Although his position was not financially profitable, Park later wrote: "I probably learned more about human nature and society in the South under

Booker Washington than I learned elsewhere in my previous years" (Park 1950: vii–viii). Most significantly, he (along with Monroe N. Work) wrote *The Story of the Negro* (1909), *My Larger Education* (1911), and collaborated with Washington in the writing of *The Man Farthest Down* (1912). It was at the end of his tenure at Tuskegee that he told Washington: "I have never been so happy in my life as I have since I have been associated with you in this work. Some of the best friends I have in the world are at Tuskegee. I feel and shall always feel that I belong in a sort of way to the Negro race and shall continue to share, through good and evil, all its joys and sorrows. I want to help you in the future as in the past in any way I can" (Raushenbush 1975: 63). Nonetheless, after surveying Park's writings during his Congo Reform Association-Tuskegee Institute period, the sociologist John H. Stanfield has written "although Park was very aware and concerned about exploitation and control of indigenous African peoples by Europeans, this concern was transformed into an apologetic position when the issue was African Americans in the South." Furthermore, Stanfield states correctly that "although Park described at length the adaptive function of Tuskegee and similar institutions in developing the black masses, he was silent about how the model could be applied in Africa without inflicting the very kind of imposition of control he criticized" (Stanfield 1985: 42).

While writing *The Story*, Park, the radical reformer, wrote to Washington:

> As introduction on to chapter second I wish you would dictate something about your acquaintance with Africa through books and through persons.
>
> What was the first book aside from a geography you read about Africa or any one who had come from Africa? Did you ever discover when you were young any one of the books, written before the war, to prove the abilities of the Native African? If so, what impression did they make on you?
>
> What Africans have you known. [?] Have you met Dube? Did you know Dr. Edward W. Blyden? Any personal reminiscences you can give me of these men or anything that connects you directly or indirectly with Africa I can use in the second chapter.
>
> Do you know any of the Liberian people?
>
> Please let me have whatever you can along this line as soon as possible.
>
> I got a good story from the Fayette Silk Mills, though we ought to see the proprietor, who is in New York before we write anything.
>
> I am very truly Robert E. Park.
>
> P. S. Don't you know of some colored man who went out to Africa with high hope of settling there, or of reforming and civilizing the natives and who returned, disenchanted?
>
> (Washington Papers: 2 June 1908)

In response to Park's first question, the following passage appeared in the first volume of *The Story of the Negro*:

> What I was first able to hear and to learn did not, I confess, take me very far or give me very much satisfaction. In the part of the country in which I lived there were very few of my people who pretended to know very much about Africa. I learned, however, that my mother's people had come, like the white people, from across the water, but from a more distant and more mysterious land, where people lived a different life from ours, had different customs and spoke a different language from that I had learned to speak. Of the long and terrible journey by which my ancestors came from their native home in Africa to take up their life again beside the white man and Indian in the New World, I used to hear many and sinister references, but not until I was a man did I meet any one, among my people, who knew anything definite, either through personal knowledge or through tradition, of the country of the people from whom my people sprang. To most of the slaves the "middle passage," as the journey from the shore of Africa to the shore of America was called, was merely a tradition of a confused and bewildering experience concerning whose horrors they had never heard any definite details. Nothing but the vaguest notions remained, at the time I was a boy, even among the older people in regard to the mother country of my race.
>
> (Washington (1909) 1940, 2: 5–67)

> After I began to go to school I had my first opportunity to learn from books something further and more definite about my race in Africa. I cannot say that I received very much encouragement or inspiration from what I learned in this way while I was in school. The books I read told me of a people who roamed naked through the forest like wild beasts, of a people without houses or laws, without chastity or morality, with no family life and fixed habits of industry.
>
> It seems to me now, as I recall my first definite impressions of my race in Africa, that the books I read when I was a boy always put the picture of Africa and African life in an unnecessarily cruel contrast with the pictures of the civilized and highly cultured Europeans and Americans...in order to put the lofty position to which the white race has attained in sharper contrast with the lowly condition of a more primitive people, the best among the white people, was contrasted with the worst among the black.
>
> (Washington (1909) 1940, 1: 8–9)

Washington did not respond to Park's second and third questions but in *The Story* he mentioned reading Henry Barth's *Discoveries in North and Central Africa* (1850) in reference to the "intermingling of racial stocks" in

Africa. In response to Park's question concerning the Africans he knew, the "Wizard" named some "pure blood" students who received honors at Tuskegee; and prominent "pure" black African-Americans such as J. C. Price, Isaiah T. Montgomery, Charles Banks, W. W. Brown, Major R. R. Moten and Paul Lawrence Dunbar. He then proceeded to tell a story of a Tuskegee student who was part Bushman and part Hottentot who talked about and even showed pictures that demonstrated his people were "the victims of circumstances" (Washington (1909) 1940, 1: 24). The last of Park's questions was excluded from *The Story*.

By 1909, Washington's conception of Africa changed once again. On 29 April 1909, James H. Breasted, an Egyptologist who taught at the University of Chicago, wrote to Washington. Breasted had been born into a Congregationalist family in 1865 in Rockford, Illinois. He had received a BA from Northwestern (now called North Central) College in Naperville, Illinois; attended Chicago Theological Seminary and Yale University; and received the MA and PhD in Egyptology from the University of Berlin in 1894. The nation's leading Egyptologist believed that Ethiopia, "long supposed to have been the source of Egyptian art and civilization, actually received its culture from the Egyptians" (Breasted 1943: 176). Nevertheless, he told Washington:

Since 1905 I have carried out an expedition on the upper, or Nubian Nile which has brought back for the first time, exhaustive copies of all the historical monuments now surviving in that distant country. At the same time the recent discovery of papyrus documents containing translations of the New Testament into the ancient Nubian tongue is enabling us to decipher the hitherto undeciphered inscriptions of the early Nubians. The importance of all this is chiefly: that from these documents when deciphered, we shall be able to put together the only surviving information on the early history of a dark race. Nowhere else in all the world is the early history of a dark race preserved.

(Washington Papers: 29 April 1909)

Washington replied to Breasted on 6 May 1909 with the astute comment:

I have noticed one fact…which lends a special interest to your discoveries: This is that traditions of most of the peoples whom I have read, point to a distant place in the direction of ancient Ethiopia as the source from which [African people] received what civilization they still possess. This is true, I think, of the people of the Western Sudan and equally true of the Lake Regions.

Could it be possible that these civilizing influences had their sources in this ancient kingdom to which your article refers?

(Washington Papers: 6 May 1909)

In short, by the end of the 1900s, Washington's position had moved through three stages. Influenced by nineteenth-century racist conceptions of Africans throughout his childhood and most of his adult life, Washington initially conceived of his African ancestors as primitive barbarians. As he became more involved in African affairs and came under the influence of Monroe N. Work, Franz Boas, and Robert E. Park, Washington modified his position to acknowledge the contribution of Africans to world civilization. And finally, influenced by James H. Breasted, he had come to the position taken by nineteenth-century African-American nationalists: that Ethiopia was the disseminator of knowledge to West Africa. As a result, in his last address before the American Missionary Association, Washington had abandoned the myth of persons of African descent and replaced it with the idea of the African American as a normal human stock. "There is sometimes much talk about the inferiority of the Negro," he stated. In practice, however, Washington asserted, "the idea appears to be that he is a sort of superman. He is expected with about one fifth of what whites received for their education to make as much progress as they are making" (Washington 1932: 282).

III

To conclude, it is tragic that Washington sustained the myths of his age to such a great extent and for so long a period. Publicly espousing a philosophy that white–black conflict could be eliminated by the gradual uplift of African Americans through industrial education, Washington assumed that racism in the marketplace with its discriminating employers and unions was incompatible with an industrial economy. Believing the industrial economy with its insatiable demand for highly specialized skills and services was based upon the merit principle, Washington preached a philosophy suggesting that individuals with those skills would be upgraded and, as a consequence, eliminate the problems stemming from white fears of black competition (Brotz 1992: 17).

Historical hindsight allows us to see the limitations of Washington's publicly espoused philosophy. By isolating the economy from other institutions and other social arrangements, Washington analyzed only one trait of a complex of characteristics. In other words, racism, I would argue, was and is so deeply embedded in the white psyche that any attempt to resolve the social problem of that period required a reformation in the cultural, economic, and political domains.

BIBLIOGRAPHY

Breasted, C., (1943) *Pioneer to the Past: The Story of James Henry Breasted: Archaeologist*, New York: Charles Scribner's Sons.

Brotz, Howard, (1992) *African-American Social and Political Thought, 1850–1920*, New Brunswick, NJ: Transactions Publishers.

Boas, F., *Papers*, Philadelphia: American Philosophical Society.

Fredrickson, G., (1971) *The Black Image in the White Mind: The Debate on Afro-American Character and Destiny, 1817–1914*, New York: Harper and Row.

Guzman, J., *Papers*, Tuskegee, Alabama: Tuskegee Institute Library.

Harlan, L. (1972). *Booker T. Washington: The Making of a Black Leader, 1856–1901*, New York: Oxford University Press.

Hemenway, R., (1972) *Introduction to the Booker T. Washington Papers*, Urbana: University of Illinois Press.

Hemenway, R. (1977) *Zora Neale Hurston: A Literary Biography*, Urbana: University of Illinois Press.

Lyman, Stanford M., (1992) *Militarism, Imperialism, and Racial Accommodation: An Analysis and Interpretation of the Early Writings of Robert E. Park*, Fayetteville: The University of Arkansas Press.

Matthews, Fred H., (1977) *Quest for an American Sociology: Robert E. Park and the Chicago School*, Montreal: McGill-Queen's Press.

McMurray, L., (1985) *Recorder of the Black Experience: A Biography of Monroe Nathan Work*, Baton Rouge: Louisiana State University Press.

Meier, A. (1963) (1968) *Negro Thought in America, 1880–1915: Racial ideologies in the age of Booker T. Washington*, Ann Arbor: University of Michigan Press.

Moses, W., (1978) (1988) *The Golden Age of Black Nationalism, 1850–1925*, New York: Oxford University Press.

Park, R., (1950) *Race and Culture*, New York: The Free Press.

Raushenbush, Winifred, (1975) *Robert E. Park: Biography of a Sociologist*, Durham, NC: Duke University Press.

Stanfield, J., (1985) *Philanthropy and Jim Crow*, Westport: Greenwood Press.

Thornbrough, E., (ed.), (1990) *Booker T. Washington*, Englewood Cliffs, NJ: Prentice Hall, Inc.

Washington, B., (1899) (1968) *The Future of the American Negro*, New York: Haskell House.

——, (1901) (1986) *Up From Slavery*, New York: Penguin Books.

——, (1907) (1968) *Frederick Douglass*, New York: Haskell House.

——, (1907) (1970) *The Negro in the South: His Economic Progress in Relation to His Moral and Religious Development*, New York: Carol Publishing Group.

——, (1909), (1940) *The Story of the Negro: The Rise of a Race from Slavery*, New York: Haskell House.

——, *Booker T. Washington Papers*, Washington, DC: Library of Congress.

Washington, E. (ed.) (1932) *Selected Speeches of Booker T. Washington*, Garden City, NY: Doubleday, Doran and Company, Inc.

Work, M., *Papers*, Tuskegee, Alabama: Tuskegee Institute Library.

12

GEORGE EDMUND HAYNES AND THE OFFICE OF NEGRO ECONOMICS

James B. Stewart

INTRODUCTION

This chapter examines the contributions of George Edmund Haynes to the application of economic concepts and associated analytical techniques for studying the dynamics of black employment during the first two decades of the twentieth century. Particular attention is focused on Haynes's activities as Director of Negro Economics for the US Department of Labor during the First World War. In this role Haynes was charged with advising "the Secretary and the directors and chiefs of the several bureaus and divisions of the department on matters relating to Negro wage earners, and to outline and promote plans for greater cooperation between Negro wage earners, white employers, and white workers in agriculture and industry" (Haynes, 1921: 12). The analyses and activities of this office are recorded in the volume *The Negro at Work During the World War and Reconstruction* (Haynes, 1921). The report reflects Haynes's unique ability to synthesize case studies, statistical and qualitative survey information, and provides useful insights on issues of contemporary import.

The report appropriately recognized large scale migration of blacks to the North as a potentially incendiary ingredient in race relations in the context of the competition for jobs. As a consequence, the program of the Office of Negro Economics incorporated three components: 1 "the organization of cooperative committees of white and colored citizens in the States and localities where problems of Negro labor arise, due to large numbers of negro workers," 2 the development of a publicity campaign to foster harmonious race relations; and 3 the appointment of African American staff in selected states and local areas to promote the program of the office (Haynes, 1921: 12–13).

Provision of assistance to the large numbers of African Americans migrating to the North was one of the particular concerns of Haynes's office. In pursuing the charge of the Office of Negro Economics Haynes drew heavily on his previous theoretical and empirical work examining migration, employment discrimination, and labor market segmentation. He viewed the migration of blacks during the First World War period as simply one case of a general process that had occurred in different places during different periods in time (Haynes, 1918). He hypothesized that the movement of the white and black populations toward cities was coincident and concluded from his empirical work that, in fact, "the general movement of the Negroes...does not seem to have been very different from that of whites" (Haynes, 1912: 14). This conclusion informed a policy perspective that "the problems which grow out of his [blacks'] maladjustment to the new urban environment are solvable by methods similar to those that help other elements of the population" (Haynes, 1912: 14).

Haynes's perspectives on employment discrimination and the distribution of workers across occupations presaged modern theories of discrimination and labor market segmentation. His approach to policy design and implementation also exhibits parallels to contemporary approaches.

The theoretical and empirical work that informed Haynes's activities under the auspices of the Office of Negro Economics is discussed in the second section. The study itself is then examined in detail in the third section, including a re-analysis of selected data reported by Haynes. That exercise is designed to facilitate the exploration of the extent to which Haynes's work remains relevant for contemporary concerns. The re-examination of the data also confirms important elements of his theoretical framework that were not supported because of limitations in the original analysis.

The analysis concludes with a general assessment of Haynes's contributions including a discussion of his activities subsequent to the demise of the Office of Negro Economics.

FOUNDATIONS OF HAYNES'S ANALYSIS OF "NEGRO ECONOMICS"

George Edmund Haynes graduated from Fisk University in 1903 with an AB Degree and received an AM degree from Yale University in 1904. He also studied at the Yale Divinity School prior to undertaking doctoral studies at Columbia (Ellison 1990). Ellison (1990) identifies him as the first African American to receive a PhD in Economics from Columbia University (1910).[1] Haynes was also a charter member of the NAACP and a founder of the National Urban League, serving as the League's Director of Education until 1918. Concurrent with these activities he organized and chaired the Social Science Department at Fisk University from 1910 until 1920, taking a leave of absence from this position to assume the responsibilities of Director of the Office of Negro Economics in 1918 (Ellison, 1990).

Haynes's dissertation, *The Negro at Work in New York City: A Study in Social Progress*, was published in 1912 as study number 3 in the Columbia

University Press "Series in History, Economics and Public Law" (Haynes 1912). This case study followed in the tradition of W. E. B. Du Bois's *The Philadelphia Negro* and *The Atlanta Publications* in the use of the case study method, with heavy reliance upon interviews to generate data and form interpretations.[2] One of Haynes's principal foci was the migration of both African Americans and European Americans from rural to urban areas.

This focus on migration was extended to generate a composite aggregate assessment in "Conditions Among Negroes in the Cities" (1913). Here Haynes identified "Three facts [that] should be placed in the foreground in looking at the economic conditions of the segregated Negro in the city" (Haynes, 1913: 112). The first fact was that "the masses of those who have migrated to town are unprepared to meet the exacting requirements of organized industry, and the keen competition of more efficient laborers" (Haynes, 1913: 112). This statement constitutes an argument about the competitive disadvantage of black workers in local labor markets with respect to industrial employment. Theoretically, training programs could constitute one vehicle for reducing the disadvantage; however, the second fact discussed by Haynes was the lack of effective vocational training for migrants. The absence of such programs, he argued, led to a "drift hit or miss into any occupations which are held out to their unskilled hands and untutored brains" (Haynes, 1913: 112).

The sub-optimal employment profile of blacks was reinforced by "the prejudice of the white industrial world" (Haynes, 1913: 112). Haynes argued that "This prejudice, when displayed by employers, is partly due to the inefficiency indicated above and the failure to discriminate between the efficient individual and the untrained throng. When exhibited by fellow wage-earners, it is partly due to fear of probable successful competition and to the belief that the Negro has 'jus place' fixed by a previous condition of servitude" (Haynes, 1913: 112–13).

This perspective on employer and employee discrimination invokes behavioral theories similar to those associated with modern statistical theories of discrimination. However, Haynes believed that both employers and employees shaped their responses to black workers largely on the basis of a "taste for discrimination" à la the Becker model: "But in the cases of many employers and employees...the opposition to the Negro in industrial pursuits is due to a whimsical dislike of any workman who is not white and especially of one who is black!" (Haynes, 1913: 113). Haynes also recognized that employee discrimination was often manifested through labor unions (Haynes, 1913: 113).

Interestingly, one of Haynes's proposed interventions to address the patterns of discrimination and competition was the discouragement of blacks from migrating to the North "unless by education and training [they are] prepared to meet the exactions of adjustment to city life"

(Haynes, 1913: 118). This approach was illustrative of Haynes's tendency, discussed by Stewart (1991), to sublimate discussions of discrimination and blame the victims of discrimination for their plight. Haynes did, however, call for the establishment of community race relations programs and "a square deal in industry, in education and in other parts of the common life," which he characterized as "equality of opportunity" (Haynes, 1913: 118–19).

Many of the elements of Haynes's analyses described above were replicated in a case study of blacks in Detroit published co-temporally with his appointment to the position of Director of Negro Economics (Haynes, 1918). In addition, however, the Detroit study presents more comprehensive discussions of critical economic and social processes affecting the status of African Americans.

Haynes (1918) used a general push–pull model to analyze migration that also incorporated social as well as economic forces (Haynes, 1918). As noted by Stewart (1991), these social causes included poor housing, poor schools, Jim Crow segregation, disfranchisement, discrimination in the criminal justice system, and mob violence. Haynes argued that there was a direct correlation between adverse economic conditions and the size of the migration stream.

The basic "push" forces were augmented by "pull" forces associated with a shortage of labor created by the First World War and the disruption of European emigration. Haynes maintained that the size of the black migration was not optimal, in part because black workers were responding to a money illusion, i.e. "thinking in terms of money wages not real wages" (Haynes, 1918: 7). According to Haynes this money illusion resulted from inaccurate information regarding wage rates in the North provided to prospective migrants by labor agents. He also noted that free transportation was often used as an incentive to induce migration. Haynes's aversion to large scale migration was motivated in part by the horrid housing and public health conditions that many blacks encountered in the North.

The case study of Detroit also includes an assessment of the structure and functioning of urban labor markets that is similar to, but more comprehensive than, those found in his earlier works (Haynes, 1918). In modern parlance, the framework would be characterized as a segmented labor market model. Haynes described the primary sector as being dominated by industrial firms while service occupations provided the bulk of employment options in the secondary sector. Blacks were relegated disproportionately to the secondary sector and, in particular, to the worst jobs in that sector. Improvements in the distribution of blacks across occupations in both the primary and secondary sector could occur, in his view, from increases in aggregate demand and improvements in labor market conditions in specific locales.

A comparison of the case studies of New York and Detroit provides a useful perspective on the impact of the First World War on employment opportunities for black Americans. The interviews conducted for the New York study revealed that most blacks were employed in domestic and personal service occupations (Haynes, 1912: 77). The age distribution of black workers in New York suggested to Haynes that "They are either killed off by the conditions under which they work and live, or drift away from the city at a premature old age" (Haynes, 1912: 57). In contrast, blacks in Detroit were found to be involved in a much wider range of occupations (Haynes, 1918: 15). Haynes observed, however, that before the advent of the First World War, blacks in Detroit had been confined to the same types of occupations as in New York and, in fact, were "probably losing ground until the industrial demand of the Great War came" (Haynes, 1918: 12).

The relegation of black workers to the secondary sector was seen as having several effects. In general, Haynes characterized the outcome of occupational segregation as a downward spiral of diminished economic well-being. Already low wages were reduced by an increased number of labor force participants seeking employment in the secondary sector, resulting in reduced attainable standards of living. Haynes argued that mothers of young children were in a particularly deleterious position. This special jeopardy derived in part from the fact that many women were forced into the labor market and many families were forced to rent rooms to non-relatives to supplement income. From Haynes's perspective, the low income of many families "forces...the necessity of completing the rent by means of lodgers, deprives the children of mothers' care, keeps the standard of living at a minimum, and thus makes the family unable to protect itself from both physical and moral disease" (Haynes, 1912: 89).

Haynes's concerns about the impacts of migration on the status of blacks, industrial race relations and disruption of the supply of workers to the agricultural sector were shared by federal policy makers. In 1916 W.B. Wilson, Secretary of Labor, commissioned a study of the emigration of blacks from the South. The principal investigator chosen for the study was James Dillard, formerly of Tulane University and then head of the Slater Funds for Negro Education in the South. This study was precipitated by concerns about "a great migratory stream of Negro wage earners... flowing out of southern and into northern States, arousing the fears of wage earners in the North on account of the potential competition for opportunities to work and consequent depressions of wages which it threatened, and exciting consternation in the South among employers who feared a loss of crops from lack of customary labor" (Dillard et al., 1919: 7). The study included three reports focusing on the migration during the period 1916–17 from the states of Mississippi, Alabama and North Carolina, and Georgia, an overview of the emigration from the South and a report on the status of black migrants in the North.[3] The perspectives on migration contained in this report bear strong similarities to those advanced by Haynes although he was not directly associated with this effort. In fact Haynes's case study of New York (Haynes, 1912) is cited in the report on migration from Alabama and North Carolina (Dillard, *et al.*, 1919: 76).

The Secretary of Labor's review of Dillard's study led to an assessment that the Department needed "continuous expert advice upon economic problems involving wage-earning labor in its relation to the Negroes of the country and their employers, and especially with reference to an effective prosecution of the war" (Dillard *et al.*, 1918: 8). The position of Director of Negro Economics was created to provide this expertise and George Haynes was appointed with a starting date of May 1918.

On 16–17 February 1919 a national conference was convened in Washington by the Secretary of Labor that generated several recommendations for what was described as a "program of national work." The components of that program were: "1 [a] survey of Negro labor conditions; 2 The getting of Negro workers into industry; 3 Holding Negro workers in industry, including the improving of living and working conditions in both agriculture and industry; 4 Training the next generation of workers; and 5 The general advancement of Negro wage earners in the United States" (Haynes, 1921: 16–17).

The Dillard study of black migration was also released in 1919 under the auspices of the Office of Negro Economics. It provided much of the foundation upon which the subsequent assessment of the status of black workers in the North was based.

GEORGE HAYNES ON THE NEGRO AT WORK DURING THE WAR

The first chapter of *The Negro at Work During the War and Reconstruction* is entitled "Migration" and consists of a little over one page that basically summarizes and references the earlier report on migration. According to the summary, the "Shortage of labor in northern industries was the direct cause of the increased Negro migration during the war period. This direct cause was, of course, augmented by other causes, among which were the increased dissatisfaction with conditions in the South – the ravages of the boll weevil, floods, change of crop system, low wages, and poor houses and schools" (Haynes, 1921: 10).

The introductory material also articulates several critical assumptions that undergird the interpretation presented in the report. The principal source of racial tensions in the workplace was identified as the combination of a high volume of migration and pre-existing prejudices: "The two races are thrown together in their daily work...These conditions give rise to misunderstandings, prejudices, antagonisms, fears and suspicions" (Haynes, 1921: 13). This statement is easily identified with modern theories of employee discrimination in the Becker tradition.

A second assumption, also reflecting parallels to modern theories, maintained that "Any plan or program should be based upon the desire and need of cooperation between white employers and representatives of Negro wage earners, and, wherever possible, white wage earners" (Haynes, 1921: 13). An implied assumption in this statement is that employee discrimination is a more fundamental problem than employer discrimination.

A third key assumption articulated in the report was that "the problems are local in character... arising between local employers and local employees" (Haynes, 1921: 13). This assumption implies that the general national situation of blacks and the status of blacks in a given industry as a whole had only limited spillover effects on the situation of black workers in specific establishments.

As part of the inquiry by Haynes's office, the Inspection and Investigation Service conducted a study of employment patterns in several basic industries for 1918–19. The survey was limited to selected firms in Illinois, Ohio and Pennsylvania but yielded detailed information for 4,260 white males and 2,722 black males employed in 194 occupations in twenty-four firms in six industries.[4] The six industries covered by the survey were foundries, slaughtering and meat packing, automobiles, coke ovens, iron and steel and their products, and glass manufacturing.

Originally a much broader survey was envisioned, but was shelved due to the failure of Congress to appropriate the necessary funds. Despite the regional limitations, the data collected provide significant detail regarding the employment of black and white workers. The data included average number of hours worked per week, average earnings per week and average hourly earnings by occupation for black and white workers. Information about the skill levels of individual occupations was also collected using the categories of skilled, semi-skilled and unskilled.

Although the report includes a table containing the detailed data, the analysis was limited to crude comparisons. Specifically, Haynes tabulated the cases where blacks earned (worked) more, less or the same wages (hours) vis-à-vis whites. He restricted the tabulations to occupations in which at least five black and five white workers were employed. Eighty-five of the 194 occupation/firm observations in the sample met this criterion. Only in the case of skilled workers was there any effort to interpret the data. Haynes observed that the foundries "were the only plants that employed any considerable number of Negroes in skilled occupations" and suggested that this phenomenon probably resulted partly from the fact that "Negroes have probably had longer industrial experience in this industry than the other occupations... except possibly coke ovens" (Haynes, 1921: 41–2).

The distributions of hours worked, average weekly earnings and average hourly earnings for all three skill classifications reported by Haynes are summarized in Table 12.1.

Table 12.1 Comparison of hours worked and earnings of black and white male workers by skill classification in six basic industries, 1918–19[1]

Measure	Unskilled occupations			Semi-skilled occupations			All occupations[2]		
	Number of cases where blacks exceed whites	Number of cases where blacks equal whites	Number of cases where whites exceed blacks	Number of cases where blacks exceed whites	Number of cases where blacks equal whites	Number of cases where whites exceed blacks	Number of cases where blacks exceed whites	Number of cases where blacks equal whites	Number of cases where whites exceed blacks
Average hours worked per week	23	13	16	8	12	5	35	25	25
Average weekly earnings	18	12	22	8	12	5	28	24	33
Average hourly earnings	18	12	22	8	12	5	28	24	33

Notes: 1 The data for individual occupations can be found in Table 12.2: a comparative table of "average hours of work" and average earnings of male white and Negro employees engaged in specified occupations of six basic industries, 1918–19 (p. 224)
2 Sum of unskilled, semi-skilled and skilled occupations

Source: George Haynes, The Negro at Work During the World War and During Reconstruction (Washington: Government Printing Office 1921, reprinted Negro Universities Press, 1969)

The data suggest a reasonably tight distribution that approximates parity for blacks and whites. Haynes's decision to forego a more detailed analysis may have been informed by this lack of obvious patterns of inequality in the distributions. However, this apparent equity may have masked serious conflicts related to the response of employers and white employees to black migrants seeking employment.

This possibility is suggested, in part, by the race riots that erupted in Chicago, Omaha, Washington, DC and other places during the Summer of 1919. The report, in fact, includes a reasonably detailed summary of Haynes's investigation of the Chicago riot in which he concluded that "The disturbance in Chicago seems to have grown out of complex fundamental conditions, mainly economic. Some of the factors are not altogether labor factors, but are largely the results of the labor and other economic conditions" (Haynes, 1921: 26). Conflicts over efforts to unionize black workers in the stockyards were also identified as one precipitating cause of the riot.

There are also indications in each of the field reports from Haynes's staff that suggest discrimination and racial tensions were more prevalent than the statistical data would seem to imply. To illustrate, in the report on conditions in New York it was noted that "Investigations were made of charges of discrimination against colored workers and steps were taken, in each case where the facts warranted, to remove the handicap" (Haynes, 1921: 96). In a similar vein, a conference on Negro labor sponsored by Haynes's office in Ohio recommended an "Investigation into the difficulties arising from discrimination against Negroes by local labor unions" (Haynes, 1921: 106).

With this background, a re-examination of Haynes's data is undertaken in an attempt to identify patterns of inequality that eluded his crude empirical techniques. The focus of the re-analysis is to ascertain how, if at all, the movement of black workers into various occupations influenced the relative levels of compensation and hours worked between blacks and whites. OLS regression analysis is used to analyze factors associated with variation in the relative hourly earnings (RELWAGE) and weekly hours worked (RELHRS) for black and white males in Haynes's sample. The individual values of the dependent variables consist of the averages for all black and white workers in a given occupation in a specific firm reported by Haynes (Haynes, 1921: 45–8).

As noted previously, Haynes restricted the original analysis of the data to cases where at least five black and five white workers were employed in a given occupation in a specific firm. This decision unfortunately restricted his ability to discuss the issue of occupational segregation by introducing sample selection bias problems. In the re-analysis of the data all cases are included and individual observations are weighted by the total number of black and white workers in a given occupation/firm.

The basic model used to re-analyze the data reported by Haynes takes the following general form:

$$\left.\begin{array}{l} \text{RELWAGE}_{ijk} \\ \text{RELHRS}_{ijk} \end{array}\right\} = f(\text{SKILL}_{ijk}; \text{ IND}_{ik}; \text{ TEMP}_{ijk}; \text{ TOTEMP}_{jk};$$

$$\text{PCTBLOC}_{ijk}; \text{ PCTFRMBK}_{jk}) \qquad \text{(Eqn 12.1)}$$

As noted above, in Eqn 12.1 RELWAGE_{ijk} and RELHRS_{ijk} refer, respectively, to the relative hourly wages and weekly hours of black and white workers in occupation i ($i = 1, \ldots 194$) in firm j ($j = 1, \ldots 24$) in industry k ($k = 1, \ldots 6$). SKILL_{ijk} refers to the level of skill required for occupation i. SKILL_{ijk} is operationalized using a set of dummy variables designating, respectively, skilled, semi-skilled or unskilled. Unskilled occupations serve as the reference group. This specification allows a more detailed examination of variation across skill levels than Haynes was able to perform. It will be recalled that Haynes was particularly restricted in examining skilled occupations because of the few cases that satisfied his selection criterion. It would be expected, however, given the concerns expressed about union discrimination that blacks in skilled occupations would experience more discrimination than those in unskilled and semi-skilled occupations. Consequently, the sign of the coefficient of the dummy variable for skilled occupations should be negative.

IND_{ik} represents a set of dummy variables for those six industries represented in the sample. Foundries are used as the reference group. This specification corresponds to the structure of Haynes's investigation. However, unlike his cursory comparative assessments, statistical estimation can yield direct comparisons of the relative magnitudes of inter-industry differences if they exist.

TEMP_{ijk} and TOTEMP_{jk} are, respectively, the total employment in occupation i for firm j and the total employment in all occupations in firm j. PCTBLOC_{ijk} and PCTFRMBK_{jk} are the corresponding percentages of the occupational and firm workforces comprised by blacks. The subscript k is required to distinguish those cases where a firm has operations that cut across more than one industrial classification. Inclusion of these variables enables an assessment of the sensitivity of relative wages and relative hours worked to workforce size and composition. Consistent with the hypotheses offered by Haynes regarding employee and employer discrimination, it would be anticipated that employers might respond to the need to hire more blacks by offering whites longer hours and higher wage rates. Such a pattern could result from at least two distinct motivations. First, employers might have a preference for white workers and seek to recruit as many as possible using available incentives (wages/hours) before hiring blacks. Second, confronted with white workers with a Becker-type "taste for discrimination," employers hiring black workers may be forced to provide additional compensation to white workers to maintain harmonious race relations. Alternatively, if the discrimination faced by black workers is "statistical" in character, then as more blacks are hired into occupations wage and hour differentials should erode. In addition, to the extent that black workers become increasingly critical to the production process, they may use this bargaining power to press for equalization of compensation. Finally, an additional strategy that could be used by employers to reduce racial tension could involve reorganization of the production process by introducing more occupational specialization. Creating new "occupations" could be used either to increase or reduce occupational segregation. It is unlikely, however, that the management of race relations would be the principal reason for increasing the number of occupations. Rather this phenomenon is principally related to firm size and complexity of the production process.

At the same time, the prior discussion of the high levels of conflict in specific cities suggests that racial tensions could be manifested in management decisions related not only to compensation and labor supply, but also to organization of the production process. To capture these effects if they exist requires introduction of three additional variables. OCCINT is constructed by interacting TEMP and PCTBLOC and measures how REL-WAGE (RELHRS) responds to variations in the mix of total employment in a given occupation and the racial composition of the occupational workforce. FRMINT is the counterpart to OCCINT at the firm level and is constructed by interacting TOTEMP and PCTFRMBK. Finally, the variable NOCC measures the number of occupations in a given firm. As noted above, employers may attempt to reorganize production by increasing occupational specialization. However, depending on an employer's taste for discrimination and the relative bargaining power of black workers, the result could be increases rather than decreases in relative wages. Nondiscriminating employers could use occupational segregation to "hide" wage equity from white workers. Well-organized black workers could use threats of production disruption to exact wage increases from recalcitrant employers. As a consequence of these multiple possible scenarios the expected sign of the coefficient of NOCC is also uncertain.

A detailed description of all variables and the means and standard deviations are presented in Table 12.2.

Two observations about the summary statistics are in order. First, the mean values of RELWAGE and RELHRS are approximately 100, consistent with Haynes's analysis. Second, the mean values of PCTBLOC and PCTFRMBK are almost identical although the standard deviation of PCTBLOC is significantly higher. This is the type of pattern that would be associated with a staffing pattern of occupational segregation constrained by the need to satisfy overall staffing requirements.

In addition to estimating the basic model, a modified model is also estimated that is designed to examine the extent to which firm-specific factors also contributed to observed variations. In the revised specification a set of twenty-three dummy variables (EST 1–23) are added and the

Table 12.2 Variable labels, weighted means and standard deviations*

Variable label	Description	Mean	Standard deviation
RELWAGE	Ratio of average hourly wage for black and white workers (b/w × 100)	101.331	47.788
RELHRS	Ratio of average hours per week for black and white workers (b/w × 100)	99.057	58.754
SKILLED	Dummy variable = 1 for skilled occupations; 0 otherwise	0.161	2.209
SEMSK	Dummy variable = 1 for semi-skilled occupations; 0 otherwise	0.273	2.680
UNSK	Dummy variable = 1 for unskilled occupations; 0 otherwise	0.566	2.981
TEMP	Total number of black and white workers in an occupation	108.591	583.720
TOTEMP	Total number of black and white workers in a firm	506.596	2061.312
PCTBLOC	Percentage of workers in an occupation who are black (× 100)	38.986	145.571
OCCINT	TEMP × PCTBLOC/100	46.517	353.173
PCTFRMBK	Percentage of workers in a specific firm who are black (× 100)	38.966	95.987
FRMINT	TOTEMP × PCTFRMBK/100	194.154	861.742
NOCC	Number of occupations in a given establishment	12.763	77.816
FOUNDRY	Dummy variable = 1 for foundries; 0 otherwise	0.226	2.517
MEAT	Dummy variable = 1 for slaughterhouses; 0 otherwise	0.115	1.920
AUTO	Dummy variable = 1 for automobiles; 0 otherwise	0.228	2.522
COKE	Dummy variable = 1 for coke ovens; 0 otherwise	0.095	1.764
IRON	Dummy variable = 1 for iron/steel; 0 otherwise	0.316	2.796
GLASS	Dummy variable = 1 for glass manufacturing; 0 otherwise	0.020	0.837

Note: *Variable means are weighted by the variable TEMP firm; 0 otherwise

variables TOTEMP, PCTBLOC and PCTFRMBK are excluded to avoid multicollinearity problems.

Only the results for the estimation of RELWAGE are presented. None of the variables in the RELHRS regression had statistically significant coefficients although the intercept was significant and had a value of 98.4. The insignificance of all of the explanatory variables suggests that given the overall environment of labor shortages, it was not feasible to organize the production process in ways that allowed differentiation in hours worked on the basis of race. The results of both estimations for REL-WAGES are presented in Table 12.3.

The results for the estimation of the basic model suggest that when controls are introduced for skill level, industry and workforce size and

Table 12.3 Regression analysis of factors affecting variation in relative
wages of black and white male workers

Variable	Base analysis		Modified analysis	
	Coefficient	t-value	Coefficient	t-value
Constant	99.439*	32.992	100.150*	31.719
SKILLED	−3.109*	−2.230	−3.909*	−2.961
SEMI-SKILLED	0.397	0.336	0.010	0.009
TEMP	0.049*	3.641	0.028*	2.549
TOTEMP	−0.019*	−2.666	−	−
PCTBLOC	0.030	0.980	−	−
PCTFRMBK	−0.099	−1.534	−	−
OCCINT	0.008	0.307	0.017	0.779
FRMINT	−2.240	−1.284	−	−
NOCC	0.220*	2.722	−	−
AUTO	−2.240	−1.284	−	−
COKE	5.080*	1.938	−	−
GLASS	−5.344	−1.596	−	−
IRON	4.360*	2.761	−	−
MEAT	−1.374	−0.759	−	−
FIRM DUMMIES				
(EST 1-EST 23)				
*SIG (+)		−		3
*SIG (−)		−		3
*INSIG		−		17
ADJ R²		0.437		0.573
F		11.680		10.599
Standard error		35.872		31.221
N		194		194

Note: *Significant at the 95% level of confidence or better

composition, at the sample mean black workers earned wages virtually
identical to those earned by white workers. The negative sign of the
coefficient of SKILLED is consistent with the hypothesis of greater discrimination in such occupations. The premium for whites in skilled occupations is about 3.1 per cent at the mean. The relative wages of black
workers are greater in those occupations employing larger numbers of
workers. The effect is about 5 per cent at the sample mean. Conversely,
higher levels of total employment in the firm are associated with lower
relative wages for black workers. The effect is about 9.5 per cent at the
sample mean. Neither the racial composition of the occupational distribution nor of the firm's workforce were statistically significant and
neither of the interaction terms, OCCINT and FRMINT, had statistically significant coefficients. The coefficient of NOCC is positive and statistically significant and at the sample mean the effect is about 2.8 per
cent.

With respect to inter-industry variation, only the coefficients of COKE and IRON are statistically significant and both are positive. The effect in both cases is on the order of 5 per cent.

The expanded model produced a better fit than the basic model. Again, the coefficients of SKILLED and TEMP are statistically significant and have the same signs as in the base estimation. Six of the twenty-three firm dummies (26 per cent) are statistically significant. This result would seem to confirm Haynes's hypothesis that local factors play an especially significant role in conditioning employment outcomes for black workers.

Additional analysis was undertaken to further explore how relative wages were affected by patterns of occupational segregation and the organization of the production process. First, paired sample t-tests were used to determine the range of values of PCTBLOC where statistically significant differences in mean values for RELWAGE occur. The critical level of representation of black workers is approximately 60 per cent of the occupational employment. This suggests that the possibility of black workers exercising sufficient bargaining power to achieve wage parity requires a substantial degree of occupational segregation.

Efforts were also made to determine how larger numbers of occupations in a firm contribute to wage parity. The distribution of NOCC is bi-modal with all but ninety-eight of the individual occupations in firms with less than ten occupations. Paired sample t-tests failed to identify any critical range of values of NOCC that yielded statistically significant differences in the mean value of RELWAGE in comparison to the remainder of the sample. The simple correlation coefficient of NOCC and PCTBLOC is −0.108. Thus, without introducing controls, larger numbers of occupations in a firm were weakly associated with less black representation in individual occupations. It appears, then, that employers did not use re-organization of the production process as a means to manage race relations. As would be expected, there is a direct linkage between the numbers of occupations in the firm and the size and complexity of the production process. The correlation coefficient of NOCC and TOTEMP is 0.740. In general, then, the results of the supplemental analysis failed to identify the transmission mechanism associated with the positive and statistically significant coefficient of NOCC.

In summary, the re-evaluation of Haynes's data suggests that conditions of strong labor demand are likely to facilitate more equitable wage offers for blacks. Blacks were found to have faced more inequities in skilled occupations than in either semi-skilled or unskilled jobs. Greater occupational specialization and/or proliferation of unskilled and semi-skilled jobs was associated with increased parity for blacks although the transmission mechanism was indeterminate. Larger employment in individual occupations was associated with greater parity for black workers. In contrast, larger overall employment in the firm was associated with less parity for black workers. These effects appeared to operate independently of the racial composition of the workforces associated with either individual occupations or the firm as a whole. Some statistically significant variations in wage equity were found across industries. Black workers apparently suffered a relative disadvantage in automobile manufacturing, glass manufacturing and slaughterhouses.

The results of the re-analysis confirm the importance of Haynes's insistence on focusing on the examination of local forces affecting the employment status of blacks. In fact, the reassessment of the data undertaken above is in the spirit of the recommendations offered by Haynes in the original report. It was recommended, in part, that the Division of Negro Economics take steps in conjunction with the other units in the Department of Labor "to develop cooperation for securing statistical data on labor matters from other departments... with reference to Negro workers and their relations to white workers and employers" (Haynes, 1921: 135). It was further recommended that "through the cooperation of the other agencies of the Federal Government some plan for the investigation of Negro affairs and race relations in as many localities as possible be undertaken as a means of having information and advice to improve conditions and race relations" (Haynes, 1921: 136).

THE LEGACY OF GEORGE HAYNES

George Edmund Haynes left the Office of Negro Economics in 1921. As fate would have it, he did not return to his post at Fisk and assumed the position of administrator of the Harmon Foundation's Negro Awards. Haynes was appointed executive secretary of the National Interracial Conference in 1928 and served as secretary of the Commission on the Church and Race Relations of the Federal Council of Churches of Christ during the 1930s. Haynes completed his professional career at the City College of New York, serving as a member of the faculty from 1950 until his death in 1960 (Ellison, 1990).

Haynes's extensive involvement in religious non-governmental organizations subsequent to his Directorship of the Office of Negro Economics probably contributed to the relative obscurity of his contributions and the limited extent to which his work provided models for future investigations. The preceding analysis has identified several areas where Haynes's work could have informed investigations that tracked the progress of blacks from the First World War up through the beginning of the modern Civil Rights movement. As an example, studies of more recent waves of black migration could have benefited substantially from the use of the type of comparative perspective advocated by Haynes and from the analytical framework that guided his investigations. More modern theories of migration exhibit remarkably little advance over Haynes's conceptions.

227

Haynes's work is also relevant for contemporary investigations of the status of blacks. As noted previously, Haynes's theoretical analysis of discrimination displays remarkable parallels to modern formulations and, in most respects, is equally sophisticated. In a similar vein, although most contemporary empirical investigations of the status of black workers utilize complicated statistical techniques to examine large national samples, there may be a renewed role for the type of analyses undertaken by Haynes. As rules regarding standards of evidence change in employment discrimination litigation, there is likely to be a need for greater emphasis on firm and occupation specific analyses that make extensive use of qualitative information in the tradition of the studies published by the Office of Negro Economics.

Haynes's approach to the implementation of policies based upon research findings also has modern counterparts. Haynes advocated the active involvement of community-based organizations in training activities and in monitoring and improving race relations. He also emphasized cooperation among employers, potential beneficiaries and governmental bodies charged specifically with catalyzing improvements in the status of blacks. Contemporary examples of programs that reflect Haynes's approach to training include the self-help training initiatives of Leon Sullivan's Opportunities Industrialization Centers that emphasize cooperation with the private sector and the more recent Private Industry Councils (PICs). Local Human Relations Commissions that are adjuncts to state level commissions and the Equal Employment Opportunity Commission are examples of the type of cooperative approach to monitoring the status of blacks in general and employment discrimination specifically.

Another legacy of George Haynes is a conservative approach to advocacy for social change. As observed previously, Haynes had a tendency to place principal responsibility for adaptation on black workers with relatively less emphasis on structural change and combating institutional discrimination (Stewart, 1991). Contemporary economists who adopt a similar posture include Thomas Sowell and Walter Williams (Sowell, 1981; Williams, 1982).

Finally, it is significant to note that one of Haynes's last major studies focused on Africa, which he described as "The Continent of the Future" (Haynes, 1950). In this study he demonstrated a recognition of the growing international division of labor and offers a positive vision for the future: "European and American workers may well ponder what will happen when factories... begin to ship their products made with cheaper wages and raw materials, to the world markets in vessels built in African shipyards" (Haynes, 1950: 20–1).

This perspective suggests that the principal message of George Edmund Haynes to peoples of African descent and those concerned with race relations may well be that where there is no vision and no industrial struggle there can be no progress.

NOTES

1 Ellison (1990) reports that Haynes received the PhD in 1911. Other sources indicate that the degree was received in 1910.
2 See W. E. B. Du Bois, "The Atlanta Conferences," *Voice of the Negro* (1) (March 1904), pp. 85–90 and W. E. B. Du Bois, *The Philadelphia Negro, A Social Study*, (Philadelphia: University of Pennsylvania, 1899).
3 The authors of the reports included in the study were R. H. Leavell, T. R. Snavely, T. J. Woofter, T. B. Williams, and F. D. Tyson. Minimal biographical information about each is included as a note on page 5 of the volume.
4 Haynes actually lists twenty-three firms but one firm was involved in operations that fit under two different industrial clasifications. It is treated as two distinct entities in the present study.

REFERENCES

Dillard, James *et al.*, (1919) *Negro Migration in 1916–17* (Washington DC: US Government Printing Office). Reprinted in 1969 by Negro Universities Press.

Du Bois, W. E. B., (1899) *The Philadelphia Negro, A Social Study*, (Philadelphia: University of Pennsylvania).

——, (1904) "The Atlanta Conferences," *Voice of the Negro* (1), pp. 85–90.

Ellison, Julian, (1990) "Ten Black Economists of Note. 1850–1950." A Report prepared for the Board of Governors, Federal Reserve System. (Gaithersburg, MD: Mid-Atlantic Economic Research Corporation).

Haynes, George, (1912) "The Negro at Work in New York City, A Study in Economic Progress," *Studies in History, Economics and Public Law*, XLIX (3).

——, (1913) "Conditions Among Negroes in Cities," *Annals of the American Academy of Political and Social Science*, XLIX (September), pp. 105–119.

——, (1918) *Negro New-Comers in Detroit Michigan, A Challenge to Christian Statesmanship, A Preliminary Survey* (New York: Home Missions Council). Reprinted in 1969 by Arno Press.

——, (1921) *The Negro at Work During the World War and During Reconstruction* (Washington: Government Printing Office). Reprinted in 1969 by Negro Universities Press.

——, (1950) *Africa: Continent of the Future* (New York: The Association Press).

Sowell, Thomas, (1981) *Markets and Minorities* (New York: Basic Books).

Stewart, James, (1991) "The Rise and Fall of Negro Economics: The Economic Thought of George Edmund Haynes," *The American Economic Review Papers and Proceedings* (May), pp. 311–14.

Williams, Walter, (1982) *The State Against Blacks* (New York: New Press).

13

SOUNDINGS AND SILENCES ON RACE AND SOCIAL CHANGE

Abram Harris, Jr. in the Great Depression

William Darity, Jr.

INTRODUCTION

Abram Harris, Jr., (1899–1963) was the first black American economist to attain academic prominence in the United States. He left his mark – although not a sufficiently recognized mark – on developments in the areas of economic anthropology, black studies, institutional economics, the history of economic thought, and, paradoxically, on both black radical and neoconservative thought.[1] A 1930 PhD in economics from Columbia University, Harris taught at Howard University from the late 1920s until 1945.[2] Thereafter, Harris was at the University of Chicago, although he never held a regular appointment with the faculty of the economics department there. His position was exclusively with the faculty of the undergraduate college. One can presume race was a factor in this turn of events.[3]

Harris underwent what appears to have been a striking transition in perspective, moving from advocacy of a multiracial working-class movement in his youth to advocacy of the precepts of nineteenth-century English liberals during his later years. This was not an altogether unusual change of heart for intellectuals of his generation. Numerous contemporary neoconservative ideologues have journeyed from Trotskyism in their early years to their current status as disciples of Norman Podhoretz.[4] Whether Harris's transformation from radical to liberal was a matter of convenience, opportunism, or conviction remains unclear. Was it discomfiture with Soviet experiment? Was it the pressures of emerging McCarthyism? But Harris's transformation was so seemingly complete that by the time he became ensconced at the University of Chicago there was little evidence of his prior radicalism. Certainly there was no evidence of it for Milton Friedman who has attributed Harris's conversion to the persuasive powers of Frank Knight:

As to your question, how well was [Abe Harris] accepted as an economist who had written extensively in the Marxist tradition, by the time I knew him he was no longer writing in the Marxist tradition. On the contrary his interests had shifted primarily to the history of economic thought. He would not have been described by anyone at the University of Chicago as a Marxist or as writing in the Marxist tradition. I believe that characterized his earlier work but not his subsequent work. It may well be that this change owed much to the influence that Frank Knight had upon him.[5]

Given Harris's notorious ego and independence of will it is doubtful that even as forceful a figure as Frank Knight could be held responsible for Harris's apparent conversion. Still the change was dramatic enough for Knight, who had known Harris since the latter's tenure at Howard, to make note of it in the 1963 obituary Knight wrote for Chicago's student newspaper:

It should be stressed that Abe "grew" intellectually and spiritually throughout life. In early years he was a "radical" both on labor–capital relations and on the "race" issue. But he became more conservative as well as temperate, as he came to understand the issues. He finally decided that propaganda activities would not mix well with objective scholarly work. In particular, he came to realize that negroes as well as others can be intolerant and stupid, and ceased to work directly for the negro "cause." I recall his saying that it is as bad for the negro to be held always in the right as always in the wrong.[6]

Dr. Michael Winston has observed that Harris and the political scientist-later-to-be diplomat, Ralph Bunche, were the two leading Marxists at Howard during the 1930s. While Bunche's shift to the right came much faster than Harris's, Winston contends that Harris also became hostile toward Marxism and even "flirted with Hayek."[7] Indeed, Harris had been involved with the libertarian Mount Pelerin Society in the 1950s, whose membership included Hayek, but it is unclear how great his enthusiasm ever was for Hayek or Hayek's perspective. After all this was the same Abram Harris, albeit of more radical vintage, who made the following comment in a 1936 letter to Frank Knight, during Harris's visit to the London School of Economics:

I have met Hayek, McGregor, Harrod, and some of the younger men including Lerner, Meade, and Radice. I think the London School of Economics is going to seed under the influence of Hayek and Robbins. The place has no vitality.[8]

Still others have suggested that Harris actually never changed intellectual streams. Robert Auerbach, an economist at the University of California at

Riverside whom Harris spurred to enter the field, describes Harris as having no definite ideological commitment. The late Joseph Houchins, a long-time professor of economics at Howard University, said that Harris really remained on the left throughout his entire life. On the other hand, another one of his colleagues at Howard, the statistician Edward Lewis, reportedly said that Harris had shifted toward nineteenth century liberalism before he left Howard, which may or may not suggest it was an ideological turn made with calculation.[9] Harold Lewis who joined the Howard faculty in 1930 two years after Harris to teach economic history, characterizes Harris as being "left of center at Howard" but definitely "not a prisoner of anyone's ideology."[10]

Harris certainly conveyed the impression in the 1950s that his outlook had undergone a transformation. Aside from his participation in the "Austro-libertarian" Mount Pelerin Society, Harris made the following seemingly revealing observation in his 1958 collection of critical essays on various economic thinkers' proposals for social reform:

> In the late 1920s when I began studying their [Marx and Veblen's] works, I was just emerging from a state of social rebellion and still adhered somewhat to socialistic ideas. Although I did not agree with many of their theories, I was more or less in sympathy with their evaluation of our system of business enterprise, or capitalism, as Marx called it. But I came to believe that while Marx and Veblen had made some important contributions as critics and historians of capitalism, their conception of the basic defects of the system was mistaken and that their programs of economic reorganization, designed to increase industrial efficiency, lessen economic inequality, and create greater "effective" freedom for the masses of men, would achieve none of these things, but would probably create greater "evils" than those attributed by them to capitalism.

The oddity in Harris's remark is his recollection that he already was "emerging from a state of social rebellion [while] still adher[ing] somewhat to socialistic ideas"[11] by the late 1920s. The implication is that by the close of the decade, Harris already viewed himself as having begun his move from the left. There is a measure of disingenuity here, since in 1930 Harris prepared a pamphlet for the Conference for Progressive Labor Action proposing the initiation of a multiracial national labor party in the United States, in 1931 Harris published *The Black Worker* with Sterling Spero which contained a similarly militant statement of the need for multiracial labor solidarity, and in 1936 Harris published *The Negro as Capitalist*, which included a devastating attack on the social consequences of the actions of black-owned financial institutions on the black masses.[12]

While Harris harbored no illusions about the negatives of the Soviet experiment and wrote openly about the dangers of state and collectivist planning in the 1930s, he did not link these reservations to Marx's vision of social change.[13] Indeed in the mid-1930s, Harris prepared a paper for the Wesley Clair Mitchell *festschrift* that constituted a defense of Marx's analytical framework against unfounded criticisms from mainstream economists.[14] It was not until the mid-1940s that Harris published an essay explicitly critical of Marx on the basis of what Harris claimed were ethical shortcomings in Marx's misguided utopianism.[15]

Harris's intellectual and political activities during the interwar years is the issue at hand. Considering the substance of these activities, Harris seems to have been quite solidly on the left throughout the 1930s, to the point of advancing a critique of New Dealism for its failure to address the fundamental problem of class inequality in the United States. The timing of this apparent reorientation of his views coincides far too closely with the timing of his move from Howard to Chicago to discount the hypothesis that sheer careerism played a key role in his ideological conversion.

THE HOWARD RADICALS

The precise timing of Harris's conversion aside, and regardless of the depth of his sincerity in changing his perspective, certainly Harris's commitment to radical labor solidarity – evident in his writings in both the 1920s and 1930s – was neither naive nor overly romantic. His research on black coal miners early in the 1920s had showed him the strength of racial antagonism within the working class and the use of trade unions as a central mechanism to facilitate exclusion of blacks from the mining sector by white labor.[16] This insight was generalized to the entire run of blue collar occupations in a paper Harris prepared for *Current History* in 1926.[17]

His most famous work, coauthored with Sterling Spero, *The Black Worker*, provided the definitive study of white labor's attempt to exclude blacks from the workplace. Although such exclusionary practices had been largely successful, Spero and Harris felt that the roots of racial antagonism in the working class had sources that could be overcome: first, distrust of blacks by whites dated from slavery times; second, many blacks were recent urban immigrants with a peasant background that led them to be ignorant of trade unionism; and third, the anti-union ideology of the black middle-class leadership of such organizations as the National Urban League fostered racial division among the working classes.[18] The first two problems would evaporate with the passage of time and with active efforts at working-class enlightenment from progressive labor organizations. The latter problem could be overcome by new patterns of education of younger, university-trained blacks who would form the core of the next generation's middle class.

Equally telling were Harris's activities in authoring a controversial policy paper, that quickly came to be known as "the Harris report", for the

NAACP in the aftermath of the storied 1933 Amenia conference. In August of that year the NAACP called together numerous members of black America's "intellectual elite" to examine the race problem in the context of the Great Depression.

This gathering, known as the Amenia conference, was held at the Hudson River estate of NAACP president Joel Spingarn. As James Young reports, for three days the younger wave of black intellectuals, including Ralph Bunche, E. Franklin Frazier, and Harris himself – the Howard University social sciences triumvirate – "denounced the tactics and ideologies of their elders."[19] Indeed, Meier and Rudwick have noted that "At Howard there had been *since the 1920s* an important contingent of socialist oriented professors, including economist Abram L. Harris, political scientist Ralph J. Bunche, and sociologist E. Franklin Frazier."[20] These three were key actors at the Amenia conference.

The young Turks charged that W. E. B. Du Bois and James Weldon Johnson, in particular, were "'race men'", ethnic provincialists who "looked at all problems and solutions with a racial perspective."[21] Instead, the status of blacks should be considered from a wider perspective, encompassing larger issues of concern to the nation.[22]

From the vantage point of the conditions of the Great Depression, the younger intellectuals advocated a shift to a class perspective rather than a wholly racial perspective. Industrial capitalism, in their estimation, was a failure – a failure evidenced by the collapse of the US economy. The focus on racism and civil rights considerations should be subordinated to an emphasis on what they saw as the fundamental problem, "the exploitation of labor by private capital." In fact, the young Turks openly rejected "older, liberal methods of agitation for civil rights." They further contended that "The older leadership...had practically ignored the basic economic needs of the black masses."[23] Economic power for the black masses had to be the first objective that needed to be addressed, rather than civil rights.

There were three possible routes given their analysis, following European models of economic organization. Capitalism could be replaced by fascism, communism, or socialized democracy. The first two alternatives were deemed unacceptable by the Howard radicals, since "fascism would most certainly 'crystallize the Negro's position at the bottom of the social structure', and...communism would demand a monumental transformation in the psychology of both white and black workers in the United States..."[24]

The preferred path, described by Young as a choice of "reform over revolution," was to pursue the third route, the development of social democracy in the US, via a mass, multiracial labor movement.[25] Thus, the Howard triumvirate advocated unity among all workers. These premises lay at the heart of the plan written in 1934 by Harris for the NAACP, charting a new course of action, a plan that ultimately was ignored.

James Young's suggestion that the young intellectuals were naively optimistic is inaccurate.[26] While Frazier continued to call for black "internal unity" in private, he tended to subordinate race to class in his published writings.[27] Neither Bunche nor Harris, as indicated above, harbored illusions about either the white trade unions or the black masses.[28] And Young himself indicates that Frazier held no particular empathy toward the black masses.[29] Neither did Bunche nor Harris, for that matter.

Nevertheless, in the interval 1929–40 Bunche's rhetoric and vision certainly bore the stamp of a Marxist inspiration, so much so that in 1963 James J. Kilpatrick would accuse Bunche of being procommunist in the years up to 1940. Bunche's record that led to Kilpatrick's accusation included Bunche's articles in Howard's house organ, the *Journal of Negro Education*, his fiery pamphlet *A World View of Race*, his status as founding member of the leftist National Negro Congress, and his association with the scholarly Marxist journal, *Science and Society*, as well as the Institute for Pacific Relations and even Alger Hiss.[30] Biographer Charles Henry says that Bunche's essential vision never changed but his strategies and rhetoric moderated. Bunche's own reply to the Kilpatrick accusation was to declare he was never a member nor a supporter of the Communist Party and to point out the irony that he could not get a room in a Mississippi hotel where Soviet foreign minister Andrei Gromyko had been able to stay.[31]

Still Brian Urquhart's recent biography of Bunche is devoted far more to his diplomatic career than to the Howard years. Nevertheless, Urquhart is direct in his observation that in the 1930s "Bunche's analysis of colonialism, as well as the problems of black Americans, was informed by a strong Marxist strain of economic determinism."[32] But Bunche always had managed to keep his distance from the Communist Party, a fact that became vitally important when his loyalty was questioned in the 1950s.[33]

Bunche certainly had practical reasons to maintain an image distanced from the radicalism that characterized his views expressed in the 1930s as his star rose on the international stage. Better to dismiss it all as a youthful peccadillo rather than deep-seated beliefs about fundamental flaws in American society. Bunche had even more to lose politically and professionally than Harris by being tarred with the dreaded red paint brush. Frazier's radicalism always was more muted than that of the other two; his most critical attack actually was directed against W. E. B. Du Bois![34]

Harris, Bunche, and Frazier formed the remarkable core of Howard's Social Sciences group which also included Charles Thompson, Alain Locke, and even, on occasion, the biologist Ernest Just. Bunche's house on campus was the site of the gatherings. It was Harris, with justification, who "was seen as the intellectual leader of the group...."[35] Bunche was most often the public voice of the core group, especially in the pages of the *Journal of Negro History*. Frequently, he would simply echo positions conceived by and taken by Harris elsewhere.

Harris vehemently rejected the black nationalist concept of the "group economy" or "black economy" which had gained some currency at the time. The concept resurfaces at regular intervals. For example, the economic philosophy of the Nation of Islam from Elijah Muhammad to Louis Farakkhan and the economic plan proposed by journalist Tony Brown are squarely in the black economy tradition. Harris's study of black banking in *The Negro As Capitalist* was in large part an attempt to disprove the validity of the group economy as a strategy for black liberation.[36]

In this context, it should be noted that Harris produced loyal and enthusiastic students but not necessarily uncritical disciples. For example, his one-time student Frank Davis eventually penned *The Economics of Black Community Economic Development* which appears to have been Davis's attempt, without mentioning Harris, to put to rest Harris's position that the group economy/ghetto economy is not a viable route toward black advancement.[37]

Bunche functioned in many respects as Harris's intellectual lieutenant for many years. But this relationship terminated when Bunche agreed to work with Swedish economist Gunnar Myrdal in the 1930s on the report that eventually became *An American Dilemma*. Harris had refused to participate on the project. George O. Butler, a former student of Harris's, said that "Harris would not genuflect" while Bunche would yield and compromise. Why should a *Swedish economist* be given the leadership role on this project, when Harris, a black American, had devoted many years of research to investigation of the economic status of "the Negro"? Then there was the issue of money; Harris was unwilling to accept a fee of $1500 when he had learned that at least $20,000 had been set aside to hire research consultants.[38]

Bunche *did* make use of Harris's research while working on the Myrdal project. But by the close of the 1930s Bunche was reshaping his image. He had broken with the National Negro Congress by 1939, ostensibly because of its excessive ties to the Communist Party. He had joined with Myrdal to help produce *An American Dilemma*, which offered a fairly positive assessment of the New Deal.[39] Given Bunche's brilliant, angry attack on New Dealism published in 1936, in a piece where Frazier's and Harris's influences were strongly evident, this was a striking accommodation.[40] Bunche was on his way to international fame, while Harris was destined to remain an academic, with attendant comparative obscurity. Harris was one of the few, if not the only, Howard scholar with no contractual ties to the Myrdal project.

But through the mid-1930s, Bunche continued to borrow heavily from Harris's analytical approach, coupled with his own hegemonic view of the ruling class. Representative of Bunche's pre-Myrdal era posture on these dimensions is a 1935 essay published in the *Journal of Negro Education* outlining and critiquing the strategic options available to black Americans.[41]

In the essay, Bunche partitioned the basic options between violent and nonviolent strategies. The former included "direct rebellion and secession by force" and "[c]ooperation with other dissentient elements toward immediate or ultimate revolution." The violent strategy of "rebellion and secession" was deemed impractical by Bunche due to small numbers of blacks relative to whites and the dispersal of blacks across the United States. The violent strategy of "cooperation with other dissentient elements" toward the end of revolution also was dismissed because "the Negro masses are so lacking in radical class consciousness...so conservative and deeply imbued with a peasant psychology and the lingering illusion of the American Dream...."[42]

Note how similar the latter passage is to Harris's concluding observation in his review of Du Bois's *Black Reconstruction*, where Harris sustains the Amenia conference charge that Du Bois was a "racialist:"

> And the persistence of the Negro's belief in the possibility of economic and social advancement by means of business enterprise and the accumulation of property by individual members of the race, not to mention his abiding faith in the good will of the wealthy white man, has until this day confined his radicalism to militant civil libertarianism.[43]

In his essay, Bunche goes on to refer to the "indifferent success" of the Communist Party in proselytizing blacks and holds out the hope that black and white workers would see the unity of their interests and form a racially united "militant labor movement."[44]

The six non-violent strategies Bunche considered were the Garvey "Back to Africa" movement, economic passive resistance, economic separatism, civil libertarianism, interracial conciliation, and the courts. The Garvey "Back to Africa" movement was described derisively as "Negro Zionism" by Bunche; he borrowed the phrase directly from the rhetoric used by Harris and co-author Sterling Spero in *The Black Worker*.[45] This is ironic, given Bunche's later key diplomatic role in the formation of the state of Israel! Nevertheless, Bunche found Garveyism wanting on grounds of its ephemerality:

> Like all programs of this character, Garveyism offered the Negro an emotional escape from oppressive conditions. Also like other such programs it was impractical, for attractive land for such a venture was no longer available, due to the consuming greed and the inexorable demands of imperialist nations. The Garvey movement could offer only Liberia to the American Negro – one of the most backward and unhealthy territories of an altogether uninviting West Africa. Moreover, the Liberians themselves did not want the American Negroes.[46]

A second nonviolent strategy discussed by Bunche was economic passive resistance, a variant in his eyes of the Gandhi movement. Bunche anticipated that this strategy would be even less effective in the industrialized countries than in India because economic boycotts would result in a self-imposed lower standard of living for the boycotters. Therefore, such movements would be hard to sustain. In addition, the "business rulers" were bound to act against it. For instance, if blacks tried to found their own "group cooperatives" they would be confronted with counter-boycotts, denial of credit and other impediments to success: "The legal and police forces of the state would be aligned against them, and, in addition, they would be subjected to the characteristic gangster attacks which have recently proved so helpful to employers in labor disputes."[47]

Bunche also referred to a "mild version of this form of economic passive resistance" that took the form of the "Don't-buy-where-you-can't-work" movement. Bunche offered the following critique of the attempt by blacks to boycott stores where blacks were not hired: 1 the "Don't buy-where-you-can't-work" movement would not create net new jobs; 2 the movement would displace white laborers if successful; and 3 the movement would displace blacks working in white communities due to white retaliation. Bunche referred to the emergence of a "vicious cycle of job displacement." The economic system would not generate enough new jobs in the first place for either whites or blacks and the boycott effort would merely undercut prospects for black–white working class solidarity.[48]

In the closing pages of *The Negro as Capitalist* (1936), Harris contended in parallel fashion that "...pushed to its logical extreme, 'Don't-Buy-Where-You-Can't-Work' ends by strengthening the forces of the segregated economy."[49] While Garveyism would be viewed as the racial chauvinism of the black masses, "Don't-Buy-Where-You-Can't-Work" constituted, in Harris's view, "the racial chauvinism [of] the black middle class." It[50] was the black capitalist who was, in Harris's eyes, the greater villain than the white capitalist.

An additional peculiar charge lodged by Harris in print (and by Bunche and Harris in public presentations) was the claim that the actions of the New Negro Alliance in DC (led in part by one of Harris's students, John A. Davis), the Citizens' League for Fair Play of New York, and the Citizens' Committee of Baltimore were anti-semitic.[51] Davis recalled that his response to Harris's criticisms in an essay in the National Urban League's journal *Opportunity* was comparatively subdued in tone only because of his great respect for his Howard professor.[52]

The Howard triumvirate's views were not limited to their own writings. Another Howard student, Emmett Dorsey, repeated almost verbatim Harris's charges against the "Don't-Buy-Where-You-Can't-Work" movement in a *Journal of Negro Education* paper published in 1936.[53] The paper also echoes Bunche's attack on New Deal social planning. Dorsey was an Oberlin graduate who had studied at Columbia and was teaching political science at Howard. He was the subject of Harris's patronage and intercession with the administrators of the Rosenwald Fund. In a letter dated 25 February 1932 Harris added his support to that of W. E. B. Du Bois and Ernest Just on behalf of Dorsey's application for dissertation fellowship support.[54] Eight years later Bunche and Harris sent a letter to the Rosenwald Fund ranking the applicants from among Howard University faculty for Rosenwald Fellowships. Dorsey was ranked first by Bunche and Harris, followed by Eric Williams, later to be the first Prime Minister of Trinidad, James Mitchell, and Vincent Browne and William Davis both placed fourth.[55]

The third strategy in the non-violent column listed in Bunche's paper was *economic* separatism, the black capitalism advocated by Booker T. Washington and Major Moten. Both Bunche and Dorsey quoted exactly the same passage from Spero and Harris's *Black Worker* (1931) to refute this approach:[56]

> The ideal of an independent black economy within the confines of the white is a living force in every black community in the land. Yet how such an independent economy is to rise and function when the white world outside controls credit, basic industry and the state is something which the sponsors of the movement prefer to ignore. If such an economy is to rise it must do so with the aid of white philanthropy, and will have to live upon white sufferance. If the great white banks and insurance companies decide that they do not want Negro business it is hard to see how the little black institutions can compete successfully against them. The same holds for the chain stores and various retail establishments. They will be able to undersell their Negro competitors if they want to, and the Negro world will not continue indefinitely to pay higher prices for its goods merely out of pride of race. Basic industry will continue to remain in the hands of the white world, for even the most ardent supporters of an independent black economy will admit that there is no prospect of the Negro capitalists amassing enough wealth to establish steel mills, build railroads and pipe lines, and gain control of essential raw materials.[57]

Dorsey adds in his essay that the independent black economy is no more than an "economic will-o-the-wisp" supported, nonetheless, by the NAACP, the Garvey movement, black churches and lodges, and the National Urban League.[58]

The fourth nonviolent strategy within the actual range of tactical considerations for "the Negro," according to Bunche, was the civil libertarian strategy, very much in the spirit of *eighteenth-century* liberalism. Here the objective is to utilize Constitutional protections, in particular the Bill of Rights and the 13th, 14th, and 15th Amendments, to establish conditions of political-cum-legal equality for African Americans. The limitation of this approach is its failure to acknowledge fully that Constitutional guarantees only are as good as the social context in which they are implemented and enforced:

> The Constitution is thus detached from the political and economic realities of American life and becomes a sort of protective angel hovering above us and keeping a constant vigil over the rights of all America's children, black and white, rich and poor, employer and employee and, like impartial justice, blinded to their differences. This view ignores the quite significant fact that the Constitution is a very flexible instrument and that, in the nature of things, it cannot be anything more than the controlling elements in American society wish it to be...[59]

Again borrowing from Harris's rhetoric, Bunche identified a fifth non-violent strategy, "interracial conciliation." The objective here was to improve the black condition by gaining the support and sympathy "among influential elements in the controlling [white] population."[60] But, according to Bunche, the difficulty with this strategy was, since it involved appeals to members of the dominant group, its successes would breed reduced aggressiveness to continue to maintain and extend the gains. Winning more and more support would necessitate still greater passivity or, as Bunche put it, with this strategy, blacks "...can be militant but only politely so; they can attack, but not too harshly...They must politely play the game according to the rules even though they have no stakes. In other words, they play cricket."[61]

Finally, Bunche considered the nonviolent strategy of reliance upon the courts as the avenue for racial progress. This subject was Bunche's bailiwick. He engaged in a detailed discussion of court decisions involving "Negro rights," the upshot of which was a demonstration that courts generally had not made decisions favoring blacks. But, even if the courts did make decisions supporting black rights, they could not enforce them.[62]

The latter three tactics – the civil libertarian strategy, interracial conciliation, and the courts – comprise the core of the principles underlying the civil rights revolution of the 1950s and 1960s, spearheaded by Martin Luther King, Jr. But along with the other tactics listed above, all three were dismissed by Bunche and Harris in the 1930s as affording little relief for blacks in America. Almost by default they settled on their case for a trade union political movement transcending racial lines. Dorsey's paper was even more direct on this point, concluding with an enthusiastic discussion of the Harris plan for a transformed NAACP, intended to shift the NAACP toward multiracial radical trade unionism.[63] But the Harris plan in all its essentials died still-born.

Harris always was an inveterate critic of programs for social reform advanced from various quarters. He was particularly skeptical about the purported civil libertarian/civil rights route to black progress. In the 1930s

Harris's criticism was posed from the left. He argued that the drive for legal equality left untouched the material basis for racial inequality, which found its origins in the American economic structure. The prohibition of black labor from preferred occupations via an elaborate system of racial exclusion was not to be overcome by a program focusing on legal rights.

But in Harris's later years his critique of the civil libertarian path shifted from the radical posture to the standpoint of orthodox economic theory in a manner echoed recently by the black neoconservative economist, Thomas Sowell.[64] For Harris, writing in the early 1960s, the legal avenue to black economic progress left untouched racial differences in human capital endowments, attributable to differences in familial socialization processes in black and white homes, linked, in turn, to differences in social class background.[65] Thus, Harris remained predisposed to question the premises of the civil rights movement – ironically, first from the perspective of militant labor solidarity and later from the perspective of post-Second World War University of Chicago economics.[66]

During the interval of the 1920s through the early 1940s Harris produced a voluminous output on matters concerning race relations. His writings on economic theory – on institutionalist economics and on economists' views on social reform – dated from the 1930s to the end of his life. When Harris left Howard his published work on race relations all but ceased, apart from the paper published posthumously on the history of black education in the US that served as the vehicle for the aforementioned neoconservative-styled critique of the civil rights approach that he adopted during his later years.[67]

"I DID NOT KNOW THAT I COULD BE SO GOOD"

Oddly enough, despite Harris's twin research interests in the history of economic thought and race relations in the 1920s and 1930s, he never merged the two to address the work other American economists had done earlier on "the Negro problem." His inquiries into doctrinal history in economics were confined largely to the ideas of German or German-educated economic theorists – Sombart, Veblen, Marx, his former professor Wesley Clair Mitchell, and the neo-scholastic Catholic economist, Heinrich Pesch. But Harris never undertook a study of the economists' work on racial difference during the entire phase where his research agenda still included racial issues.

Indeed, there was an enormous body of work by economists on racial differences – a stomach-curdling literature with a drumbeat theme of black inferiority – dating from the time of the formation of the American Economic Association in the 1880s. Walter Willcox of Cornell and his students and disciples Charles Tillinghast, Frederick Hoffman, and Alfred Holt Stone all prepared major monographs, published by the American Eco-

241

nomic Association, that were paeans to the intellectual and moral deficiencies of black people.

During the late nineteenth and early twentieth centuries, the pages of the *Journal of Political Economy (JPE)* and the *Quarterly Journal of Economics (QJE)* were filled with studies by anthropometrists ranking the relative qualities of racial groups on both physical and mental dimensions. The distinctive nineteenth-century concept of race blended nationality, culture and genetics to distinguish human groups. Craniometry was a popular subject matter in *economics* journals of the day. The anthropologist Carlos Closson of Los Angeles, firmly convinced that blacks ranked at the bottom of a putative human evolutionary scale, published frequently in both the *JPE* and *QJE* in the period 1890 through 1920.[68]

It is puzzling that at a time when disciplinary fields were seeking to establish separate identities – and political economy already had carved out a distinct domain by the mid-nineteenth century due to the prominence of the English Classical school – so much material influenced by nineteenth-century anthropometry found its way into economics journals at the turn of the century. With respect to the *JPE* a partial explanation may be the interests of Thorstein Veblen, who was managing editor of the journal between 1896 and 1906.

Veblen made a twisted and ingenious use of the concepts of nineteenth-century anthropology to construct an analysis of the "dolicho-blond race" that led him virtually to predict the First World War.[69] Veblen also was one of the few to say next to nothing about blacks when employing the theoretical apparatus of this brand of anthropology. Harris, despite his extensive investigations of Veblen's work, had little to say about this aspect of it aside from the dismissive comment that "The anthropology from which Veblen derived his theory of three European racial types – that differ in both physical and mental characteristics – has long been discarded."[70]

Behind Harris's slender comment lay a great deal more. Although Harris had done his PhD at Columbia in economics as a graduate student, he had worked as a research assistant with the anthropologist Melville Herskovits, before Herskovits left Columbia for Northwestern. Herskovits, in fact, tried unsuccessfully to lure Harris away from economics to anthropology. Eventually, Harris was to be Herskovits's principal tutor on economics when Herskovits wrote the first major text in economic anthropology, *The Economic Life of Primitive People*. Nevertheless, Herskovits neglected to acknowledge Abram Harris's help in the preface.[71]

The Columbia tradition in anthropology, identified with Franz Boas, professed a certain cultural neutrality and self-consciously positioned itself as the antithesis of nineteenth-century anthropometry. His immersion in Columbia anthropology may have led Harris to believe that the nineteenth-century presumptions were genuinely dead. He was, therefore, unlikely to have been alert to its recrudescence in the form of the human capital explanation for racial inequality which he came to embrace himself at Chicago.[72] It was not to occur, but it certainly would have been interesting to have had Harris mount an analysis of the anthropo-economic view of "the Negro problem" that pervaded the American economics in the early years of the American Economic Association, especially in light of his own embrace of human capital doctrine later in his career.[73]

Perhaps blinded by his personal and philosophical commitment to individualism, he naturally would have viewed the human capital explanation for racial inequality as non-paternalistic, and hence, positive. He was, after all, even late in life a self-styled advocate of an individualistic brand of socialism patterned after J. S. Mill. Harris, despite his transformation into an anti-Marxist economist, never dropped the claim that he was a socialist who favored appropriate government intervention, along the dimensions indicated by J. S. Mill.[74]

Harris, as the cliché had it, did not suffer fools gladly. To have the force of his intellect applied to the manifestations in the economic literature of nineteenth-century conceptions of race and racial difference would have been compelling. Particularly in his arrogant and fiery youth Harris did not let intellectual rivals up off the mat. Apparently, many were incapable even of entering the ring with him.

Consider Harris's own description of his participation in Hubert Herring's Interracial Seminar banquet held at the Whitelaw Hotel in Washington, DC in November 1930 in a letter from Harris to the journalist Benjamin Stolberg:

> In the morning it [the seminar group] was addressed at Howard University by [Alain] Locke, [Mordecai] Johnson [then president of Howard] and Kelly Miller. I had planned to have nothing to say. But Mordecai W. Johnson and Hubert Herring requested me to speak at the banquet. In other words I *was* the speaker. Callie [California McGuinn, Harris's first wife] persuaded me to accept and I did. Man I raised a hornet's nest. I let everyone there know where I stood. I talked on "The Black Man and This Economic World." The first speaker was Mr. Crampton, Member of Congress and Howard University's best friend. I followed, I talked about the prospects of the black bourgeoisie, the exclusive and reactionary tactics of the American Federation with respect to Negro labor and white unskilled workers, white philanthropy as the means of delaying Negro labor consciousness, the separatist tactics of Negro leadership, the other-worldly religiosity of the Negro church, and the attempt of the Negro intellectual to get away from the mass.
>
> Dr. George Haynes of the Federal Council of Churches and I clashed. Boy it was a hot time. When I finished with Haynes I had him proving that the Negro church and leaders like himself had been

the employers' greatest friend and the Negro workers' worst enemy. The issues were clear cut. And there was no quibbling. Locke told me that he had never seen such a scrap before. Mordecai W. Johnson told me that he did not know that I could take such good care of myself in the give and take of debate. And when I had finished with Haynes, President Johnson asked me to elaborate more fully on the prospects of petty capitalism within the race. Anson Phelps-Stokes, lover of black humanity and peace, sat beside me. Man you should have seen him frown and squirm when I said that the white philanthropists had encouraged the Booker T. Washington philosophy and that as the traditional ally of the Negro, the Negro business league was looking to such philanthropists as Rosenwald and Rockefeller for financial assistance in establishing a chain of Negro retail stores. I said "evidently these Negroes believe that Negro business should take its place alongside Urban Leagues, Y.M.C.A.'s and day nurseries as another worthy charity." Do you think Mr. Rosenwald will reasonably do anything that will cut the profits of Sears-Roebuck? I can tell you no more. I will let you read the speech when I see you. I did not know that I could be so good.[75]

But of course, he "could be so good." Following the banquet speech, the sociologist Charles Johnson came home with Harris, wanting to talk further. Johnson was an old friend with whom Harris had worked on the Urban League's journal, *Opportunity*, in the early 1920s. The visit led to the following exchange of views on methodology, race relations research and research funding, again described by Harris in the same letter to Stolberg:

Well Dr. Johnson and I talked things out. He asked me if I had read his book [*The Negro in American Civilization*]. This question led to the whole question of research and scientific method. He said that he thought my stuff was always very good, but that I always tried to fit my philosophy into the facts that come under my observation. So I asked what in the hell was science anyway and did a mere presentation of facts mean that the writer was as much of a scientist as the one who actually interpreted the facts? I also asked if he did not think that the man who actually perceived certain valid conclusions in his facts and refused to draw them was not only dishonest but an intellectual hypocrite. Of course he said no. He said that he looks upon the researcher as one who gathers the facts and leaves it to others to draw conclusions. Well we got nowhere with our argument. When I told him that the foundations paid liberally for his stuff because he refused to draw conclusions and refused to finance my work because I do draw conclusions he said that I had a persecution complex. He also said that Ben Stolberg had said as much about him. And while he did not agree with that statement made by Stolberg, he did agree with the statement that the book gives no picture of Negro life or offers social criticism. With that we parted.[76]

Stolberg had condemned Charles Johnson's book in a review in the New York *Herald Tribune* earlier during the same year, characterizing it as an "important book...not...because it is a good book" but because it represents "the most competent example of a certain type of very bad book." Stolberg complained that Johnson's book was "[b]owdlerized of the faintest trace of opinion or conclusion, as though a social outlook were almost an indecent thing in social research" and that after a person had read the book "you know no more about [the Negro's] life than you know about American society after you have read the Almanac."[77]

Such aggressively safe, largely descriptive social science research on race matters lives on in such forms as the annual National Urban League report *The State of Black America* or the recent National Research Council assessment of the status of black Americans, *A Common Destiny*. Indeed, while employed in 1925–6 as executive secretary of the Minneapolis Urban League – just before the advent of his academic career – Harris produced a monograph on black Minnesotans that greatly resembled the type of work he decried that came from Johnson's pen.[78]

But Charles Johnson may have been stung by Harris's and Stolberg's criticisms and spurred to modify his approach. The report Johnson prepared, summarizing the findings of the 1933 Conference on the Economic Status of the Negro, contains passages that sound very much like Harris's interpretation of the "facts" in the 1930s. The report documents labor union racial exclusionary practices and virtually advocates the promotion of a multiracial working-class movement![79] Of course, such overtures toward radicalism probably had a more acceptable resonance to the officials of the Rosenwald Foundation, who funded the conference, in the midst of the Great Depression than they would have had at an earlier time. Indeed, by then even the National Urban League had moved to temper its enthusiasm for strikebreaking and anti-unionism.

Harris's youthful fire gave way to a reserve in his later years. The mature scholar may have displayed more dignity and a considerably less overt argumentative style. But the young Harris's incandescence bore an exciting ferocity that tore into conventional beliefs about schemes for racial progress with an unparalleled force. When the older Harris attacked economists' views on social reform the intellectual acuity was no less present, but the lowered flame made the effort somewhat less fascinating. In a way, the older Harris while still exceptionally good had forgotten how good he actually could be – tempered by his, in all likelihood, convenient gravitation toward the intellectual matrix of neoconservatism long before the ideology was given its contemporary label.

NOTES

1 See William Darity, Jr., and Julian Ellison, "Abram Harris, Jr.: The Economics of Race and Social Reform," in *History of Political Economy*, vol. 22: 4, 1990, pp. 611–27.

2 This was a remarkable period at Howard. Racial segregation of faculties in higher education in the US restricted black scholars to appointments at black colleges and universities. Howard in Washington, DC, in particular assembled an array of outstanding scholars as a result: Ernest Just in biology, Franklin Frazier in sociology, Alain Locke in philosophy, Ralph Bunche in political science, Eric Williams and William Leo Hansberry in history, among others.

3 William Darity, Jr., "Introduction: The Odyssey of Abram Harris From Howard to Chicago," in *Race, Radicalism, and Reform: Selected Papers of Abram L. Harris*, William Darity, Jr. (ed.), (New Brunswick NJ: Transaction, 1989, pp. 3–6).

4 This includes Podhoretz himself.

5 Personal correspondence dated 18 February 1986 from Milton Friedman to myself.

6 Frank Knight Papers, Box 47, Folder 11, Joseph Roegenstein Library, University of Chicago.

7 Correspondence with Rodney Green dated 25 February 1986, reporting on conversations he had with Michael Winston and the late Joseph Houchins.

8 Correspondence from Harris to Frank Knight dated 18 May 1936 (Knight Collection, Joseph Roegenstein Library, University of Chicago).

9 Correspondence with Rodney Green, *op. cit.*

10 Telephone conversation with Harold Lewis in November 1986.

11 Abram Harris, Jr., *Economics and Social Reform* (New York: Harper and Row 1958, pp. xiv–xv).

12 Abram L. Harris, Jr., *The Negro Worker: A Problem of Vital Concern to the Entire Labor Force Movement*, Pamphlet No. 3, Progressive Labor Library (New York: Conference for Progressive Labor Action, 1930); Sterling Spero and Abram Harris, Jr., *The Black Worker: The Negro and the Labor Market* (New York: Columbia University Press, 1931); and Abram L. Harris, Jr., *The Negro as Capitalist: A Study of Banking and Business Among American Negroes* (Philadelphia: The American Academy of Political and Social Science, 1936).

13 Abram L. Harris, Jr., "Government and the U.S.S.R.," *The Nation*, vol. 117: 3694 22 April 1936, pp. 518–20 and Abram L. Harris, Jr., "The Totalitarian Tide" *The Nation*, vol. 146:7 and *The Nation*, 12 February 1938, pp. 188–90.

14 Abram L. Harris, Jr., "The Marxian Right to the Whole Product," in *Economic Essays in Honor of Wesley Clair Mitchell* (New York: Columbia University Press, 1935).

15 Abram L. Harris, Jr., "The Social Philosophy of Karl Marx," *Ethics*, Part 2, February 1946.

16 Abram L. Harris, Jr., "The Plight of the Negro Miners," *Opportunity* vol. 3: 34 October 1925, pp. 303–4 and "The Negro in the Coal Mining Industry," *Opportunity* vol. 4:38 February 1926, pp. 45–7. Harris's research on black labor in mining originated with the work he did for his master's thesis at the University of Pittsburgh "The Negro Laborer in Pittsburgh" (1924). Also see Dennis C. Dickerson's fine study *Out of the Crucible: Black Steelworkers in Western Pennsylvania, 1875–1980*, Albany: State University of New York Press 1986, which makes good use of Harris's research.

17 Abram L. Harris, Jr., "Negro Labor's Quarrel With White Workingmen," *Current History* vol. 24:6 September 1926, pp. 903–8.

18 Spero and Harris, *The Black Worker, op. cit.*
19 James O. Young, *Black Writers of the Thirties* (Baton Rouge: LSU Press, 1973, p. 3). Also see Raymond Wolters, *Negroes and the Great Depression* (Westport: Greenwood Press, 1970, pp. 219–29).
20 August Meier and Elliot Rudwick, *Black History and the Historical Professions 1915–1980* (Urbana: University of Illinois Press, 1986, p. 102), emphasis added.
21 Young, *op. cit.*, p.3.
22 *ibid.*, pp. 3–4.
23 *ibid.*, pp. 4–5.
24 *ibid.*, p. 4. Also see Ralph Bunche, "Current Events of Importance in Negro Education," *Journal of Negro Education*, October 1933, pp. 516–17.
25 *ibid.*, p. 4.
26 *ibid.*, p. 5.
27 *ibid.*, p. 5 and Wolters, *op. cit.*, pp. 224–5.
28 Charles Henry, "Civil Rights and National Security: The Case of Ralph Bunche," in Benjamin Rivlin (ed.), *Ralph Bunche: The Man and His Times* (New York: Holmes and Meier, 1990, p. 53).
29 Young, *op. cit.*, p. 53.
30 Henry, *op. cit.*, p. 50.
31 *ibid.*, pp. 50–3.
32 Brian Urquhart, *Ralph Bunche: An American Life* (New York: W. W. Norton, 1993, p. 56).
33 *ibid.*, pp. 246–56.
34 Young, *op. cit.*, pp. 49–54.
35 Henry, *op. cit.*, p. 53.
36 Harris, *The Negro As Capitalist, op. cit.*
37 Frank Davis, *The Economics of Black Community Economic Development: An Analysis and Program for Autonomous Growth and Development* (Chicago: Markham Publishing Company, 1970).
38 Interview with George O. Butler, Washington, DC, 4 March 1987. David W. Southern (*Gunnar Myrdal and Black–White Relations: The Use and Abuse of An American Dilemma 1944–1967* (Baton Rouge: LSU Press, 1987, p. 14)) reports that Bunche originally asked for $9500 a year or the equivalent of $73,000 in 1986 dollars but eventually settled for $5000 or the 1986 equivalent of about $40,000.
39 John B. Kirby, "Race, Class, and Politics: Ralph Bunche and Black Protest," in Benjamin Rivlin (ed.), *Ralph Bunche: The Man and His Times* (New York: Holmes and Meier, 1990, pp. 37–8).
40 See Ralph Bunche, "A Critique of New Deal Social Planning As It Affects Negroes," *Journal of Negro Education*, vol. 5, January 1936, pp. 59–65.
41 Ralph Bunche, "A Critical Analysis of the Tactics and Programs of Minority Groups," *Journal of Negro Education*, vol. 4, July 1935, pp. 308–20.
42 *ibid.*, p. 312.
43 Abram L. Harris, Jr., "Reconstruction and the Negro," *The New Republic*, vol. 83: 1079, August 7, 1935, p. 368.
44 Bunche, "A Critical Analysis," *op. cit.*, p. 312.
45 Spero and Harris, *The Black Worker, op. cit.*, pp. 387–8.
46 Bunche, "A Critical Analysis," *op. cit.*, pp. 312–13.
47 *ibid.*, p. 313.
48 *ibid.*, pp. 313–14.
49 Harris, *The Negro As Capitalist, op. cit.*, p. 182.
50 *ibid.*, p. 184.
51 *ibid.*, p. 184.

52 Telephone conversation with John A. Davis in February 1986. Davis's response to the critics of the "Don't-Buy-Where-You-Can't-Work-Movement" appears in "We Win the Right to Fight for Jobs," *Opportunity*, vol. 16: 8 August 1938, pp. 230–7. John A. Davis is not to be confused with John P. Davis, who formed the National Negro Congress with Bunche in 1936. Bunche was to break with John P. Davis and the Congress in 1940 due to the organization's growing alliance with the US Communist Party. John P. Davis, who later joined the Communist Party, offered key testimony during Bunche's loyalty hearings, confirming that Bunche had never joined the Communist Party nor attended a Party meeting. See Urquhart, *op. cit.*, pp. 59, 60–1, 93–4, 253–4.

53 Emmett E. Dorsey, "The Negro and Social Planning," *Journal of Negro Education*, vol. 5, January 1936, pp. 107–8.

54 Correspondence from Abram Harris Jr. to Edwin Embree dated 25 February 1932 (Rosenwald Fund Papers, Amistad Research Center, Tulane University).

55 Correspondence from Bunche and Harris to George Reynolds dated 7 February 1940 (Rosenwald Fund Papers, Amistad Research Center, Tulane University).

56 Bunche, "A Critical Analysis," *op. cit.*, p. 314 and Dorsey, *op. cit.*, p. 106.

57 Spero and Harris, *The Black Worker, op. cit.*, p. 466.

58 Dorsey, *op. cit.*, pp. 106–7.

59 Bunche, "A Critical Analysis," *op. cit.*, p. 315.

60 *ibid.*, p. 316.

61 *ibid.*, p. 326.

62 *ibid.*, pp. 316–20.

63 Dorsey, *op. cit.*, pp. 108–9.

64 For example, see Thomas Sowell, "Economics and Black People," *The Review of Black Political Economy*, Winter/Spring 1971, especially pp. 5 and 7. For an additional representative sample of Thomas Sowell's views, see his book *Civil Rights: Rhetoric or Reality?* (New York: William Morrow and Company, 1984). Also see the discussion in Darity and Ellison, "Abram Harris, Jr.," *op. cit.*, pp. 614–17.

65 On Harris's later views on the civil rights strategy for black progress see Abram Harris, Jr., "Education and the Economic Status of Negroes in the United States," in *100 Years of Emancipation*, ed. Robert A. Goldwin (Chicago: Rand McNally, 1964, 129–57). Reprinted in *Race, Radicalism and Reform*, Darity, ed., *op. cit.*

66 A. W. Coats, the economic historian, who was a personal friend of Harris, speculates that Harris "opposed any kind of anti-discrimination laws (positive discrimination was not then usual, or to my knowledge even heard of), as though he had managed to 'make it' despite all the obstacles, and didn't really see why others couldn't, given the effort." Coats does add that such an inference might be "unfair" to Harris. (Personal correspondence from A. W. Coats dated 3 November 1989).

67 See Mark Aldrich, "Progressive Economists and Scientific Racism: Walter Willcox and Black Americans, 1895–1910," *Phylon*, 40, no. 1 (Spring 1979): 1–14; Robert Cherry, "Racial Thought and the Early Economics Profession," *Review of Social Economy*, 34, no. 2 (1976): 147–62; and Mark Aldrich, "Capital Theory and Racism: From Laissez-Faire to the Eugenics Movement in the Career of Irving Fisher," *Review of Radical Political Economy*, 7, no. 3 (Fall 1975): 33–42.

68 Thorstein Veblen, *The Place of Science in Modern Civilization and Other Essays* (New York: Russell and Russell, 1961, 457–96).

69 Abram L. Harris, Jr., "Veblen and the Social Phenomenon of Capitalism," *American Economic Review*, 41, no. 2 (May 1951): 66.

70 Melville Herskovits, *The Economic Life of Primitive People* (New York: Alfred A. Knopf, 1940, viii–ix). In correspondence dated 29 July 1935, Herskovits wrote Harris as follows, revealing the scope of Harris's influence on his project: "I am writing to ask for some of your later reprints, for I am getting at my book on primitive economics, and I shall want your things badly. I only have the first paper from the *Journal of Political Economy* [Harris's essay, "Types of Institutionalism," *JPE*, 1932]. I know you published at least one other ["Economic Evolution: Dialectical and Darwinian," *JPE* 1934] and then there is the paper from the Wesley Mitchell volume ["The Marxian Right to the Whole Product," in *Economic Essays in Honor of Wesley Clair Mitchell*, 1935]. I hope you have your reprints sufficiently handy to send me these as well as any others. I have been having a great time getting into the material. At first I was confused by most of the theory that I read, but I finally decided that I would have to trouble very little with the Classical, Neo-Classical, and German historical theories. It seems to me that the Institutionalist approach is the only one, and the problems that I shall take up will be of a general nature – the relationship between the natural environment and economic life; economic determinism; the question of individualism and collectivism in primitive society. I am also planning a section to discuss the matter of economic surplus and its appropriation by the leisure class in those societies in which technology permits such a surplus to be produced. These classes, I think, in primitive society are primarily the governing and priestly groups, and I expect to discuss at some length the manner in which their position is validated by the conspicuous consumption of valuable goods" (Herskovits Collection, Northwestern University Archives). Through Harris's filter, Herskovits apparently absorbed Veblen's vision of "the leisure class," those persons performing ideological leadership, mystical, and mystification functions, supported out of the social surplus to which they make no direct productive contribution.

71 The human capital approach ascribes the lag in black economic performance to deficiencies in attributes that enhance individual productivity in the workplace.

72 Another odd silence in Harris's career is the lack of communication with sociologist Oliver Cox whose work had immense potential for cross-fertilization.

73 On Mill's libertarian socialism see especially Abram Harris, Jr., "J. S. Mill on Monopoly and Socialism: A Note," *Journal of Political Economy*, vol. 67:6 December 1959, pp. 604–11 and Abram Harris, Jr., "John Stuart Mill's Theory of Progress," *Ethics*, vol. 46:3 April 1956, pp. 157–75.

74 Correspondence from Abram Harris, Jr. to Benjamin Stolberg dated 12 November 1930 (Stolberg Collection, Columbia University Archives).

75 *ibid.*

76 *ibid.*

77 Benjamin Stolberg, "Review of Charles S. Johnson's *The Negro in American Civilization*," Books Section, *New York Herald Tribune*, 22 June 1930. W. E. B. Du Bois approvingly quoted Stolberg's review of Johnson's book in Du Bois's book column in the September 1930 issue of *The Crisis*; see *Book Reviews by W. E. B. Du Bois*, ed. Herbert Aptheker (Millwood: Kto Press, 1977, p. 149).

78 Abram L. Harris, Jr., *The Negro Population in Minneapolis: A Study of Race Relations* (Minneapolis: Minneapolis Urban League and Phyllis Wheatley Settlement House, 1926) reprinted in part in *Race, Radicalism and Reform*, Darity (ed.), *op. cit.*

79 Charles S. Johnson, *The Economic Status of Negroes* (Nashville: Fisk University Press, 1933).

14

FORMULATING THE NEGATION

Abram Harris, Jr. as critic

Julian Ellison

In the evolution of economic ideas there is evidence of a kind of dialectic at work.*

Much of Abram L. Harris's writing represented a critique of received economic doctrine. His positive theory comprised a much smaller, though not less significant, part of his *oeuvre*. As he spent much of the last third of his life teaching philosophy, it is not inappropriate to characterize the critical part of his work in philosophical terms as a process of expressing the antithesis, or "formulating the negation."

It is also of some interest that the field of the history of economic doctrine to which Harris contributed his most well-regarded work consists of the analysis and criticism of existing systems of thought. By choosing this field in which to work, Harris committed himself to the life of a critic.

Harris was introduced to the critical frame of mind in scholarship by Clarence Maloney, his economics professor and debate team coach at Virginia Union University. Debate comprises the application of the opposition relationship of deductive logic to selected topics, and Maloney taught him this application of logic. In the curriculum of European medieval universities, this application had been contained in the courses on rhetoric.

At New York University in 1922–23, Harris was first exposed to the application of this idea to the history of economic doctrine by Lewis Henry Haney of the economics department, a student of Richard T. Ely at Johns Hopkins University. For Haney criticism meant the application of the Hegelian dialectic to the history of economic thought, as he demonstrated brilliantly in a long chapter of his book entitled *The Evolution of Economics as a Science*.[1] Haney showed that economic thought evolved in triadic

---

* A. W. Coats, "John R. Commons as a Historian of Economics: The Quest for the Antecedents of Collective Action," in Warren J. Samuel (ed.), *Research in the History of Economic Thought and Methodology. A Research Annual*, vol. 1, Greenwich, CT: Jai press, 1983, p. 154.

cycles, the engine of development of which was the necessary opposition of successive theories. In the fourth edition of the book, published in 1949, Harris would be cited as one of the authorities on institutionalist thought.[2]

Harris's immediate motivation in choosing this field might well have been his admiration for the work of his Columbia University professor and mentor Wesley Clair Mitchell. Harris had taken Mitchell's class in the history of economic doctrine, Types of Economic Theory, in which Mitchell introduced him to the work of Karl Marx. The full English title of Marx's *magnum opus* was *Capital: A Critique of Political Economy*. The subtitle is not often cited, but its influence on Harris's thought should not be underestimated.[3] Harris apparently took from Mitchell both the idea of extensive intellectual biographical sketches, and the title of his first article published in the *Journal of Political Economy* in 1932. That first article echoed the title of Mitchell's class, being called "Types of Institutionalism."

Harris's principal themes and literary style also warrant equally extensive analysis, but space prohibits undertaking that analysis here. Suffice it to say that in his career, Harris critiqued three principal types of theories using the dialectic: 1 theories of black economic development; 2 theories of African Americans as world isolates; and 3 "institutionalist" economic theories. The theories concerning blacks *per se* were very important, but as he wrote to Frank Knight early on, critique of them alone could not of itself make his reputation. The status of Africans in the world at that time, and the academic study of that status, did not command the high respect sought by Harris. As he predicted, he is remembered most for his critique of "institutionalist" theory. The effect of this critique in his case ultimately was a return to classical economics. His style was rhetorically dialectic.

In this article, the sense in which Harris was a critic is explored by analyzing only one aspect of his work – his method.

NEGATION: THE HARRIS METHOD FOR THE HISTORY OF ECONOMIC DOCTRINE

Understanding Abram L. Harris's method of analysis requires an understanding of philosophy, its fields of study and their interrelationships. Most importantly, it requires an understanding of traditional and dialectical logic. Dialectical logic is Hegelian and Marxian. Harris adopted the Marxianized Hegelian dialectic, and Marx's application of that logic to the study of history under capitalism, to analyze economic theories.[4]

Harris on philosophy

Philosophy as presently studied has six fields – ontology, cosmology, epistemology, ethics (morals), logic, and esthetics. Harris, in his first article in a professional economics journal in 1932, whenever he was specific about

251

philosophy, mentioned morals (ethics) and logic. Each economic theory, he implied, has an ethic and a logic and theories are to be contrasted with regard to differences in ethics and in logic. Finally, theories are compared and contrasted as to their epistemological status – as idealist or materialist.

On ethics

Harris therefore judged each theory he analyzed by its affirmation or negation of an ethical norm, the economic equality of all members of society.[5]

The classical economic research agenda, studying the determinants of value, is one part of normative ethics, or moral philosophy. Bentham's theory of value, utilitarianism, which constituted a major pillar of classical economics, was one theory in moral philosophy, a monistic theory in that there was only one principle determining "good."[6] That principle was the pursuit of individual "utility." When utility was constrained to be "happiness," or "pleasure," its pursuit was transformed into hedonism.[7] To achieve effective reform, Harris would implicitly conclude, one needed to begin again with moral philosophy and construct a new economic theory.

For Harris, therefore, reform of classical economics meant the substitution of other philosophical premises, other monistic theories of value, and the explication of the ideological implications of these new theories of value. Harris's theory of value was the principle of economic equality as the only principle determining "good." By economic equality, he intended to convey equality of the result of economic activity for all races and classes. He did not anticipate the current drive for gender equality.

On logic

Harris primarily used dialectic in his analysis.[8] It would help to clarify his method by digressing a moment on this form of logic.

Logic is the study of the validity of different kinds of inference. Traditional logic is defined here as that study from Pythagoras to Hegel. For most of this period, Aristotelian logic and commentaries on it dominated philosophical treatment of the subject. Hegel represents a rupture with the European Aristotelian tradition.

Conventionally, traditional logic begins with Aristotle's treatise *Categories*, which posited ten divisions of essence, i.e. being as such, necessary in order to make literal sense in philosophical discourse about the world. Aristotle said that every uncombined expression refers to one or more things falling into at least one of these categories. The Aristotelian categories were substance, quantity (singular, universal, particular, indefinite), quality (affirmation, denial), relation, activity, passivity, place, time, situation, and state.[9]

Aristotle's table of categories was supplanted most influentially by that of Immanuel Kant in his 1781 *Critique of Pure Reason*. Kant's table consists of what Thompson refers to as a "fourfold division of triads." The four principal categories were: 1 quantity, which could be of the types singular (unity), plural, and universal; 2 quality, with types affirmative, negative (negation), and infinite; 3 relation, with types categorical, hypothetical, (conditional, causality), and disjunctive; and 4 modality, with types problematic (possibility), assertoric (actuality) and apodictic (necessity). These categories referred not to essential *being*, however, but to *phenomena* (appearances). They classify not uncombined expressions as in Aristotle, but expressions of statements or judgements.[10] The fourth Kantian category, modality, may be considered to contain the seven Aristotelian categories other than quantity, quality and relation.

Aristotle defined the concept of simple proposition to mean a proposition that has no other proposition as a constituent part. The most important kinds of simple propositions are the subject–predicate proposition, and the relational proposition. The first affirms or denies that something is a member of a class or has a certain property. It consists of one subject term, one predicate term, and one copula (connective). The copula is a form of the verb "to be." The relational proposition affirms or denies that a certain relationship holds between two or more objects.[11]

Beginning with Aristotle, traditional logic consists fundamentally of analysis of the opposition relationship. The reason for this will be seen below. Opposition can be expressed as one of the four Aristotelian "laws of thought" – the law of contradiction. This law is "A is not-A." That is, contradiction is the relation of a universal proposition of one quality and the particular proposition of the opposite quality, such that both cannot be true, or both cannot be false.

Contradiction, however, is only one possible relation of opposition. Others are contrary opposition, subcontrary opposition, and subaltern opposition.[12] The contrary relationship is one between two universal propositions of opposite qualities, in which both may be false, but both cannot be true. The subcontrary relationship is one between two particular propositions of opposite qualities, in which both propositions may be true, but both cannot be false. The subaltern relationship is that between a universal proposition and a particular proposition, the two having the same quality. The proposition of universal quantity is called the subalternant, and the proposition of particular quantity the subalternate. The subaltern relationship traditionally was interpreted to mean that the universal proposition implied the particular proposition, but the particular did not imply the universal.[13]

As thus suggested, the opposition relationship in traditional logic is defined as the relationship between two propositions having the same subject and the same predicate, but different quantity, quality, or both.[14]

It can be illustrated with the assistance of the "square of opposition" used in deductive logic. This is a geometric figure the corners of which are denoted "A" (top left), "E" (top right), "I" (bottom left), and "O" (bottom right). The square of opposition depicts the *relationships* among *quantity* and *quality*. Following Aristotle, A and E represent *universal* quantities, A *affirming the universal* proposition, E denying or *negating it*. I and O represent *particular* quantities, I *affirming the particular* proposition, O denying or *negating it*. Hence, the top and bottom sides of the square refer to quantity, and the left and right sides refer to quality.

Sixteen relations between pairs of categorical propositions are possible: AA, AE, AI, AO; EA, EE, EI, EO; IA, IE, II, IO; and OA, OE, OI, OO. The four relations AA, EE, II, and OO are affirmative relations, and are not considered here. Hence, three-quarters of all possible relations are opposition relations – AE and EA; AI and IA; AO and OA; EI and IE; EO and OE; and IO and OI – making opposition the quantitatively most important form of relation among two propositions in traditional logic, as Aristotle had determined.

A is related to E as a contrary, and I is related to O as a subcontrary. In these two relationships, there are only quality differences.

A is related to I as a subaltern, and E is related to O as a subaltern. In these two relationships there is only a quantity difference.

A is related to O as a contradiction, and E is related to I as a contradiction. In these two relationships, there are differences in both quantity and quality, and so contradiction may be considered the relationship with the greatest degree of opposition between two propositions.

Thus, the square of opposition can be used to determine valid syllogisms. Aristotle created the syllogism as a method of analysis of the relationships among propositions. As seen above, only universal and particular propositions were required for the Aristotelian syllogism.[15]

Following Aristotle, in traditional logic, an argument must be conducted in the form of a syllogism, or system of three propositions: a major thesis, minor thesis, and conclusion. The minor thesis may affirm or oppose the major thesis; if opposed, no specific form of opposition is required.

It will be noticed that the square of opposition analyzes propositions in terms of the Kantian categories quantity, quality and relation, but not the fourth Kantian category modality. Analysis of the fourth category is known as *modal logic*.

Hegel created a form of logic in which the syllogism consisted of a thesis, antithesis, and synthesis. The minor thesis is *required* to be in opposition to the major thesis. Opposition is the only *possible* relationship. The synthesis (conclusion) constitutes a new thesis in an ever unfolding sequence of logical relationships. Thus, Hegel applied the apodictic (necessary) type of the fourth Kantian category modality to the study of logic. The Hegelian dialectic is a form of modal logic.

That Hegel's dialectic had such a problematic existence for much of the 150 years or so between its creation and Harris's death was due to factors in religious and political history. Modal logic had been treated extensively by the Greek and Roman logicians in terms of the seven Aristotelian categories, but the early Catholic Church hierarchy thought it theologically dangerous. This was due to its use, for example, to question the logical validity (necessity, truth) of certain papal and Church pronouncements. It, therefore, was developed largely by the *Muslim* logicians Avicenna and Averroes, and later by Christian Scholastics, especially *Thomas Aquinas*, in an attempt to refute the Muslims. With the defeat of the Muslims in the fifteenth century, it was largely ignored in Europe after the Renaissance.[16] Hegel's reintroduction of modal logic to the mainstream of the European logical tradition thus was taken to be anti-Christian in intent, and rigorously suppressed. Only the left-wing Hegelians, including Karl Marx, pursued research into the dialectic, and they were largely barred from posts in academia and government. Of all Hegel's works, the logic has been the most recently translated into English.

The syllogisms of Aristotle and all logicians before Hegel referred to forms and not content of argument. Hegel's dialectic posited the inseparability of form and content. The subject of the proposition, including material things, as well as the proposition itself, was affected by the dialectical process.[17]

The proof of this aspect of Hegel's dialectical logic had seemed to be abstract or idealist, but had been developed by Marx and Engels to refer to the evolution of ideas out of material things, for as seen below an idea (ideology) was determined by material entities and relations among them. In the development of this extended proof of the Hegelian dialectic, Marx and Engels followed the triadic pattern of Hegel.

It was in this Marxianized form that Harris used the Hegelian dialectic, for in his writings in economics journals, he applied it strictly to economic thought. Thus, Harris's method of analysis suggested that the evolution of economics (the science of the material evolution of human society) can be viewed as movement from systems of universal propositions to systems of particular propositions and back to systems of universal propositions, i.e. as the opposition of systems of economic propositions. The universal is the material world; economic thought is one of its necessary particulars. Economics has not been moved by systems of affirmative propositions, either at the universal or particular levels of quantity.

On epistemology

Harris was concerned that traditional economic theories were idealist, in that their propositions were not empirically testable. Their truth or falsity (modal category) could not be determined. The institutionalist theorists claimed to address this failing by casting their own theories as materialist theories. Thus, Harris in the final stage of his critique analyzed institutionalist theories as to their epistemological status. He would conclude that these theories did not differ in this respect from traditional economic theories, and hence could not serve as a sound basis for economic reform. There were no materialist economic theories.[18]

Harris on ideology

Ideology is a word of relatively recent French origin, meaning "science of ideas." Karl Marx adopted the program to create a science of ideas, his contribution being a belief that scientific statements could be made about the *succession of ideologies* in history.[19]

Thus, ideology is defined by Marx, according to one analyst, as "the beliefs that motivate members of society to heed the essential requirements of the *legal* relations among themselves, in the course of putting resources, capital equipment and technology into operation." In short, ideology is a system of beliefs about society, including the economy, that originate in specific social classes, that have an instrumental purpose, and that may be true or false.[20]

As a look at the whole body of his work plainly reveals, Harris adopted this Marxist definition of ideology, the model of the working of ideology in society, and the model of the evolution of ideologies through time. His objective in applying the Marxian model of the succession of ideologies to economic theories was to determine if these theories (ideologies) facilitated institutional reform. By so doing, he provided an explicitly rational justification for the procedure initially used by Haney thirty years before.

Classical economics he viewed as an ideology because "the body of knowledge derived from [its] preconceptions [natural law and hedonism] is an apologia for the status quo."[21] Veblen had attacked the classical ideology by attempting to discredit its logic and its moral (ethical) justification.[22] Hence, Harris adopted these aspects of philosophy as the basis of his criticism. Similarly, marginal productivity theory also was an ideology, because it was a "dogmatic defense of the competitive economic system."[23]

Harris's adoption of the Marxian model of the relationship of ideology to the forces and relations of production meant that his analysis of ideology had definite, specific implications for economic and political events. According to the Marxian model of ideology that he used, a given ideology can exist only if certain means and relations of production exist. Thus, in discussing current economic ideologies, Harris actually was discussing current economic events.

256

The Harris methodological scheme: summary

Harris's writings consist of the dialectical analysis of economic theories. Traditional economic theorists used primarily deductive logic, and institutional theorists used largely nondeductive (inductive and dialectical) logic.

Most *economic* theories are systems of *Kantian categorical* syllogisms. That is, the propositions that constitute the premises and conclusions are assertions about phenomena. In order to criticize such a theoretical system, it is necessary to *isolate* each syllogism in the system, and subject each to strict analysis. Analysis means separation of an intellectual whole (the syllogism) into constituent parts (implicit premises and conclusions) for individual study. This separation and study Harris accomplished by the use of the dialectic.[24]

Dialectic never has been the preferred mode of analysis of the economics profession. However, Harris was lucky. The 1930s decade was a period of experimentation as to analytic method, because the ruling paradigm of economics, using a deductive methodology, had failed to predict accurately the movement of the real economy. Conversely, the dialectical method, embodied in the Marxian paradigm, seemed to more accurately predict the times. Hence, the profession for one of the few periods in its history was receptive to wide and deep research based on the Marxian paradigm.

Still, Harris had to pay homage to the reigning paradigm. Even an approach in which direct comparison of the dialectical and the deductive paradigms was made was not acceptable. A comparison of alternatives to the reigning deductive paradigm was acceptable, however, and so Harris for this reason adopted an *unstated* dialectical mode of analysis. Although his method was *objectively* dialectical, he nowhere cited Marx's master Hegel with regard to the dialectic. Indeed the term dialectical itself does not appear in the indexes to any of his books. Moreover, he mentions Hegel only in connection with the thinkers he discusses, although since most of these are German or Germanophile, the name Hegel appears frequently. Thus he is mentioned in connection with Marx and Engels, Veblen, Sombart, Pesch and John Stuart Mill.

The classical school as thesis

Harris began his written work by stating clearly the essence of classical theory, the analysis of the determinants of value, which was a question of ethics or moral philosophy. Classical economics, especially the works of Adam Smith and David Ricardo, and much later John Stuart Mill, thus represented for him the thesis for his research.

Economic reform, the antithesis

He differentiated the work of the individuals he discussed by their departure from this central focus. Any departure was considered "reform," and adherence was considered an "apologetic." Departures, reforms constituted negation, opposition, antithesis.

The method was complex, however, for each doctrine antithetical to classical economics became itself a new thesis, and departures from them new antitheses. The later doctrines he examined departed not directly from classical economics, but from a new synthesis carrying classicism forward – neoclassicism. Thus, in Harris's analytic scheme, reform meant opposition to either or both classical and neoclassical theories.

Having identified departures from these two doctrines in temporal order using the method of opposition, he defined all departures as institutionalism. Thus, Marxism and Keynesianism became institutionalist.

Finally, institutionalist theories were assessed as to their status as epistemologically materialist or idealist.

Harris's critical method led him, therefore, to consider in turn *all* economic reform theories beginning in the late eighteenth century. His fame rests in the mastery of "institutionalist" theories his method provided for him. For these were the most important "reform" theories before Keynesianism.

On the adequacy of institutionalism

The institutionalist school of economics proposed to study: 1 the empirical "laws" governing economic relationships, by describing these relationships statistically (Mitchell); 2 the formal, stated rules (political laws) governing permitted economic relationships (Commons); and 3 the psychological and anthropological "laws" governing economic relationships (Marx, Pesch, Veblen, Sombart and Keynes).

Harris concluded by 1953 that all reform theories had failed to achieve the necessary logical connection between philosophical premises and ideological implications or conclusions, that all reform theories were idealist constructs, just as was the traditional economic theory, and that therefore an adequate reform theory must be developed anew by returning to the classical economists' philosophical sources and proceeding positively from there. This last conclusion would not be communicated to the public until the publication of his 1958 book.

The ethical norm or moral philosophy of the new Harris economics was economic equality. The logic was dialectic. The epistemology was materialist. The ideological implication was social and political liberty for Africans and their relatives in the Americas.

APPLICATIONS OF THE DIALECTICAL METHOD IN HARRIS'S ANALYSIS OF INSTITUTIONALIST ECONOMICS

As we have seen, Harris defined economic institutionalism as the negation of "traditional" economics, by which he meant classicism and neoclassicism.

But just as there are different modes of opposition in traditional logic, Harris identified different types of institutionalism, or different ways in which traditionalism was negated. Three classes of institutionalists were identified: 1 the quantitative-statistical theorists (Mitchell); 2 the critical-genetic theorists (Veblen, Sombart and Pesch); and 3 the class-struggle theorists (Marx). He suggested that this classificatory scheme could be elaborated further, but never did so in print.

In general, the class-struggle category can be considered to be in contradictory opposition to classical economics, in the logical terms employed above. Critical-genetic theorists can be considered in contrary opposition to neoclassical economics. The quantitative-statistical theorists can be considered in subcontrary opposition to neoclassicism. This will become more apparent as we proceed.

Harris wrote twenty-four essays on institutionalism, stretching temporally from 1932 to 1963. Indeed, all his economic writing was on institutionalism, for he defined all the men he studied as reformers of one sort or another, and hence as institutionalists. However, in this chapter, we will consider only his essays on Marx, Pesch, Veblen, Mitchell, Commons, and Sombart. A consideration of his treatment of Keynes, in terms of this categorical scheme, also is presented here. Harris published seven major articles on Marx, six on Veblen, one on Mitchell, four on Commons, four on Sombart, and two on Pesch. The first essay was counted above for each of those named; if it is counted only once, the total number of essays reduces to nineteen.

Harris's methodology was conceptually complete by the time he first published professionally in 1932. He had already: 1 identified reformers; 2 amalgamated them all into one category called institutionalist; and now was engaged in 3 considering the ideological implications of the economic philosophies of those in this category. Thus in the scheme of institutionalism presented in "Types of Institutionalism," Mitchell came first, Veblen, Commons and Sombart second, and Marx last. In temporal and dialectical sequence, however, Marx comes first, followed by Veblen, Commons, Sombart and Mitchell. A decade later he would add Heinrich Pesch, a contemporary of Veblen, to the critical-genetic category. He never categorized Commons and Keynes in this scheme, except as generic institutionalists. Here that characterization is made.

On Mitchell as institutionalist

Wesley Clair Mitchell's propositions were of the O type, and were directed against I type propositions. This relationship of subcontrary opposition to traditional economics is the one depicting perhaps the least logical opposition among categorical propositions. Harris, therefore, wrote less on the ideas of Mitchell than he did on any important institutionalist.

Nevertheless, he considered Mitchell first because the latter was his mentor in institutionalist analysis.[25]

On the economic theory of K. H. Mordechai/Karl Marx

Harris's critique of Marxist economic theory is contained in seven essays published from 1932 to 1958.[26] In the first essay, Harris classifies Marx as a type of "class-struggle theorist."

Marx's critique of economic theory lay on the level of ethics, logical method, and the empirical accuracy of the institutional matrix assumed by the classical economists. His ethical norm was economic equality. His logical method was the dialectic. The application of the Hegelian dialectic to empirical history led him to construct the theory of dialectical materialism, a new economic theory suggested by his reading of Hegel.

Marx's critique, in the logical terms used above, was in the relation of contrary, subcontrary and contradictory opposition to classical theory. It began with a negation (change in quality of) universal (quantity) propositions of classical economic theory, taking the "E" position against tradition's "A." It then negated (changed the quality and quantity of) the particular (quantity) conclusions derived from the universal premises. That is, it took the "E" position against the "I" position of tradition. Finally, it negated (changed the quality of) particular (quantity) propositions reflecting institutional detail. That is, it took the "O" position against the "I" position of traditional theory. It thus was the most thoroughgoing of the critiques in a logical sense, explaining Harris's relatively greater emphasis on Marx as compared to other institutionalists.

On Veblen as institutionalist

Veblen's economic theory Harris considered a synthesis of Darwin's biology, Gobineau's anthropology, James–McDougall instinct-habit psychology, and Marx's ethics. Harris focused most in his critique on the biological and psychological theories used by Veblen.[27]

Veblen's theory negated traditional economic theory at the level of its general premises, or at the level of universals. Thus it was in contrary opposition to traditional theory. That is, it took the "E" position relative to tradition's "A" position.

Harris's critique of Veblen ended with the statement that Veblen, though belonging to the "quantitative-descriptive" school by his own lights, had an implicitly preferred human behavior that underlay his theory, and thus vitiated its scientific character and rendered it idealist. Fundamentally, it was of the same epistemological order as the traditional theory.

On Commons as institutionalist

An important Commons contribution was to identify government regulation of the economy as an acceptable activity, and to steer his students toward influential positions in the government bureaucracy so that it could be made to respond affirmatively to his left-center policy suggestions. Commons thus probably was the most important of the institutionalists in terms of his impact on US economic history, even if perhaps not in terms of the history of doctrine.

Commons's students developing his institutionalist legacy include Malcolm P. Sharp and Kenneth R. Parsons at the University of Wisconsin itself. Sharp later taught law at the University of Iowa Law School, University of Wisconsin Law School, and the University of Chicago Law School, where he became close to Harris.

It was the Commons institutionalists at Harvard, with their anti-traditionalist orientation, who proved decisive in the adoption and spread of Keynesianism in the United States. Keynes appeared to them as a very effective theoretical institutionalist.[28] These institutionalists in turn accomplished the adoption of Keynesian analysis as the basis of federal government fiscal policy in the late 1930s and 1940s.

Particularly important in this regard was Lauchlin B. Currie, a native of Nova Scotia. Currie received the PhD in economics from Harvard in 1931, and became a naturalized US citizen in 1934. Entering the federal government, he was assistant director of research and statistics at the Federal Reserve Board from 1934 to 1939, and the first official economic assistant to the President from 1939 to 1945.[29]

Harris quoted, cited and had connection to Commons, his students and the students of his students, on many occasions, from 1924 to 1958.[30] These citations primarily documented discussions of trade union and labor issues, rather than institutionalist theory. In the articles in which he explicitly set out to criticize Commons's theory of institutionalism (1952, 1958), Harris claimed to find it "baffling," "perverse," and "obscure," despite his sympathy with Commons. He focused his critique of Commons on the latter's central contribution to institutionalist thought – the theory of the relationship between the law of property and other economic activity.

This body of law was a principal defining institution of capitalism according to many institutionalists, the central institution in determining the contours of what Marx had called the "relations of production." It was largely common law, or judge-made law, rather than legislation. This body of law was more important in the US than elsewhere, because the US Supreme Court was the ultimate arbiter of the meaning of legislation and lower court decisions. Thus, Supreme Court justices were for Commons the "first faculty of political economy."

Harris's critique of Commons consisted largely of a reinterpretation of the history of the law of property traced by Commons. He did not treat

Commons's analytic scheme of institutionalism as set out in *Institutional Economics*, a work which sought to present a twentieth-century economic paradigm of the type and quality of *The Wealth of Nations* in the eighteenth century, and *Das Kapital* in the nineteenth century.

For Harris, therefore, the Commons critique of traditional economics was at the level of particulars, and as such was in subcontrary opposition to traditional theory, like that of Mitchell. Harris's conclusion on the Commons theory was that it was "abounding in metaphysical abstractions,' a phrase he quotes from I.L. Sharfman's review of a Commons book.[31] In more simple language, the theory was idealist.

Harris was not alone in not welcoming Commons's book, and there was one apparent reason for this neglect, the alternative synthesis of Keynes, which appeared two years later. Commons's theory was nearly forgotten. Thus Harris in the full triumph of Keynesianism could dismiss Commons as "baffling." Nevertheless, he said, Commons anticipated Keynes by advocating a fiscal policy of "public spending to counteract cyclical fluctuations."[32]

On Keynes as institutionalist

This is Harris's only known reference to Keynes in print, although Keynes by Harris's definition could be considered an institutionalist economist. To the extent that Keynes was an institutionalist, therefore, he was a follower of the Commons variant of the doctrine.[33]

By Harris's definition, however, there might have been some ambiguity concerning Keynes as an institutionalist. The most important element of ambiguity was Keynes's use of the marginalist calculus to develop his ideas. His achievements – the abandonment of Say's Law of Markets, leading to an underemployment equilibrium; the distinction made between "microeconomics" and "macroeconomics;" and the specification of the relations between the microeconomy and the macroeconomy – were not opposed to the traditional objective of determining value in markets. Say's Law of Markets, an important premise of traditional economics, had not been a target of either the Marxists or other institutionalists. From their standpoint, one could observe that Say's Law was a minor premise of what was considered capitalism's apologetic ideology, and Keynes's triumph over it, therefore, a minor tactical success. What was more important, by adopting the idealist marginalist method, Keynes upheld the major premise of the traditional synthesis – that material economic wellbeing depended upon such psychological and hence unobservable phenomena as the marginal propensity to consume, the marginal efficiency of capital, and the demand for money, especially liquidity preference. Moreover, Keynes did not take the opportunity to present a long-term growth (accumulation) model, but only a means to reduce the amplitude of periodic fluctuations in economic activity. Thus, Harris ignored Keynes because: 1 he did not depart from the principal feature of neoclassicism, its epistemological idealism; and 2 he did not address the principal concern of the institutionalists – cumulative economic change. Like Commons, his theory was at the level of subcontrary opposition to traditional economics.

On Sombart as institutionalist

Harris wrote two major pieces on Sombart.[34] In his first article on institutionalism in 1932, he had classified Sombart with Veblen as representatives of the critical-genetic variant of the doctrine, because Sombart argued in favor of collective (state) control of the economy, rather than *laisser faire*. At that time, Sombart was considered something of a Marxist, and certainly an opponent of traditional economics. In his 1942 article, Harris attempted to read Sombart out of institutionalism, because of Sombart's defense of Naziism in his 1934 book, *Deutscher Sozialismus*.[35]

Like that of Mitchell and Commons, Sombart's theory was in the relation of subcontrary opposition to traditional theory, being concerned primarily with historical details of specific economic institutions. Harris's critique of Sombart, like his critiques of all other institutionalists assessed so far, concluded by labelling him an idealist.

On Pesch as institutionalist

Harris also wrote two major articles on Pesch, a German Jesuit economist.[36] The views represented by Pesch were considered by Harris to fall into his category of institutionalist because they were more concerned with the collective rather than with the individual as the unit of economic analysis. But while Commons was concerned with collectivities that existed between the individual and the state executive, Pesch was concerned with substituting the Church for the nation as the primary unit of governance in society. His views, and those of Sombart, led toward what Harris called corporatism, a form of Catholic solidarism, and ultimately to fascism.

His critique of traditional economics thus was in the relation of contrary opposition to traditional economics, or at the level of the universal quantity and negative quality.

What was new in Harris's critique of Pesch was a systematic analysis of modern Catholic economic thought, a research program in which he was nearly unique among non-Catholic economists in the United States. Only Jacob Viner, of Canadian Jewish background, might be considered an exception, and he published nothing in this regard during his lifetime.

On institutionalism: summary and conclusion

Harris's economic institutionalists have shaped the role of the government in the market economies of capitalism profoundly in this century. They have thus had a great impact on economic history, as well as on the history of economic thought. They altered the structure of the economy, by means of altering the functions of governmental institutions with respect to economic matters.

In the US, the economic institutionalists were important in creating agencies of the central government having regulatory authority over the economy, and in developing systems of statistical records by which control of the economy could be achieved by those agencies.

After the Second World War, five students of the institutionalists Commons, Mitchell and Hamilton served on the President's Council of Economic Advisors (CEA) – Leon Keyserling, Roy Blough, Arthur F. Burns, Walter W. Stewart and Walter W. Heller. Keyserling, Burns and Heller served as chairmen in successive presidencies, the first Democratic, the second Republican, the third Democratic. Blough and Heller were Commons's students, and "kept the faith," so to speak. Whether or not Mitchell's students Keyserling and Burns, and Hamilton's student Stewart remained attached to institutionalism during their service on the CEA is more difficult to assess.[37]

Despite the great *policy* influence wielded by the institutionalists-Keynesians, however, Harris found their intellectual systems lacking in soundness. All were guilty of the sin of idealism, which placed them in epistemological agreement with traditional economics. To the extent that there was this agreement in principle, no basis in institutionalist economic *theory* existed for economic reform. Moreover, either their conclusions failed to accord logically with their premises, or sound logic referred only to relations among particular, i.e. empirical, phenomena.

With the construction of the antithesis to traditional economics, the second stage of Harris's work was finished. Following the completion of his criticism of the institutionalists, therefore, Harris decided to return to the classical economists to critique them directly himself, and perhaps in that way to construct a viable economic reform theory based on a new moral philosophy. Rather than consider all the strands of classicism, he chose John Stuart Mill, who had constructed the most widely accepted synthesis of classical thought.

A TEMPORAL INVERSE ANTITHESIS: HARRIS ON MILL

Harris first referred to Mill in print in the article on Sombart in 1942. He subsequently published five substantial pieces on Mill, and had partially completed two other manuscripts on him before his own death.[38]

Interestingly, of the five pieces only one, a note, was published in a US economics journal. Perhaps a part of the explanation for this was Harris's focus on the socialistic elements in Mill's thought, the features of his system that permitted the Fabian Socialists to claim him as their progenitor. For neoclassical orthodoxy, there was the danger that the man they also claimed as the best synthesizer of the individualist doctrine would be brought into the lists as the champion of the opponent. Harris was fighting the traditionalists for Mill's soul.

For in this series of articles, Harris focused on Mill's belief in social and economic equality, and the policies he advocated to achieve such equality. Thus Mill was to be used to construct the new moral philosophy on which an adequate economic reform theory could be built. This new moral philosophy was to be the foundation of the work of constructing a new synthesis. Unfortunately, Harris died as the foundation was laid down.

NOTES

1 Lewis Henry Haney, *History of Economic Thought*, 4th edn, New York: Macmillan Company, 1949, pp. ix–xxii.
2 Haney, *History of Economic Thought*, pp. 720–2.
3 Wesley Clair Mitchell, *Types of Economic Theory; from Mercantilism to Institutionalism*, ed. by Joseph Dorfman, New York: Augustus M. Kelley, 1969, p. vii, n. 1.
4 On the pervasiveness of the opposition relationship, see Heinrich Scholz, *A Concise History of Logic*, tr. by Kurt F. Leidecker, New York: Philosophical Library, 1961; S. Koerner, "Laws of Thought," *Encyclopedia of Philosophy*; Alasdair MacIntyre, "Ontology," in same; Hans-Georg Gadamer, *Hegel's Dialectic. Five Hermeneutical Studies*, tr. by P. Christopher Smith, New Haven: Yale University Press, 1976, p. 81; Will Durant, *The Story of Philosophy*, New York: Washington Square Press, 1969, p. 295. See references to George Boole, William De Morgan, William Hamilton, W. Stanley Jevons, and John Stuart Mill, in Harris, "Introduction," (Harris, *Economics and Social Reform*, pp. 18–21, 94, 95 n). It is of some interest here that classical economist John Stuart Mill in his two volume 1843 book *System of Logic* (New York: Longmans, Green and Company, 1930), was the first to *name*, if not use, the opposed concepts deductive and inductive logic. But see also Harris's references to "the principle of covering needs" in his 1946 article "The Scholastic Revival: Heinrich Pesch," *Journal of Political Economy (JPE)*, February 1946, pp. 45–6. Here, however, Harris views Pesch's use of this principle as rooted not in medieval logic, but in medieval ethics. In his first published professional economics article, Harris stated: "The distinctions separating [traditional economics and institutionalism, and individual institutionalists] are philosophical and ideological." See Harris, "Types of Institutionalism," *JPE*, 1932, p. 752.
5 Harris, "The Marxian Right to the Whole Product," in Simon S. Kuznets (ed.), *Economic Essays in Honor of Wesley Clair Mitchell*, New York: Columbia University Press, 1935, pp. 154–9.
6 Kai Nielsen, "Ethics, Problems of," *Encyclopedia of Philosophy*; D. H. Monro, "Bentham, Jeremy," in same; Richard T. Garner, "Ethics," *Encyclopedia Americana*.

7 On the evolution of the concept of public "happiness," see Garry Wills, *Inventing America. Jefferson's Declaration of Independence*, Garden City, NY: Doubleday & Company, Inc., 1978, chs 17–18.

8 Dialectic meant logic in traditional usage. It was with Hegel that the use of the term logic was adopted by mainstream logicians. See Scholz, *Concise History of Logic*, pp. 7–13. Hegel developed a specific form of dialectic, however, that was little understood in his lifetime, and largely opposed thereafter. Left-wing Hegelians, especially Marxists, adopted the traditional term dialectic to refer to Hegel's work in logic, and to their own. Non-Marxists adopted the new term largely to differentiate subsequent work in this field from that of Marx.

9 Boruch A. Brody, "Logical Terms, Glossary," *Encyclopedia of Philosophy*; Manley Thompson, "Categories," in same.

10 A. N. Prior, "Logic, History of: The Heritage of Kant and Mill," *Encyclopedia of Philosophy*; Thompson, "Categories."

11 Brody, "Logical Terms, Glossary," *Encyclopedia of Philosophy*.

12 Vincent Edward Smith, *The Elements of Logic*, Milwaukee: Bruce Publishing Company, 1957, ch. 14, esp. pp. 100–5; Morris R. Cohen and Ernest Nagel, *An Introduction to Logic and Scientific Method*, New York: Harcourt, Brace and World, 1934, pp. 65–75. Neither of these works was available to Harris in 1932. Available sources in 1932 on traditional logic and the dialectic included John Stuart Mill, *A System of Logic* (1843; 8th ed. 1872); William Stanley Jevons, *Pure Logic, or The Logic of Quality Apart from Quantity with Remarks on Boole's System and on the Relation of Logic and Mathematics* (1863); Jevons, *The Substitution of Similars* (1869); Jevons, *Elementary Lessons in Logic* (1870); Jevons, *The Principles of Science; a Treatise on Logic and Scientific Method* (1874); John Neville Keynes, *Studies and Exercises in Formal Logic* (1884, 1887, 1894, 1906); William Ernest Johnson, *Logic* (1921, 1922, 1924); John McTaggart, *Studies in the Hegelian Dialectic* (1896, 2nd ed. 1922); McTaggart, *A Commentary on Hegel's Logic* (1910); and G. W. F. Hegel, *Wissenschaft der Logik*, tr. by W. H. Johnson and L. G. Struthers as *The Science of Logic*, 2 vols, (1929); Marx, "Critique of the Hegelian Dialectic and Philosophy as a Whole;" and Engels, "Review: *A Contribution to the Critique of Political Economy*, by Karl Marx." Also see Acton, "Dialectical Materialism;" McInnes, "Marxist Philosophy." All these except Johnson and McTaggart were economists. Harris's likely sources included Marx, Hegel, Johnson, and McTaggart, whom he had discussed in correspondence with Benjamin Stolberg. Johnson was particularly illuminating on the opposition relationship in traditional logic.

13 Brody, "Logical Terms, Glossary," op. cit.

14 Smith, *Elements*, p. 100.

15 Czeslaw Lejewski, "Logic, History of: Ancient Logic," *Encyclopedia of Philosophy*.

16 A. N. Prior, "Logic, Modal," *Encyclopedia of Philosophy*; Ernest A. Moody, "Logic, History of: Medieval Logic," in same; Stuart MacClintock, "Averroes," in same. Averroes was of Moroccan-Spanish origin. His works, *The Incoherence of the Incoherence*, and *On the Harmony Between Religion and Philosophy* (between 1159 and 1195) argued that there were three intellectual roads to truth, including dialectic, and not only one – implicitly Christian dogma.

17 Manley Thompson, "Categories."

18 Harris, *Economics and Social Reform*, pp. 13–15.

19 David Braybrooke, "Ideology," *Encyclopedia of Philosophy*.

20 Emphasis added. This is possibly the source of Richard T. Ely's and hence his student John R. Commons's research program in the law of property as the key to other economic relationships. This Marxian concern for the legal relations of

capitalism can be taken as the basis for the research agenda of John R. Commons in institutionalism. These are part of the "relations of production," the part related to the role of the state under capitalism. Because Marx considered the state as part of the "superstructure," he never developed a theory of the state, and Commons's agenda was to develop an economic theory of the state.

21 Harris, "Types," p. 728.

22 Harris, "Types," pp. 728–9.

23 Harris, "Types," p. 727, n. 14.

24 As a note here, to isolate a theoretical phenomenon is to describe its properties minutely, and to state explicitly the properties that differentiate it from other phenomena. In critical thought about socio-economic phenomena, the isolated phenomenon (system) is succeeded by its opposite. In noncritical thought, the isolated phenomenon can be extended in its similars, i.e. it can be succeeded by similar phenomena. Critical thinkers have considered noncritical thinkers to be engaged in "apologetics" on behalf of the initially isolated phenomenon, which since the eighteenth century in Europe has been the capitalist socio-economic system.

25 Mitchell was treated only in Harris, "Types of Institutionalism," *JPE*, December 1932.

26 Harris, "Types of Institutionalism," *JPE*, December 1932; Harris, "Economic Evolution: Dialectical and Darwinian," *JPE*, February 1934; Harris, "The Marxian Right to the Whole Product," in Simon Kuznets (ed.), *Economic Essays in Honor of Wesley Clair Mitchell*, (1935); Harris, "Pure Capitalism and the Disappearance of the Middle Class", *JPE*, June 1939; Harris, "The Social Philosophy of Karl Marx," *Ethics*, vol. 58, no. 3, part 2 (April 1948); Harris, "Utopian Elements in Marx's Thought," *Ethics*, January 1950; and Harris, "Karl Marx: The Utopia of Classless Democracy," in Harris, *Economics and Social Reform*, New York: Harper and Brothers (1958).

27 Harris, *Economics and Social Reform*, pp. 152–5; Harris, "Types of Institutionalism," p. 741 and n. 62.

28 Harris, "Veblen and the Social Phenomenon of Capitalism," *American Economic Review (AER)* (Papers and Proceedings), vol. 41, no. 2, May 1951, pp. 71–4; also see Julian Ellison, "Abram L. Harris, Frank H. Knight and the Development of the Idea for the Mont Pelerin Society," unpublished paper delivered at ASSA annual convention, Chicago, 28 December 1987. But see below for Harris's reaction to Keynes.

29 See Galbraith, *A Life in Our Times*, pp. 69, 98, 102, 109; Galbraith, *Economics, Peace and Laughter*, pp. 13 n., 47–8, 54; *Contemporary Authors*. In 1958, Currie moved to Colombia and became a naturalized citizen of that Latin American country. In 1982, he completed the cycle begun in 1939, becoming economic advisor to the President of Colombia.

30 Harris, "Negro Migration to the North," *Current History Magazine* (September 1924, p. 921); Harris, "The Negro and Economic Radicalism," *Modern Quarterly* (February 1925, p. 201 n.); Harris, "A White and Black World in American Labor and Politics," *Social Forces*, December 1925, p. 378 n. 7; Harris, "Economic Foundations of American Race Division," *Social Forces* (March 1927, p. 472 n.); Commons and his student John A. Fitch read Harris's dissertation before publication, at the request of Columbia University Press, 1930–1; Sterling D. Spero and Harris, *The Black Worker*; Harris, "Types of Institutionalism," *Journal of Political Economy* (1932); Harris, "Review: *The Economics of Collective Action*, by John R. Commons," *Ethics*, October 1951; Harris, "John R. Commons and the Welfare State," *Southern Economic Journal* (October 1952, paper originally presented at November 1951 annual conference of Southern

Economic Association held in Knoxville, TN); Harris, "The Corporate State: Catholic Model," in Harris, *Economics and Social Reform* (1958), p. 309 n. 2. (This article was published originally as "The Scholastic Revival: The Economics of Heinrich Pesch," *Journal of Political Economy*, February 1946, without the reference to Commons); Harris, Introduction, in same; Harris, "John R. Commons: The Theory of Collective Democracy," in same.

31 Harris, *Economics and Social Reform*, p. 271.

32 Harris, "Review: *The Economics of Collective Action*, by John R. Commons," *Ethics*, October 1951, p. 63; Harris, "John R. Commons and the Welfare State," pp. 223 n. 3, 231 and n. 25.

33 Harris did appear on a 1945 American Economic Association panel on "New Frontiers in Economic Thought." On that panel, Frank Knight and Clarence Ayres discussed Keynes extensively, although Harris did not comment on their presentations. He and Galbraith discussed a paper by Ralph H. Blodgett. On Keynes as an institutionalist, and his respect for Commons, see Charles H. Hession, *John Maynard Keynes*, New York: Macmillan Publishing Company, 1984, p. 203; Seymour E. Harris, "Introduction: The Issues," in S.E. Harris (ed.), *The New Economics. Keynes' Influence on Theory and Public Policy*, New York: Alfred A. Knopf, 1950, p. 4; Seymour E. Harris, "Three Problems in the *General Theory*," in same, p. 40; Seymour E. Harris, "In Relation to Classical Economics," in same, p. 57; Gottfried Haberler, "The General Theory (4)," in same, p. 164 n.; Seymour E. Harris, "Introduction [to Part Eight]: Keynes' Attack on Laissez Faire and Classical Economics and Wage Theory," in same, p. 554. A personal connection between Commons and Keynes was provided by Alvin Harvey Hansen, who earned the MA and PhD under Commons at the University of Wisconsin in 1915 and 1918, respectively, and who became the premier US champion of Keynes's ideas as professor of economics at Harvard University from 1937 to 1962. Hansen visited Keynes in 1941 in connection with the Bretton Woods process, at the behest of the US State Department. This was apparently the only time the two met in person. On this visit, see Harrod, *Keynes*, p. 527.

34 Harris, "Sombart and German (National) Socialism," *JPE*, December 1942; Harris, "Werner Sombart: From Capitalism to True Socialism," in Harris, *Economics and Social Reform*, 1959.

35 Harris, "Sombart and German (National) Socialism," p. 807.

36 Harris, "The Scholastic Revival: The Economics of Heinrich Pesch," *JPE*, February 1946; Harris, "The Corporate State: Catholic Model," in Harris, *Economics and Social Reform*, 1958.

37 But see Burns's statement in a 1980 interview: "...I think that relying on economic history, on close statistical studies of an historical sort, will yield better forecasts than relying on econometric models. These models are bankrupt..." in *The President and the Council of Economic Advisors: Interviews with CEA Chairmen*, ed. by Edwin C. Hargrove and Samuel A. Morley, Boulder, CO: Westview Press, 1984, p. 121.

38 Harris, "Sombart and German (National) Socialism," *JPE*, vol. 50, no. 6, December 1942, pp. 805–35; Harris, "John Stuart Mill's Theory of Progress," *Ethics*, vol. LXVI, no. 3, April 1956, pp. 157–75; Harris, "John Stuart Mill: Liberalism, Socialism and Laissez Faire," in Harris, *Economics and Social Reform* (1958), pp. 24–118; Harris, "J.S. Mill on Monopoly and Socialism: A Note," *JPE*, vol. 67, no. 1, December 1959, pp. 604–11; Harris, "Mill on Freedom and Voluntary Association," *Review of Social Economy*, vol. 18, no. 1, March 1960, pp. 27–44; Harris, "John Stuart Mill: Servant of the East India Company," *Canadian Journal of Economics and Political Science*, vol. 30, no. 2, May 1964, pp. 185–202. In

addition, Harris had two unpublished book manuscripts on Mill nearly completed at his death. These were Harris, *John Stuart Mill: Servant of the East India Company* (1963), and Harris (ed.), *The Dispatches of John Stuart Mill to the Government of East India* (1963).

15

THE POLITICAL ECONOMIC THOUGHT OF OLIVER C. COX

Herbert M. Hunter

THE HISTORICAL BACKGROUND

The recognition Oliver C. Cox attained as a scholar came mainly from the field of sociology. His magnum opus, *Caste, Class, and Race*, published in 1948, became one of the few books to seriously challenge many of the mainstream conceptualizations of race relations in the 1940s, particularly his critique of both the caste school of race relations espoused by Robert E. Park, W. Lloyd Warner and their associates and the seminal work of Gunnar Myrdal, *The American Dilemma*.[1] Cox's main objective in *Caste, Class, and Race* was to demonstrate how racial antagonisms were essentially linked to the class struggle between capital and labor rather than, as conventionally explained, caused by the racial-caste system presumed to exist in the southern United States. It was his contention that the application of the Hindu caste system to model the race problem in the United States served to mystify both the origins and process of racial antagonisms in a capitalist society. In a similar fashion, he argued, Gunnar Myrdal's distinction between the ideals of the American democratic creed and the racist practices of white Americans led Myrdal to uncritically settle for an acceptable normative interpretation of race relations. Thus, adopting a Marxist theoretical framework in his early work, Cox was labeled a Marxist and thereby ignored by many of his sociology contemporaries. Nor was Cox to receive much recognition in the field of economics from institutional economists, political economists, or economic historians.[2]

Less known by many sociologists and economists, however, are three major volumes on capitalism published in the late 1950s and 1960s: *The Foundations of Capitalism* (1959); *Capitalism and American Leadership* (1962); and *Capitalism as a System* (1964). This trilogy of works traces the origins, growth, and development of capitalism as a world system from its beginning in medieval Venice to the ascendancy of American capitalist leadership in the post-Second World War period. Based on a theoretical analysis of economic history, congressional committee reports, and secondary sources, these works go beyond the interests and competencies of many of Cox's sociological peers.

Cox's early training in the field of economics is relevant to the kind of work he chose to do. In 1930, following a year and a half recovering from an attack of poliomyelitis (from which he never fully recovered), he entered the Department of Economics at the University of Chicago, believing that academic work "would not require too much footwork." Among the economic courses he studied were Economic History, Economic Theory, Labor Problems, Economic History of European Civilization, and International Economics under very prominent Chicago economists such as John U. Nef, Frank H. Knight, Jacob Viner, and Harry A. Millis. Well versed in economic history and theory and strong advocates of a multi-disciplinary approach to scholarship[3] these economists had a significant influence on Cox. Jacob Viner, for example, wrote extensively on the history of economic thought and international trade, subjects which influenced Cox's writings on capitalism. Frank Knight was an economist and philosopher and held positions in both the economics and social science departments at the University of Chicago in the 1930s. Knight, too, was a translator of Max Weber's *General Economic History*, and consequently, some observers such as Harry Elmer Barnes have noted that Knight "was especially responsible for Professor Cox's appreciation of the value of a sound historical perspective."[4]

Despite these influences, however, Cox was to receive his doctorate in sociology in 1938 and not in economics. From the little evidence we have on this decision, it appears that it was the Depression and the failure of economics to predict this great catastrophe that may have caused Cox's displeasure with the field of economics. He offered the following observation about his decision to pursue sociology:

> I received my MA in economics and then I changed over to sociology. The Depression caused me to change to sociology. I felt that if economics did not explain what I wanted to know; if economics did not explain the coming of the Depression; if economics did not help me to understand that great economic change then I felt I did not need it. Thus, I changed over to sociology.[5]

However, as this paper will demonstrate, much of Cox's work on the social organization and dynamics of capitalism draws on economic history and theory as well as sociology. We first focus on Cox's argument that medieval Venice in the thirteenth century was the first city-state to reflect the institutional and cultural patterns peculiar to capitalism. Next, attention is drawn to Cox's contributions to world-system theory, focusing on the various arguments he used to explain why capitalism has always been a world-wide economic system from its inception and how it continued in successive capitalist societies that gained and lost leadership as more powerful nations came to the fore. Thirdly, we look at his argument regarding the rise of capitalism in England in the seventeenth century, which for Cox marked the rise of the first nation state to achieve capitalist leadership. Lastly, attention is drawn to his assessment of the ascendancy of American leadership in the capitalist system following the First World War and the unique role the United States played in stabilizing capitalism in the post-Second World War period in the face of decolonization and the rise of socialism.

Altogether, this paper will demonstrate why Cox's version of world-system theory is an important forerunner to the contemporary conceptualization of this perspective, which gained a great deal of popularity among sociologists in the 1970s. For example, there are remarkable parallels between Immanuel Wallerstein's world-system perspective and Cox's model discussed below.[6] Both Cox and Wallerstein view capitalism as a geographically stratified world economy. As noted below, Cox's early ranking of the early city-states, towns, and territories, and his subsequent model of leader, subsidiary, progressive, and passive countries, are similar in method to Wallerstein's ranking of core, semiperipheral, and peripheral areas. Cox was especially interested in demonstrating how the internal organization of a society was related to its capacity to develop as a capitalist society and its position in the world economy. As in Wallerstein's analysis, Cox's leader national cities or nation-states have strong state apparatuses, wage labor, strong cities, a strong and indigenous bourgeoisie, and culturally homogeneous ideologies and policies; while the opposite conditions exist in the "backward" areas of the system. Also, Cox's argument that economic and political imbalances between the component societies provide opportunities for capital accumulation in the dominant nations and shape the nature of a dependent society's economy are central tenets in contemporary world-system theory.

ON THE ORIGINS OF CAPITALISM

There has been a great deal of debate among economic historians over the origin and development of capitalism, and Cox entered into this controversy. As discussed below, his explanation of the origins of capitalism diverges significantly from those writers who believed that capitalism had been firmly established with the decline of feudalism in Western Europe and the expansion of industrialization, especially in countries such as England. England represented the first mature capitalist nation, but Cox believed that by the time of its ascendancy, most of the institutional patterns of a capitalist society and a capitalist world-economy had been firmly established – as early as the thirteenth century in medieval Venice.

Henri Pirenne, the economic historian, viewed capitalism as firmly planted in the medieval cities of Europe and intensified at later stages of capitalist development in Britain's Industrial Revolution. Cox, following this approach, took as his model the medieval city of Venice and showed how the basic character of capitalist culture emerged there.[7] Like Pirenne,

Cox demonstrated that the commerce of ancient societies was quite differ-ent from the patterns of trade that evolved among the Venetians and earlier city-states.[8]

Thus, Cox's thinking on the origins of capitalism differed from the classical economic historian Werner Sombart and the sociologist Max We-ber, both of whom represent an idealist tradition in economic thought. Both Sombart and Weber tended to attribute the essence of capitalism as derived from a *geist* or *spirit*, where states of mind and the rational pursuit of profit reached their fruition under capitalism.[9] Sombart argued, for example, that capitalism had emerged in the Medieval Age, but he believed that such developments as "a greed for gold," the "development of ways and means of money getting," and a "bourgeois temperament" were the essential basis for capitalist economic formations.[10] Sombart, too, unlike Cox, did not see the spirit of capitalism as arising out of a peculiar type of economic organiza-tion, but from an "entrepreneur spirit" that laid the foundation for capitalist development. "It goes without saying," wrote Sombart, "that at some time in the distant past the capitalist spirit must have been in existence – embyro, if you like – before any capitalist undertaking could become a reality."[11] In a similar fashion, Cox disagreed with Weber's thesis that the foundation for capitalist development was based on Calvinism – a religious value system – that generated the "spirit of capitalism."[12] From Cox's standpoint it was the other way round; capitalism permitted religion to flourish. The unique difference was that the church always had to submit to the secular object-ives of a capitalist society.

There is also a clear departure between Cox's theory of capitalism and those Marxist writers who make a distinction between commercial and industrial capitalism. Like many contemporary world system theorists, Cox's view was that commercial and industrial capitalism were two sides of the same coin. From the very beginning, capitalism was commercial, and domestic industrial production was dependent upon it for prosperity. Moreover, all capitalist societies had some form of industry, in which case commerce was inseparable from the former. The Industrial Revolution in the eighteenth century, therefore, marked a great scientific and technolo-gical breakthrough, but was not responsible for the beginning of capitalism. What it did do was enhance the development of capitalism even further, although the essential features had already existed in earlier societies. Cox viewed Marx and his followers as making some important contributions in asking critical questions about the nature of capitalism, but Marx's preoc-cupation with the class struggle between capitalists and labor prevented him from giving sufficient attention to the more global nature of the capitalist system. According to Cox, Marx's focus on a *national society*, principally England, and not the *capitalist system*, a "world-wide system," prevented him from seeing the importance of capitalist leadership and the dominant role of foreign trade in capital accumulation.[13] Cox also observed that

Lenin, Maurice Dobbs, and other Marxist writers had missed the point in thinking that imperialism was a more recent capitalist trend, prompted by declining profit. Instead, Cox argued that this was a principal force at work in early capitalist societies such as Venice where the absence of trade resulted in the loss of leadership to more commercially dominant nations in a capitalist world-economy. Whereas Lenin had addressed imperialism at the stage of monopoly capitalism – where declining profits and the growth of capital via large scale accumulation was the motive for imperialism – for Cox, imperialism had the purpose of dominating markets and was an integral feature of capitalist societies from their inception.

There are also some disagreements between Cox and contemporary world-system theorists such as Immanuel Wallerstein in determining the time at which the capitalist world-economy first emerged. Cox claimed that the embryonic design of the first capitalist world-system originated in medieval Venice and the component societies were gradually included as the system expanded.[14] Feudalism was eventually undermined by the superior organization of capitalism, but during its early development it was possible for capitalism and feudalism to coexist side by side. In contrast, Wallerstein argued that the catalyst for the capitalist world-market was the failure of feudalism and the Hapsburg empire in the early sixteenth century to compete against a more dynamic and productive capitalist world economy. In addition, Wallerstein argued that the capitalist world economy, once formed, became the dominant mode of social organization and it was no longer possible for feudalism and capitalism to coexist.[15]

Cox's examination of the social organization of medieval Venetian society and other territories enabled him to identify several conditions which, in combination, facilitated the development of capitalism in this early city state. First, it was essential that a capitalist society should have access to the sea because of the necessity for foreign trade. Second, the government of the society must be accessible to the dominant business classes, and not controlled by a feudal aristocracy. This required the head of state to be controlled by election or impeachment to allow for the removal of uncooperative political leaders who did not support the aims of the entrepreneur. Third, religion was tolerated, but unlike the role of the church in feudalism, it was removed from politics and economics. There should exist a class of bureaucratic functionaries to administer the affairs of state. And, culturally, "a capitalist ethos or pattern of values, i.e., a communal determination to make an active foreign commerce the vital core of the economic life of the community so that social status, religious and legal ideology, art, science, and war all contribute to this end."[16] These basic postulates play a prominent role in Cox's analysis of the emergence of capitalist leadership in different societies. He attempted to show the degree to which various societies displayed these characteristics in their social organization as the capitalist world-system evolved. His key operational proposition was this:

the more a city-state or nation manifested these conditions, the greater was its opportunity to establish capitalist leadership in the wider system.

A crucial factor contributing to the development of capitalism in Venice, therefore, was the absence of traditional forms of social organization such as feudalism. Venice, Cox explains, created something approaching a parliamentary form of government, where the ruling bourgeoisie openly took control over the membership of the Venetian legislature. As well, "The very nature of the Venetian social order necessitated a relatively elaborate system of civil, criminal, and international law" to protect its industry and commerce.[17]

The fundamental economic underpinnings of Venice were commerce, colonization, labor, business enterprise and finance. Commerce, Cox argued forthrightly, was indispensable, and like all capitalist societies to follow, the Venetians had to trade or perish. Lacking arable land to provide for her own consumption needs, Venice had to seek agriculture staples from other areas, but the foreign trade she was to engage in was not equal. In the very process of providing for its own consumption needs, typical of future capitalist market economies, Venice brought the provisioning of others under its control. This placed Venice in the position of securing both consumption goods and raw materials for her industries, whereas exported finished products were sold to the dependent areas. Consequently, Cox pointed out, the Venetians regulated and planned their commerce and industry very astutely to enhance their monopolistic position over more dependent traditional areas.

Venetian workers, as is the case with all capitalist leader societies, benefited from Venetian economic prosperity, were nationalistic, and contributed to the domestic economy. However, due to the power of the economic oligarchy, they were politically insignificant. On the other hand, the main catalyst was foreign trade and it was business people who controlled it: "Among them there were, as in all subsequent leading captalist nations, the great aristocrats of foreign trade and the much larger number of lesser merchants and traders who participated mainly in derived domestic commerce. Capitalism set in motion its foreign trade, and produced all sorts of consumption demands at home, which were naturally satisfied by the trader. Venetian industry created a demand for labor and supplied buying power," but essentially, it was foreign trade that gave Venice its prosperity.[18] The purpose of foreign trade, however, was not solely to provide for the consumption needs of the Venetians, but to export goods for the consumption needs of others.

The Venetians, Cox asserts, clearly demonstrated a peculiar pattern found in capitalist societies. Specifically, they regulated and planned their commerce and industry to enhance their monopolistic position over more dependent and less capitalistically developed areas. For example, "It was ...in regard to rules of navigation that the Venetians reached the height of their mercantile wisdom. They guarded carefully the secrets of ship construction, limited the sale or rental of galleys to foreigners, regulated the carriage of foreign goods in their ships, excluded outsiders from association with their citizens in overseas ventures...determined competitive strategy with other communities, and laid down the laws of conduct at sea."[19] Forms of money holding and money changing existed in ancient societies but, as Cox explained, in Venice money played a more vital part. The Venetian golden ducat set the monetary standard in international trade. "It [Venice] gradually evolved fundamental banking practices; its stocks circulated as obligations ultimately backed by the state; and it served as a source of investments. It is," Cox reasoned, "a characteristic of leading capitalist nations that investment capital tends to flow towards them; hence foreigners sought as a privilege, to invest in these gilt-edged securities."[20] This demonstrated to him how important it was for later capitalist leader countries to set the standard for international currency flows which inordinately moved toward the leader nation. Other features he examined were the role of treaties, ambassadors and consuls, and the immigration of labor, which would later be significant to future capitalist leader nations. From all this, Cox surmised that in a capitalist society there is a strain toward colonization and exploitation.

Cox believed, therefore, that Venetian culture was much more highly developed than other parts of Europe that were mired still in the darkness of the Middle Ages. Unlike other feudal societies then existent in Europe, Venice had no serfs, no vassals or laws regulating landownership. Moreover, as is characteristic of capitalist societies, there were unprecedented opportunities in Venice for enterprising individuals to acquire wealth.

By the thirteenth century, Cox maintains, capitalism was firmly established in the world and its culture irreversible. With Venetian eminence firmly assured, its splendor diffused into other areas such as Holland and the United Provinces. Eventually, Venice would be a model for these latter areas which would assume leadership with Venice's decline.

From the Venetian experience, Cox shows there were several recognizable patterns that marked the decline of capitalist leadership, the most important being the loss of commercial advantages. While the historical situation differs from society to society, the general pattern is the same. Venice's loss of leadership resulted from the discovery of the Cape route to the East and the attractiveness of the American continent to other European countries, which expanded their foreign trade. Secondly, defeat in wars meant the loss of vital trade routes, her famous and powerful arsenal, and Venice's place as the outstanding shipyard in the world, as Holland took on the role of building most Venetian ships. Lastly, another typical feature appeared: "the tendency to export capital to the new leader for more efficient uses." Cox believed that a key sign of a declining capitalist nation is the reversal of capital flows from the old to the new, emergent, capitalist leader nation.

With the decline of Venetian capitalism, Cox saw other capitalist city-states such as Florence and Genoa emerging and making their individual contributions in banking and finance. These cities, he notes, were never able to assume capitalist leadership because of the persistence of their feudalism and their inability to achieve a stable form of government. To the north, on the other hand, the Hanseatic League in the late thirteenth century managed to achieve leadership status because of its preeminent commercial interests, its exploitation of the most backward areas in Europe and Asia, and its protection of foreign trade and industry. Next, the Dutch cities (the United Provinces) came to the fore and were "the first to integrate their feudal ruler into their capitalist social structure; though not completely so. Clustering in a commercially strategic area, their capitalist traditions developed in the hard school of competition with the (Hanseatic) League. Further, certain imponderable historical events in their struggle with Spain made it possible for these cities, together with the intervening feudal authority, to form sovereign federal unions that were the nearest approach to the modern capitalist nation before England became organized."[21]

A WORLD SYSTEM THEORY OF CAPITALISM

When Cox wrote the preface to *The Foundation of Capitalism*, he believed that capitalism represented a unique form of societal organization in displaying its own distinct institutional patterns. Unique to capitalism – and this is where fresh ground is broken – was the formation of a "worldwide system" involving both capitalist and noncapitalist societies. This system was hierarchically arranged in a territorial division of labor of dominance, dependency, and exploitation.[22]

To demonstrate the territorial organization of the early formation of capitalism as a "world wide system," Cox begins his analysis with a typology illustrating how the system had been first established among a group of functionally interdependent medieval cities and towns. His classification is based upon ranking five general types of capitalist cities and towns which are the principal components forming a structural pattern of the first capitalist system. These include the *national*, the *dependent-subject*, the *fairs*, the *kontors*, or *staples*, and the *emporia* areas in the system. The various subtypes Cox incorporated in his scheme of analysis are also listed below.

Cox defines the dominant areas in the system as the *national-capitalist* city-states – the centers of organization and commerce. Capitalism flourished in cities of this type because they were able, at different points in time, to separate themselves from feudal control and create a distinct political and economic order. Included in this category were the "sovereign" cities of Venice and to a lesser degree Amalfi; the "autonomous leagued cities", represented by the Hanseatic league: Lubeck, Hamburg,

Bremen, and Cologne; and the "sovereign federal" cities of the United Provinces under the Dutch, including Amsterdam. Cox believed that most of the national-capitalist cities managed to assume some semblance of independence but, as mentioned, they were often unable to resolve totally the problems of feudalism, national integration, and leadership in the capitalist system. Therefore, they never attained the national sovereignty and capitalist leadership achieved by Venice.

Subordinate areas, such as the *dependent-subject* cities and towns represented by the French communes, the English boroughs, and London are described as "caught up in the stream of developing capitalism" but "remained relatively dependent and subject, particularly because of the settled stagnancy of their feudal overlordship."[23] Thus, capitalism had developed rather late in these areas owing to the persistence of feudalism and their inability to establish an internal bourgeois government. In England, especially, the king's authority over trade provided privileges for foreign traders at the expense of the English merchants, rendering powerless for a period "a comparatively feeble but relentlessly growing English bourgeoisie striving to assimilate commercial privileges through their borough institutions."[24]

Fair towns served as distribution centers in the capitalist system. In effect they became "the foci of commerce and financial transactions."[25] As middlemen in the capitalist system they were not integrated into the national capitalist economy, but operated more as subordinated municipalities organized as self-interested entities. Though in the fair towns "the most advanced principles and techniques of the market of the capitalist system were largely worked out," they were more dependent "upon the commercial activities and patronage of the national capitalist cities for their prosperity. They were not, therefore, initiators of capitalist commerce."[26] Within this category Cox listed what he called the "periodic" fair towns of Bruges and Antwerp.

The *kontors* or *staples* were the trading outposts of the national cities. They were less sophisticated than the fair towns and functioned mainly in collecting and distributing goods in the capitalist system: "The staples were indispensable to capitalist commerce because they served as protective communities from which capitalist merchants might negotiate with peoples in more or less backward countries."[27] These centers were either of the "concessionary" type, as in the case of London (before 1450), Batavia, Calcutta, Canton, Novgorod, and Archangel, or of the "subject" type, including such cities as Tyre, Calais, Bergen, Goa, and Shanghai.

The most subordinated areas in the system, the *emporia*, served as great marts and warehouses. They are described as being patronized and/or established by the national-capitalist cities. "The emporia, as such cities may be designated," Cox writes, "were reservoirs for commercial products of a given area. They were patronized by capitalist merchants not particularly with the purpose of consummating a commodity exchange, but rather that of replenishing stocks."[28] Examples include such towns as "Wisby on the Swedish island of Gothland and Ormuz on its island at the head of the Persian Gulf." Cox concluded at the time "the islands of Hong Kong and Curaçao appear still to retain significant features of the emporium."[29]

By the thirteenth and fourteenth centuries, Cox explains, commercial trade among these areas constituted a "worldwide" capitalist system involving five essential market situations: "(a) that between the advanced capitalist and noncapitalist peoples; (b) among the advanced capitalist cities; (c) between the advanced cities and minor European towns; (d) in the highly competitive situations at the fairs; and (e) in domestic transactions."[30] The Venetians were at the focal point of this trade, dominating the Adriatic and Mediterranean seas, while the Hanseatic League in the north controlled the trade of the Baltic region.

Cox argues convincingly that these societies were all early formations of capitalism. A system of international communities was "'cradled' and hence its traits may be recognized far more simply in them than the more complex modern nations."[31] Accordingly, capitalism emerged, not as a mature system, but from its earliest prototype in Venice, and advanced through a succession of cities and federations including the Hanseatic League, the United Provinces, and Great Britain. The latter's distinction was that it became the first capitalist nation-state.

THE ESTABLISHMENT OF THE FIRST CAPITALIST NATION

Cox's main objective in his analysis of capitalist leadership in England was to demonstrate how the first capitalist nation-state was created and to show what the industrial revolution had contributed to this development. He also made more explicit his views of mercantilism, which are found in various parts of his writings, arguing that the mercantilists were probably more correct than any other economic doctrine in their understandings of capitalism and the essential role of foreign commerce in enhancing the wealth of a nation.

Cox notes that the movement of England toward achieving capitalist leadership was inhibited by the feudal authority of a king, who like other leaders in backward areas, acquired wealth through allowing more progressive capitalistic-oriented foreigners to dominate commerce. For centuries, Cox observed, England was placed in the position of being a dependent staple controlled by alien merchants from capitalist leader cities such as Venice, the Hanseatic League, and the United Provinces. However, several events changed England's status. The rise of a national capitalist movement among the indigenous merchants was critical since this enabled them to resist the intrusion of foreign traders. The establishment of a sovereign parliamentary system of government significantly reduced the power of the king. The organization of merchant companies paved the way for foreign exploitation of other nations and territories in the world economy. Finally, with the organization of domestic commerce and industry, England was on the way to becoming one of the first capitalist societies to absorb a feudal structure into a national state.

By 1600, Cox observed, English trading companies such as the East India Company had expanded English foreign trade throughout the world as the human and national resources of backward countries became open to exploitation. As well, domestic production in England became naturally geared to foreign markets. English merchants exchanged their economic surplus with other areas. This enabled them to provide for the domestic consumption of England, while also effectively determining the productive situation of more dependent areas in Africa, Asia, and Russia. England, therefore, achieved all of the significant features of a capitalist nation by the end of the seventeenth century.

Cox devoted substantial space to mercantilism in his analysis of English capitalism. He argued that before the Industrial Revolution mercantilist thinkers and writers played a key role in providing the ideological basis for English capitalism, since it became their responsibility to further "...convince and win over the non-capitalist authority in their community."[32] But mercantilism as a school of thought, Cox cautioned his readers to note, represented mainly a formalization of early capitalist practices, which had already been put into action in the national cities and was not a new development accompanying the rise of English capitalism.

Mercantilism was not simply an advocacy of the regulation of economic activities. It was not a movement against laissez-faire. Mercantilism, Cox believed, supported free trade because it was in the self interest of a nation to pursue such a policy, while simultaneously taking a protectionist position against imports into the home country. The mercantilist recognized the significance of maintaining leadership in the capitalist system and the necessity of exporting manufactured goods in exchange for raw materials that produced wealth literally "out of nothing." Characteristic of capitalist economies, the mercantilist also knew the advantages to be accrued through forcing dependent areas to gear their economies to the demands of the domestic manufacturing of the capitalist leader country. Thus, Cox suggested, foreign trade was seen as greatly facilitating the domestic economy of the leader nation, not the reverse as the classical economists had argued in thinking that the source of wealth was mainly to be found in the domestic economy. For Cox, the expansion of manufacturing did not displace the role of foreign commerce, but enabled a nation to take leadership in foreign commerce.

Further, the mercantilist had definite ideas as to the role of labor in capitalist societies as well as in the dependent areas. "Colonies were considered economic appendages to England; and defined in reference to the latter's labor laws, raw materials, and manufacturing requirements."[33] A similar attitude taken toward the English working class was applied to labor in the colonies in that neither had the mercantilist freedom of the English business class. In those colonial areas where slavery existed, "Negroes, as the plantation labor force, came within the same self-interested calculations as the English worker, but with compounded pressures upon them." They experienced the added burden of racial antagonism that supported the exploitation of people of color throughout the world.[34] Thus, for the Mercantilists, labor was considered an exploitable natural resource and its price was determined by supply and demand. Surplus value was realized either through increasing the work of labor, lower wages, or improving the techniques of production. But these conditions were not to be seen as unconnected to foreign commerce, which significantly augmented domestic industries.

The decline in Britain's leadership, Cox points out, was the consequence of several factors: the impending rivalry of younger and more resourceful emerging capitalist nations, such as the United States, Germany and Japan offered a formidable challenge; and so did the movement of colonial peoples to resist British colonial domination and exploitation. Significant, too, was England's involvement in two costly and unproductive world wars which reduced the country almost to bankruptcy and gradually dispossessed her of her colonies.[35]

From his examination of the early city-states and England, Cox was able to draw many significant generalizations and conclusions about the nature, growth, and development of capitalist societies. The drive of capitalist societies toward imperialism and colonization did not begin with the exploitation of colored peoples of the world. Instead, it was an inherent feature of capitalism that took on new significance with the contact of Europeans with people of color in the fifteenth and sixteenth centuries. While countries such as Portugal and Spain had taken the lead in colonizing Africa and the New World, their capitalist development had been restricted by the continuance of feudalism. Capitalist leader societies had a propensity to create a territorial division of labor advantageous to their position in the wider world system, which was disadvantageous to the backward areas of the world economy. It was very necessary, therefore, for backward countries to specialize and produce raw materials for the dominant nations in the system, while the latter diversified their production. No leading capitalist nation, Cox submitted, had historically placed itself in the position of specializing and becoming a producer of raw materials. This was the position of the mercantilist, and was certainly demonstrated by the early national cities, which lacked consumption goods, but were able to import all that was required for their own prosperity. Nor did this imperialist imperative mean the same thing for all societies in the world economy. At one extreme, the superior economic advantages accrued by the capitalist leader meant a higher standard of living, greater freedom for citizens, and a more complete existence. At the other extreme, for the great masses of people in the world, the consequences were poverty, forced labor, and racial humiliation.

THE DECLINE AND TRANSITION OF AMERICAN CAPITALIST LEADERSHIP

Cox further expounded upon his views of capitalism by extending his analysis of the capitalist world system in two other works, *Capitalism and American Leadership* (1962) and *Capitalism as a System* (1964). In part, the purposes of these volumes were to demonstrate how more recent capitalist leader nations, facing an unstable world economy, were now required to utilize policies and practices that were uncommon in the earlier capitalist city-states and Great Britain. Secondly, Cox offered an account of what he believed was the inevitable transition of capitalism to socialism, focusing on the problems confronting socialist development in the back-ward areas of the world. Thirdly, he reformulated his model of the capitalist system to reflect the territorial organization of the contemporary world situation in the twentieth century.

The major categories in Cox's conceptualization of a modern world capitalist system now included such designations as the *Leaders*, the *Subsidiaries*, the *Progressives*, the *Dependents* and the *Passives*. The new rival leader nations were now the United States, Great Britain, and Germany. According to Cox's calculations, these nations represented only 12 per cent of the world's population. While Great Britain had set the pace for capitalist leadership in the nineteenth century, by 1914 the United States had taken the lead. Germany's imperial conquest brought that nation into a rival status in the capitalist system, but Germany alone never captured leadership. The second group of nations – the *Subsidiaries* – included " ... a few advanced European nations and Japan, each with varying potentialities for growth and differing competitive capacities," each imitating the national-istic sentiments of the leader nations. Subordinated to the subsidiaries were the *Progressives*: " ... a group of 'new nations' – the British Dominions and Argentina – each with large stocks of natural resources relative to popula-tion and with ambitions and capabilities for development somewhat similar to those of the United States."[36] Unlike the United States, "The progress-ives ... did not have the same open road to success as the United States; and their growth was already limited by a plethoric industrial capacity in Canada and Latin America. Basic industries in Canada and Latin America, for example, were mostly financed by United States capital and managed by American corporations."[37] The two largest categories constituting most of the world's population were the *Dependents* and *Passives*, those areas most open to capitalist exploitation. In the *Dependent* countries, such as pre-revolutionary Russia, China, the Near East, and the rest of South America, commercial development was limited and they were subject to the self-interest of the dominant leaders. Cox states that "The *Passives* constituted virtually all of Africa, the rest of Asia, the West Indies; and the islands of the Pacific. They were regarded by the leading powers as having no international rights. Their peoples were thus voiceless, and their resources were organized directly with a view to the enhancement of the economic welfare of any active capitalist nation that was able to establish and maintain control."[38]

Cox claimed that following the First World War, capitalist leadership in the United States signaled a period of decline in the capitalist system. The United States had "become not only the most powerful, magnificent, and uncontestable leader the capitalist system has ever known but also, apparently, the terminus of [its] development."[39] A critical factor leading to the decline of capitalism in the United States was the rise of new forms of social organization, which forced the country to deviate from the traditional modes of capitalist behavior. The world movement of the backward countries toward self-determination and the appearance of socialism placed restrictions on American commercial expansion and direct exploitation. In particular, Cox suggested, the Bolshevik Revolution of 1917, the Chinese Revolution of 1948, and the emergence of nationalism and socialism in Third World countries came at the very time the United States was assuming leadership status. In addition, unknown to the earlier national cities was the inability of American capitalism to shake off periodic depressions and the need to rely upon "pump-priming" measures such as maintaining a defense economy, farm price supports, and public works programs, all Keynesian policies which Cox characterized as socialists' efforts to prop up American capitalism.

Another important sign of decline was the fact that American foreign investments had become a major instrument for enhancing the sale of American products abroad. Now, markets for manufactured goods could be secured only through large investments in the dependent countries importing those goods. Thus, Cox's assessment led him to believe that the United States began the post-First World War period by supporting its capitalist development in a way quite different from the earlier national cities. While capital accumulation had been derived earlier from a direct exploitative situation, American business now had to convince its own community, the public, and the government that they had to invest abroad or stagnate. The more foreign lending that was precipitated abroad, the greater the opportunity for selling American products to foreign countries.

Cox viewed the decade of the 1930s as a period of frustration, as American capitalist leaders began to face a default on its foreign securities, thereby depressing both the domestic and foreign markets. Foreign lending by the United States tapered off, which concomitantly affected the borrower's ability to pay and the power of the American domestic economy to dispose of its products. After the money market collapse had been fully exposed during the great Depression, "capitalism as a patient" would be stabilized by the Second World War and the New Deal.

To also overcome the limitations on expansion and the drift toward stagnation, Cox viewed the national defense economy created by the US government after the Second World War as a major stabilizing force which allowed American capitalism to continue. Tied both to the domestic and foreign market, he explained that militarization and preparation for the eventuality of open conflict were extreme measures, but they provided many important subsidiary values against economic crises. These measures also created optimistic expectations of recapturing the non-capitalist areas of the world and could be a show of force to those dependent areas of the world that might become restive or seek to remove themselves from the capitalist system.

The United States could not take a leading role in providing a model for the "backward areas" of the world whose economic development had been restricted by colonialism and imperialism. Consequently, the main objective of American capitalist leadership, Cox argued, was keeping underdeveloped countries within the orbit of the world capitalist system. Furthermore, its policies were directed primarily toward perpetuating the private enterprise system and opposing communism and movement toward planned economies. This has been the historical posture of capitalist nations toward backward countries.

Cox was not naive about the problems confronting those countries who chose to remove themselves from the capitalist system. The establishment of a socialist society was a difficult task and some countries might have an easier time at it than others. He affirmed that in order for a viable socialist society to be established there are several conditions that must exist: "...a relatively large, sophisticated governmental bureaucracy, a tractable military establishment, at least a nest egg of native scientists and technicians, a certain critical size of population and quantity of natural resources, and a people capable of being inspired and motivated to endure privation and to labor unremittingly for a millennium which they may never live to enjoy."[40] Undoubtedly, with the fall of communist regimes in the last decade or so, the legitimacy of socialism had been seriously undermined by economic collapses throughout the communist world and by the failure to promote liberal democracy.[41]

Writing during the Cold War period, Cox also understood the implications of a country removing itself from the capitalist world system and taking a socialist path. Serious economic dislocation was likely, particularly among the one crop and mineral producing countries, which could be placed in a serious state of deprivation with the closing of markets. Thus, there were few opportunities for small, undeveloped countries to become independent socialist states. As Cox saw the dilemma, "The smaller countries must expect to remain forever satellites – or become merged into large regions. No nation of the West Indies or mainland Caribbean, for example, can ever hope to profit progressively by the economies of scale inherent in the heavy industries, in production for its necessarily domestic consumption. They must, so far as it is possible to envision, always import the consumer goods which flow from these industries. As part of a larger region involving free population mobility, however, they may become conscious contributors to the total productive process."[42]

In South America and Sub-Saharan Africa, Cox observed that resources and population were sufficient for socialist development, but these countries were confronted with national and tribal disunity. "As individual countries – unless it is perhaps Brazil and the Congo – they must continue to suffer the inadequate rate of development, or even decline, imposed by imperialist contrivances, or else make desperate individual attempts at socialism perhaps only to become aware of a deadend ahead."[43] On the other hand, the opposition of the advanced sectors of the capitalist world created few opportunities for trade in the less-developed sectors of the world economy.

Nonetheless, writing at a time when many Third World countries were undergoing decolonialization and in the aftermath of the Chinese and Cuban Revolutions – two major revolutions that occurred in his lifetime – Cox was quite optimistic about socialism in the Third World. The initiative for class struggle could not come from the working class in the more advanced capitalist countries. They were beneficiaries of the wealth of the leader nation, which meant that capital "...is not entirely, or sometimes even mainly, accumulated from the exploitation of domestic workers."[44] Further, their aim was in reforming the social structure for a larger share of the national wealth and not revolutionary change that would undermine their privileged position. Hope for revolutionary action did come from the more disadvantaged groups in the underdeveloped countries, who were the real proletariats in the capitalist system. In short, "the class struggle...becomes not simply a violent clash between workers in the most advanced capitalist nations and their ruling classes (as Marx argued), but a conflict between the masses of people, mainly in the more organizable backward countries, led by native socialists or nationalists [against] their weak, domestic bourgeoisie or feudality supported by the system."[45]

In addition, he saw several exogenous possibilities that could serve as a catalyst for the transition from capitalism to socialism. First, as mentioned earlier, Cox believed that stagnation in the capitalist system required the capitalist leader nation to take negative holding actions, in which normal capitalist expansion and exploitation were no longer possible. Capitalist leader succession had not only ended, but capitalist institutions were being transformed in the process as non-market solutions became necessary to stabilize the system. Second, socialist societies could benefit from the more positive aspects of capitalism especially the latter's science, technology, and rationalism. The adaptation of these advances had the unintended effect of giving underdeveloped countries the confidence that planned economies were attainable. Third, the transition was enhanced through competition between capitalist and socialist nations. The Soviet Union was a major industrialized country Cox recognized as issuing "a resounding challenge" in matching the technological superiority of the United States; a situation with which earlier capitalist cities did not have to contend. Fourth, the relative growth rates between the United States and the Soviet Union indicated the transition. Cox believed that because GNP in the USSR by 1958 was less than half that of the United States, the Soviet economy was growing at a faster rate with a more dynamic system of resource allocation.[46] Fifth, another sign of the transition was the regional restructuring of the capitalist world, the encouragement of European cooperation through the Marshall Plan, and the formation of the European Common Market. Though organized to sustain the stability of the capitalist system, this was a movement toward economic cooperation. Cox observed that "Since the Second World War this movement has gained considerable momentum. Indeed, the *region* has become widely recognized as the basic unit of co-operative, self sustaining productive growth. Unlike the capitalist nation its psychological drive is directed internally, and its major concern is with development through the exploitation of regional resources."[47] Furthermore, "Regionalism...becomes an initial way out of capitalist stagnation. It envisages an economy large enough to benefit from the normal expansibility flowing from a relatively unlimited reliance upon science and technology."[48]

At the time, Cox saw several significant movements toward regionalism, which for him were demonstrations of economic cooperation that were uncharacteristic of traditional capitalist societies. According to Cox, at the time, "The Soviet Union, India, and China could be regarded as highly integrated transitional regions. The European Common Market and the potential for a Latin American Common Market seemed more or less on the way to achieving regional unity, while Pan Africa, the Arab Region, Southeast Asia, and the West Indies represented less developed movements toward regionalization."[49] Although the economic and political leadership of the United States opposed economic cooperation among the underdeveloped areas, Cox noted that movement toward regionalism and trade based upon the social needs and plans of the various countries (opposed to producing for the needs of capitalist nations) would progressively transform the world-system of capitalism.[50]

CONCLUSION

With the fall of Marxist–Leninist regimes throughout the world, and the persistence of capitalism and liberal democracy, it is seriously doubtful that, in the foreseeable future, socialism alone is likely to offer Third World nations a viable alternative to economic development as Cox envisioned.[51] In fact, as it seems, market-oriented economies such as Taiwan, South Korea, Thailand, Hong Kong, Singapore, and other countries in eastern Asia, which open themselves up to multinational corporations, have progressively produced economic growth rates that currently exceed industrialized countries like the Soviet Union, albeit an authoritarian political system has been the rule. Many writers, such as Cox in the post-Second World War era, viewed the Soviet Union as a proven example that socialism was a model for the future in less developed areas of the world. They ignored the totalitarian aspects of the Soviet Union and the means by which it had industrialized so quickly. Moreover, Cox could not see the inability of a Soviet style command economy to adjust to a post-industrial high technology era, requiring more flexibility and international ties than the Soviet system could offer.

Dependency theory in the 1950s and 1960s gained in popularity and argued that "The advanced countries controlled the world terms of trade and, through their multinational corporations, forced Third World countries into what was called 'unbalanced development'." In contradiction, classical liberal trade theory argued that trade was equally beneficial to all.[52] Perhaps both theories are correct. Through the eyes of today, a powerful argument can be made that, while a capitalist world system may be responsible for the emergence of underdevelopment in Third World countries with a history of colonialism, it may be also argued that the continuation of underdevelopment in a global economy can also be laid at the feet of restrictive trade barriers and culture patterns in the Third World, which have been inimical to capitalism, industrialization, and liberal democracy. Nonetheless, Cox's writings on capitalism warrant attention in the context of the dependency–modernization debate emerging in the decade of the 1950s, as well as his substantive contributions to our understanding of the evolution of capitalism as a society and as a world-wide system.

NOTES

1 As an invited paper prepared for this volume, most of the analysis in this chapter has been revised from previous work done by the author for the purpose of drawing attention to Cox's contributions to political economy. See especially Herbert M. Hunter, "The Life and Work of Oliver C. Cox," PhD thesis, Department of Sociology, Boston University, 1981; "The World System Theory of Oliver C. Cox," *Monthly Review* (October, 1985), pp. 43–53; and Herbert M. Hunter and Sameer Abraham, *Race, Class, and The World System: The Sociology of Oliver C. Cox*, New York: Monthly Review Press, 1987.
2 Notable examples of political economists who *have* given limited space to Cox's ideas on capitalism would include Samir Amin in *Unequal Development: An Essay on the Social Foundations of Peripheral Capitalism*, New York: Monthly Review Press, 1976, p. 174, and Paul Baran and Paul M. Sweezy, *Monopoly*

Capital: An Essay on the American Economic and Social Order, New York: Monthly Review Press, 1969, p. 178.

3 The historical sociologist Harry Elmer Barnes has written "In the economic field, he [Cox] studied under Professors John U. Nef, Frank H. Knight, Jacob Viner and Harry A Millis, experts in economic history, economic theory and labor problems." See Harry Elmer Barnes, "Foreword," *The Foundations of Capitalism* by Oliver C. Cox, New York: Philosophical Library, 1959, p. 11.

4 *ibid.*, p. 11.

5 Interview with Oliver C. Cox by Elmer P. Martin, Morgan State University, 22 June 1977. Also see Elmer P. Martin, "The Sociology of Oliver C. Cox: A Systematic Inquiry," MA Thesis, Department of Sociology, Atlanta University, May, 1971. It may also be noted that Cox served as professor of economics at Wiley College of Marshall, Texas, from 1932 to 1944.

6 See for example, Herbert M. Hunter, "The World-System Theory of Oliver C. Cox," *Monthly Review* (October, 1985), pp. 43–55.

7 Henri Pirenne, "The Stages in the Social History of Capitalism," *American Historical Review*, 19 (April, 1914), 494–515.

8 Henri Pirenne, *Medieval Cities: Their Origins and the Revival of Trade*, translated by Frank D. Hasey, New York: Doubleday and Company, 1956.

9 Maurice Dobb, *Studies in the Development of Capitalism*, New York: International Publishers, 1947, p. 5.

10 Werner Sombart, *The Quintessence of Capitalism: A Study of the History and Psychology of the Modern Businessman*, edited and translated by M. Epstein, New York: Howard Teritg, Publisher, 1967.

11 *ibid.*, p. 344.

12 Oliver C. Cox, *Capitalism as a System*, New York: Monthly Review Press, 1964, pp. 57, 58.

13 While contending that Marx understood the international structure of capitalism, Paul A. Baran and Paul Sweezy in a footnote reluctantly lend support to Cox's criticism of Marx's inattention to the international dynamics of capitalism. They point out that "There is, therefore, justification for the criticism expressed by Oliver C. Cox in his *Capitalism as a System*...and value in his reiterated insistence that the international character of capitalism has always had a decisive effect on the nature and functioning of the national units which compose it" (Baran and Sweezy, *Monopoly Capital*, p. 178).

14 *Capitalism as a System*, 1964, p. x.

15 Immanuel Wallerstein, *The Modern World System: Capitalist Agriculture and the Origins of the European World Economy in the Sixteenth Century*, New York: Academic Press, 1974, p. 92.

16 Cox, *Capitalism as a System, op. cit.*, p. 8.

17 Oliver C. Cox, *The Foundations of Capitalism*, New York: Philosophical Press, 1959, p. 45.

18 *ibid.*, p. 78.

19 *ibid.*, p. 91.

20 *ibid.*, p. 81.

21 *ibid.*, pp. 204, 205.

22 There are remarkable parallels between Wallerstein's world-system perspective and Cox's model. Wallerstein goes beyond the conventional analysis of social systems and delineates two types of world-system: the world-empire, which includes culturally different groups administered by a single political authority (such as Rome, Pisa, and Greece) and the world-economy that includes multiple political units forming a world system. This is similar to the distinction Cox made between ancient societies and the system of national capitalist cities and

nations. Further, in Wallerstein's analysis the world economy constitutes a geographical division of labor among different states and areas of the world: *Core states* become the most advantageous countries in the world system; *semiperipheral areas* act as middle-trading regions; and the *peripheral areas* become the weaker and exploitable countries and areas (depending upon whether they are in a colonial or neo-colonial situation). See Immanuel Wallerstein, *The Modern World-System: Capitalist Agriculture and the Origins of the European World-Economy in the Sixteenth Century*, New York: Academic Press, 1974. As will be shown in detail in this and the next sections of the paper, Cox had envisioned a similar global stratification of early and modern capitalist leader societies and dependent areas.

23 *The Foundations of Capitalism, op. cit.*, p. 27.
24 *ibid.*, p. 252.
25 *ibid.*, p. 27.
26 *ibid.*, p. 27.
27 *ibid.*, p. 27.
28 *ibid.*, p. 275.
29 *ibid.*, p. 276.
30 *Capitalism as a System, op. cit.*, p. 8.
31 *The Foundations of Capitalism, op. cit.*, p. 25.
32 *ibid.*, p. 325.
33 *ibid.*, p. 384.
34 *ibid.*, pp. 384, 385.
35 *ibid.*, p. 475.
36 *Capitalism as a System, op. cit.*, p. 5.
37 *ibid.*, p. 5.
38 *ibid.*, p. 6.
39 *Capitalism and American Leadership, op. cit.*, p. xv.
40 *Capitalism as a System, op. cit.*, p. 241.
41 For an excellent discussion on the fall of authoritarian and totalitarian regimes in the post-Second World War era see Francis Fukuyama, *The End of History and the Last Man*, New York: Macmillan, Inc., 1992.
42 *Capitalism and American Leadership.*, p. 242.
43 *ibid.*, p. 243.
44 *ibid.*, p. 190.
45 *ibid.*, p. 196.
46 *ibid.*, p. 269, 270.
47 *ibid.*, p. 277.
48 *ibid.*
49 *ibid.*, pp. 277, 278.
50 Interestingly, although many of the member countries of the OPEC oil cartel remain within the orbit of capitalism, it serves as an example of the potential impact regional movements can have on capitalist economies.
51 The conclusion of this chapter has been greatly influenced by the recent work of Francis Fukuyama, *The End of History and the Last Man*, 1992, particularly pages 98–125.
52 *ibid.*, p. 100.

16

FROM THE NEW DEAL TO THE GREAT SOCIETY

The economic activism of Robert C. Weaver

Cecilia A. Conrad and George Sherer*

The election of Franklin Delano Roosevelt in 1932 ushered in not merely a new head of government, but also a new vision of the role of government. Government, through bold experimentation, became an activist in the search for economic stability. Government programs for job creation would include the Civilian Conservation Corps and the massive investment of the Tennessee Valley Authority among others. Regulatory activity would eventually extend into nearly every industrial sector. However, there was one area of private economic relations that Roosevelt's New Deal appeared to neglect – the racial segregation of workers by occupation and industry. Employment programs like the WPA tended to reinforce racial and gender based employment systems.[1] Many localities excluded blacks from the employment programs under their control, despite an announced federal policy of nondiscrimination. The Negro workers, confined to positions as unskilled laborers, were left unprotected.

It was this neglect of the economic problems of Negro workers that indirectly led Robert C. Weaver to his first government post. In 1933 while completing the requirements for a PhD in economics at Harvard University, Weaver joined with John P. Davis to form the Negro Industrial League. Initially, the League consisted of just Davis and himself.[2] As representatives of the League, Weaver and Davis testified before Congressional hearings on the National Industrial Recovery Act. Their activities introduced Weaver to Clark Foreman[3] whom Harold Ickes, Secretary of the Interior, ultimately appointed as his adviser on Negro affairs. Clark Foreman hired Weaver as associate adviser. Weaver later replaced Foreman as the chief adviser in 1935. During the Second World War, Weaver became director of the Negro Manpower Service in the War Manpower Commission.

*Alisia Gill provided valuable research assistance in making this chapter possible. We also wish to thank Robert C. Weaver for his valuable assistance and for devoting time to checking our facts.

Like the architects of the New Deal, Weaver was an advocate of economic activism. Skepticism regarding the ability of competitive markets to solve social problems characterizes much of his career – a career which spanned from Roosevelt's New Deal to Johnson's Great Society. His distrust of laissez faire economics derives not only from the economic conditions in which he reached maturity, but also from his observations of the economic experiences of African Americans. As an example of the inability of private markets to end economic discrimination, he offers the failure of private employers to hire Negro workers during the early days of the Second World War despite their successful employment during the First World War. He laments the lack of freely competitive housing markets. In an essay on neoconservatism, Weaver writes, "...to assume a free and competitive market in a situation of de facto widespread residential segregation is to assure such market-approved discrimination."

The strength in Weaver's research is not its imaginative development of economic theory, but its systematic analysis of the practical problems of policy implementation. Weaver was a passionate advocate for the concerns of Negro workers, but he was also a pragmatic social scientist. In an authoritative volume on blacks in the Roosevelt administration, John B. Kirby contrasts Weaver's style with that of Mary McCleod Bethune.

> Seldom did he express himself on the subject of the "Negro problem" in the sweeping, moralistic manner for which she was noted; nor did he reflect her extreme states of euphoric optimism or bitter disillusionment.... Weaver made his appeal not to the moral conscience of America but to its rationality.[4]

Weaver based his appeal to rationality on traditional neoclassical concepts of economic efficiency. Discrimination implies a waste of productive resources. A country in which discrimination is widespread cannot be operating on its production possibility frontier. In *Negro Labor*, published in 1946, Weaver offers example after example of how the exclusion of Negro workers inhibited wartime production. In *The Negro Ghetto*, published in 1948, he depicts how racial segregation of housing leads to an inefficient allocation of urban space. Ultimately, his concern with the Negro ghetto broadened to a concern with America's cities.

Weaver is a prolific scholar, amazingly so given his almost continuous employment outside academia. We do not attempt an exhaustive survey of his work here. Instead, we focus on the three issues that consumed most of his energy – the plight of Negro workers, the Negro Ghetto, and the plight of urban America.

THE PLIGHT OF NEGRO WORKERS

Although Weaver is primarily known for his work in urban economics, his early research focused on the problems of the Negro worker. While in the

Department of the Interior, he completed a study of the status of skilled Negro workers during the depression, *The Urban Negro Worker in the United States, 1925–1936* (United States Department of the Interior, 1938–9), and he published a number of articles on the role of Negro labor in the war effort. By far, his major work in the field of labor economics was *Negro Labor*, a detailed analysis of the integration of Negro workers into wartime industries. The first half of the book documents the barriers to Negro employment; the second analyzes how these barriers were overcome through case studies of specific industries.

Weaver identifies two barriers to Negro employment in wartime production – discrimination in training and discrimination in employment. Although the United States Office of Education announced a policy of nondiscrimination in federally funded vocational education programs, local authorities set the admission criteria and determined curriculum. They could systematically exclude Negro workers from programs offering training needed for work in defense and as Weaver documents, they frequently did. In the South, where there were separate vocational schools for whites and blacks, the majority of blacks received agricultural training while whites were equally divided between agricultural programs and training for crafts and industry. The latter training prepared whites for opportunities in defense related industries. During the first two years of defense training, Negroes held no more than 6 per cent of the slots in pre-employment courses. Weaver assigned part of the blame for the exclusion of blacks with the Office of Education's failure to press for Negro participation in defense training. The Office of Education established no guidelines to insure the equitable distribution of equipment and collected no records on Negro participation in defense training until the end of the war.

Even if Negro workers had access to vocational training it did not guarantee employment. Skilled Negro workers were routinely denied employment in defense related industries. Perhaps in no industry was the discrimination as blatant as in the aircraft industry. A letter from one California based company addressed to a Negro organization stated, "I regret to say that it is not the policy of this company to employ people other than of the Caucasian race, consequently, we are not in a position to offer your people employment at this time" (*Negro Labor*, p. 109). In a Kansas City plant, management expressed a willingness to hire Negro workers, but only as janitors (*Negro Labor*, p. 110). Management was often aided and abetted in its maintenance of segregated work forces by craft unions and by acquiescence on the part of the United States Employment Service.

In the early years of the war, unions possessed market power and clearly exercised it to exclude African Americans from employment. In an oral interview, Weaver, asked whether unions or employers posed the biggest obstacle to integration, emphatically answers, "Unions."[5] Yet Weaver's stance in *Negro Labor* is never anti-union. He warns in the preface that "there can be no sound generalization about unions' contribution, since organized labor is made of many units" and concludes in a later chapter that "the introduction of Negroes into platform jobs in transportation can be much more readily accomplished if the union is a strong one whose officers and members mutually respect and trust one another" (*Negro Labor*, p. 187). Weaver advocates a practical approach to unions – one which utilizes the power of unions whenever possible to ease the transition to an integrated workplace. Years later he described his strategy:

> our approach was to say to the employer, look, your responsibility is to hire these men and we will work it out with the union, so we wouldn't get them to blame it on the unions and then the unions blame it on the employers. Of course, they tried to do it, but this was the way we went about it.[6]

The color bar did bend. Black men and, in the last year of the war, black women held a large number of defense industry jobs, dramatically altering the color caste system of employment. For Weaver, the expansion of Negro employment during the Second World War was the product of two factors – tight labor markets and an activist anti-discrimination policy by the federal government under the auspices of the FEPC and the War Manpower Commission. Weaver does not overstate the role of the federal government. There are chapters devoted to the role of management and of trade unions, chapters relevant to the debate over affirmative action today. But, in case after case he documents FEPC hearings, investigations, and negotiations that resulted in an expansion or upgrading of Negro employment. Sometimes there was resistance by both management and unions, as happened with Philadelphia's transportation workers. In cities like Chicago where, according to Weaver, management and unions assumed leadership roles, the transition went smoothly. However, it was Weaver's contention that without an activist stance by the federal government the changes may never have taken place.

Weaver emphasized that the enforcement of anti-discrimination policy required a definition of discrimination and a means to prove it. While in the Interior Department, Weaver devised one solution: the insertion of a minimum percentage clause into contracts for the construction of public housing under the Public Works Administration (PWA).[7] The minimum percentage clause required that projects within a specific unit of the PWA hire a certain percentage of skilled black craftsmen based on the total number of skilled black craftsmen within that locality. Failure to do so constituted prima facie evidence of discrimination. This program was the forerunner of modern day affirmative action.

For Weaver, the conclusion was clear. Given the extraordinary resistance to Negro employment in a time of tight labor markets and political crisis, there was little hope for maintenance of those employment gains during reconversion without a persistently activist role by the federal government. He warned of the large displacement of Negro workers as industries contract and as workers with greater seniority return to reclaim their prewar jobs. Weaver advocated a two pronged postwar strategy: 1 government action to maintain full employment; and 2 a peacetime equivalent of the FEPC. Against Weaver's advice, the FEPC was disbanded at the end of the war, but nearly twenty years later it was reincarnated as the Equal Employment Opportunity Commission.[8]

THE NEGRO GHETTO

Through his work on the problems of integrating Negro workers into the wartime economy, Weaver became more and more interested in the problem of housing. Again, his weapon was statistics and his strategy, an appeal to rationality.

In *The Negro Ghetto* (1948), Weaver provides an exhaustive nationwide study of the racial segregation in housing markets and its consequences. He describes the northward and westward migration of blacks that occurred at the turn of this century; the hostility, on the part of whites, toward the newcomers; and the failure of the private sector to provide adequate housing for black households. Discriminatory housing covenants, which specified that sales of existing structures be made only to buyers from a specific racial group, were a clear impediment to the normal movement of black people to other areas commensurate with the changes in their income. As a result, more and more blacks were squeezed into existing urban "Black Belts." Housing prices were initially bid up and quality deteriorated.

Discriminatory housing covenants and government acquiescence impeded the workings of the free market and in so doing posed a danger to the economy as a whole (*The Negro Ghetto*, p. 235). The case of a public housing project in Buffalo illustrates dramatically the potential cost to society of this pursuit of racial segregation:

> Two years were consumed by Federal and local authorities looking for a site for Negro war housing. Meanwhile several thousand units of public war housing in the Buffalo area were unoccupied, since there were no qualified white applicants. Finally a solution was reached. The Negro public housing project was expanded. This action, however, violated all the announced policies of war housing. It involved demolition of over a hundred units of existing shelter, remodeling of two buildings, and slum clearance. It used critical materials unnecessarily; it wasted hundreds of thousands of taxpayers' dollars;...the final solution involved construction of 300 dwelling units in order to increase supply by 200 net units. This occasioned the additional expenditure of $400,000.
>
> (*The Negro Ghetto*, p. 95)

With remarkable prescience, Weaver predicts that the continued crowding of blacks into black belts and the deteriorating conditions within those communities would lead to anger, the degradation of social relationships, and ultimately to urban violence. To avert this urban disaster, Weaver urged an activist role for government. He envisioned government as the one American institution that could insert itself into the gap left by the private sector. He advocated three specific policies: one, government action to encourage private sector investment in these communities; two, a commitment to nondiscrimination in publicly assisted housing projects; and three, legal action to eliminate discriminatory housing covenants.

In some respects, Weaver's proposal called for a reversal of course by the federal government. Heretofore, the Supreme Court had failed to dismiss discriminatory housing covenants on constitutional grounds. A fascinating chapter details how the policies of the Federal Home Loan program required a lower assessment of housing values in racially mixed neighborhoods, thereby inhibiting integration of neighborhoods. The failure of local authorities to implement policy decisions reached in Washington was a source of continual frustration, but Weaver could also document instances in which the government acted as a catalyst in the creation of a desegregated living environment. A low cost housing project in Marin County was one example:

> Marin County became one of the most successful war projects on the West coast...From the start management was careful to see that there was no segregation. When, for example, some whites objected to Negro neighbors in the dormitories included in the project, the executive director of the local authority was requested by the dormitory council to move the objecting whites into a special building. He refused to tackle the problem on the basis of race and asked what was the objection to the Negroes. On being told that it was because of their alleged noisiness, he established the fact that some of the whites were noisy too. His solution, which worked, was to move those who were likely to make noise, regardless of color, into a separate building. If whites objected to living with Negro neighbors, as a few did, management told them that they could move out, but no white family was allowed to move from one house to another to avoid living in the same building with Negroes.
>
> *(The Negro Ghetto*, p. 168)

By firmly imprinting a non-discriminatory stamp on family selection and placement decisions within any publicly assisted housing project, a progressive and activist government could create areas within which the rationale of desegregation could be proven. With proof in hand these communities could become showcases to the rest of the country.

The overarching point of Robert Weaver's *The Negro Ghetto* is that the dismantling of the discriminatory barriers in the housing market would at one stroke both enhance the national economy and advance the living standards of black people. The former would be accomplished by ridding the housing market of price and quantity stickiness resulting directly from racial prejudice. The latter would be accomplished as a by-product of black and white people living together. With housing desegregation, Weaver asserted, daily observation of black family life would erode white stereotypes of black behavior. In Weaver's view, these ends could not be accomplished without an activist role for government. If, however, the federal government failed to overrule discriminatory tendencies at the grass roots, or at the state or local level, then segregation would become entrenched.

THE PLIGHT OF AMERICA'S CITIES

Despite Weaver's warnings, racially segregated housing continued as the norm in most urban areas. The stereotypes held by whites of blacks were not eroded through integration, but instead were strengthened by the association of the problems of the inner city with race. Crime, family instability, and the physical decay of neighborhoods became not just urban problems, but black urban problems. While he resisted this association of ethnicity with urban decay, the conceptualization of the Negro problem as an urban problem led Weaver to focus on the broader question of the rehabilitation of the center city and ultimately to his appointment as the first Secretary for Housing and Urban Development.

The Urban Complex (1964), clearly meant as a textbook for students of urban policy, delves into the details of rational, regional planning. The book, Dilemmas of Urban America (1965), offers a spirited defense of policies Weaver pursued as head of the HHFA. Weaver's role as an architect of housing policy in the Kennedy and Johnson administrations influenced his thinking, but did not prevent his giving a balanced analysis of both the costs and benefits of specific programs.

Again, Weaver relies on traditional neoclassical analysis to rationalize the need for government intervention. For Weaver, the cities are a collective good. Vital utilities and services that the suburbs require to survive emanate from the center cities. They are cultural centers and centers of economic activity. Weaver warns suburbia that it must reckon with the refurbishment of the inner city or face a diminished standard of living at home:

> We may not be able soon to overcome the current inclination to neglect urban and shelter needs. But we can and should emphasize the unique role of cities in our society and the high priority Americans accord adequate and attractive housing. That priority suggests the danger a democracy confronts when it fails to supply even the minimum standard of housing to a significant segment of the population. Nor can we afford to neglect further the existing urban infra-

structure, the cultural facilities cities traditionally have provided, or the economic and social ills that beset cities. To do so would substantially degrade the quality of life for many Americans of varied economic and social levels.

("The First Twenty Years of HUD," p. 472)

Weaver's writings concentrate on two specific concerns: 1 the decline of the central city as a hub of residential and business activity for the total population; and 2 the need to design urban renewal programs which minimize the costs of dislocation. Weaver offers a single prescription for both problems – the harmonization of municipal planning with that of the greater metropolitan community. Weaver stresses the need for comprehensive planning of land use and development to mitigate the effects of urban sprawl. Through coordinated planning efforts, the objective of urban renewal could be integrated with that of highway planning among other public projects so as to minimize the dislocation caused by any one project. The federal government would assist this process by linking federal funds to regional planning. Federal grants which would normally cover up to 20 per cent of the total cost of a local development project would cover up to 30 per cent of the cost if the project was carried out in conjunction with regional planning efforts (*The Urban Complex*, p. 147). The federal government's role is to nudge the cities and their suburbs into working as an integrated whole.

Urban renewal was, and still is, a contentious issue. The policy, requiring as it did the coerced relocation of families to facilitate the destruction and subsequent rebuilding of decaying areas, was often-times a source of pain for the people it might have benefited. Once tenements were razed they were replaced by housing for upper-income buyers. Particularly in a tight housing market, urban renewal led to increased crowding of the poor as the stock of affordable housing decreased. Urban renewal was often accompanied by increasing degradation of the areas within which the poor were forced to live.

In *Dilemmas of Urban America*, Weaver staunchly defends urban renewal. He argues that its critics exaggerate its disruptive effects, citing a Census Bureau statistic that 94 per cent of those relocated had been relocated to standard housing. He challenges the "romantic illusion" that urban renewal disrupts stable neighborhoods "to which residents have strong ties" (*Dilemmas*, pp. 57–8). Even with the benefit of twenty years of hindsight, Weaver writes, "Urban renewal, although unable to achieve its multiple, often conflicting goals and fulfill its unrealistic promises, has made a positive contribution to revitalizing downtown America and has left a legacy of technical expertise in land clearance, assembly and redevelopment" ("The First Twenty Years of HUD," p. 472).

Urban renewal appealed to Weaver for two reasons. Not only would it aid the revitalization of depressed urban centers, but the vacant land created the opportunity to replace segregated neighborhoods with racially integrated ones. Weaver could revisit his vision of achieving racial equality through blacks and whites living together.

However, Weaver also recognized that the goal of integrating neighborhoods was sometimes in conflict with the goal of improving the housing conditions of African Americans. If a ghetto was razed and replaced with integrated, higher cost housing, where would the excess blacks go? Weaver was aware that, for many African Americans, urban renewal was a euphemism for Negro renewal. Yet, he also saw the dilemma in political terms. The pursuit of racially mixed housing frequently meant the delay of badly needed expansion on new construction of low income housing. A site selected outside of the black ghetto would guarantee a political battle and delay the project. A site selected inside the ghetto perpetuated existing patterns of residential segregation. It was a dilemma that Weaver never resolved to his satisfaction ("The First Twenty Years of HUD," p. 471).

THE ECONOMIC PHILOSOPHY OF ROBERT WEAVER

Weaver championed government activism throughout his writings. In "Black Americans and Neoconservativism," (1980), Weaver refutes the neoconservative argument that government should minimize its role in society and the economy. Harking back to his experiences starting with the New Deal, he notes that accompanying this ideological movement away from an activist government was a deceleration, and in some areas a reversal, in the gains that had been made by black Americans during the previous decades. He describes the ongoing campaign to repudiate and rescind the Great Society programs as a "cop out" by neoconservatives who, he implies, lack the political courage to confront the problems faced by local governments in an honest manner. For Weaver, the failures of urban policy under the Great Society program were not an indictment of activist policies, but an indictment of the management of HUD under the Nixon, Ford and Reagan administrations. He criticizes the stop and go policies under Nixon:

> new HUD Secretary George Romney (1969–73) pushed some programs too fast. In the Section 235 homeownership program, for instance, Romney failed to take time to correct fraud, dishonest appraisals, abuses by speculators, and shoddy construction, then abruptly terminated the program. In the area of racial integration Romney pushed so hard as to create a congressional backlash, then was forced to retreat from that effort.
>
> ("The First Twenty Years of HUD," p. 464)

The backlash in Congress led the White House to retreat from its initial enthusiasm in enforcing the goals for new housing established in the 1968

Housing and Development Act and to declare a moratorium on the construction of new housing. Congressional backlash also forced Romney to weaken fair housing legislation. In Weaver's view, this waffling on policy coupled with a lack of philosophical support from the White House undermined HUD's credibility. Weaver's evaluation of the Reagan administration's efforts was even more negative. He described it as a nadir for the image and credibility of HUD. In Weaver's view, the lack of a clear agenda under the Nixon administration, the cutbacks under the Reagan administration, and the generally conservative mood of the nation contributed to the demotion of HUD in status and in influence.

Weaver was an urban economist before urban economics was a recognized field of study, using theory to develop an activist policy agenda. In testimony to his political savvy and his prescience, much of this agenda was eventually implemented. Equally remarkable was his ability to function simultaneously as an administrator and as a policy analyst. He was a prolific writer – analytical and deliberative in his attempt to evaluate the impact of policy, weighing both the social and efficiency consequences. Weaver's papers present no formal economic models, yet they embody a high level of technical sophistication. His policy prescriptions reflect both this technical sophistication and a recognition of the political and practical problems of implementation.

Our profession typically measures the stature of an economist by the length of his publication list, by the number of times he is cited in the literature and by the prestigious awards he has received. Robert Weaver offers these credentials and more. The homes constructed under the turnkey program, the families housed under the Section 8 program, and the federally subsidized urban rehabilitation projects jointly offer tangible evidence of his lasting influence on the formation of economic policy in urban America.

NOTES

1 This was particularly true for black women as documented by Jacqueline Jones in *Labor of Love, Labor of Sorrow*, 1985. Weaver details the exclusion of black women from the war effort until near the end of the war.
2 The League evolved into the Joint Committee on National Recovery.
3 Clark Foreman was a white civil rights activist.
4 John Kirby, *Black Americans in the Roosevelt Era: Liberalism and Race*, Knoxville: The University of Tennessee Press.
5 "Robert Weaver Oral History Interview," Frances Hardin, interviewer. Labor–Management Documentation Center, Martin P. Catherwood Library, Cornell University, 30 November 1973, p. 4.
6 ibid.
7 Weaver in *Negro Labor* does not take personal credit for this innovation. The Hamiltons (1986) credit Weaver with the program and identify him as the originator of the concept of affirmative action.
8 Herman Belz in *Equality Transformed: A Quarter Century of Affirmative Action* (1991) provides an extensive discussion of the evolution of equal employment

opportunity law since the Second World War albeit from a less sympathetic perspective than Weaver's.

REFERENCES

Belz, Herman, *Equality Transformed: A Quarter Century of Affirmative Action*, New Brunswick NJ: Social Philosophy and Policy Center and Transactions Publishers, 1991.

Hamilton, Charles V. and Dona, C. "Social Policies, Civil Rights and Poverty," in *Fighting Poverty: What Works and What Doesn't*, edited by Sheldon H. Danziger and Daniel H. Weinberg, Cambridge, MA: Harvard University Press, 1986.

Jones, Jacqueline, *Labor of Love, Labor of Sorrow*, New York: Basic Books, 1985.

Kirby, John, *Black Americans in the Roosevelt Era: Liberalism and Race*, Knoxville: The University of Tennessee Press, 1980.

Perkins, Frances, "Robert Weaver Oral History Interview," Frances Hardin, interviewer. Labor–Management Documentation Center, Martin P. Catherwood Library, Cornell University, 30 November 1973.

United States Department of the Interior, Office of the Adviser on Negro Affairs, *The Urban Negro Worker in the United States, 1925–1936*, Washington, DC: US Government Printing Office, 1938–9.

Weaver, Robert, *Negro Labor: A National Problem*, Port Washington, New York: Kennikat Press, 1946. Reissued in 1969.

——, *The Negro Ghetto*, New York: Harcourt, Brace Jovanovich, 1948.

——, *The Urban Complex: Human Values in Urban Life*, New York: Doubleday, 1960, 1961, 1963, 1964.

——, *Dilemmas of Urban America*, Cambridge, MA: Harvard University Press, 1965.

——, "The Role of Government in Urban America," in *The Urban Environment: How It Can Be Improved: The Charles C. Moskowitz Lectures, School of Commerce, New York University*, New York: New York University Press, 1969.

——, "Black Americans and Neoconservatism," in *The Social Welfare Forum*, 1980, New York: Columbia University Press, 1981.

——, "The First Twenty Years of HUD," *Journal of Housing*, Autumn 1985, pp. 463–74.

BIOGRAPHY OF DR. ROBERT CLIFTON WEAVER

Born in 1907 in Washington, DC, Robert Clifton Weaver became the first Secretary of Housing and Urban Development. Appointed by Lyndon Baines Johnson in 1966, he was the first black to hold a cabinet level post.

Weaver received his PhD in economics from Harvard University in 1934. From 1933 to 1944, he served in the administration of Franklin Roosevelt first as an advisor on Negro Affairs to Secretary of the Interior Harold Ickes (1933–7) and later as a special assistant in the US Housing Authority (1937–40). During the Second World War, Weaver was the director of the Negro Manpower Service in the War Manpower Commission (1941–4). Between 1954 and 1961, Weaver held a variety of positions in New York state and city governments, including Deputy Commissioner of Housing for the State of New York, State Rent Administrator and Vice Chairman of the New York City Housing and Redevelopment Board. His appointment to Johnson's cabinet was preceded by a stint as the administrator of the Housing and Home Finance Administration, the predecessor of HUD.

Dr. Weaver was president of Bernard Baruch College in New York City from 1968 to 1978 and he is currently professor emeritus at Hunter College.

Weaver is a prolific scholar, having published over 175 articles and four books: *Negro Labor* (1946); *The Negro Ghetto* (1948); *The Urban Complex* (1964); and *Dilemmas of Urban America* (1965).

INDEX

Note: entries refer to African Americans unless otherwise stated.